# THE ELEMENTS SHALL MELT
# WITH FERVENT HEAT!

Unless otherwise noted, all scriptural citations are from the New King James Translations 1990, 1985, 1983, Thomas Nelson, Nashville, Tn.


ISBN 978-1-937501-07-5



Produced by JaDon Management Inc.
1405 4ᵗʰ Ave. N. W. #109
Ardmore, Ok. 73401

Cover Design by
Kim Lester
P. O. Box 33741
Amarillo, Tx. 79120

# THE ELEMENTS SHALL MELT WITH FERVENT HEAT

## A STUDY OF 2 PETER 3

**By Don K. Preston**

First published in 1990 as *2 Peter 3: The Late Great Kingdom*

# FOREWORD

It has been 16 years since I wrote the first edition of this book. Those familiar with that work know that it was then entitled *2 Peter 3: The Late Great Kingdom*. The first edition sold out quickly, yet, interest in 2 Peter 3 has not abated. If anything, it has grown as more and more Bible students have been introduced to the principles of preterism. I constantly receive requests for the original book. That first book spanned 126 pages. As you can see, this volume is almost 300 pages. The passing of the years and more in-depth research has yielded the book you now hold.

I don't have to tell you that 2 Peter 3 is the foundational text for proving that the physical cosmos is going to one day end in a fiery conflagration. I was raised believing that, and as a young minister I preached that. However, I came to realize that my main mistake was not honoring the proper context of Peter's thought world. Peter was a Jew trained in the Old Testament prophetic language. He was a Jew longing for the fulfillment of the hope of Israel.

While I grasped *some* of this in the first edition, I must confess that I did not then fully appreciate the importance of this issue. The mistake of most commentators is to approach 2 Peter 3 from the perspective of a modern cosmology. They approach the text with the idea that Peter is concerned with the fulfillment of God's promises to the church, not His promises to Israel. They seek to fit Peter into a Greek world view, instead of grasping that Peter, like Paul and the majority of the other New Testament writers, was a *Hebrew*. He did not think in Hellenistic ways. He was focused on the fulfillment of God's faithfulness to His covenant people, Israel. In this revised work, I will show how, if we are willing to pay attention, this Hebraic, covenantal, prophetic context of 2 Peter 3 will guide us into a proper understanding of what Peter was saying.

In my first edition, I proposed that 2 Peter 3 is not about the end of time, or the end of the physical cosmos. Rather, Peter was predicting the end of the Old Covenant world of Israel, that came to an end with the fall of Jerusalem in A.D. 70. *I am more convinced than ever* that this is the proper view of 2 Peter 3. Biblical eschatology is not about the end of history, i.e. Historical Eschatology, but the end of the Old Covenant that could never bring life and righteousness. Thus, Biblical eschatology is "Covenant Eschatology."

# TABLE OF CONTENTS

# THE ELEMENTS SHALL MELT WITH FERVENT HEAT!

Accenting to the most popular reading of 2 Peter 3, our planet is doomed to one day perish in a fiery cataclysm that will bring human history, indeed, all material creation, to an end. After all, Peter did say, "The earth and the elements therein shall be burned up with fervent heat," didn't he? And yet, great scholars in every age have rejected the "popular" view, and believed instead that 2 Peter 3 was a prediction of the end of the Old Covenant world of Israel that occurred with the fall of Jerusalem in A. D. 70. We will show that this is the proper interpretation of 2 Peter 3.

## SETTING THE CONTEXT

To properly understand 2 Peter 3, we must first investigate the purpose of the epistle itself. Chapter 3 does not stand alone in its discussion of the *Day of the Lord*. It is within the context of the apostle's overall purpose. Peter does not leave us in the dark about this, his reason for writing is to respond to scoffers questioning the reality of the *parousia*, (*parousia* is the Greek word that is translated as coming, and refers to what is popularly called today, the Second Coming of Jesus Christ).

"For we have not followed cunningly devised fables, when we made known unto you the power and coming (Greek parousia, παρουσια), of our Lord Jesus Christ, but were eyewitnesses of his majesty. For he received from God the Father honor and glory, when there came such a voice to him from the excellent glory, This is my beloved Son, in whom I am well pleased. And this voice which came from heaven we heard, when we were with him in the holy mount. We have also a more sure word of prophecy, whereunto ye do well that ye take heed, as unto a light that shineth in a dark place, until the day dawn, and the day star arise in your hearts." 2 Peter 1:16-21 (KJV)

Peter tells us that he was writing his epistle because there were some who were claiming that the prediction of Christ's coming was a fable, a myth not to be believed. The *Expository Greek Testament* says, "The false teachers in 2 Peter have brought a new idea into the field...They cast doubt on the Christian eschatological expectation"[1] Peter responds, first of all, by saying that Christ's coming was not a myth, because the apostles, specifically he, along with James and John, were eyewitnesses to a vision of the parousia when they witnessed the Transfiguration.

To appreciate the significance of the Transfiguration, and its impact on the proper interpretation of 2 Peter 3, we must investigate that *Mountain Top* experience of the apostles.

If Peter saw the Transfiguration as a proof of the parousia, it seems odd that so little attention is given to that event in eschatological studies. As Johnson says, "It is surprising to discover the omission of the theological significance of the Transfiguration in the standard systematic theologies."[2]

Peter's claim is tremendously important for our study about the Day of the Lord in 2 Peter 3. This is true because whatever it was the scoffers (2 Peter 3:3) were denying, Peter says he and the other apostles knew it was going to happen because of the Transfiguration. Boobyer correctly notes, "2 Peter as a whole is concerned to buttress hope of the second advent, and in 1:16-18 itself the writer desires above all to show that the Lord's *dunamis (power) and parousia (coming)* were not 'cunningly devised fables.' They were not, because he and others had actually been 'eyewitnesses of that glory.' If this was to be of any value as a proof of the coming *dunamis and parousia* it must have been something of the parousia greatness that the eyewitnesses on the 'holy mount' saw."[3] In other words, if the Transfiguration was not a vision of the parousia, then it would have no apologetic power against those denying the parousia. The Transfiguration therefore *defines the parousia* being anticipated by Peter and denied by the scoffers.

What did they see on the Mount? What is the Transfiguration all about? Well, Peter says it was a vision and confirmation of Christ's coming. It was a vision of what the scoffers were denying. It behooves us therefore, to carefully examine that mountain top experience.

## WHAT THEY DID NOT SEE!

Before proceeding to examine what the disciples saw on the Mount, it will first of all be profitable to notice what they did not see.

The majority of Bible students today, whether premillennial, amillennial, or postmillennial, believe that Christ's coming is *the end of the Christian age.* Among postmillennial and amillennial students, it is held that at Christ's appearing the material cosmos is burned up in a "moment, in the twinkling of an eye." While these are the traditional paradigms, they are in direct conflict with the Transfiguration vision.

If the epiphany of Christ is an end of time, earth burning event, and if the apostles saw a vision of that phenomenal cataclysm, then surely, when we examine the Transfiguration scene, we will find a description of the end of time, the conflagration of the earth, etc., correct? The trouble is, the Transfiguration scene contains not one thing espoused by the traditional theories of the "time of the end!" To aid our understanding of the vision, then, let's take a look at what the disciples did not, in fact see.

**A.)** The disciples did not see a vision of the destruction of material creation. As just seen, the traditional view of the parousia insists that Jesus' coming is to destroy the physical universe, yet the disciples saw no such thing on the Mount. Why is that?

**B.)** The Transfiguration did not include a vision of a literal gathering of every individual of every nation into one geographical location. Yet we are told this is integral to the final judgment.

**C.)** On the Mount there was no sounding of a literal trumpet or literal shout of an arch-angel.

**D.)** The disciples did not see a vision of a resurrection of physically dead human corpses coming out of the terra firma.

**E.)** The Transfiguration was not a vision of Jesus on the physical throne of David in Jerusalem.

**F.)** As a corollary to the previous point the Transfiguration was not a vision of the reestablishment of national Israel. This is devastating to the millennial view. Millennialists claim that the Transfiguration was a vision of Christ's coming to establish the millennial reign with the re-establishment of Old Covenant Israel, along with the Temple sacrificial cultus. *This is the direct opposite of what the apostles saw!* What they saw was the *passing* of the Old Covenant world, *not its re-establishment.* Now, if the Transfiguration is a vision of the parousia, at beginning of the millennium per our millennial friends, then the Transfiguration scene is a total refutation of the idea of a restoration of Israel.

Make no mistake, the disciples *did see* a vision of the parousia. The Transfiguration was to Peter the proof positive ("we have the prophetic word made more sure," 2 Peter 1:19), of the Advent of Jesus Christ. When we concentrate on what the disciples did see we find the true Biblical definition of the parousia.

## WHAT THE DISCIPLES SAW

On the Mount the disciples were amazed to see Jesus' countenance changed into a glorious appearance so bright they could not gaze upon him.

3

Then, incredibly, Moses and Elijah appeared with the Lord. What an awe inspiring vision!

Peter was so moved by the occasion that he offered, "let us make here three tabernacles: one for You, one for Moses, and one for Elijah" (Matthew 17:4). It does not take much to understand the significance of Moses and Elijah.

Moses was the Lawgiver "par excellence," Elijah was the epitome of the Old Covenant prophets. Ramsey correctly notes, "By appearing together Moses and Elijah sum up the entire drama of the old order from its beginning to its end, the one is the predecessor, the other is the precursor of the Messiah."[4] Peter's suggestion that three tabernacles be made suggests that he saw Jesus, Moses and Elijah as equals. But this was not to be.

Matthew says, "While he (Peter, DKP) was still speaking, behold, a bright cloud overshadowed them: and suddenly a voice came out of the cloud, saying, 'This is my beloved Son, in whom I am well pleased. Hear Him!'" What is it that Peter and the other disciples are seeing? To borrow the words of Boobyer, "the Transfiguration was a divine confirmation of the Messianic status of Jesus in the form of a visionary forecast of the parousia of Jesus--that moment when his divine Sonship and Messianic glory would be displayed in all their majesty as he came from heaven." (*Transfiguration*, 29). But contra Boobyer we believe the contextual definition of the parousia--the time of the revelation of the Sonship and Messianic Glory of Jesus--was not perceived by Peter or the other writers as an "end of time event," rather *it is the surpassing of the Old Covenant-- the law and the prophets--by the transcendent glory of Jesus the "mediator of the New Covenant."*

Both Moses and Elijah appeared *in glory* with Jesus (Luke 9:30-31), but the glory of Jesus out shined the glory of those two grand spokesmen of the Old Covenant. There could be no mistake, the Father removed Moses and Elijah, Jesus alone remained and the Father's voice clarified the issue: "This is my beloved Son, in whom I am well pleased: Hear Him!" What Peter and the other disciples witnessed was the passing of the Old Covenant glory and the establishing of the surpassing New Covenant glory of Jesus. Now let us bring 2 Peter 1 back to the discussion and formulate our argument for simplicity and ease of understanding.

In 2 Peter 1 the parousia was still future to the apostle. But Peter said the Transfiguration made the prophetic word, i.e. the prediction of the parousia, more sure--established it beyond doubt, for on the Mount they saw a vision of the parousia. But the Transfiguration was a vision of *the*

4

*transformation from the Old Covenant Glory of Moses and the Prophets to the New Covenant Glory of Jesus the Messiah.* Therefore, the Biblical definition of the Parousia of Jesus is the complete transformation from the Old Covenant world of Moses and Elijah to the New Covenant world of Jesus. This clearly has incredible implications for the study of eschatology.

The great majority of the religious world believes that the parousia, the Second Coming of Christ is a matter of *Historical Eschatology.* That is, it brings human history as we know it to an end. However, the Transfiguration was a vision of Christ's coming. And *the Transfiguration was not a vision of Historical Eschatology.* It was a vision of the end of a covenant age or world. This radically redefines our view of "last things."

---

**The Transfiguration was a vision of the parousia being denied by the scoffers of 2 Peter 3. Yet, the Transfiguration was not a vision of the end of time, or the destruction of planet earth. It was a vision of the change from the Age of Moses to the Age of Christ. This means the parousia being denied by the scoffers was the Covenant change from Moses to Christ!**

---

There can be no mistake. Peter undeniably did appeal to the Transfiguration as a positive refutation of the scoffers denying the parousia. When we accept Peter's definition of the Day of the Lord as defined by the Transfiguration, it becomes apparent that the scoffers were not concerned with the coming of Christ at the end of time. They were denying the end of the Old Covenant world of Moses.

Our argument, simply stated, is this:

Peter offered the Transfiguration as a vision of Christ's coming, the coming being denied by the scoffers (2 Peter 1:16; 3:3).

The Transfiguration–a vision of Christ's coming--was a vision of the end of the Old Covenant age of Moses and the Law (Matthew 17).

Therefore, the coming of Christ being denied by the scoffers was the end of the Old Covenant age of Moses and the Law.

The fact that Peter posits the Transfiguration as a vision of what the scoffers were denying is proof positive that the scoffers were not denying the coming of Christ at the end of time, and the dissolution of material creation. *They were denying the passing of the Old Covenant world of the Law and the prophets.*

5

Peter's affirmation that the Transfiguration was a vision of Christ's "Second Coming," and that coming is what the scoffers were denying, proves beyond successful refutation that 2 Peter 3 has nothing whatsoever to do with the end of time, or a literal, bodily coming of Christ. As we proceed in this study, this will become increasingly more evident, for as we will see, the Bible never predicted the end of material creation or the end of time.

## SETTING THE CONTEXT: 2 PETER 2 AND CHAPTER 3

Far too often in popular discussions of 2 Peter 3, the previous chapter is virtually ignored. Yet, the discussion of chapter 3 is the continuation of Peter's discussion from chapter 1 onward. Peter's entire epistle is for the purpose of refuting those who were denying the *parousia* of Christ. Chapter 2 is no exception to that theme and purpose. With that in mind, when we see what Peter says in 2 Peter 2:1-3, we are forced to conclude that if in fact chapter 3 is a continuing discussion of the issues of chapter 2, then chapter 3 cannot be referent to an end of time event. It was discussing an event that was about to occur in Peter's generation.

In 2 Peter 2:1-3, the apostle wrote these words:

"But there were also false prophets among the people, even as there will be false teachers among you, who will secretly bring in destructive heresies, even denying the Lord who bought them, and bring swift destruction on themselves. And many shall follow their destructive ways, because of whom the way of truth will be blasphemed. By covetousness they will exploit you with deceptive words; for a long time their judgment has not been idle, and their destruction does not slumber."

We will confine ourselves to a few brief points on this text.

**First**, Peter is speaking in a "Jewish" or covenantal context. He points out, "there were false prophets among the people." This is undeniably referent to false prophets among Old Covenant Israel. In the preponderant number of cases, references to prophets among the people are to the prophets sent to Israel. While God (very) occasionally sent His prophets to pagan nations (e.g Jonah to Nineveh), this was extremely rare. Thus, for Peter to speak of prophets among the people sets his discussion firmly within the context of *a covenant people.* Just as there were false prophets among O. T. Israel, Peter warns God's New Covenant people that false prophets are among them as well.[5]

6

**Second**, Peter *seems* to be citing Deuteronomy 32:18 when he speaks of how the false prophets and their followers would deny "the Lord who bought them." In Deuteronomy 32, it speaks of Israel in the last days, "Of the Rock who begot you, you are unmindful, and have forgotten the God who fathered you." (v. 18). If Peter is referencing Deuteronomy 32, this posits the events of 2 Peter 2 within the confines of Israel's last days.

**Third**, what Peter is predicting is what Jesus foretold in Matthew 24:10-13. Jesus said false teachers and false prophets would come "and deceive many"; lawlessness would abound and, "most people's love will grow cold." (NASV). Jesus was speaking of the events to take place in his generation (Matthew 24:34), and of course, those events did take place. Peter was reiterating what his Lord had said, but noting the *current presence* of what was foretold.

**Fourth**, Peter affirms that the judgment of these false prophets and teachers was at hand. The false ones he is speaking about are *already present* (2 Peter 2:10f). In addition, Jude says the false teachers and immoral leaders were already present. Peter, while using the future tense, was merely reminding his readers of what the prophets said would come. It was the prophets of old that said false prophets would arise in the last days. Peter is not making a new prediction of a different last days, or different false prophets. He was living in the time foretold by the prophets, and witnessing the fulfillment of what they forecast.

Notice that Peter says "they shall bring swift judgment on themselves." The word for swift is *taxinos*, and as Bauckham says, "And bring swift destruction upon themselves does not mean 'sudden,' but, 'coming soon, imminent.' Probably the author has in mind the false teacher's jibe that the Lord is slow in coming to exercise judgment (3:9), and therefore the sense will be that judgment at the parousia is imminent."[6] In other words, the wicked prophets that were forecast for the last days, were already at work, and their prophesied judgment, that had "slumbered" for a long time, was now awake and ready to fall.

Nicoll says the judgment of the ungodly, "whose judgment has for a long time not been nactive, (sic) although there is the appearance of delay. This delay is the argument used by the false teachers....The judgment has long been gathering and is impending."[7] What Nicoll is saying is that the false prophets were going about their business, denying that judgment was coming. They were saying, "Where is the promise of His coming?" They were saying, "Peace, and safety!" (1 Thessalonians 5:2). Peter's response is that the judgment may have appeared to slumber, i.e. delay, due to the

7

fact that it was actually foretold so long ago (by the O.T. prophets), but now, the time had come. As Alford's Greek Testament says, the judgment from God, "is awake and ready to seize them."[8]

Are the wicked teachers of 2 Peter 2 the same as the scoffers of chapter 3? If not, where is the delineation in the text? Both were foretold by the Old Testament prophets. Both scoffed at the idea of judgment. In both chapter 2 and chapter 3, the time for the judgment was short (2:1-3 / 3:12). If the false teachers of chapter 2 and the scoffers of chapter 3 are the same, then since chapter 2:3 says the judgment was now at hand, no longer slumbering, this means the Day of the Lord of 2 Peter 3 was near.

This is devastating for the futurist eschatologies. For instance, Keith Mathison has edited a book seeking, vainly, to refute the ideas held here and by other preterist authors. Mathison has a strange dilemma. In his book, he writes a chapter seeking to explain away the eschatological temporal statements in the N. T.. However, he *normally* takes the view that when the NT posits an eschatological event as near, *it refers to the A.D. 70 judgment of Israel*. But, Mathison posits 2 Peter 3 as predictive of the end of time and human history.[9] So what is the problem?

Here is Mathison's problem, simply stated, in light of the affirmation of the nearness of the judgment in 2 Peter 2:

All New Testament eschatological prophecies that affirm the nearness of the event are predictions of the Lord's coming in judgment of Israel in A.D. 70 (Mathison).

But the judgment of 2 Peter 3, being the same as the judgment of 2 Peter 2, was coming quickly. (i.e. it is an eschatological prophecy that affirms the nearness of the event.)

Therefore, the judgment of 2 Peter 3, being an eschatological prophecy that affirmed the nearness of the event, was a prediction of the Lord's coming in judgment of Israel in A.D. 70.

If Mathison cannot prove beyond doubt that 2 Peter 3 is discussing a different *parousia* of Christ in judgment from that found in chapter 2, then since chapter 2 says the judgment of the wicked was "awake and coming quickly," then this means the judgment of 2 Peter 3 was referent to the A.D. 70 judgment of Israel.

So, what has the context of 2 Peter 3 established?

We have seen that Peter presents the Transfiguration as an eye witness vision of the coming of Christ being denied by the scoffers. As a vision of the parousia of Christ, the Transfiguration was a vision, not of the end of time, or of a bodily coming of Christ, but of the passing of the Old

8

Covenant age of Moses and the Law, and the establishment of the transcendent glory of Christ's New Covenant. This definition of the parousia proves that 2 Peter 3 is not a prediction of the end of planet earth.

We have shown that 2 Peter 2 discusses the wicked that 2 Peter 3 says was to be judged, and we have seen that 2 Peter 2 affirms that the judgment was coming soon.

So, the context of 2 Peter 3, as set forth in 2 Peter 1 and 2, is the impending judgment of Israel. She was in her last days, her age was about to end. A proper understanding of the context of 2 Peter 3 forbids its application to our future, and to the dissolution of planet earth.

# CHAPTER 2
## WHO ARE THE PROPHETS?

**"This Second Epistle I Write unto You, (In Both of Which to Stir up Your Pure Minds by Way of Reminder), That You May Be Mindful of the Words Spoken Before by the Holy Prophets."** (2 Peter 3:2, NKJV) Peter says that he was going to remind his readers of what "the prophets" had earlier written. Who are the prophets to whom he alludes? Are these Old Covenant prophets or New?

The term "the prophets" is used 88 times in the NT. Of those 88 times it is used only 17 times in reference to New Covenant prophets. In each of those cases there can be little controversy as to the identity of the prophets being considered. For instance, Jesus said he would send prophets to Jerusalem (Matthew 23:34). In Matthew 24:24, he warned of the coming of false prophets. In Acts, we are told of Agabus and Barnabas, (13:1f), as well as Judas and Silas (15:32). I Corinthians 12:28-29, and 14:29,32 speak unequivocally of church prophets as does Ephesians 2:20, 3:5, 4:11. John, in I John 4:1, told of many "false prophets" that were then present. (Incidentally, why aren't the "false prophets" that John said were already present, *whose presence proved the end was near* (1 John 2:18), not the same false prophets spoken of by Peter in 2 Peter 2? Peter's declaration, "the end of all things has drawn near" is the direct equivalent to John's,"it is the last hour." Thus, the issue was the same, and the time statement was the same: the end was near.)

In each of these cases, as noted, there is always clear contextual identification that the prophets under view are contemporary prophets of the first century. When the New Testament simply uses the term "the prophets," and does not delineate whether old or new, the reference is always to Old Testament prophets.[10]

### WHAT'S THE POINT?

The identification of *the prophets* is important for the proper exegesis of 2 Peter 3. Peter specifically tells us he is only reminding his readers of what *the prophets* have said earlier. If these were Old Covenant prophets we can draw some preliminary conclusions about 2 Peter 3.

First of all, if the prophets Peter alludes to are the prophets of Israel, then it is evident that Peter's prediction is an inherent part of *the promises made to Israel*. Just as Paul preached nothing but what was written in "Moses and the prophets" (Acts 24:13-15), Peter likewise preached only what, "Samuel and all the prophets, yea all that have spoken" had foretold. *To attempt to interpret 2 Peter 3 outside the framework of God's promises to Israel is to miss the apostle's purpose and point.* This means the eschatology of 2 Peter 3 is the eschatology of Israel's aeon, i.e. *Covenant Eschatology*, and not *historical eschatology*, i.e. the end of time and space. We will have more to say on this issue as we proceed, but for now, we need to take note of the fact that all interpretations of Biblical eschatology that are divorced from Israel and her last days, are doomed to fail. This can hardly be overstated.

> **Any eschatology that is divorced from Israel and her last days is doomed to failure and confusion.**

It is now being recognized by an increasing number of scholars that God's promises to Israel did not include the prediction of the end of time, nor the end of the material universe. Nanos says,

> "Within the mainline Jewish writings of this period, covering a wide range of styles, genres, political persuasions and theological perspectives, there is virtually no evidence that Jews were expecting the end of the space-time universe...What then did they believe was going to happen? They believed that the present world order would come to an end--the world order in which pagans held power, and Jews, the covenant people of the creator god, did not."[11]

N. T. Wright comments on the questions of Jesus' disciples in Matthew 24:2, about the "end of the age,"

> "As far as the disciples, good first century Jews as they were, were concerned, there was no reason whatever for them to be thinking about the end of the time-space universe. There was no reason, either in their background or in a single thing that Jesus had said to them up to that point, for it to even occur to them that the true story of the world, or of Israel or of Jesus himself, might include either the end of the time space universe, or Jesus or anyone else floating down to earth on a cloud."[12]

11

The western literalistic mind-set that sees the end of time and the material cosmos in 2 Peter 3, is completely overlooking the Jewish source and nature of the language of this great chapter. Jewish prophetic literature is highly metaphoric, hyperbolic, and figurative. We shall discuss this in-depth below, but it is essential to introduce this concept early on.

This issue of the source of Peter's prediction is crucial. Many people mistakenly believe the Old Covenant was removed at the Cross and that God's promises to Israel were all fulfilled at that juncture.[13] It is held that post-Pentecost, Jehovah was no longer bound to any of His covenant promises to Israel, and that, consequently, the eschatology found in the New Testament books is found in *new* promises made to the church exclusive of Israel. This is egregiously wrong.

Peter was the apostle to the Jews (Galatians 2:5f). Like Paul, he proclaimed *the hope of Israel*. Israel's prophetic hopes were the foundation of Peter's gospel (Acts 3:19f, more on this later). Further, he declared that the time of the fulfillment of those prophetic promises had arrived, because Moses and all the prophets "foretold these days" (Acts 3:24). Peter knew and preached that the last days foretold by the prophets had arrived (Acts 2:15f), and that has a direct bearing on our understanding of 2 Peter 3.

When speaking of the appearance of the last days scoffers Peter was not speaking of a distant age or time. He knew the last days were *his* "these days." Remember that on Pentecost Peter cited the "last days" prediction of Joel 2, "This is that which was spoken by the prophet Joel." So, the O. T. prophets foretold the events of the last days, including the appearance of the false prophets, and Peter said "this is that!" The last days were Peter's generation.

This is proven by considering the following:

The very purpose of 2 Peter, as we have noted, was the refutation of those denying the parousia. In other words, Peter wrote 2 Peter to refute the scoffers who were already saying "where is the promise of His coming?" Now, was Peter writing his epistle to counter one set of scoffers who just happened to be denying the same thing that another generation of scoffers, millennia removed, would also deny?

As we have seen, the scoffers of 2 Peter 3 were denying what Peter affirmed, "The end of all things has drawn near" (1 Peter 4:7). Now, if Peter was affirming the imminence of what the scoffers in chapter 3 were denying, then the passing of 2000 years has validated the scoffers and falsified Peter!

12

To avoid this dilemma, one has to divorce chapter 3 from the rest of Peter's epistles in order to project 2 Peter 3 into a time far removed from Peter. In other words, although Peter tells us the purpose of his epistle is to respond to the skeptics denying Christ's coming, his affirmation of its nearness and its validity *had no contemporary application*, because the scoffers of chapter 3 were not to come for at least two millennia. Is the eschatology of 2 Peter 3 unrelated to the eschatology of 1 Peter and 2 Peter 1-2? This cannot be, for Peter tells us that 2 Peter 3 was a reminder of what he had already written.

If the scoffers in 2 Peter 3 were in fact denying what Peter affirmed in 1 Peter and 2 Peter 1-2, then this is proof positive that the last days of 2 Peter 3 were already present, and the scoffers were already denying what Peter affirmed. Peter was not interacting with two separate groups of scoffers, one already present and one 2000 years away. And, if this is true, it strikes a crushing blow to the postmillennial view.

Postmillennialists tell us the "final" coming of the Lord may yet be 25-30,000+ years in the future. More on this below. If this is true then Peter must have been preaching this 2000 years ago. But, if the apostles were saying the parousia was so far off, why in the world would Peter have to write 2 Peter to refute the scoffers denying that "the end of all things has drawn near"? Why would Peter even bother? Why did Peter not write, "Listen you scoffers, the apostles have never said the Lord's final coming is near. Why are you even asking, 'Where is the promise of His coming?' We have always said the final coming is a long time off!" The fact that Peter affirmed that his contemporaries were "hastening the Day," and that Peter wrote his epistle to refute the then contemporary scoffers is *prima facia* refutation of postmillennial eschatology.

Peter knew nothing of two last days periods. He proclaimed that his generation was the last days foretold by the O. T. prophets. Those days were the days for the fulfillment of all things spoken by all the prophets (Acts 3:23-24). Thus, 2 Peter 3 does not anticipate another last days period, in fulfillment of other O. T. prophets. He was living in those predicted last days, and this proves that the scoffers of 2 Peter 3 were already present, and would perish at the Day of the Lord.

Unlike Mathison, therefore, who says that, "in some sense, then, the last days were already present immediately after the first coming of Christ." (*When*, 189), Peter had no ambiguity about when the last days were. He said the last days foretold by the prophets were present. He also said the consummation of those days was near (1 Peter 1:5f, 4:5, 7, 17).

Demonstration that Peter does have the O.T. prophets in mind is seen in verse 13 where he says "according to the promise, we look for a new heavens and new earth." The promise of the new heaven and earth is to be found in Isaiah 65-66.[14]

Proof that Peter has the Old Covenant prophets in view is also found in his terminology, that is, in how he refers to the prophets. He says he writes to remind his readers, "of the words which were spoken before by the holy prophets." When the NT writers refer to the prophets which have spoken or written *before* it is *always* allusion to OT prophets. See for instance Matthew 5:12; Acts 2:31, 3:20. Also study Matthew 2:23, Luke 24:25, Acts 3:21-24, 13:40. Do not forget the famous text in Hebrews 1:1.

Still further proof that Peter has Old Covenant *prophets–and the fulfillment of God's promises to Israel--* in mind is found in the fact that he quotes Psalms 90:4 in verse 8.

The main conclusion to be reached, based upon the identification of "the prophets" as Old Testament prophets, is that, whatever 2 Peter speaks of, it has already been fulfilled and has, therefore, no reference to our future.

Unless you are, **1.)** Able to demonstrate that "the prophets" is a reference to New Testament prophets, who made predictions totally unrelated to the Old Prophets, or, **2.)** Willing to say that parts of the Old Covenant have not yet been fulfilled, then you must believe 2 Peter is fulfilled. There is no alternative! Why is this true?

**First**, in Luke 21:20-22 Jesus spoke of the destruction of Jerusalem that was to occur in 70 AD. He said of that catastrophe, "these be the days of vengeance in which all things that are written may be fulfilled." It is sometimes objected that Jesus was speaking only of the fulfillment of O.T. prophecy. However, this is irrelevant because in reality, *all New Covenant eschatology is based solely on the eschatology of the Old Covenant.*

**Paul** said his doctrine of *the resurrection of the dead* was nothing but what Moses and the prophets foretold (Acts 24:14f:26:6f, etc.).

**Peter** said his doctrine of the coming of the Lord and the new creation was prophesied by the Old Covenant prophets (2 Peter 3:1-2, 13).

**Hebrews** says the judgment it foretold was to be the fulfillment of O. T. prophecy (Hebrews 10:33f).

**Jude** said his doctrine of the coming of the Lord was foretold by the O. T. prophets (v. 10-14)..

**John** said his doctrine of the last things was what the prophets foretold (Revelation 10:7f; 22;6f).

14

What we have then is that all N. T. eschatology is the reiteration of the Old Covenant promises God made to Israel. *There are no "new" eschatological prophecies in the N. T.*. So, when Jesus said that in the fall of Jerusalem, "all things that are written must be fulfilled," this means that all eschatological promises would be fulfilled at that time.

The tragic failure to grasp the covenantal significance and context of eschatology is exemplified by Pentecost, "Eschatological studies are not concerned with...the Mosaic Covenant made by God with man, inasmuch as all these are temporary and non-determinative in respect to future things, but only with the four eternal covenants given by God, by which He has obligated Himself in relation to the prophetic program."[15] As you can see from the list just above, the New Testament writers undeniably posited the consummation of the Abrahamic and Edenic promises at the time of the fulfillment of God's promises to Israel. To sever eschatology from the end of Israel's covenantal aeon therefore is completely misguided.

Daniel 9 proves this. That prophet was told that by the end of the pivotal 70 Weeks, i.e. *in the fall of Jerusalem* (v. 26-27), one of the things to be accomplished would be "seal up vision and prophecy." This phrase means the comprehensive fulfillment of all prophecy.[16] Luke 21:22 is a divine commentary on Daniel 9, telling us that all prophecy would be fulfilled by the time of Israel's demise. Thus, Daniel foretold the fulfillment of all prophecy by the time of, and in the passing of the Old Covenant world. Jesus, in predicting the destruction of Jerusalem, said "all things that are written" would be fulfilled in that catastrophe. Perfect correlation.

Mathison seeks to avoid the power of Luke 21:22 by claiming, "We can get a better idea of what Jesus actually meant by examining what he said in Luke 18:31. In this text, Jesus tells his disciples, "Behold, we are going up to Jerusalem and all things that are written by the prophets concerning the Son of Man will be accomplished.' Now, if we use hyper-preterist hermeneutics to interpret Luke 18:31, we are forced to conclude that the Second Coming occurred when Jesus went up to Jerusalem with the disciples, since 'all things' prophesied about the Son of Man would be accomplished at that time." (*WSTTB*, 172)

One can only wonder why Mathison failed to call his reader's attention to Luke 18:32, "For He will be delivered to the Gentiles and will be mocked, and insulted and spit upon, and they will scourge Him and put Him to death. And the third day, he will be raised from the dead." Notice the particle "for"; it is *explanatory* of what has just been said. The point is that in v. 32 Jesus clearly quantified the "all things" concerning the Son of

15

Man that were to be fulfilled. Mathison has conveniently omitted the very text that modifies Jesus' "all things!" Why would Mathison omit such a critical, defining text?

What is the difference between Luke 21:22 and Luke 18? The difference is between "all things that are written," and all things *concerning the suffering of the Son of Man.* The difference is between a *modified* "all things" and a *comprehensive* "all." The difference is also timing.

In Luke 18 Jesus is speaking, undeniably, of his passion. Note again that it is not a comprehensive statement that "all things that are written must be fulfilled." It is a limited, qualified statement. Furthermore, in Luke 21, Jesus is undeniably speaking of events to occur long after his passion. Since, Luke 21 is speaking of events to occur long after the passion, and since the terminology of Luke 21 is far more comprehensive than the terminology of Luke 18, Mathison's argument is invalidated.

Now, we can imagine someone objecting by saying, "Luke 21:22 is only speaking of the fulfillment of all things concerning wrath coming on Israel. That was fulfilled in A.D. 70, but that has nothing to do with the *real* end." The problem is, this argument *assumes* an eschatology divorced from Israel, and, *ignores* the fact that as we have just seen *all Biblical eschatology,* including resurrection, are inextricably linked with the time of the judgment of Israel.

Some (i.e. amillennialists and postmillennialists) argue that New Testament eschatology is *not* based on Old Testament predictions.[17] This claim is false, as we have shown. The Old Testament is the source for the predictions of the *resurrection* (Daniel 12:2; Acts 24:14-15, 1 Corinthians 15:54f), and Peter emphatically declares that his prediction is from the Old Covenant prophets. Thus, New Testament eschatology is Old Testament eschatology restated. They are part and parcel of the same cloth.

Peter, in 2 Peter 3 reminds his readers of Old Testament prophecies of the Day of the Lord. But Jesus, in Luke 21 said all Old Testament prophecies would be fulfilled by the destruction of Jerusalem in A.D. 70. Therefore, Peter's prediction of the Day of the Lord, which had been predicted by the Old Testament prophets, was fulfilled by the destruction of Jerusalem in 70 AD.

**Second**, since Peter affirms that his prediction of the Day of the Lord and passing of the "heaven and earth" is from the Old Testament prophets, Matthew 5:17-18 becomes a vital passage. Jesus declared that not one jot or tittle, *not the smallest particle*, could pass from the law until it was all fulfilled. Simply put, this means *the Old Law would not pass until it was all*

16

*fulfilled.* When it was all fulfilled, then and only then would it be completely done away.

Peter tells us the Day of the Lord, was an Old Testament prophecy. This means that if 2 Peter 3, a recapitulation of O.T. prophecy is not yet fulfilled, then the Old Law has not yet passed away.

The rejoinder will be offered that Jesus took the Law away by his death (Romans 7, Ephesians 2, etc). Without question his death was the *ground and power* for that removal, but the Law was not removed at the Cross.

As noted, Jesus said the Law and prophets could not pass away until it was all fulfilled. In A.D. 33 Jesus looked beyond Calvary to the fall of the Jewish polity in 70, and said in that demise all prophecy would be fulfilled. Therefore, Jesus well knew the Law would not fully pass until then.

Further, the New Covenant teaches that the passing of the Law was an on-going process.[18] In 2 Corinthian 3:13 Paul said the Law was "being abolished," and they were living, several years subsequent to Calvary, in "hope" of the coming New Covenant. In Hebrews 8:13 inspiration says the Old Law was "nigh unto vanishing away" or in the process of vanishing. Hebrews 12:22f speaks of the system that was being shaken so that the unshakable kingdom, that was in the process of being delivered, might remain. Each of these texts illustrates that the passing of the O.T. was not completed in one singular action at the Cross. Again, that was the *power* behind the Law's demise, but other prophecy had to be fulfilled to complete that abrogation. The passing of the O.T. occurred over a period of time as it's prophecies were fulfilled and as the New was given and confirmed. Other verses confirm this.

In Romans 11 Paul affirmed in no uncertain terms that God's covenant with Israel would stand firm until the coming of Christ in fulfillment of Jehovah's promise to take away Israel's sin *and make the New Covenant with them* (Romans 11:25-27). The promises cited by Paul are Isaiah 27, Isaiah 59, and Jeremiah 31. Now, if God's Old Covenant promises to Israel remain valid until the parousia of Christ, as Paul affirms, then, if the Second Coming has not occurred, Israel remains as the chosen people of God. Further, if the coming of the Lord has not occurred, in fulfillment of God's promises to Israel, then most assuredly all of the Old Law, not some of it, not a little bit of it, not even most of it, but *all of it remains in force.*

The point of referring to Romans 11 is the fact that God's covenant with Israel would remain valid until He had kept His promises of bringing redemption to her. Many people miss the connection between Romans 9:28 and Romans 11:25-27. The salvation of Israel would be consummated with

17

the salvation of the remnant (Romans 11:5f). The salvation of the remnant had begun in the first century, and was on-going as Paul wrote. However, the climax of that process of bringing Israel's salvation history to a close was not to be a protracted event. The consummation was near, "For He will finish the work and cut it short in righteousness, because the Lord will make a short work on the earth" (Romans 9.28).

Now, since none of the Law could pass until all of God's promises to Israel were fulfilled, and since Paul said God's eschatological promises to Israel–i.e. the bringing in of her salvation–were to be fulfilled shortly, this means the passing of the Law was near when Paul wrote.

The postmillennial paradigm of Mathison, Gentry, and others falls in the face of Paul's unequivocal statements about the imminent consummation of Israel's hopes. Postmillennialism says Romans 11:26f is yet to be fulfilled near the end of the Christian age. This is patently not what Paul says. Naturally, Paul's statements falsify the dispensational eschatology as well. If the salvation of Israel was at hand when Paul wrote, then patently, it was not 2000 years away.

In the Apocalypse, John sees the reality of the soon to be fulfilled O.T. prophetic hopes of Israel. In chapter 1 he is told the future events are at hand and must shortly come to pass. In chapter 10:6-7 he hears what is to happen in the days of the seventh angel. He is told,"the mystery of God should be finished as he declared to his servants the prophets." As we have seen, when the term "the prophets" is used in the New Testament, unless there is clear contextual demonstration to the contrary, the reference is always to *Old Covenant prophets*. Thus, *John sees the imminent fulfilling of all Old Covenant prophecy.* (We are reminded of Daniel's prophecy of 70 weeks determined to "seal up prophecy and vision" meaning both the revelation and fulfilling of divine revelation. Daniel saw it for his distant future. John saw the fulfillment of that prophecy as imminent.) Importantly, John realized that the Old Covenant, since it was not yet fulfilled, was still anticipatory, thus still standing.

In the face of these declarations of Holy Writ it can scarcely be averred that the Old Law was done away at Calvary. Jesus said it would not pass until it was *all* fulfilled. It was not fulfilled until all prophecies contained therein were realized. All those prophecies were not realized until the fall of Jerusalem (Luke 21, Revelation 10).

In regard to 2 Peter 3 then, his declaration that his prediction of the Day of the Lord was a reminder of Old Covenant prophecy leads inescapably to the following conclusions which we hope do not sound repetitious.

18

The Law and Prophets (the Old Law) could not pass until they were all fulfilled (Matthew 5:17-18). 2 Peter 3 is a reiteration of the prophets (2 Peter 3:1-2). Therefore the Law and Prophets could not pass away until 2 Peter 3 was fulfilled.

The Law and Prophets (the Old Covenant), could not pass until it was all fulfilled (Matthew 5:17-18). 2 Peter 3 is part of the Law and Prophets. 2 Peter 3 is not yet fulfilled, per the modern interpretation. Therefore, it must be true that the Law and the Prophets have not been done away.

It is interesting that the opponents of Covenant Eschatology become so desperate in their attempts to refute this paradigm that they are willing to affirm the continuity of the Old Law. Mathison (*When*, 190), seeking to prove a yet future consummation of redemption at the end of time, posits Romans 2:13 as proof of that yet future event, "For not the hearers of the Law are justified before God, but the doers of the Law will be justified." The problem is, *Romans 2:13 is a direct reference to the Mosaic Law*. It is not a reference to obedience to the Gospel of Jesus Christ!

Of course, as a Theonomist, Mathison does in fact believe in the continuing validity of the Old Law. He believes Matthew 5:17-18 affirms the continuity of the Law until the passing of literal "heaven and earth." However, in 1997, David Chilton, a former Theonomist and former postmillennialist, explained why he had abandoned both those views and embraced the full preterist view. Among other things, he cited Matthew 5:17-18 pointing out that the very passage that the Theonomic school appeals to for proof of the continuing validity of the Law demands, *prima facia*, that not one iota of the Law, *including the sacrificial system*, could pass until the complete fulfillment. Therefore, if any of it is still valid, all of it, *sacrifices included*, must remain valid and obligatory.[19]

Where does obedience to *the Law of Christ* enter the picture, if it is obedience to "the Law" that is the ground for justification at the eschatological consummation? If the consummation of redemption is linked with the fulfillment and obedience to "the Law" where does grace enter? Those under "the Law" are not the recipients of grace; they are under the curse (Galatians 3:10f). Paul emphatically said "life and righteousness" are not through the Law (Galatians 3:21). Per Mathison's application of Romans 2:13 to the eschatological consummation therefore, he has mitigated the gospel of Jesus Christ, and reaffirmed justification by the works of "the Law!" Such careless exegesis, or such inconsistent doctrine, is characteristic of those who seek to refute the truth of Covenant Eschatology.

19

> **Mathison has affirmed the absolute necessity for faithful observance of the Mosaic Mandates until the "end of time!" What about animal sacrifices then??**

Related to the discussion of the passing of the Old System is the discussion of miraculous gifts, their purpose, and the establishment of the kingdom.[20] It is maintained by the opponents of the views set forth herein, that the church was completely established in fullness, power and glory on Pentecost. It is maintained that anything less than full establishment is failure. This contention is inconsistent with Biblical truth, and strangely enough, the arguments some of these detractors have made.

In my library, I have several debate books on the topic of miracles. Invariably, the cessationists argued that the charismata were part of the infancy state of the church. Passages such as I Corinthians 13 and Ephesians 4 are used to prove this, and correctly so. It is noted that miracles were for the purpose of equipping the church for the ministry until all revelation had been given and confirmed (Ephesians 4:8-16). When all revelation had been delivered and confirmed, when the "perfect" (I Corinthians 13:8f), had arrived then miracles would end. In the meantime miracles were part of the "partial," the "immature," state of the church.

But now, when, as noted above, preterists insist the church was not full grown until all prophecy was fulfilled, until the Old System was taken out of the way, they are labeled as heretics. Suddenly it is to be believed that the church was established full grown on Pentecost. But there are some severe consequences to such a claim.

If miracles were to equip the church to do the work of the ministry until the church came to maturity, and, if the church was established in full completeness and maturity on Pentecost, then it must be true that miracles were to equip the church to do the work of the ministry only until Pentecost. If this be true, then the church must have been established well before Pentecost!

If all revelation and confirmation of the Word had to happen before the church would come to maturity (Ephesians 4:8-13),[21] and if the church was established in full completeness and maturity on Pentecost, then *all the Word had been revealed and confirmed prior to Pentecost.* This implies that the entirety of what we call the New Testament, since written after Pentecost, is not divinely revealed and inspired!

If the church was established in full glory and completeness on Pentecost, and, if the church was established on Pentecost *prior to the conversion of the Gentiles*, then it must be true that the conversion of the Gentiles was not essential to the establishment of the church in full glory and completeness. Those who are familiar with Old Covenant prophecies know this is not the case. See Isaiah 2,11,35,65,66, etc.

If the church was established in full power and completeness on Pentecost, and, if the church was established *without elders*, then it must be true that elders were not essential to the full establishment of the kingdom. This means the church was fully grown, but not fully organized.

These are but a few of the logical ramifications of denying the period of time from Pentecost onward was a time of transition, of fulfilment, of maturation for the church. The Old Law was not all fulfilled on Pentecost, all revelation was not complete on Pentecost. The church had to grow up.

The only way to disprove the above is to, **1.)** demonstrate that the Old Law did not have to be fulfilled before it could pass. But this is contradicted by our Lord. **2.)** Prove that 2 Peter 3 is not a recapitulation of Old Covenant prophets. But Peter tells us he *is* referring to Old Covenant prophets. Taken together then, Luke 21:22 and Matthew 5:17-18 when viewed in reference to the fact that 2 Peter 3 is a restatement of Old Covenant prophecy, constitute strong proof that 2 Peter 3 is fulfilled. If not, *the Old Testament is still in effect.*

There is something else. It is interesting that partial-preterists such as Gentry argue against the present reality of the charismata, insisting that the gifts terminated in the first century.[22] Yet, notice what he also believes:

**1.)** Gentry believes we are in the last days.

**2.)** Gentry believes the consummate Day of the Lord is still future.

Gentry's view opens the door for the Pentecostal position that miracles are still operative. Joel said the Spirit would be poured out in, that is *during, the last days before the Day of the Lord. Miracles would continue until the day of the Lord.* (This is precisely what Paul said in I Corinthians 1:4-8.) If miracles were to be given in the last days and endure until the Day of the Lord, and if we are in the last days, and the Day of the Lord has not come, then *there must be miracles today.* By rejecting the Biblical testimony concerning the frame-work and time of the last days, Gentry is defenseless in the face of the charismatic world that he opposes.

21

Our point in this chapter is extremely important, and yet, too often overlooked. Many simply do not grasp the significance of the fact that Biblical eschatology is inextricably linked with the last days of Israel. Let me illustrate very quickly by delineating the traditional eschatologies.

**1.) Amillennialism:** This view says God was through with Israel at the Cross, and starting on Pentecost, God essentially started all over with a new set of prophecies and promises.

Engelsma iterates the Reformed Amillennial view by insisting that the O. T. prophecies must be fulfilled *at the end of the Christian age,* completely divorced from any connection to Old Covenant Israel. Biblical eschatology is, then, *Christian Eschatology,* Historical Eschatology. It is not about the fulfillment of God's promises to Israel.[23]

*Amillennialists have no place in their theology for the consummation of Israel's promises at the end of the current Christian age.*

**2.) Postmillennialism:** This view *ostensibly* honors the fact that Biblical eschatology is related to Israel, but, in reality, it does not do so. Postmillennialists, based on Romans 11:25f, posit a yet future conversion of "all Israel," but, it is *at the end of the Christian age*, not at the end of Israel's Aeon. Thus, postmillennialism has a "mix and match" eschatology. The problem is that the salvation of Israel foretold in Romans 11, is based squarely on the Old Covenant promises made to Israel (i.e. Isaiah 27:10f; 59:17f; Jeremiah 31), that would be fulfilled at the time of God's judgment of Israel for shedding innocent blood (Isaiah 59:3, 6-7), and the time when God made the New Covenant with Israel (Jeremiah 31).

Interestingly, postmillennialists say Israel was judged for shedding the blood of the martyrs in A.D. 70, and they even claim God fulfilled His promise to make the New Covenant with Israel, in the first century. Yet, they still place the coming of the Lord of Romans 11 in the future. This is anachronistic and inconsistent.

Postmillennialism does not have a place in its theology for a yet future destruction of Israel at the end of the Christian age, and at the time of the resurrection. Yet, the Old Covenant prophets placed the resurrection at the time of the end, at the time "when the power of the holy people is completely shattered" (Daniel 12:2,7).

**3.) Premillennialism:** Standing in opposition to the amillennial and postmillennial constructions, premillennialism does in fact, see the unbreakable link between eschatology and God's promises to Israel. Unfortunately, dispensationalism ignores or denies the proper time-frame for the fulfillment of those promises to Israel, maintains a woodenly literalistic approach to those prophecies, and says God could not and did not fulfill His promises to Israel at the time foretold.[24] This denies the emphatic declarations of the N. T. writers that they were living in the days foretold by the O. T. prophets, and that the promises to Israel were being fulfilled "in these days" as Peter put it.

The traditional eschatologies do not honor the unbreakable connection between Biblical eschatology and Israel, or they deny the proper time for the fulfillment of those promises. That is why we have taken the time in this chapter to drive this point home. Traditionally, Biblical eschatology is defined as *historical eschatology*. It is supposed to be about the end of human history. In fact, Biblical eschatology is *Covenant Eschatology*. It is about God's promises to Old Covenant Israel. Thus, when Peter says he was anticipating the fulfillment of the Day of the Lord prophecies of the Old Testament, including the promise of the new heavens and earth, the fact that he was speaking of the Old Testament prophetic corpus demonstrates that he was not speaking of the end of the Christian age, the end of time, or the end of human history. The Old Testament prophets never foretold anything remotely like the end of time, nor did they predict the end of the Christian age. On the contrary, they affirmed that the age of the Messiah would be without end (Isaiah 9.6f; Daniel 2.44).

We have shown that Jesus taught that not a single particle of the Old Covenant could pass away until every iota was fulfilled. This means without doubt that since the prediction of the Day of the Lord in 2 Peter 3 is part of "the Law and the prophets," if Peter's prediction has not been fulfilled, the entirety of the Old Law, including the animal sacrifices, Levitical priesthood, carnal washings, all of it, is still binding today. You simply cannot delineate between Peter's prediction and the Old Covenant prophecies, and blithely say 2 Peter 3 is still future, without demanding the continuing validity of the Old Covenant. If 2 Peter 3 remains unfulfilled, the Old Testament prophets remain unfulfilled, and valid.

23

## CHAPTER 3
## PETER'S PREVIOUS PREDICTIONS

**"This Second Epistle I Write to You, in Both of Which to Stir up Your Holy Minds by Way of Remembrance."** (2 Peter 3:1)

Simon says he is reminding his audience of what was written in the first epistle concerning the Day of the Lord. This is significant because when we examine 1 Peter we find unequivocal statements as to the expected time for the parousia, i. e. the Day of the Lord.

In I Peter 1:5, he speaks of their salvation and says it was *"ready to be revealed in the last time."* The word *ready* is from *hetoimos* (Strong's #2092), and has the meaning of *"ready, prepared."* This word indicates imminence. This same word is used in Revelation 21 to speak of the New Jerusalem descending out of heaven as the bride "prepared for her husband" (Revelation 21:2). The idea is that the bride was all dressed up for the wedding. Now ask yourself, how imminent is the wedding when the bride is all dressed up?[25]

Notice the fisherman says the salvation was, "ready to be revealed in the last times." He says they greatly rejoiced in this prospect, but before it could become a reality they must suffer "for a little while" (v. 7). In other words, the salvation which was ready to be revealed would be revealed *when their suffering was perfected, and that was only going to be a little while.* This is confirmed in chapter 5:10, "But may the God of all grace, who called us to His eternal glory by Christ Jesus, after you have suffered a while, perfect, establish, strengthen, and settle you." (NKJV)

These statements establish an unmistakable chronological frame work for the expectation of Peter's readers.[26] They longed for the salvation that was to be revealed, and it was *ready to be revealed.* They knew that salvation could only be revealed after they had suffered. They are reassured by Peter (inspiration) that the suffering would only be for a little while longer. (See our discussion of 2 Thessalonians below). Peter was not addressing the church, timeless and universal. He was addressing *living, breathing humans,* suffering for their faith, assuring them that the reward for their faithfulness was to be given in a short time.

Corroboration of this is to be found in Revelation 6:9-11. The apostle of Jesus' heart sees the fifth seal opened. Under the altar he sees the souls of slain martyrs. They have died for their faith and testimony. They cry out for vindication, "How long, O Lord, dost thou not judge and avenge our blood on those who dwell on the earth?" Unlike those to whom Peter wrote, these have already died. Like Peter's readers they are looking for something. They want *vindication*.

They are given robes and told to rest "a little while longer, until both the number of their fellow servants and their brethren, who would be killed as they were, was completed" (Revelation 6:10). Take note that these have died and want vindication. They are told they must wait for just a little while because there are others who must also die for their faith. Thus, their vindication was near. In Peter those who were at the very time suffering for their faith, (and which persecution was to intensify, I Peter 4:12), want relief and salvation. They are assured it is ready to be revealed as soon as they have suffered for just a little while. Peter's sufferers, and their contemporary brethren are the ones of whom Revelation 6:11 speaks.

In both texts we find suffering, some past, some present. In both there is the earnest desire for salvation. In both passages salvation is said to be "in a little while." In Peter, Jesus was "ready to judge the living and dead," "the end of all things is at hand," and, "the time is come for judgment to begin at the house of God" (1 Peter 4:5, 7, 17). In Revelation "the time is near." (Revelation 1:3 )

This scenario of suffering and the promise of imminent vindication is found in other passages. In Matthew 23 Jesus accused Jerusalem of being guilty of killing all the prophets and righteous (Matthew 23:31f). He said he would send prophets who would be killed as well. He then threatened: "On you may come all the righteous blood shed on the earth, from righteous Abel to the blood of Zechariah, ... Assuredly, I say to you, all these things will come upon this generation" (Matthew 23:33-36). Thus, Jesus foretold the coming persecution of his saints. (Remember Paul's words that he must fill up what was lacking in the suffering of Jesus, Colossians 1:24?) But Jesus also said the judgment of the persecutors of his people would occur in that first century generation.

In Luke 18:1-8, Jesus spoke of the suffering martyrs that "cry out day and night" for vindication, and he says they would be vindicated *speedily*. Who are these that cry out? Are they not the righteous of Hebrews who were sawn asunder, mocked, stoned, slain, tormented, and afflicted? These all looked for the "better resurrection" (Hebrews 11:35). Are they not the ones under the altar in Revelation 6? Surely this is true, and the promised vindication, the promised redemption, was to occur at the coming of Jesus in that generation. See Luke 21:7-33 where there is the warning of persecution (v.12), the promise of deliverance at the coming of Jesus (v.27), and the promise it would happen in that generation (v.32). This

25

theme of the imminent vindication of the suffering saints is found in a text that is the favorite of "end times" preachers, 2 Thessalonians 1:6f . We need to take a brief, but important look at that text to see how it fits into the picture before us.[27]

In writing to the church at Thessalonica, Paul was addressing a church undergoing severe persecution, so much so that Paul was concerned they would give up (1 Thessalonians 3:1-3). The Jews were the movers and shakers of that persecution (1 Thessalonians 2:15-17).

Notice Paul's reference to "those who are troubling you." Now, historically, this was not the Romans, who did not persecute the church until Nero, almost two decades later. It most assuredly could not have been the Roman Catholic Church that many suggest. It was not some unknown entity. It was the Jews and the Jews only who were "those who are troubling you." This is indisputable.

2 Thessalonians 1 contains emphatic declarations about when Christ was to return in aid and comfort of the Thessalonians, and yet, its declarations are virtually ignored by so many Bible students.

"So that we ourselves glory in you in the churches of God for your patience and faith in all your persecutions and tribulations that ye endure: Seeing it is a righteous thing with God to recompense tribulation to them that trouble you; And to you who are troubled rest with us, when the Lord Jesus shall be revealed from heaven with his mighty angels, In flaming fire taking vengeance on them that know not God, and that obey not the gospel of our Lord Jesus Christ: Who shall be punished with everlasting destruction from the presence of the Lord, and from the glory of his power; When he shall come to be glorified in his saints, and to be admired in all them that believe (because our testimony among you was believed) in that day." (KJV)

We need to take note of several facts:

**First**, the Thessalonians were currently undergoing intense persecution. Paul uses the word *thlipsis* as well as *pasxo*, (suffering) to describe what they were enduring. Paul was not speaking of the church suffering persecution throughout the ages. He was writing to living, breathing humans being persecuted in their home town. Paul was not referring to the mundane human existence as *thlipsis*. He was not referring to heart disease, cancer, financial difficulties, or even problems with teenage children! He was speaking of persecution for believing in Jesus as the Son of God.

**Second**, Paul promised the Thessalonians rest (from *anesis*, which means relief from pressure[28]), from their persecution.

26

**Third**, Paul said *their persecutors would be persecuted* at the same time the Thessalonians received relief (v. 6-7). In other words, the tables would be turned, the persecutors would become the persecuted.

**Fourth**, Paul said the promised relief from persecution would come, "when the Lord Jesus is revealed from heaven, in flaming fire taking vengeance on those that know not God" (v. 7-8).

*Notice what Paul did not say*:

**First**, *he did not say* the Thessalonians would receive relief from their persecution by *dying*. He said their promised relief would come at the coming of Jesus.

**Second**, *he did not say* the *church* thousands of years later would eventually receive relief from persecution. He said the *Thessalonians*, those who were being persecuted when he wrote, would receive relief from their persecution. Thessalonians is an "occasional letter" which means that a very specific historical occasion prompted Paul to write to them. And, it was the urgency of the occasion that prompted Paul's promise of relief from that very real, very personal, very contemporary, occasion.

Our choices here are very limited:

**First**, the Thessalonians are either still alive being persecuted, if the Lord has not come, or they are dead. It is pretty clear they are dead.

**Second**, if the Thessalonians are dead, then the Lord either came in their lifetime and gave them relief from their persecution, or he did not come in their lifetime and give them the promised relief.

**Third**, if the Lord did not come in the lifetime of the Thessalonians and give them relief from their persecution, then Paul's prediction failed.

**Fourth**, if Paul's promise/prediction failed, then he was a false prophet, and the inspiration of scripture is destroyed.

**Fifth**, it is a fact of history that the Jews were the instigators of the persecution of the Thessalonians (Acts 17:1f), and it is a fact of history that in the war of A.D. 66-70, the Jews went from being the persecutors of the Christians–and inciting the Romans to do so as well–to being persecuted by the Romans.

So, just as Paul said in 2 Thessalonians 1, the persecutors would become the persecuted, and the Christians would receive relief. In other words, Jesus did come in judgment of the persecutors (Israel), and gave relief to the persecuted brethren.

This is harmonious with I Peter 1 and the salvation which was to be revealed in the last time, and the fact that their deliverance would come in "a little while." It helps us clearly posit the last times in which the salvation was to be revealed as not the distant future from Peter's readers, but the very generation in which they lived. Since 2 Peter 3 is, according to Peter in vs.1-2, but a reiteration of these matters it seems undeniable that the events of 2 Peter 3 were to be fulfilled in that generation.

There is yet another confirmatory factor here, and that is the identity of the scoffers. The scoffers were not scientists, affirming the doctrine of uniformitarianism. The scoffers were, in all probability, either apostate Christian Jews, or the unbelieving Jews, and, this is important. They were not simply challenging the veracity of the parousia doctrine. They were *persecuting the church*! Now, if that claim will hold up, then the time frame and the frame-work for the Day of the Lord in 2 Peter 3 is undeniably set within the first century, when Jesus was going to come in judgment of the persecutors of his body, and vindicate the martyrs. That was to be in the judgment of Old Covenant Israel in A.D. 70 (Matthew 23).

The time frame for "the last time" is not left to open question in other passages either. In I John 2:18 John tells us, "we know it is the last hour." The writers of the New Testament knew they were living in the last days. Peter said their salvation was, "ready to be revealed in the last times." John says they were living in the "last *hour.*" Therefore, that salvation must have been not only prepared to be revealed, but on the point of being revealed as well. This is corroborated by other verses that Peter penned.

In chapter 4:5 Peter says Jesus was "ready to judge the quick and the dead." The same word *ready* is used here as in chapter 1 noted above. It is often asserted Jesus could not have been ready, in the sense of imminence, to judge in the first century because this would require a radical alteration of our concept of the judgment and the resurrection. While it is true it requires such an alteration, the change brings us in tune with the Bible, and this is never wrong. Jesus clearly taught he was going to judge the dead in the first century (Matthew 23:29-39, Revelation 11, 20,22).

To make the point even clearer, Peter emphatically declares in I Peter 4:7, "The end of all things is at hand." (Literally, *has drawn near*, from *engeken*, the perfect tense of *engus*). When we combine the words of verses 5 and 7 it is irrefutable proof of the expectation of the soon return of Christ. Interestingly, Mathison lists 1 Peter 4:7 as one of, "several passages in the epistles of the New Testament that describe the end as near." (*When*, 202). Well, what end was near? It was the end, when the living and dead were ready to be judged (1 Peter 4:5). This is the resurrection!

In fact, Mathison affirms, "If the epistles of the NT were written before the fall of Jerusalem in A.D. 70, then they too could have referred to the

28

coming end of Israel as simply 'the end.'" (*WSTTB*, 202) Would Mathison deny that the books of the NT were written before A.D. 70? His ambiguity in this regard is indicative of his approach in his book. He lists one alternative explanation after another, including the amillennial and premillennial, and in some cases refuses to even take a firm stand. It seems as if he is saying, "I will accept *any view* except the 'hyper-preterist' view![29] Take your choice of the following possibilities, but remember that the full preterist can't be one of the choices!"

Finally, for our current investigation, is chapter 4:17. Inspiration said, "the time is come for judgment to begin at the house of God." This passage is important for the understanding of 2 Peter 3, since it speaks of the same judgment being anticipated in that chapter (2 Peter 3:7). Consider the following thoughts in regard to 1 Peter 4:17 and the judgment.

In about 64 A. D. Peter said, "The time has come for the judgment to begin at the house of God, and if it first begin at us what will be the end of those who do not obey the gospel." (1 Peter 4:17)

Peter said "the *time* has come," the word "time" is from *kairos*, (Strong's #2540), and means *appointed* or *designated* time. It is *specific time* as opposed to generic time. Earlier in that generation the apostle Paul had said, "God has appointed a day in which he will judge the world (literally "is about to judge," from *mello*, Acts 17:30-31). Here is the *appointed time* Peter had in mind. And notice that Peter used the definite article. It is "*the* time," not generic time. See more on this judgment and the Greek definite article below.

Kistemaker attempts to use the word *kairos*, as used in Revelation, as a refutation of preterism. He notes that when John said "the time is at hand" he used the word *kairos*. It is claimed that *kairos* is "the motif of God-ordained phases relating to the end of time."[30] For Kistemaker, *kairos,* "conveys the meaning of eschatological time, expressed not in chronological periods, but in terms of principle." (*WSTTB*, 238)

Kistemaker says that while, "We could say that the fulfillment of Jesus' promise, 'I am coming soon,' is long overdue, if it has not taken place. But consider the concept of 'soon' in the light of Old Testament prophecy." (*WSTTB*, 247). He then claims the Old Testament prophets spoke as if the coming of Christ and the end was near, when in fact, of course, it was hundreds of years off. These claims are false.

Peter emphatically says "the *kairos* has drawn near." So, in truth, it does not matter how you define *kairos*, Peter said unequivocally the *kairos* had arrived. This means that all attempts to negate the imminence of the *kairos* are misguided.[31] If *kairos* was a mere principle, then the principle had arrived (how does a "principle" arrive?).

The apostle also said the time has come for "*the* judgment." Unfortunately, many translations do not take note that the definite article appears before judgment. They render it "the time has come for judgment." (Compare for instance NASV, NRSV, NKJV, etc.). Peter was not saying a time had come for "a judgment," it was time for "the appointed time" of "*the* judgment!" What judgment did he have in mind?

In 1 Peter 1 he was eagerly anticipating the arrival of the salvation foretold by the Old Testament prophets. Those prophets had been told they were not predicting events for their day (1 Peter 1:10-12). But Peter said that salvation, that would come at the revelation of Jesus, was "ready to be revealed in the last time" (1 Peter 1:5-7). And Peter emphatically said he was living in the last days (Acts 2:15f, 1 Peter 1:18-20). In 1 Peter 4:5 the writer said Jesus was "ready to judge the living and the dead." In verse 7 he said "the end of all things is at hand."

Peter was not predicting the end of time or material creation. He was predicting the coming of Jesus at the end of the Old Covenant age in the fall of Jerusalem in A.D. 70. Jesus said he was coming in that generation (Matthew 24:29-34), and redemption would be brought at that time (Luke 21:20-28). Peter was writing later *in that very generation,* and said Christ's coming for redemption was at hand. The time had come!

Upon what basis do we today say the judgment has not occurred? *Peter said the time for the judgment had arrived 2000 years ago.* Was Peter wrong, just deluded? Peter *did not say,* "I *hope* the time for the judgment has come. *He said it had arrived.* If he was wrong he was not inspired!

Traditional concepts are difficult to change. But if we are going to be serious students of the Word we must accept its inspired decrees. If we are going to *reverence* God's authority we must accept its decrees instead of our preconceived ideas. The question is: Was Peter right or wrong?

For Peter, therefore, there was no controversy, he and his readers were living in the time when they expected Jesus to return and judge the living and the dead. (Cf. Matthew 5:17-18 with Acts 24:14-15.)

# CHAPTER 4
## *THE LAST DAYS*

### "There Shall Come Scoffers in the Last Days."

What does the Bible mean by the term "the last days?" If you have read the *Left Behind* books, you may, like millions, believe we are in the last days. There is not a more critically important study than this, for all eschatology belongs to the "last days." Be sure to see my book, with contributions from John Anderson, entitled, *The Last Days Identified*, for a full discussion of this vital topic.[32] You need to read the entirety of that book to appreciate the importance of the topic at hand. If we can properly identify the last days, and demonstrate that the last days have nothing to do with the last days of the Christian age, or the last days of time, then any suggestion that 2 Peter 3 is referent to a yet future termination of time or human history is misguided.

The dispensational view is that the term "last days" refers to two different periods. **First,** when the *Old Testament* speaks of the last days, it refers exclusively to the last days of Israel i. e.. the climactic 70th Week of Daniel 9. The millennialists claim "the church was an unrevealed mystery in the Old Testament."[33] **Second,** the term *last days* is identified, by both millennialists, amillennialists and postmillennialists, as the entirety of the Christian age. **Third,** the term *last days* is often defined by the dispensationalists as *the last generation* of the Christian age.

One thing to keep in mind initially is this–and this may sound strange at first, but read carefully-- if the Old Testament never predicted the Christian age, then *the New Testament* never speaks of the Church Age. Ludicrous you say? How could we make such a statement? Here is why.

---

If the millennialists are right, that the O. T. never speaks of the church, or the last days of the church age, it therefore follows that the N. T. never speaks of the church or the church age. The N. T. writers repeatedly affirm that their last days doctrine is exactly what the O. T. prophets foretold. Therefore, if the O. T. never mentions the church age, then the N. T. never mentions the church age. And that, of course, is patently false.

---

31

All of the New Testament writers affirm, in the clearest manner possible, that the gospel they preached was taken strictly from and based squarely on the *Old Testament prophecies.* Paul's doctrine of the resurrection –and that is eschatology *exemplified,* is it not?– was nothing but what Moses and all the prophets predicted (Acts 24:14f). Now, if Paul's eschatology was Old Testament eschatology, and if the Old Testament never predicted the Church in any way, then it must be true that Paul's doctrine of eschatology relates exclusively to Israel, *and that it has nothing to do with the church.* This is devastating for the view–that includes amillennial and postmillennial– that the *parousia* of Christ, the Day of the Lord of 2 Peter 3, is to be the end of the current Church Age.

Peter likewise affirms, as seen above, that his eschatology is taken directly from the Old Testament prophets (cf. Acts 3:19f; 1 Peter 1:10f). John in the Apocalypse affirms the same thing (Revelation 10:7f; 22:6).

Thus, all New Testament eschatology is Old Testament eschatology *reiterated–not redefined!--* and placed within the context of Jesus as Lord. The last days spoken of in the Bible are the last days of Israel.

The amillennial and postmillennial view is that "the last days" is a technical term for the entirety of the Christian age. Gentry[34] and Mathison, (*WSTTB,* 189) postmillennialists, also believe that the last days is the entirety of the Christian age. Amillennialists concur.[35]

Mathison presents a confused view of the last days. He says: "In some sense then, 'the last days' were already present immediately after the first coming of Christ." (*When,* 189) And furthermore, he admits that the last days under consideration were, "the last days foreseen by the prophet Joel."(*WSTTB,* 189) This is a vital admission, but there is more.

Perhaps seeing the danger of admitting that the last days foretold by the Old Covenant prophets were present, Mathison then suggests:

"There are, however, other New Testament texts that seem to refer to 'the last days' as something yet to come. Paul for example, warns Timothy that 'in the last days perilous times will come' (2 Tim. 3:1; cf. 1 Tim. 4:1). Peter warns his readers, that scoffers will come in the last days" (2 Peter 3:3). It should be noted that neither Paul nor Peter explicitly says that 'the last days' are future in these texts. What they do say is that 'the last days will be a time in which something that is future will happen. The coming of 'perilous times' and of 'scoffers' is explicitly said to be future. The future times during which these things will come is called 'the last days." The

32

implication is that 'the last days' referred to in these texts are still future." (Mathison, *WSTTB*, 189-190)

There are numerous problems with Mathison's assessment.

**First,** to suggest that the last days foretold by the Old Testament prophets were present in the first century is to demand that they were living in the time of fulfillment. In Acts 3:19f, the apostle emphatically said all the prophets that had written before hand "foretold these days." (*kateggeilan tas hemeras tautas*). What *days* did the Old Covenant prophets foretell? The last days. Thus, there can be no doubt that the last days foretold by the Old Testament prophets were in fact present in the first century. Peter even affirms this in 1 Peter 1:5-7, 20.

**Second,** did Paul and Peter anticipate a protracted last days? Is Mathison correct to suggest that what Peter and Paul foretold did not take place in the first century?

Mathison has conveniently ignored the fact that in Paul's prophecy of the last days (1 Timothy 4, 2 Timothy 3), he explicitly warned Timothy to prepare *himself* to confront the dangers being foretold. If the events were for the far off future, this was a pointless exhortation. The truth is that every danger mentioned by Paul and Peter was present in the first century. Robertson has noted: "As a matter of fact, the false teachers described in 2 Peter (and thus in Paul, DKP), suit the first century precisely if one recalls Paul's troubles with the Judaizers in Galatia and Corinth and with the Gnostics in Colossae and Ephesus. 'Every feature in the description of the false teachers and mockers is to be found in the apostolic age' (Bigg)"[36] This being the case, Mathison's argument that the scoffers and false teachers were future is wrong. The last days foretold by Peter and Paul were in the first century.

Furthermore, to divorce the last days of 1 Timothy 4 and 2 Timothy 3-4 from the "hope of Israel" creates a disjunction in Paul's message. Remember that Paul taught nothing but the hope of Israel. His gospel was nothing but that found in Moses and the prophets (Acts 24:14f; 2621f; 28:16f). Thus, attempts by Mathison, Gentry, et. al. to divorce 1 Timothy 4, 2 Timothy 3-4 from that context are misguided. The result of this kind of hermeneutic is the creation of two eschatons, two hopes, two gospels.

**Third,** in our exegesis of 2 Peter, based on Isaiah 28, it is clear that Peter was not predicting that "one of these days by and by" the scoffers would come. He was reminding his audience that what the prophets had foretold long ago was true. He was telling them they were in the time foretold by the prophets. See our discussion above on the relationship

33

between Jude and 2 Peter. Jude positively said the scoffers foretold by the Old Testament prophets, and the apostles, *were already present and at work in his day*. Now, if the scoffers foretold by the Old Testament prophets, *and by the apostles*, were already present, then Mathison's claim that the last days foretold by Peter are yet future is falsified.

Those who insist the last days started on Pentecost overlook the very prophecies which spoke of them. Isaiah 2:2 said the house of the Lord would be established *in* or *during* the last days. Joel said the Spirit would be poured out *in* or during the last days. Now since the kingdom was to be established and the Spirit given *during*, that is, *while the last days were in progress*, it is inconsistent to say those last days did not even start until Pentecost. The prophecies did not say these events would initiate the last days. These events would occur *while the last days were in progress*.

To put it another way, the *church age* was to be established in the last days. This means that *one age was to be established* during or while another age was in existence. Again, the church age was to be established in or during the last days. If the "last days" is referent to the Christian age this means the Christian age was to be established in the Christian age. In other words, if the last days are equal to the Christian age then the Christian age was to be established while it was already ongoing. This would have Isaiah and Joel saying, in the Christian age, the Christian age will be established. Does the Bible use such useless redundancy?

Isaiah 2-4 is not a prediction of the *founding* of the last days, but of events to occur *in the last days of Israel*. Isaiah 2-4 is a united prophecy. It predicted the last days (2:2-4), consummating in the Day of the Lord (2:10f, 19-21). Mathison claims the prophecy is still unfulfilled today, at least finally. (*WSTTB*, 166)

Isaiah 3 describes the events of the Day of the Lord, and it cannot be an "end of time" event, since it would be a time of famine, warfare, and, more importantly, the time when God would judge Israel (3:13f), when Israel's men would fall by the edge of the sword (3:24f). Significantly, this Day of the Lord would be *when Jehovah would purge Israel from her bloodguilt, the guilt of shedding innocent blood* (4:4f). This is no other time than the first century. It is impossible for Mathison and the postmillennialists to extrapolate beyond the Day of the Lord in Isaiah 2-4. Yet, the Day of the Lord of Isaiah 2-4 was to be when Israel was judged for her blood guilt. Jesus said Israel would fill the measure of her sin– the sin of shedding innocent blood– and be judged in his generation (Matthew 23:29f). Thus, the events of the last days, consummating in the day of judgment against

34

Israel for shedding innocent blood, belong exclusively to the last days of Israel. This contradicts Mathison's postmillennial paradigm, for he, somewhat like the millennialists, sees a yet future *restoration of Israel*, not a cataclysmic judgment.

> **Isaiah's prediction that the kingdom would be established *in the last days*, before the Day of the Lord, was a prediction that the kingdom would be established in the last days of Israel before she was judged in A.D. 70.**

What this means of course, is that one of the key texts appealed to by the amillennialists and postmillennialists to prove that the last days began on Pentecost, proves just the opposite. It proves the last days were already in existence on Pentecost, and that they refer to Israel's last days, not the last days of time or human history.

Let us frame it in simplified form. The church was to be established in the last days spoken of by Isaiah 2-4. But the last days foretold by Isaiah 2-4 were the last days of Israel before her judgment in A.D. 70. Therefore, the church age was to be established in the last days of Israel before her judgment in A.D. 70.

If the last days spoken of by Joel and Isaiah were already in existence when the church age was established, the church age cannot be the last days spoken of by Joel and Isaiah. The last days spoken of by Joel and Isaiah *were* in existence when the church age was established. Therefore, the church age cannot be the last days spoken of by Joel and Isaiah.

Consider the significance of Isaiah 2-4 for the traditional eschatologies.

Isaiah 2-4 refutes dispensationalism, because it speaks of the last days judgment of Israel for shedding the blood of the saints. Millennialism has no place for this in its eschatology.

Isaiah 2-4 refutes postmillennialism because it speaks of the last days judgment of Israel for shedding innocent blood, at the Day of the Lord, yet, postmillennialism believes in the restoration of Israel in the future, not the judgment of Israel.[37]

Isaiah 2-4 refutes amillennialism because amillennialists have no place for Israel in the future. Yet, Isaiah is undeniably about Old Covenant Israel.

Only the preterist view of Isaiah 2-4 properly posits the events of Isaiah 2-4 within the confines of the last days of Old Covenant Israel, and her judgment for shedding innocent blood, at the Day of the Lord in A.D. 70.

35

## THE SONG OF MOSES AND THE LAST DAYS

Another text to help us identify the last days is Deuteronomy 32. This great chapter is called the *Song of Moses*, and is one of the most significant, yet overlooked prophecies in the Bible. I am currently working on a book about the Song to demonstrate how this prophecy is interwoven into the very fabric of the New Testament, and specifically, of Biblical eschatology. For the time being, we can focus only on a few salient points from this prophecy to help us identify the last days. What follows is an edited excerpt from my book: *The Last Days: Identified!*

**First**, the prophecy has to do with *the last days of Israel*, not the last days of time. Moses called on Israel to consider, "what their end will be...that they would consider their latter end" (Deuteronomy 32:20; 29).

**Second**, Moses said that in Israel's last days, she would, "become utterly corrupt and turn aside from the way which I have commanded you, and evil shall befall you in the latter days" (Deuteronomy 31:29). Since Deuteronomy 31:29 serves as the introduction to the Song of Moses, we are including our examination of it in our comments on chapter 32.

**Third**, in the last days, Jehovah would bring in the Gentiles in order to provoke Israel to jealousy (V. 21f).

**Fourth**, God said that in the last days, "The Lord shall judge His people" (v. 36). He would judge Israel because, "Her vine is the vine of Sodom" (v. 32).

**Fifth**, as a result of Israel's sin, the Lord said, "A fire is kindled in My anger, and shall burn to the lowest hell, it shall consume the earth with her increase, and set on fire the foundations of the mountains." (v. 22).

**Sixth**, in the last days, El Shaddai would, "Avenge the blood of His servants and render vengeance to His adversaries" (v. 43).

There are many other issues we could explore, but for brevity, we will confine our comments to these issues. Let us begin by taking special note of **the first point**, that the focus of the prophecy was *the last days of Israel*. To interject the consummation of the Christian Aeon, or the end of time into the chapter is without merit.

Moses said (**second point above**), that in the last days, Israel would become *utterly corrupt*, and evil would befall her. Here, we are on safe ground in identifying the framework and time of the last days.

In Acts 7:52, Stephen stood in the Temple and castigated the Jews for their long, bloody history of killing the prophets: "Which of the prophets have you not slain?" Jesus had earlier said that they would, by killing the apostles and prophets he was going to send, fill up the measure of their sin.

They were going to become *utterly corrupt*, just like Moses predicted they would "in the last days!" (Deuteronomy 31:29) Finally, Jesus said judgment for that full cup of sin would be poured out in his generation (Matthew 23: 34-36). Remember the parable of Matthew 21 and the wicked husbandmen. They exhausted the patience of the master by killing the servants sent to them. The harmony with Deuteronomy is direct.

Thus, Moses said that in the last days, Israel would become utterly corrupt, fill the measure of her sin, and be judged. Jesus, who appeared in the last days (Hebrews 1:1), said Israel would fill the cup of her sin and be judged in her generation. It is clear Jesus was not speaking to or about the church. He was not speaking about any so-called end of time. He was speaking of what was going to happen *to Israel*, in his generation. This means, unequivocally, that the *last days* foretold by Deuteronomy 32 would be in existence during Jesus' generation, but would come to consummation when she was judged. And, it should go without saying that the judgment Jesus was referring to was the judgment that fell on Jerusalem in A.D. 70.

Moses said that in the last days, Jehovah would call the Gentiles to Him in order to make Israel jealous. Remember that Moses was speaking of *Israel's* last days, not the last days of time or the church. And, he said that in Israel's last days God would call the Gentiles. (God was not promising to call the Gentiles in order to make the *church* jealous).

According to millennialists, the 70th week of Daniel 9, and the famous 70 weeks prediction, was suspended, and Israel's last days were put on hold. The 69th week supposedly ended when Jesus rode into Jerusalem, being hailed as king. Thus, from that point forward, Israel's last days are in abeyance until the Rapture, "At His first advent, the Lord Jesus Christ came to offer the Kingdom promised in the Old Testament. When Israel rejected her Messiah, the Old Testament program was held in abeyance."[38] But here is the problem.

Moses said that in Israel's last days, Jehovah would call the Gentiles to Him. However, the Gentiles were not called to Jehovah by the preaching of the Gospel until some 10 years after the day of Pentecost. The conversion of Cornelius (Acts 10), signaled the ministry to the Gentiles, and then, the conversion of Paul began the Gentile mission in earnest.

As a matter of fact, Paul was the special apostle to call the Gentiles, and, here is what is so important, he specifically quotes from Deuteronomy 32 to justify his ministry to the Gentiles (Romans 10:19)! In other words, Paul saw his ministry to the Gentiles as the fulfillment of the Song of Moses. But if Paul's ministry was the fulfillment of the Song of Moses, this means

37

the last days of Israel were in existence during Paul's ministry, long after the so-called suspension of the last days of Israel. This is absolutely devastating to the premillennial view!

If the last days foretold by Moses in Deuteronomy 32 were in existence during Paul's ministry,[39] then undeniably, the countdown of Israel's last days was not suspended as our premillennial friends say. If the countdown of Israel's last days was on-going during Paul's ministry, then since Jesus placed the consummation of those last days at the fall of Jerusalem, as we have just seen, this means the last days of Israel cannot in any way be placed in the future!

Further, since Paul's ministry to the Gentiles was the fulfillment of Deuteronomy 32, this means the last days foretold by that prophecy was the focus of his ministry as well. This means that when Paul said, "the time has been shortened" (1 Corinthians 7:26f), and, "the end of the ages has come upon us" (1 Corinthians 10:11), that we need to see these statements in the context of *Israel's last days*. After all, isn't it pretty clear Paul was *not* saying, "The end of the Christian age has drawn near"? If he was, he was patently wrong, and, if he was wrong, Christianity falls.

It cannot be over-emphasized that the focus of Deuteronomy 32 is *the last days of Israel*. To apply that prophecy to the last days of the current age is wrong. Yet, most commentators, when speaking of the conversion of the Gentiles in Romans, focus on the Christian age. This is anachronistic. It removes Paul's discussion far beyond the temporal and covenantal parameters of Deuteronomy and the Old Testament prophecies he cites. Paul was focused on the fulfillment of God's promises to Israel.

**Our third point** is that Moses said that in the last days, "The Lord shall judge His people," and the reason for that is, "Their vine is the vine of Sodom" (Deuteronomy 32:32, 36). A great deal could be said about these two verses from Deuteronomy. We will only note a few things.

Paul, in Romans 12:19, comforted the Christians being persecuted by quoting from Deuteronomy 32:35. In Hebrews 10:30, in the identical context of persecution, he quotes the same verses. Now, it is important to see that the persecution against the church in the first century was primarily instigated by the Jews. So, in both Romans and Hebrews, Christians were being persecuted by the Jews. Paul promised the Christians relief from that persecution by quoting the promise of Moses that in Israel's last days, they would be judged! Paul was applying the last days prophecy of the judgment of Israel to *his contemporary generation*, and applying that prophecy to the Jews of his day who were persecuting the True Israel of God.

38

In Hebrews 10, the impending judgment on the persecutors and the attendant salvation for the faithful, was coming, "in a very, very little while" (Hebrews 10:37, Greek, *hosan, hosan micron*). The last days judgment of Israel foretold by Deuteronomy 32 was the judgment being promised by Hebrews. Hebrews said it was very, very near. Therefore, Israel's last days were present in Hebrews 10.

**The fourth point** is that Moses said Israel was to be judged because her vine was, "the vine of Sodom" (Deuteronomy 32:32). This brings us again to see the beautiful harmony in the Bible. In Revelation, we find the judgment of the harlot city. Remember, this is, "where the Lord was slain" (Revelation 11:8). This harlot city was also, "spiritually called Sodom"! So, Revelation, which is about the fulfillment of God's promise concerning Judah and Shiloh, is also about the judgment of Jerusalem, whom He calls *Sodom*, because the prophecy of Moses was being fulfilled in her!

Here is something amazing. The only city, in all the Bible, that is ever spiritually called Sodom was *Old Covenant Jerusalem*! As a matter of fact, the only city, other than historical Sodom, to *ever* be called Sodom at all, was *Jerusalem!*[40] See Isaiah 1:9-10, Jeremiah 23:14 and Ezekiel 16:35-49. So, here is what we have. Moses said that in the last days, Israel would bear the fruit of being the vine of Sodom. John, writing about the last days, says, "Babylon"–the city where the Lord was slain– was spiritually called Sodom, and was about to be destroyed. John had the fulfillment of Deuteronomy 32 in mind. By the way, he refers to the Song of Moses more than once in the Apocalypse, so, like Paul, John was concerned with the fulfillment of that prophecy of Israel's last days.

**The fifth point** above is that in Israel's last days, Jehovah would be so angry at that nation that He would *burn up the earth* (Deuteronomy 32:22). Here is an interesting question: Does *anyone* teach that at the so-called end of time, or at the end of the Christian age, the literal earth is burned up *because God is angry with Israel*? Answer: No! I am unaware of any school of eschatology that teaches that at some point in the future, God will be so angry at Israel that He will destroy the literal cosmos.

Well, what does this mean then? This is metaphoric language. It means that in Israel's last days, Jehovah would destroy Israel's land, her Temple, her *world*! God would destroy Israel's "heaven and earth." He would destroy her *covenant* world.[41] Unless you are willing to posit a future destruction of Israel at the end of the Christian age, or at the end of the millennium, then you must take the language metaphorically. The beauty of this is that we have Jesus' words that in his generation, Israel's "heaven

39

and earth" was indeed going to be destroyed, *at his coming in judgment of Jerusalem* (Matthew 24:29-34). Thus, Moses said that in Israel's last days, Israel's sin would lead to the destruction of "creation." Jesus, who appeared in the last days, predicted the destruction of Israel's "heaven and earth!"

Note again that Peter tells us his discourse on the Day of the Lord and the events of the last days are taken from the Old Testament prophets (2 Peter 3:1-2). Now, if Peter is in fact drawing upon Deuteronomy 32, as he often does in his writings, then since it is undeniable that Deuteronomy 32 has nothing whatsoever to do with the last days of time or material creation, this means 2 Peter 3 is a referent to the last days of Israel.

**Our sixth and final point** from Deuteronomy 32 is that Jehovah said that in the last days, He would, "Avenge the blood of His servants" (v. 43). This is an important promise, and one present throughout scriptures. In my book *Like Father Like Son, On Clouds of Glory,* I develop at length the Biblical theme of the vindication of the martyrs, the Law of Blood Atonement, Filling the Measure of Sin and Suffering, and similar motifs. We cannot develop these motifs here, but refer you to that work.[42]

What did Adonay (*Adonay* is one of the names for God), mean by the promise to vindicate the blood of His saints? It refers to the fact that historically, He had sent His prophets to Israel, to call them to repentance and holiness. In response, Israel had repeatedly rejected and killed the prophets. Nehemiah recounted Israel's history: "They were disobedient and rebelled against You, cast Your law behind their backs and killed Your prophets who testified against them" (Nehemiah 9:26; see 1 Kings 18:4).

Repeatedly, the Lord accused Israel of having hands red with the blood of His saints (see Isaiah 1:15; Isaiah 59, 3, 6, 7; Jeremiah 2, 22:17; Ezekiel 22, etc.) Israel was judged in B. C. 721, and Judah was judged in B. C. 586 for killing the righteous. However, Deuteronomy 32 looked to the last days and the "final" judgment for killing the Lord's servants.

Do you remember what Jesus said in Matthew 23? We have shown how Jesus, who appeared in the last days, stood in the temple, and recounted Israel's history of killing the righteous, "O Jerusalem, Jerusalem, thou that killest the prophets, and stones them that are sent unto her!"

In his parable of the Importunate Widow (Luke 18), Jesus spoke of the righteous, suffering at the hands of their persecutors. He said the martyrs, "Cry out to Him (God, DKP) day and night." Their cry was for *vindication,* the identical word (*ekdekeesis*), used in Deuteronomy 32:43, in God's promise to *vindicate* the martyrs' blood in the last days. This is also the word used in Revelation 6:9-11, where we see the martyrs under the altar crying, "How long, O Lord, will you not *avenge* us on those who dwell on the earth?" (Revelation 6:9-11).

The stream of the martyrs' blood flows throughout scriptures, and it flows through the street of one city, Old Covenant Jerusalem. From Deuteronomy 32 through Revelation the stream flows, yet, in Deuteronomy 32, Jehovah promised that *in the last days*, He would finally avenge that blood. When was that promise to be fulfilled? Was it to be at the end of the Christian age, or at the end of time? Read Matthew 23:33-34:

"Serpents, brood of vipers! How can you escape the condemnation of hell? Therefore, indeed I send you prophets, wise men and scribes; some of them you will kill and crucify, and some of them you will scourge in your synagogues and persecute from city to city, that on you may come all the righteous blood shed on the earth, from the blood of righteous Abel to the blood of Zechariah, the son of Berechiah, whom you murdered between the temple and the altar. Assuredly I say to you, all these things shall come upon this generation." (Matthew 23:33-36).

If we are going to accept Jesus as Lord, and his word as authoritative, we must bow before his statement that the vindication of the martyrs was to occur *in his generation at the fall of Jerusalem*. This helps us positively identify the last days.

Moses said that *in Israel's last days* God would avenge the shed blood of His saints (Deuteronomy 32:43).

But Jesus, who appeared in the last days (Hebrews 1:1-2), said all the blood of the martyrs, all the way back to creation, would be avenged in the fall of Jerusalem in A.D. 70.

Therefore, the last days foretold by Moses, the last days of Israel, occurred in the fall of Jerusalem in A.D. 70.

We must emphasize how destructive this is to the millennial view. Remember that the millennial view is that the last days of Israel were suspended when Jesus was rejected in Matthew 12, and that the 69th week of Daniel 9 ended with the triumphant entry into Jerusalem in Matthew 21. Jack Van Impe says that when Jesus died, "At that very moment, the prophetic clock stopped as far as Daniel's vision is concerned and 70 years later the Jews were dispossessed of their country and scattered throughout the world."[43] The consummative last days of Israel will begin with the signing of the peace treaty by the anti-Christ and Israel following the Rapture, according to this view, and could not have been present in A.D.

70. If the last days of Israel were present in A.D. 70, the entire premillennial view is destroyed!

This is not an overstatement for dramatic effect. Ice, a leading dispensationalist, says in a series of articles on Daniel 9 that if there is no gap of so far 2000 years between the 69th and 70th week of Daniel, then, "the dispensational system falls apart."[44]

With this in mind, look again at our argument.

**Moses: the blood of the martyrs would be avenged** *in the last days of Israel* **(Deuteronomy 32:20f, 42).**

**Jesus: the blood of the martyrs would be avenged in the fall of Jerusalem** *in A. D. 70 (Matthew 23:29f).*[45]

**Therefore, the last days of Israel existed in A.D. 70.**

There is no escape from this argument. Israel's last days existed in A.D. 70. Therefore, "the dispensational system falls apart."

The Biblical *fact* of the time of the vindication of the blood of the martyrs, is equally destructive to the traditional amillennial and postmillennial definition of the last days. Here is why.

The amillennial and postmillennial view is that the martyrs are vindicated at the end of the Christian age. Years ago, I listened to a sermon on the last days by a professor friend of mine, an amillennialist. He quoted Matthew 23:34-35, and said, "one of these days," at the end of the Christian age, all the martyrs will be vindicated. This is *not* what Matthew 23 says!

Here is why this is so important. The amillennialists and postmillennialists say the true last days belong to the end of the Christian age. However, the Bible affirms, as shown above, that *the Christian age has no end.*

Furthermore, the Bible undeniably places the vindication of the martyrs *in the last days of Israel in A.D. 70.* This means the amillennial and postmillennial views are wrong.

The issue is actually simple. Moses and Jesus said the vindication of the martyrs would occur *in Israel's last days.* Amillennialists and postmillennialists[46] say the vindication of the martyrs will occur *in the last days of the Christian age.* Who shall we believe? I choose to accept the words of Moses, Jesus, and the New Testament writers. The vindication of the martyrs was to occur *in the last days of Israel.* This is supported by John in the Apocalypse.

Remember, in Revelation 6, we saw the martyrs crying for vindication. They were then given white robes and told to, "rest for a little while, until their fellow-brethren who should suffer as they did, should be filled." The next seal vision was of their vindication at the Day of the Lord. Let's make this short and simple.

**The vindication of the martyrs would occur with the fall of "Babylon" (Revelation 11:8-17; 18:20-24).**

**But "Babylon" of Revelation was Old Covenant Jerusalem (Revelation 11:8).**

**Therefore, the vindication of the martyrs would occur with the fall of Old Covenant Jerusalem.**

As a corollary argument to help us confirm our identification of the last days consider the following.

**The vindication of the martyrs was to occur in the last days of Israel (Deuteronomy 32:43).**

**But the vindication of the martyrs was to occur with the fall of Jerusalem Therefore, the last days of Israel occurred in A.D. 70.**

Remember, Revelation is about the "real" last days, not a preliminary last days. The last days of Revelation are the *true* last days to wrap up God's Scheme of Redemption. Thus, to identify the last days in Revelation is to identify the last days of all of eschatological focus. We have shown that the last days of Revelation are the last days of Israel that ended in A.D. 70. Therefore, the last days that are the focus of Biblical eschatology are the last days of Israel, not the last days of the Christian age.

As you can see, Deuteronomy 32 clearly establishes the identity of the last days as the last days of Israel, not the church age. This means 2 Peter 3 cannot be about the destruction of material creation or the end of the Christian age. Let me express it like this:

**The Day of the Lord to vindicate the martyrs would occur in the last days of Israel in the judgment of Jerusalem in A.D. 70 (Isaiah 2-4; Matthew 23).**

**Peter foretold the Day of the Lord, in the last days (2 Peter 3).**

**Therefore, the Day of the Lord, in the last days, foretold by Peter (2 Peter 3), was the Day of the Lord in the last days of Israel in the judgment of Jerusalem in A.D. 70.**

### END OF THE AGE

The brethren of the first century believed they were living in the last days, or the consummation of the ages. In I Corinthians 10:11 Paul said:

43

"Now all these things happened unto them for ensamples: and they are written for our admonition, upon whom the ends of the world have come." Earlier he had said, "The time is short," and, "the fashion of this world passeth away" (I Corinthians 7:29,31). Undeniably, they believed they were in the last days, not in some vague, nebulous sense as espoused by Mathison, but concretely. Further, in Hebrews we have the express statement of Holy Writ that Jesus came in the consummation of the age (Hebrews 9:26). Was this not the same "end of the ages" that the Corinthians were experiencing? Were there two ends of the ages present?

There are three quick points to be made here.

**First**, Jesus and his Jewish contemporaries, only believed in two ages.[47] The two ages were "this age," and "the age to come."

**Second**, "this age" was the age of Moses and the Law, while "the age to come" was the age of Messiah, the New Covenant, and the kingdom.

**Third**, "this age" was to end, but "the age to come" was to be endless. There was some controversy among the Jews as to the duration of the Messianic Age, (Schurer, 536), but, in scripture that controversy does not exist. The age of the Messiah is endless (Isaiah 9:6f; Luke 1:32f).

Now if we are today in the Messianic Age, as the amillennialists and postmillennialists insist, then since scripture affirms that *the Messiah's Age will never end*, just how do they then affirm that Peter was predicting *the end of the endless Christian age*? If the New Testament writers believed in only two ages, and they clearly did, then the fact that they say they were living in the end of the age, is *prima facia* proof that they were anticipating the end of the age of Moses and the Law, and the establishment of the unending kingdom of the Messiah. This completely falsifies the idea that 2 Peter 3 is a prediction of the end of the Christian age.

**The throne and kingdom of the Messiah will never end (Isaiah 9; Luke 1; Matthew 24:35, etc.)**
**But the current Christian age is the age in which Messiah sits on his throne in his kingdom. (Amillennial and Postmillennial view).**
**Therefore, the current Christian age will never end.**

It is somewhat incredible to read the comments of the postmillennialists and dispensationalists in regard to "the age to come." Mathison, stating that the "last days" began with the first advent of Jesus, signified by the charismatic gifts on Pentecost, affirms that the current Christian age is called "this present evil age" by Paul in Galatians 1:4. (*WSTTB*, 188). Are we to believe the Christian age, ruled by the Son of God, is called "this present evil age"? Did Christ not triumph over his enemies and put them to

44

open shame (Colossians 2:14f)? Does Mathison *really* believe that the age of the Messiah is "this present evil age?"

In Matthew 13 Jesus spoke of "the end of this age" as the time of the harvest.[48] This is significant in light of Revelation 14 and the imminence of the harvest. It is also meaningful because he was living in the Jewish age when he said "harvest is at the end of the age," and, "as the tares are gathered and burned in the fire, so shall it be in the end of this world." *World* here is age. Jesus said harvest was to occur at the end of his "this age" (Matthew 13:39-40). In what age was Jesus living at the time? Galatians 4:4 tells us Jesus was born under the Law, i.e. he was born in and lived during, the age of Moses and the Law. And Jesus said the harvest would occur at the end of *that* "this age."

In Matthew 24 the disciples asked Jesus when the end of the age would come. He told them the harvest and his coming at the end of the age would happen in their generation (Matthew 24:29-34).

Since it is inescapable that *the end of the age* existed in the first century does it not follow that they were living *in the last days?* The question of course is, the end of what age? The last days of what age? Confusion on this question is often caused by the misconception that the new age was fully delivered on Pentecost while the entirety of the old age passed away on the cross. The new age did begin on Pentecost. It is equally true that it was not full grown nor perfected. It did not have its full constitution, nor was it fully organized as of yet.

It is also true that the old age was still in place. While it is true that those coming into Christ died to the law (Romans 7), this does not mean the Law itself had passed away. Those turning from the law were having the veil taken away in Christ (2 Corinthians 3), but the law was not completely passed (Hebrews 8:13). The Law was on its way out, but had not yet passed. The Bible clearly depicts the old world in the process of vanishing (Hebrews 12:23-29).

What we see in the N. T. is a transitional period in which the New Covenant was being delivered and confirmed while the Old Covenant was becoming obsolete and passing away. Two worlds were in transition. One covenant world was in its last days, a New Covenant world was born, and coming to maturity. The "new heavens and earth, wherein dwelleth righteousness" was about to fully arrive.

Undeniably, the NT writers affirm in unequivocal terms that the end of the age had arrived. They say the end was near. They believed in only two ages, the age of Moses and the Law, and the age of the Messiah, that would

45

never end. The fact that they affirmed the passing of the age of Moses, and the eternally abiding nature of Christ and his gospel proves conclusively that 2 Peter 3 could not be predicting the end of the current Christian age.

Hebrews 9:26 tells us Jesus came "in the end of the world," it is literally the "consummation of the age." In Hebrews 1:1 it says Jesus spoke "in these last days." A comparison with chapter 2:1f reveals this to be an allusion to his personal ministry. Such is also the case with the passage in 9:26 since it is speaking of him appearing in the end of the age to put away sin by sacrificing himself. In I Peter 1:19-20 Simon tells of the redeeming sacrifice of Jesus. He tells us Jesus was foreordained for this purpose, i.e. sacrifice of his blood, but was manifested in "these last days." In each of these passages then it speaks of the personal ministry or death of Jesus. (Need we say this was before Pentecost when the last days were supposed to have begun?) But while it speaks of Jesus in his ministry it says he appeared in the last days. If the last days did not start until Pentecost, how could Jesus have appeared in the last days?

This is not all. In Galatians 4:4 we find this: "But when the fullness of time was come, God sent forth his Son, made of a woman, made under the law." Jesus appeared in the last days. But he appeared under the law. Jesus appeared in the last days but *Jesus did not live even one day on earth after Pentecost*. Now since Jesus appeared in the last days, but he appeared prior to Pentecost, it follows that the last days could not have begun on Pentecost. It is logically unavoidable that the last days existed prior to Pentecost. Therefore, it is logically unavoidable that the last days were not initiated on Pentecost.

It may be rejoined that Jesus did appear in the last days, and he did appear prior to Pentecost, but the writers of Hebrews and I Peter, writing after Pentecost, say Jesus appeared "in *these* last days." In other words, they believed they were still living in the last days. That is correct, but they did *not* believe the last days started on Pentecost. What they believed was that, as shown above, they were living in a transitional period. They knew the New Covenant was being revealed and confirmed. The new system was taking shape and moving toward completion. As the new age moved close to perfection or maturity (I Corinthians 13, and Ephesians 4), the Old System stood on the brink of annihilation. Those last days started in the days of the Baptizer, and were consummated when Jesus came in judgment on the persecuting city in A.D. 70.

What we have seen then, in regard to the last days, is that they do not refer to the last days of earth, but to the last days of the Jewish Aion.

46

We concur with the following comment on the meaning of the last days, "It is important to understand that to Israel such phrases as 'the latter days,' 'the latter years, 'the time of the end,' 'the time of the iniquity of the end,' would refer to the final days--the waning years--of her theocratic life as the chosen nation. That national life ended in AD 70. None of those 'latter days' prophecies are yet future, millennialism notwithstanding. The 'latter days' do not refer to the last days of earth time, but of national time."[49]

If no "latter days" prophecies are yet future this means 2 Peter 3 cannot be future. If one argues that the latter days cannot be used by the premillennialist to speak of the future he certainly cannot then use those passages himself to speak of the end of time. Thus, when Peter said scoffers would come in the last days, he was not looking into the far off future. He was speaking of his own time, the waning days of the Jewish Age.

## "Knowing this First, That There Shall Come Scoffers in the Last Days" (2 Peter 3:3)

An examination of 2 Peter with Jude provides unequivocal proof that the last days of which Peter spoke were not in the far off future, but were a present reality when Peter wrote. This is a clear contradiction to Spargimino and others who are now saying that preterists are the last days scoffers predicted by Peter! (*Anti-Prophets*, 79)

Peter said scoffers would come in the last days. His depiction of these men can be found in detail in 2 Peter 2. One has only to compare Peter's description of these men and then study the book of Jude to see that what Peter said would happen was happening at that very time.

Read Jude verse 17, "But, beloved, remember ye the words which were spoken before by the apostles of our Lord Jesus Christ: how that they told you there should be mockers in the last time, who should walk after their own ungodly lusts."

Now without reading the rest of the book one could conclude he was simply reiterating Peter's prophecy. But look closer. In verse 4 he has said, "There *are* (emphasis mine, DKP) certain men crept in unawares." In verse 8 he speaks of *the then present* work of these corrupt workers. In verse 10 he tells how they were then speaking evil of things of which they do not understand. He says these scoffers were present at the love feasts of Jude's readers (v. 12). Undeniably, Jude views the scoffers as present realities.

If Jude says the scoffers that Peter predicted were present, then the last days that Peter predicted were present. We would put this in simple form.

Peter said scoffers would come in the last days. Jude said the scoffers which had been predicted for the last days were present. Therefore Peter's prediction of scoffers in the last days was fulfilled.

McGuiggan, in his debate with Max King,[50] insisted that 2 Peter 3 and Jude speak of different "last days." His reason for delineating between them is that Peter depicts his scoffers as being apostates whereas Jude says of his, "certain men crept in unawares." It is not possible, says McGuiggan, for apostates to be referred to as men who came in privately or unaware, therefore Jude speaks of someone different from Peter. Yet, in Galatians 2:1f, Paul says some false brethren had crept in unawares to spy out their liberty. Were these not apostates? They were certainly false brethren. Did they not creep in privately? See also I John 2:19.

48

Ellis suggests that the scoffers were "gnosticizing-Judaizing Jewish Christians."[51] If this is so, then their denial of the passing of the "heaven and earth" is consistent with the thoughts concerning the Transfiguration. If the parousia was in fact the full arrival of the New Covenant glory of Jesus Christ, at the passing of the Old Covenant glory of Moses, the Judaizers were opposed to that event. Further, they were living late in the generation that Jesus predicted would see his parousia, the passing of the old world. And yet, the Temple still stood. Jerusalem was still intact, and the priesthood and sacrifices continued unabated. The Judaizers, who insisted on the permanent application and imposition of that Old Covenant on New Covenant Christians seemed to have every right to deny the imminent passing of Jerusalem and the Temple. The longer it stood, the stronger their arguments seemed to be.

So, the scoffers were not, as some suggest, modern scientists arguing from uniformitarianism, but were Jews or Judaizers denying that Israel was in her last days. They were arguing for the continuing validity and standing of that old world.

The Judaizers fit the description of Jude and 2 Peter 2. Further, the Judaizers were strongly opposed to–they were skeptical of–the passing of the Old Covenant world. They scoffed at the passing of Jerusalem and the Temple with its cultus.

We have seen then, that the days of which Peter wrote were *his days*. 2 Peter 2 proves this, and Jude emphatically declares that the prophecies of the coming of scoffers in the last days were fulfilled. This being the case, is it not illogical to say the prophecy of Peter is yet to be fulfilled in *our* future. That would say that although Jude says the very people and the very days of which Peter spoke were present, some 2000 years later the prophecy still stands unfulfilled. This would imply that those scoffers must still be alive today! If, as Jude says, those scoffers of *his day* fulfilled Peter's prophecy, and if they are to be active just prior to Jesus' return, which it is insisted is yet future, then either those scoffers are still alive or will be resurrected to continue scoffing!

Not only did Jude insist that what Peter predicted was present, but what is often overlooked is that Peter and Jude said the scoffers were predicted in the Old Testament. So, the question is, do we know of the O.T. prophecies of the last days, and the appearance of scoffers before the destruction of "heaven and earth?" The answer is, "Yes." And the fascinating thing about that prophecy is that it has nothing to do with the destruction of physical creation. This means, of course, that 2 Peter is not about the destruction of literal "heaven and earth."

The prophecy is found in Isaiah 28:20-22.[52] In reality, we must consider the entire context of the passage to understand the promise of the scoffers. This prophecy is utilized by three NT figures. Isaiah 28 played a significant role in the teaching of Jesus, Paul and Peter. When we discover how each of them applied that chapter, we will be closer to understanding Biblical eschatology. There are several key elements of Isaiah's prophecy.

**First**, Isaiah 28 promised the salvation of the remnant (28:5).

**Second**, Isaiah 28 foretold the coming of covenantal judgment on Israel.

**Third**, Isaiah 28 foretold the time when Jehovah would lay a precious cornerstone in Zion.

**Fourth**, Isaiah 28 foretold the time when Jehovah would perform His "unusual act" of judgment although the scoffers would deny it.

**Fifth**, this act of judgment would be like when Jehovah had performed His acts of judgment at Perazim and Gibeon.

**Sixth**, This judgment would consume "the whole earth." Let us examine now how this great chapter is used by Jesus and the NT writers.

### JESUS AND ISAIAH 28

Jesus applied Isaiah 28 along with other O.T. references to the "Stone" motif to the time when Jehovah would lay the foundation stone of the New Temple. In Matthew 21, Jesus told the story of the wicked husbandman who killed the Master's servants, and finally His Son. The parable is an undeniable referent to Israel and her treatment of the prophets and Jesus. What was to be the result of that bloody history of rebellion? The "Stone," the "chief cornerstone," would fall on them and crush them, and the kingdom would be taken from them and given to another kingdom (Matthew 21:42-43).[53] Thus, Jesus applied the "Stone" motif based on Isaiah 28 to the impending judgment against Israel in A.D. 70.

It might be argued that in Matthew 21 Jesus does not directly cite Isaiah 28, but refers to Psalms 118:22 and Isaiah 8:7f instead. However, this in no way mitigates our case. In the N.T., the three key OT prophecies of the "Stone" (Isaiah 8, Isaiah 28, and Psalms 118), are all considered as prophecies of the same time period and the same framework of events. The use of any of the key "Stone" prophecies by a N.T. writer would automatically bring to mind the entire complex of thoughts associated with that motif. As Holland has noted, "The mere quotation of a short text had the effect of alerting the reader to the O.T. passage from which it had been taken. In this way these texts had a far greater significance for the first readers of the NT than is normal today. Their knowledge of these passages meant that they automatically understood the passage of the NT that they were reading in the light of the O.T. passage out of which the quotation was drawn."⁵⁴ You cannot cite one of the "Stone" prophecies in isolation from the others. They belong together thematically and temporally.

It is clear that Jesus' use of the Stone motif was in the context of impending judgment on Israel for rejecting him, the precious cornerstone. He was the stone of stumbling and the rock of offense to both houses of Israel, yet, he would crush those who had rejected him.

## PAUL AND ISAIAH 28

Like Jesus, Paul drew from Isaiah 28, and in regard to one of his most dearly held doctrines, the salvation of the remnant.

The salvation of the remnant is one of the most significant OT prophetic themes. In Romans 9-11, the apostle cites OT prophecies of the salvation of the remnant, and says that those promises were being fulfilled in his generation (Romans 9:27-28). Furthermore, he says that while the salvation of the remnant was then on-going, the *consummation* of that work was near, "For He will finish the work and cut it short in righteousness, Because the Lord will make a short work upon the earth." (Romans 9:28).That work would culminate at the *parousia* of Christ (Romans 11:25-27). This demands that Isaiah 28:5, with its promise of the salvation of the remnant, must be posited within the first century generation context. Thus, just as Isaiah 28 posited, the Day of the Lord and the salvation of the remnant belong together, and, again, Paul posited those events in the first century.

*Isaiah 28 also foretold Covenantal judgment coming on Israel.* In Isaiah 28:11, the prophet said, "with stammering lips and another tongue He will speak to this people, to whom He said, 'This is my rest with which You may cause the weary to rest,' And, 'this is the refreshing,' Yet they would not hear." The threat of "stammering lips and another tongue" is taken from the Law of Blessings and Cursings, and specifically Deuteronomy 28:49.

In Deuteronomy 28-30, Jehovah told Israel that if they kept the covenant, He would bless them. However, if/when they violated the covenant, He would bring disaster on them. One of the forms of judgment would be invasion, destruction, and deportation at the hands of their enemies. The "stammering lips and another tongue" is referent to the foreign invaders being brought by Jehovah against His rebellious people. What does all of this have to do with Paul and Isaiah 28? A great deal.

51

Just as he refers to the theme of the salvation of the remnant, the apostle directly quotes from Isaiah 28 in 1 Corinthians 14:21-22.

In 1 Corinthians 14 Paul addressed the abuses of the charismata in the church at Corinth. He seeks to address misconceptions about the purpose and place of those miraculous gifts. The Corinthians had, for some reason, exalted the speaking in tongues to a position of eminence far beyond God's intent. They had made tongues the focus of their assembly, and evidently felt that tongues were intended for the benefit of the believer. Paul corrected that misconception. He quotes Isaiah 28:11, and then says: "Therefore, tongues are for a sign, not to those who believe, but to the unbeliever" (1 Corinthians 14:22). This is highly significant.

As Palmer has noted, Paul's citation of Isaiah indicates, "he is simply applying to his day the covenantal curse of Deuteronomy 28:49"[55] Paul is not, as some might say, just snatching up, "an isolated aphorism to apply to his circumstance. He understood that judgment on Israel was the subject at hand. In short, Paul quoted Isaiah 28 because he understood the New Testament phenomenon of tongues to be the climactic fulfillment of the Old Testament prophecy...Tongues serve as a sign of covenantal curse" (Robertson, *Tongues*, 46, 47). In other words, Paul was citing Isaiah 28 to say the gift of tongues in the first century was a sign of impending judgment on Israel. Tongues were not simply for the edification of the body of Christ,[56] they were to warn Israel that her last days had come.

So, Paul alludes to the salvation of the remnant, as foretold by Isaiah 28, and applied it to his generation. In 1 Corinthians 14 he quotes Isaiah 28 and the prophecy of coming covenantal judgment, and applied it to his generation. And there is more in Paul from Isaiah 28.

Paul incorporated Isaiah 28 a third time. Isaiah foretold the time when God would, "Lay in Zion a stone for a foundation, a tried stone, precious cornerstone, a sure foundation; whoever believes will not act hastily" (Isaiah 28:16). In Romans 9 Paul discusses how Israel was at that time offended by the story of Jesus, and was rejecting the story of her Messiah. Paul says the reason they were not realizing righteousness is because *they were fulfilling Isaiah 28*. He conflates Isaiah 8 and 28 to speak of Israel's stumbling:[57] "Behold, I lay in Zion a stumbling stone and rock of offense, and whoever believes in Him will not be put to shame" (Romans 9:32-33). For Paul, Israel's stumbling at the "Stone" is the fulfillment of Isaiah 28. And that meant that judgment was coming, because those who stumbled at the stone would be crushed. In both Isaiah 8 and 28 the theme is judgment on Israel. In Romans 9 Paul laments Israel's rejection of the foundation stone. That can mean only one thing: judgment was coming, and that means Paul had the judgment of Israel in mind.

Notice another text that has a bearing on the scoffers and is directly related to the issue at hand. In Acts 13, Paul addressed the Jews, who clearly did not want to hear his message of the fulfillment of the Abrahamic blessings in Christ. As Paul perceived their rejection he warned them: "Behold, you scoffers and marvel and perish; for I am accomplishing a work in your days, a work which you will never believe, though someone should describe it to you" (Acts 13:41, NASV).

Paul is citing Habakkuk 1:5, the prediction of the destruction of "the whole earth" and all things therein in the fiery cataclysm of the Day of the Lord against Jerusalem in B. C. 586 (Zephaniah 1; 3). As Rackham says: "Habakkuk had warned the Jews of his day of a work of judgment which God was preparing for them, viz. the Babylonian invasion. But they would not believe, they despised the warning and consequently were utterly destroyed. Paul likewise knew a day of the Lord was being prepared for the unbelieving Jews.... And it came in the utter destruction of Jerusalem."[58]

In Isaiah 28 Jehovah promised to do *a strange work* that no one would believe, and that strange work was *the judgment on Israel,* when Jehovah would destroy "heaven and earth." God warned the *scoffers* not to reject the prophetic word. In Habakkuk the prophecy was that *the Day of the Lord was coming on Judah,* and warning was given to the *scoffers* not to deny *God's strange work, when He would consume the entire earth.*

Paul appeals to Habakkuk to warn Israel of his day of an impending judgment if they rejected the foundation stone foretold in Isaiah 28. Peter warned his audience of the scoffers who were denying the foundation stone of Messiah, foretold by Isaiah, and said the Day of the Lord was hastening on them to destroy "heaven and earth."

These parallels are not coincidental. I suggest that the scoffers of Acts 13 are to be closely, if not identically, identified with the scoffers of 2 Peter 3. If that is the case, then that places Peter's Day of the Lord firmly within the context of God's covenantal judgment of those who rejected the chief cornerstone, and as a result of that rejection, that Stone was about to crush them and grind them to powder. It was the Day of the Lord against Judah.

So, we have shown that both Jesus and Paul used Isaiah 28 in the same way, to speak of the laying of the precious cornerstone, Israel's rejection of that Stone, and the consequent judgment.

# PETER AND ISAIAH 28

Not only did Jesus and Paul utilize Isaiah 28, Peter applied the prophecy just as they did. In Acts 4:10f, as Peter and John stood on trial for preaching in the name of Jesus, Peter said, "This is the stone which was rejected by you builders which has become the chief cornerstone" (Acts 4:11). We must emphasize again that when the NT writers and speakers cite a "Stone" prophecy, they are not quoting it in isolation from the corpus of "Stone" prophecies. They all speak of the same time and the same events, and that was the first century.

Thus, when Peter told the Sanhedrin they had rejected the "chief cornerstone" he was, in a powerful, unmistakable manner, telling them they were going to be ground to dust (Isaiah 8; Daniel 2:44)! He was telling them, as Jesus had, they were going to be cast out. They were the ones scoffing at the cornerstone that God had laid down, and just as Isaiah said, Jehovah was going to work His "unusual work" on them for their rejection.

By the way, Peter's application of Isaiah 28 to the Jewish leaders shows us that the identity of the scoffers cannot be confined to just Christian apostates. If Peter is applying Isaiah to the Jewish leaders, this all but demands that we see them in the role of the scoffers as well. While Hillyer applies 2 Peter 3 to an "end of time" scenario, his comment about the scoffers supports a *first century application* far better: "From NT times right up to the present day, there have always been those who scoffed at this subject. So how can this be a sign of the impending *Parousia*? The scoffing Peter warns about goes beyond the utterance of mere words, for the Greek terms imply physical persecution."[59] Why do Hillyer's comments fit the first century context far better?

**First** of all, it fits because Peter is applying Isaiah's prediction to the first century Jewish leaders.

**Second**, it fits because as Hillyer notes, the word "scoffers" indicates actual persecution, and that is exactly what is happening in Acts 4 when Peter says the Jewish leaders were the ones rejecting the Stone. They are the scoffers, and they were persecutors.

**Third**, it fits because in the context of both Acts 4 and 2 Peter 3 the scoffers were going to be destroyed, punished for not only rejecting the Stone, *but for persecuting the saints.*

Now, if we identify the scoffers of Isaiah 28 with the Jewish leaders, then this means that the Day of the Lord of 2 Peter 3 was to be the Day of Christ's coming against the persecutors of his saints.

54

So, what we are saying is that the term "scoffers" cannot be confined to one single definition. Both the apostate Judaizers are labeled as the scoffers foretold by the prophets, and, the rebellious Jewish leaders are identified as the scoffers as well. Of course, both parties were scoffing at the very idea of the passing of the old world of Judaism. The Jews simply rejected the idea that the temple would be destroyed. The Judaizers saw the temple as a continuing focal point of the new world.

Not only did Peter allude to Isaiah 28 in Acts, in 1 Peter 2:4f, the apostle tells his readers, "the diaspora," "you also as living stones are being built up a spiritual house, a holy priesthood, to offer up spiritual sacrifices acceptable to God through Jesus Christ." Notice his referent to the "building stones,"and his motif of building the new temple. This is a strongly Messianic motif taken from Isaiah 2-4, Ezekiel 37, 40-44, Zechariah 6, and other prophecies. For Peter, those promises that God would dwell among His people in a New Tabernacle were now being fulfilled in Christ. Not in old Jerusalem, but in the person of Jesus.

The apostle then proceeds to discuss the foundation upon which this new temple was being constructed: "Behold, I lay in Zion a chief cornerstone, elect, precious, and he who believes on Him will by no means be put to shame." This is Isaiah 28.

In Isaiah 28 Jehovah was going to lay the precious cornerstone. He was also going to do a *strange work* and come in judgment of Israel, even though the scoffers denied this. For Peter to quote Isaiah 28:16 is to call to the mind of his audience that although the blessings of Isaiah were being fulfilled, there was a dark cloud behind that silver lining. That cloud was impending judgment on Israel. This is corroborated by the next citation about the "Stone."

In 1 Peter 2:7-8, Peter says that in fulfillment of Isaiah 28 and its promise that those of faith would be blessed, there was the other side of the coin. That meant the unbelievers would be crushed in judgment by the "Stone": "The stone which the builders rejected has become the chief cornerstone," and, 'A stone of stumbling and a rock of offense.'" This is a conflation of Psalms 118:22 and Isaiah 8:14. One message comes through loud and clear from Isaiah 8: judgment on Israel for rejecting the "Stone."

Remember that in Matthew 21, Jesus cited Psalms 118 and Isaiah 8 to predict the judgment on Israel in A.D. 70: "The Kingdom of God shall be taken from you, and given to another nation...and whoever falls on this stone will be broken; but on whomever it falls, it will grind them to powder" (Matthew 21:43-44). Thus, Jesus applied Isaiah 8, and the "Stone"

55

to the judgment on Israel. But remember, Peter, in 1 Peter 2 is quoting from *that same verse*, as well as Isaiah 28, another prophecy of judgment on Israel, to address his audience.

Consider this then:
Isaiah 28 foretold judgment on Israel for rejecting the Stone.
Jesus applied Isaiah 28 to the impending judgment of Israel for rejecting the Stone.
Paul applied Isaiah 28 to the impending judgment of Israel for rejecting the Stone.
In Acts 4 Peter applied the Stone motif to the Jewish leaders, implying their coming destruction.

Are we to believe that in 1 Peter 2 Peter applies Isaiah 28 to a totally different judgment, of a totally different people, at a totally different time from Isaiah, Jesus and Paul applied that prophecy? More, is he changing the application that he had himself made in Acts 4? If Peter was applying Isaiah 28 or Isaiah 8 differently, where is the evidence?

We need to examine Isaiah 28 a bit more closely to know the nature of the Day of the Lord being forecast. The prophet was told that it was a time when "the whole earth" would be consumed. Was this to be an end of time, earth burning, kosmos consuming catastrophe, as most believe Peter was forecasting in 2 Peter 3? What was this Day to be like?

Remember now, just as Peter said, Isaiah said the scoffers were going to come denying the reality of this Day of the Lord. Since Peter's prediction of the Day that was denied by the scoffers was from the prophets, and *the chief prophecy* of the Day being denied by the scoffers is Isaiah 28, then if we can determine the nature of the Day in Isaiah this will have a profound impact on our understanding of 2 Peter 3.

---

Isaiah 28 foretold judgment on Israel for rejecting the Stone.
Jesus *applied* Isaiah 28 to judgment on Israel for rejecting the Stone.
Paul *applied* Isaiah 28 to judgment on Israel for rejecting the Stone.
Did Peter apply Isaiah 28 in a totally different way from Isaiah, Jesus and Paul?

---

We have already seen that Jesus and Paul applied Isaiah 28 to the judgment that was coming on Israel in A.D. 70. If Jesus and Paul applied the prophecy of Isaiah 28 to the Day of the Lord coming against Judah in their generation, they patently did not see that Day as an earth burning, time ending, history terminating Day. The Day of the Lord foretold in Isaiah would be when, "The Lord will rise up as at Mount Perazim, He will be angry as in the valley of Gibeon–that He may do His work, His unusual act" (Isaiah 28:21).

So, the Day of the Lord that the scoffers would deny would be the time when God destroyed "the whole earth" in a judgment like that of Mount Perazim and the Valley of Gibeon. The question is, how had Jehovah come at Perazim and Gideon? Had He come visibly, literally, bodily? No.

The referent to Perazim and Gibeon goes back to 2 Samuel 5:17f (parallel 1 Chronicles 14:8f). The Philistines had heard that David had been anointed king and decided to rebel. David inquired of the Lord for wisdom and counsel, and was told that Jehovah would go before him and defeat the Philistines. The only "manifestation" of Jehovah was: "when you hear a sound of marching in the tops of the mulberry trees, then you shall go out to battle for God has gone out before you to strike the camp of the Philistines." (1 Chronicles 14:15).

Remember, the Day of the Lord in Isaiah 28, when Jehovah would destroy "the whole earth" would be like His coming at Perazim. Yet, Perazim was not a time ending, visible, bodily coming of the Lord. The Day of the Lord at Perazim and Gibeon, was a historical Day of the Lord. It patently was not the end of human history. Furthermore, the Day of the Lord in 2 Peter 3 is the Day of the Lord foretold by Isaiah, the Day the scoffers would deny. If the Day of the Lord foretold by Isaiah was to be like the Day of 1 Chronicles 14, and the Day of 1 Chronicles 14 was not an earth burning, time ending, kosmos destroying event, upon what basis do we make 2 Peter 3 such an event?

Another thing to be noted from Isaiah 28 is the focus of the Day of the Lord. Israel would be the object of this Day, when Jehovah would do His "unusual act." (28:21) What would be so unusual about this Day? As Barnes says:

"This is called the strange work because it would be inflicted on His people. He had destroyed their enemies often, but now He was about to engage in the unusual work of coming forth against His own people."[60]

Watts concurs that the strange work foretold by Isaiah is a judgment against Israel and Jerusalem. Israel believed that God's work was supposed to deliver them, yet,

"The vision (of Isaiah, DKP), had argued repeatedly that they were blind, uncomprehending, and unbelieving to His 'other work' which the prophets had announced, that through the Assyrians and Babylonians He was bringing total destruction to the land and exile to the people. Thus, in their eyes, this message contradicted their understanding of what they considered to be His 'real work' in and through Israel. It is no wonder they called it strange and alien. They may well have found that God Himself had become strange and alien to Israel."[61]

Isaiah was predicting the Day of the Lord that the scoffers would deny, and it was to be the Day when Jehovah laid the precious cornerstone. In other words, *the last days Day of the Lord* being foretold by Isaiah was to be of the same nature as the Day of the Lord against Perazim, and this means the last days Day of the Lord being foretold by Isaiah was not to be the end of time or human history. It was to be the judgment of Israel.

So, 2 Peter 3 is drawn from Isaiah 28 and its prediction of the scoffers who would deny the Day of the Lord. The fact that Isaiah said this Day was to be against *Israel* should definitively identify the Day of the Lord in 2 Peter 3. It would be the consummate judgment of Israel in A.D. 70. To make 2 Peter 3 a prophecy of "the end of time" a person must demonstrate that Peter was not drawing his prophecy from Isaiah 28, or that, although he did have Isaiah 28 in mind, he was now making the language literal. There is no indication that Peter was altering the nature of the prophecy of Isaiah 28. He emphatically tells us that his prophecy of the scoffers and the Day of the Lord was taken from the Old Testament. If Isaiah did not predict a literal end of time Day of the Lord, then Peter did not predict a literal end of time Day of the Lord. And we have still more. We have Peter's own earlier use of Isaiah 28 to help confirm this idea.

Remember that 2 Peter 3:1-2 informs us it is a reminder of what the apostle had written in his first epistle. In the first epistle, the apostle utilized the "Stone" motif used by Jesus and Paul to speak of impending judgment on Israel. Peter's extensive discussion of the "Stone" in 1 Peter 2 sets the stage for his prediction of the Day of the Lord in 2 Peter 3. What we have in 2 Peter 3 is a strong referent to the prophecy of Isaiah 28, with its prediction of scoffers who would deny the Day of the Lord.

So, let me repeat what we stated above.

Isaiah 28 foretold judgment on Israel for rejecting the Stone.

Jesus applies Isaiah 28 to the A.D. 70 judgment of Israel.

Paul applies Isaiah 28 to the A.D. 70 judgment of Israel.

In Acts 4 and 1 Peter 2, Peter applies the Stone prophecies, including Isaiah 28 to the judgment coming on Judah for rejecting the Stone.

In 2 Peter 3 Peter says he is reminding his readers of what the prophets said about scoffers coming in the last days, denying the parousia, and this is a reminder of Isaiah 28. But, remember, Isaiah 28 is a prophecy of the A.D. 70 judgment on Israel for rejecting the Stone.

In 2 Peter 3 Peter says he is also reminding his readers of what he had said about the Day of the Lord in his first epistle. In his first epistle he cited the Stone prophecies, including Isaiah 28, to predict the impending judgment of Israel for rejecting the Stone.

Given these facts, how is it possible to conclude that in 2 Peter 3, the apostle is predicting a different Day of the Lord from that foretold by Isaiah, Jesus, Paul, and in his own earlier writings? That is, the impending judgment of Israel for rejecting the Stone. Unless it can be shown that Peter is in no way relying on Isaiah 28, and that he is not in fact calling to mind what he had himself written about the Stone prophecy in 1 Peter, then this is strong evidence indeed that 2 Peter 3 cannot in any way be construed as a prophecy of an end of time, earth burning Day of the Lord.

We have had a good bit to say about the scoffers, but need to add a bit more. Peter said the scoffers would scoff because the parousia had not yet transpired. Their reasons for scepticism were, it seems, two-fold. First, the passing of time. They looked at how much time had elapsed since the prediction of the end and concluded since it had not happened by now, (their time), it was not going to happen.

Secondarily, the scoffers looked around and saw life continue as normal and concluded the predicted upheaval could not happen. They argued, "since the fathers fell asleep all things continue as they were." Their point was that life went on as normal. And their real point was that the "world" identified by "the fathers" was still standing. Where was the predicted upheaval and catastrophe?

On the first point, it seems that the problems cited by the scoffers point to the distinct probability that the parousia had been predicted for their generation. Consider this, if the Day of the Lord had only been forecast as to occur in the far off, vague, unknown future, the scoffers would have little upon which to base their scepticism. After all, if time means nothing to God, as some aver, why didn't Peter respond to the scoffers' claims by saying, "Listen guys, we never said the Day was at hand. It could be thousands or even millions of years away. Don't you understand that the

59

Day could be far off?" Of course, that is not what Peter said. He said they were "hastening the Day of the Lord." The Day was near!

If the judgment had been forecast to occur in a given time frame of a generation, although the day and hour had not been revealed (Matthew 24:36), as the last days of that generation approached and the event had not transpired, the greater the likelihood for sceptics. Their taunts would go something like this, "Yea, they keep saying the Lord is coming back real soon. In fact, they say he is returning in this generation. But look around! It has been over thirty years since Jesus left. You haven't seen him yet have you? Where is the promise of His coming? The time is up, and he has not made it!" The only scenario to properly explain the presence of these scoffers is that they had heard the repeated warnings that, "The coming of the Lord draweth nigh" (James 5:7-9).

If the scoffers believed, as Sproul Jr. does, that the parousia was not supposed to be, and still is not supposed to be, for thousands of years in the future, their scoffing would have been pointless. Sproul's take on the timing of the Lord's coming destroys any semblance of validity to scoffers denying the nearness or even the reality of the parousia:

"I am a postmillennialist. That means I believe that we-that is, the church of Christ-will experience a thousand-year golden age before Jesus returns to make all things right. Despite that strong conviction, I pray regularly *Maranatha, Lord Jesus*, imploring the King to come now. I'm pretty sure, however, that that prayer will not be answered, not because of my eschatology, but because of the promises of God. He tells the children of Israel in Exodus 20 that if they will refrain from idolatrous worship, He will bless them to a thousand generations. The pious, literalist dispensationalists, of course, do not think that thousand means thousand. It is a symbolic number. And they may be right. But it symbolizes a large number, not a small one. He may return after more than a thousand generations. It could even be a round number, and return after only 951 generations. Either way, if a generation is roughly forty years, that means He'll be back somewhere around 39,000 AD; two down, thirty-seven to go. If, on the other hand, He comes tomorrow, 1000 symbolizes roughly 75."[62]

Sproul Jr. says he prays daily for the Lord to come soon (*Maranatha*), but he is *"pretty sure it will not happen,"* because he believes that there are approximately 40,000 years to go! This self-contradictory logic is totally foreign to the Biblical writers. They definitely prayed *Maranatha*, but it was because they not only hoped the Lord was coming soon, they *knew* he

60

*was* coming soon, and would not delay (Hebrews 10:37). There is not a shred of evidence to support Sproul's, Mathison's, Gentry's concept of a parousia delayed for 40,000 years. Where did a single Biblical writer *ever* express the idea that they prayed for the Lord to come soon, but did not really *expect* Him to come for 30,000-40,000 years?

Sproul's admission that his eschatology and his belief in the promises of God are at odds is very revealing. *Should not our eschatology and our hope match with one another?* Should not our "hope" be grounded in our eschatological doctrine? Sproul Jr. has all but admitted that there is a disjunction between his doctrinal eschatology and his subjective hope.

But, again, the point is, that if the Lord's coming was understood by the scoffers to be that far off in the future, they could hardly complain that it had not happened on time.

The second point of the scoffers sounds similar to what Jesus said would occur prior to the destruction of Jerusalem. In Matthew 24:37f Jesus said in the days prior to the fall of that economy the people would be just like they were prior to the flood. They were, "eating, drinking, marrying, and giving in marriage." In other words, life went on as normal. They saw no cause for concern. They felt secure and comfortable. You can almost imagine scoffers in Noah's day saying, "Where is the promise of this flood? Since creation all things continue as they were!" And the scoffers of his time, Peter said, would say "since the fathers fell asleep, all things continue as they were from the beginning of the creation." They saw no reason to be alarmed. They were going about their life just like always.

It would be good to note that sceptics are also notorious rationalizers. The sceptics of Noah's days also saw no cause for alarm. All things were continuing the same since creation. Life went on. In spite of the many warnings by Noah and family they did not believe anything would happen.

Take note of the scoffers in John 8:31-34, "We have never been in bondage to any man!" So it was in the days prior to Jerusalem's demise. The church preached the message of impending doom for a full generation. Yet the unbelievers scoffed. They felt comfortable in their "city of God." They were God's people! They could point to their illustrious past and how God had protected His people and city. History reveals for us how even in the death throes of war the people clung to the firm conviction that God would never desert His city and would miraculously save them. How easy then to believe they could say, "since the fathers fell asleep all things continue as they were." It was not *true*, but since they denied what was being preached they refused to see what was before their eyes.

61

Compare the scoffers in Peter with those in I Thessalonians 5. Paul spoke of those who said, "Peace and safety," then sudden destruction would come as in the days of Noah. This is the very thing Peter is implying would happen. Jesus in Matthew 24, Paul in I Thessalonians 5, and Peter in 2 Peter 3, all speak of the same event. Jesus said he would return in that generation, (24:34). Paul and the Thessalonians believed they would live to see it (I Thessalonians 4:15,17). Peter in 2 Peter 3:12, said they were "looking for and hastening the coming of the day of God." The signs were there for the scoffers to see and heed, as in, "who hath ears let him hear," but they refused to see and heed.

The point is that the scoffers were not scientific uniformatarians looking at the creation and extrapolating from that to a denial of Christ's coming. They were looking at the (imagined) stability of their *world*. It was a world determined by "the fathers," and that was *the Old Covenant world*. The scoffers were denying that Israel's last days were near, that God was coming in judgment of the apostate nation. In addition to the identification of the scoffers already offered, Chilton suggests that the scoffers were Jewish apostates (*Vengeance, 540*).

Another thought: the scoffers were denying the very thing affirmed by Peter. This is so critical that it has to be emphasized. Peter said: "The end of all things has drawn near" (1 Peter 4:7). The scoffers said, "All things continue as they were from the beginning of creation." The question is, *who was right*? Who shall we believe? Were the "all things" that Peter said were near their end, a different "all things" from what the scoffers were denying was about to end? This cannot be true because Peter tells us in 2 Peter 3:1-2 that the second epistle is only a reminder of what was written in the first, about the events of the last days and Day of the Lord. Thus, the "all things" of 1 Peter and the "all things" of 2 Peter 3 are the same.

The fact that the "all things" of 1 Peter 4:7 and the "all things" of 2 Peter 3:3 are the same is devastating to the postmillennial view of Mathison, Sproul Jr., Gentry, et. al.. Mathison admits that 1 Peter 4:7 is advert to the A.D. 70 parousia of Christ: "There are several passages in the epistles of the New Testament that describe the end as near (e.g. 1 Cor. 7:29; Heb. 10:25; 1 Peter 4:7)...If the epistles of the New Testament were written before the destruction of Jerusalem in A.D. 70, then they too could have referred to the coming of the end of Israel as simply 'the end." (*WSTTB*, 202). Well, if 1 Peter 4:7 is referent to the A.D. 70 parousia of Christ, how does Mathison delineate between 1 Peter 4:7 and 2 Peter 3, when Peter emphatically tells us 2 Peter 3 is a reiteration of what he wrote in the first epistle and the scoffers were denying the very thing that Peter affirmed, "the end of all things"?

If Peter was predicting the destruction of material creation and the end of time, *the scoffers have been vindicated*. Peter affirmed, "the end of all things has drawn near." The scoffers said, "all things continue as they were." If they were both speaking of the same "end," and they patently were, then the passing of 2000 years has proven that Peter was wrong, and the scoffers were right! The passing of 2000 years falsifies and refutes the idea that an event had drawn near. That is, if Peter was predicting the end of time and the dissolution of physical creation. However, if we understand that "the end" in Peter's mind was the end of the Old Covenant world of Israel, then Peter was undeniably true, and the scoffers were falsified. This brings us to another consideration.

Was Peter a false prophet? We will consider this further below, but consider Luke 21:8, in the light of Deuteronomy 18.

Deuteronomy 18 of course, provides the test of a prophet: simply stated, if his predictions fail, he is false, and to be rejected. Consider now Luke 21:8: "Many will come saying 'I am he, and, the end has drawn near.' Do not go after them." Jesus was speaking to Peter, James and John. Jesus was warning his apostles against making, or against believing, *premature declarations that "the end has drawn near." * You *must* catch the power of Jesus' warnings in light of the Biblical testimony about the parousia!

*Peter* heard Jesus warn against premature declarations of the end. Yet, in 1 Peter 4.7 Peter proclaimed "the end of all things has drawn near." He used *almost the exact words* that Jesus said the false prophets would use in making their premature declarations. So, was the end truly near, or, *had Peter become one of the very false prophets Jesus warned him about?*

*James* heard Jesus warn against premature declarations of the end. Yet, James said, "The coming of the Lord has drawn near" (James 5:8). *Did James become one of the very false prophets Jesus warned him about?*

*John* heard Jesus warn against premature declarations of the end. Yet, John said "It is the last hour!" (1 John 2:18), and "These things must shortly come to pass...the time is at hand." (Revelation 1:1-3). *Did John become one of the very false prophets Jesus warned him about?*

Jesus warned against making or believing premature declarations of the nearness of the end. However, he gave his disciples signs whereby they could know when the end was near (Matthew 24.14f), and then told them, "when you see these things come to pass, then know that it is nigh, even at the door" (Matthew 24.32). Luke's record has: "When you see all these

63

things happening, know that the kingdom of God is near" (Luke 21.31). So, Jesus told them not to believe anyone who said "the end has drawn near" before the appearance of the signs.[63] However, when the signs appeared, they could know and proclaim "the end has drawn near!"

The very fact that Jesus told Peter, James and John not to make or believe premature declarations of the end, but informed them when they could declare its imminence, in light of their repeated affirmations of the nearness of the end is proof positive of one of two things. **First**, it means Peter, James and John ignored their master's warnings and made false, premature declarations of the soon coming end, *or*, it means they heeded his warnings, and when the signs of the end appeared, they proclaimed truthfully, "The end of all things has drawn near."

Take note of this, the scoffers said "the end of all things has not drawn near." They were rejecting what many consider to be a premature declaration of the nearness of the end *made by Peter*. Were the scoffers actually heeding Jesus' words to reject premature declarations of the end? Had Peter become one of the false prophets Jesus warned him about?

---

**Jesus warned *Peter, James and John* not to make or believe premature declarations of the nearness of the end.**
***Peter* later said, "The end of all things has drawn near."**
***James* later said: The Coming of the Lord has drawn near."**
***John* later said, "It is the last hour."**
**If Peter, James and John were wrong, and the end was not truly near, then they are the very false prophets that Jesus warned them about!!**

---

These are serious issues that cannot be lightly dismissed. Since I first introduced this argument sometime ago, I have not had so much as an intelligent response to it. One millennialist responded: "Well, Jesus was speaking only about false Christs who would make the false statements, and Peter was not a false Christ, so your argument does not stand." *Desperation leads to desperate arguments!* Jesus' point is not limited to false messiahs. To defend the premature declarations of the nearness of the end, because the men making the false predictions were not claiming to be Jesus is tantamount to saying, "It is okay to make false prophecies, *as long as you don't claim to be Jesus!* You can say the end is near, even if you don't have a clue if it is or not. Just don't say you are Jesus!" Was Jesus saying it is okay to make false prophecies, as long as you don't claim to be him? This kind of "logic" is patently false, and *dangerous*.

How is the church to test the prophets? Paul charged the Thessalonians to, "prove all things, hold fast that which is good" (1 Thessalonians 5.21). When some in Corinth claimed to be apostles, Paul challenged them to prove their claims, "I will know, not the words only, but the power" (1 Corinthians 4.19f). John said, "Test the prophets whether they be of God" (1 John 4.1f). Yet, the modern day view of prophecy eliminates any possibility of testing the prophets.

Here is what we mean. We are told that even though the N. T. writers affirmed the nearness of the end of the age and Christ's parousia, that God can't tell time. Time statements don't mean anything to Him. Therefore, authors like MacArthur acknowledge that the N. T. writers proclaimed that the end was near, and yet it did not come. MacArthur asks, "Why was the fact of our Lord's return presented in the language of imminency, but the exact date withheld?"[64] His answer is, "One reason was that He desired to keep His people on the very tiptoe of expectation, continually looking for Him." MacArthur admits that this failure or "delay" of the imminent expectation has caused perplexity among believers over the centuries, and has even caused skepticism. Yet, he has no problem with every generation of "prophecy experts" saying "the end has drawn near!" The problem of course, is that Jesus did have a problem with false predictions of the end!

As we shall see below, the Bible gives examples of "prophets" making false time statements, and God condemning them for it. He actually killed one prophet for making a false time prediction! Jehovah said when some things were to occur. He gave a time statement, man rejected it and gave a different time-frame. As a result, God killed the man! Doesn't that indicate that God can tell time pretty well, and that He expects man to honor His time statements?

But the question is, if God wanted to keep the church on the tiptoe of expectation throughout all the generations, how is the church to test "prophets" to know if they are true or false in regard to their predictions of the end, as Jesus commanded in Luke 21?

You see, if time statements of the end mean nothing objective, then Jesus' warnings to reject false predictions concerning the end are empty words. They mean nothing. There is no such thing as a premature declaration, "the end has drawn near" because, in the first place time statements don't mean anything. In the second place, since time statements don't mean anything, you can't know if the statement is true or false. In the third place, God wants His church to think the end is near and to stay on the tiptoe of expectation, whether the statements are true or not.

So, mitigating the objective imminence of the N. T. time statements is dangerous. It destroys any possibility of testing the prophets. Yet, the church is supposed to test the prophets. It destroys any possibility of knowing whether declarations of the end are premature. Yet, Jesus said to reject premature declarations of the nearness of the end. It destroys any possibility of knowing when the end would truly be near. Jesus said "when you see these things come to pass, then know that the kingdom is near." Yet, if time statements mean nothing, what is "near" supposed to mean, even when the signs appeared? If one day is with the Lord as a thousand years, then what did Jesus really mean when he said "when you see these things come to pass, then know that the kingdom of God is nigh at hand"?

Only by acknowledging that the time statements in the N. T. are objective indicators of the nearness of the end is there any way to understand the commands to test the prophets. Only if God can tell time was there a way to reject those who said the end had drawn near, before it had drawn near. *Only if Peter told the truth were the scoffers wrong.* But if the scoffers were wrong, and Peter was right, then the Day of the Lord was truly near in the first century, and 2 Peter 3 was fulfilled then.

The sad reality is that the modern church has seemingly lost its nerve, desire, or even ground for testing the prophets. Generations come and go, and in every generation, so-called prophecy experts arise telling us, "This is the generation that will see the coming of the Lord!"; "Our generation has more signs to indicate Christ could come in our lifetime than any generation before us" (*Charting*, 119).[65] Hal Lindsay predicted the end for 1988. Jack Van Impe predicted the end would come in 1999. The list goes on and on, and yet, the evangelical community, as a whole, sits silently by, not raising a voice against such shameful and dangerous false predictions! There is something fundamentally wrong here, and what is wrong is that the church has so bought into the false concept of a delayed, postponed eschatology, that it hardly blinks at the idea of a failed God! This is *shameful*, and *detrimental* to the very cause of Christ. It is time for the Christian community at large to wake up to the seriousness of this issue and stop ignoring the false prophets in its midst. It is time for Christianity itself to come to grips with its view of a God that cannot tell time, that cannot or will not communicate truthfully.

Jesus himself instructed and challenged his audiences: "If I do not do the works of My father, do not believe Me; but if I do, though you do not

66

believe Me, believe the works, that you may know, and believe that the Father is in Me, and I in Him" (John 10.37-38, NKJV). Please note that Jesus said faith in him comes *after* the fulfillment of the work the Father had given him. Their faith in him, indeed, our faith in him, lies on the other side of the completion of his work. No performance, no faith. If he failed to do the work, He is not to be believed. In other words, it is not wrong to put even Jesus himself to the test. He said so himself!

Consider what this means. Jesus said he was not to be accepted as the Son of God if he did not perform the work the Father had given him. Ask yourself this question: *What were the works the Father gave Jesus to do?* There are many of course, but among other things, He gave him the task of dying for the sins of the world. So, if Jesus did not die for our sins, and was not resurrected, then we are not to believe him, or to believe *in him*. Most would not have a problem with that statement, after all, Jesus was, "declared to be the son of God with power, according to the spirit of holiness, by the resurrection from the dead" (Romans 1.4). Our faith in him comes because of the fulfillment of his promises. But there is something very challenging here that is not being considered by many.

*The Father also gave Jesus the work of the Judgment and the Resurrection* (John 5:19f), "From henceforth the Father judges no one, but has committed all judgment to the Son, that all men might honor the Son as they honor the Father." So, since Jesus said we are not to believe in him unless he performed the work that the Father gave to him, and since the work the Father gave to him included the work of judgment and the resurrection (John 5:19f), *this means that faith in Christ cannot be complete unless he has completed and perfected the work of judgment* –the work of 2 Peter 3-- and the resurrection.

---

**Full faith in Christ comes only through the knowledge that he performed the work the Father gave him (John 10:37f).**
**The Father gave Jesus the work of the Judgment (John 5:19f).**
**If therefore, Christ has not performed the judgment, faith in him cannot be confirmed as complete!**

---

Consider this additional point: Peter is clearly giving a *sign* whereby those to whom he wrote could know the Day of the Lord was imminent. He told them "in the last days" scoffers would come. Is this not a sign? And if it is, what of the common assertion that there would be no signs of the final return of Jesus?[66]

Commentators, from Kik, *Eschatology of Victory*; Boettner, *The Millennium*, Coffman's *Commentary series*, and others, are quite insistent that Jesus clearly taught there would be no signs to discern the time of his coming. This view is popular in both the postmillennial and amillennial schools. If this is true it presents an insurmountable obstacle for the traditional view of more than a few passages.

If there are no signs of the final coming of the Lord, then any passage which speaks of signs to precede the coming of the Lord cannot refer to a future coming of the Lord. But 2 Thessalonians 2, I Timothy 4, 2 Timothy 3 and 4; 2 Peter 2 and 3, Jude, I John 2 and Revelation are passages which speak of signs to occur prior to the coming of the Lord. Therefore these passages cannot refer to a yet future coming of the Lord.

There is more to say about signs. The millennialists tell us that the signs of the end abound today. The events of 1948, and the establishment of the nation of Israel, are called "The Super Sign of the End" by prophecy teachers Tim LaHaye and Thomas Ice. (*Charting*, 119). In December 2004 the tsunami hit Indonesia, killing 200,000 or more. At the time of this writing, the hurricanes Katrina and Rita have devastated New Orleans, parts of Mississippi, Alabama and Texas. A massive earthquake has hit Pakistan, killing over 30,000. Pat Robertson[67] and other prophecy pundits have gone on record claiming that these events prove the end is near. However, a closer look will reveal the inconsistency in the millennial camp when it comes to the issue of signs.

On the one hand, we are told "the Rapture is a sign-less event." (*Charting*, 118) However, we are then told that the Rapture comes at the end of the current Christian age.[68] Then, we are told that since 1948 there has been a veritable "parade of signs" in fulfillment of Matthew 24:4-14. (*Charting*, 36). But *then*, we are told that, "Since Matthew 24:4-14 cannot happen until after the Rapture and the start of the Tribulation, it is wrong to say that such events are prophetically significant in our own day." (*End Times*, 167) The contradictions here are real.

The millennialists say there are no signs of the Rapture, but there are signs of the end of the current Christian age, and the Rapture comes at the end of the current Christian age. Well, if there are signs of the end of the Church Age, and the Church Age ends at the Rapture, then the signs of the end of the Church Age are, *de facto*, signs of the Rapture. There is no escape from this.

Further, where is the consistency in saying that since 1948 there has been a parade of signs in fulfillment of Matthew 24:4-14, and then saying that it is wrong to say that Matthew 24:4-14 is prophetically significant for our own day? If the signs of Matthew 24:4-14 have been fulfilled in our own day, then isn't the fulfillment of these prophecies "significant?"[69]

CHAPTER 6

## "Since the Fathers Fell Asleep, All Things Continue as They Were Since the Foundation of the World."(2 Peter 3:4)

One reason the scoffers felt secure was, "since the fathers fell asleep, all things continue as they were since the beginning of creation." Pryor, reviewing Max King's book,[70] *The Spirit of Prophecy*, insists 2 Peter cannot be speaking of the demise of Judaism because, "Peter wrote this in 65 A.D. just five years before the destruction of Jerusalem. The passing of the heavens and earth are in the distant future. In the last days (certainly not five years hence) mockers will come saying, 'Where is the promise of His coming? For ever since the fathers fell asleep all continues just as it was from the beginning of creation.' When Peter wrote this, the fathers had not fallen asleep, neither had all things gotten back to normal and continued as they had since creation."

Pryor errs in several points. **First**, he *assumes* that Peter was predicting the passing of the physical heavens and earth. **Second**, he *assumes* that it was in the distant future from Peter's perspective. **Third**, since the fall of Jerusalem was near, Peter 3 could not be reference to A. D. 70. This is what is known as *petitio principii*. What that means is that you *assume* your position to be true, without *proving* it to be true. The problem is that Pryor's *assumption* is precisely what has to be proven, not assumed. He must *prove*, not *assert*, that Peter anticipated the end of time.

Whatever it was Peter was anticipating he definitely did not think it was in the distant future. He and his audience were "looking for and hastening" that Day. By the way, one wonders how Pryor knows the destruction of Jerusalem was near to Peter, if time statements don't mean anything. Did Peter know the destruction of the old world was near? If so, how did he know? Was it not through *Jesus' time statements*, that Pryor does not believe can be understood because God cannot tell time? Pryor has Peter able to both understand God's time statements, but then affirming that God's time statements do not mean anything!

Amillennialists and postmillennialists, often appeal to the pronouns in Matthew 24. The argument goes something like this: When Jesus says "you" he is speaking of things his disciples would personally witness. When he says *they* or *them* he is referring to those in the distant future. We cannot help but wonder where that argument is when 2 Peter 3:13 is considered? Peter said *we*, that is he and his contemporaries, "look for the new heavens and earth." How do we today take it out of his lifetime when he said *they* were looking for it?

Further substantiation that the passing of heaven and earth was not in the distant future is to be found in Peter's exhortation to righteousness in view of the passing of the old heavens and earth. Peter says, "seeing then that all things shall be dissolved, what manner of persons ought we to be?" Notice the emphasis on his readers. He tells them the "heavens and earth" were going to perish. Because of this *they* ought to be righteous.

Peter's exhortation to his contemporaries to prepare themselves for the new world is powerful proof that the new creation was expected in that generation. It is much the same scenario as in 2 Timothy 3. In that passage Paul warns Timothy that in the last days corrupt men who would grow worse and worse. (Compare 2 Timothy 3 with 2 Peter 2) This was to happen in "the last days," *but Paul told Timothy to prepare himself to meet the challenge.* Paul assuredly believed that Timothy was going to see, if he was not already seeing, the reality of his prediction. If the last days were in the far distant future from them, as Pryor contends, why did Paul tell Timothy to be prepared for it? And, if the passing of the heavens and earth in the last days was in the far distant future from Peter's readers why did he tell them to have their lives in order? Peter's exhortation was not just some general moral exhortation. It was specific and direct, based upon the passing away of the heavens and earth.

See also Paul's directives in I Corinthians 7:26-31. He reminded the Corinthians that due to the "present distress," and "the time is short," "the fashion of this world is passing away," that they should remain unmarried if possible! The first century "audience relevance" of these directives cannot be ignored. This is parallel to 2 Peter 3. Was the world that was passing away in Corinthians a different world from that which was passing in 2 Peter 3? If the world was the same in both passages, then the moral exhortations must be seen as couched in the same context of imminence. Clearly, both writers were anticipating the soon coming consummation.

Pryor's argument that the last days had to be in the misty future from Peter is based upon his assertion that "the fathers had not fallen asleep." His point is that the "fathers" is an allusion to *the fathers of the church.* The father's of the church were the apostles. The apostles were still alive in the middle 60s. Therefore, Peter could not be speaking of scoffers being alive when he wrote since the church "fathers" were still alive.

This is an unfortunate error. The term "the fathers" is used some 58 times in the New Covenant. Only ten times does it NOT have reference to

71

*the Old Covenant figures.* One has but to read passages such as John 6:31, 49, 58; 7:22 in the gospels to realize this without question. And in the book of Acts see 3:13,22; 13:17,32. Especially see Acts 7 where the term is used more times than in any other single chapter. Hebrews 1:1 is a famous text which should be consulted as is 3:9 and 8:9. We cannot list all the places. Get your concordance and study it for yourself.

Bauckham, says the *consistent* Biblical and early Christian usage of the term "the fathers" is to the Old Testament fathers.[71] Although he grants the consistent usage of the term, he nonetheless claims Peter was referring to the first generation of Christians. This is untenable however, and is based on Bauckham's belief in a later date for 2 Peter.

The scoffers were not saying the early church leaders had died. They were referring to the fact that since the *Old Covenant fathers* fell asleep all things continued as they were. Pryor's position ignores how the term *the fathers* is used in the New Testament.

When one considers that *the fathers* is a reference to the Jewish fathers of the Old Covenant it places a great emphasis on the identity of the Day of the Lord. In other words, it makes the scoffers out to be Jewish scoffers, and makes it more plausible that the object of their scorn was the message of the coming destruction of Jerusalem.

Peter, like Paul, proclaimed the eschatological hopes of Israel. This is clear from verses 1-2 of this chapter. Israel's promises were covenantal promises. His allusion therefore, to the *fathers* should be seen in this light. These scoffers were denying the demise of their world based upon the historical stability of life extending back through their Jewish existence. The context of their objection was their Jewish world.

Jesus said the message of Jerusalem's fate would be preached in all the nations (Matthew 24:14). When that message was proclaimed it went, "to the Jew first and then to the Greek." Study the book of Acts, and see examples of preaching where there is the threat of coming judgment (Acts 2:40; 7; 13:41). Especially is this true when the audience is Jewish. Is it not extremely likely that as the message of Jerusalem's impending demise was proclaimed that scoffers ridiculed the very idea? Would the objection of the scoffers not be likely to come from Jewish hearers so confident of the indestructibility and eternality of their city?

72

# THE WORLD THAT EXISTED

The argument is made that Peter's illustration of the destruction of the world by flood proves he is speaking of the dissolution of the physical universe. A closer look at the text will dispel such a notion. In 2 Peter 3:4 Peter says Noah's heavens existed, the earth stood out of the water and the *world* perished. He then tells us, "the heavens and earth which now exist are kept in store by the same word, reserved for fire." The traditional argument goes thus: "God once destroyed the world by flood, but He promised to never again destroy the world by water. The next time, as Peter teaches, He will destroy the world by fire."

To properly interpret 2 Peter 3 we must examine the Noahic catastrophe, God's promise given then, and compare with what is said by Peter. A study of Genesis 8:21 is challenging: "I will never again curse the ground for man's sake, although the imagination of man's heart is evil from his youth; nor will I again destroy every living thing as I have done."

It is generally assumed that Jehovah looked down at the havoc created by the flood and said, "One of these days I will destroy all living things again but the next time I will do it by fire!" But ask yourself, was God concerned with *methods, magnitude,* or with *mercy*? Did Jehovah simply determine to change His method of inflicting universal suffering? What kind of an image of God does this project?

God said He would never again destroy every living thing. The question is, what does, "As I have done" mean? It is assumed that it means, "I will not do it by flood, but I will do it by fire." In other words, Jehovah simply determined to *change His method* of destruction. But considering the nature of God, does it not comport better with His mercy to believe He looked on all the suffering caused by the flood and vowed never again to bring such cataclysmic trauma on the earth? It is then, a question of whether God is more concerned with *methods* or *mercy*.

This construct is supported by closer examination of the Genesis text. Ask this, "*Why* did God bring the flood on that world?" In Genesis 6:5-8 we are told it was because "every intent of the thoughts of his (mankind's DKP) heart" was only evil continually. God saw man's wickedness and decided to bring cataclysm on him (Genesis 6:7). In chapter 8:21, God looked down the stream of time and into man's heart and said, "although the imagination of man's heart is evil from his youth" (NKJV), He would never again curse the ground nor destroy every living creature. *This is critical!* Catch the power of that "*although*."

73

*Although* He had once destroyed every living creature *because of man's evil*, God vowed to never again destroy every living creature *although He knew man would continue to be evil.* If the traditional posit of a universal disaster by fire, is accurate, *God has reneged*! He will, in spite of the fact that He knew mankind would still be unholy, destroy all life, only this time by fire. As a matter of fact, the traditional view insists that God will do in the future what He did not do in the flood. In the flood only the *world* perished (I Peter 2:5), but the traditional view says this time *all creation* will be consumed. This interpretation is offered in spite of the fact that Jehovah knew what man's future would be, *wicked*, and in spite of that He vowed to never again bring destruction on all living things.

While Peter speaks of Noah's heaven and earth, he asserts it was their *world* that perished. This bears on the definition of his (Peter's) heaven and earth. Peter is comparing the perishing of the *world* at the Day of the Lord in Noah's day with the coming Day of the Lord. His comparison breaks down if in Noah's day only the world perished, but in his (Peter's) coming Day of the Lord the physical universe is to perish. The heaven and earth of Noah's day were kept for the day of judgment of ungodly men. And by that word the world that then was perished. By the same word the heavens and earth which now exist, (in Peter's day), are kept for the day of judgment of ungodly men. Now since the physical universe did not perish in Noah's day, then Peter was not saying the physical universe must perish.

The chart below will show the similarities and parallels that Peter was drawing, and help us to see that Peter was not focused on the destruction of *terra firma,* but the *world* of the ungodly.

| Noah's Day | Peter's Day |
|---|---|
| Heaven and earth kept. | Heaven and earth kept. |
| Kept for judgment of the ungodly. | Kept for judgment of the ungodly. |
| Kept by power of God. | Kept by power of God. |
| Earth "perished," (Genesis 9:11) but not destroyed | Earth to perish in same sense? (There was a catastrophe on the earth) |
| *World* perished. | *World* to perish? (2 Peter 2:5) |

This helps us realize that Peter is speaking of *worlds, societies,* that had/were to perish, not physical creation.

One final thought on the word *world.* William Barclay, commenting on I John 2:15-17 observes:

"We must be careful to understand what John meant by the world, the *kosmos.* But *kosmos* acquired a moral sense. It began to mean the world apart from God. C. H. Dodd defines this meaning of *kosmos*: 'Our author means human society in so far as it is organized on wrong principles and characterized by base desires, false values, and egoism.' In other words, to John the world was nothing other than pagan society with its false values and its false gods."[72]

Other commentators take note that Peter was concerned, not so much with physical destruction as he was with the world of the wicked. Gaebelin says: "The globe was not destroyed, only its inhabitants and its ordered form."[73] Dispensationalist authors Walvoord and Zuck say: "The world (*kosmos*) refers to inhabitants, since the earth itself was not destroyed in the flood."[74]

We understand from Peter that in Noah's day the world, the moral world, or society perished. We understand that Peter foresaw the coming dissolution of another society, the Jewish world. This is exactly what happened in 70 A.D.

## WHAT ABOUT "AS LONG AS THE EARTH STANDS"?

It is sometimes objected that since Genesis 8.21 begins with, "As long as the earth stands..." that this necessarily involves a limitation to how long the earth will stand. In other words, in spite of the fact that in verse 20 Jehovah had unequivocally stated that He would never destroy the earth again, He now implies that it will be of limited duration.

This is a tenuous suggestion at best, and violates the fact that there are numerous texts that affirm the abiding nature of material creation. Some of what follows is a brief section from my book *The Last Days Identified.*[75]

John Anderson notes that there are several passages in the Bible that teach that the earth is permanent. Psalms 78:69 states, "And He hath built his sanctuary like high palaces, like the earth which He has established *forever*" (Strongs #776). This verse states that the earth is established forever. Psalms 93:1: "The Lord reigneth, He is clothed with majesty, the Lord is clothed with strength, wherewith He hath girded: The world also is established that it cannot be moved." The word, *world,* here is # 8398 in

75

Strong's Concordance and means, "the earth-the globe-the Land." Psalms 104:5. "Who laid the foundations of the earth, (Strong's #776) that it should not be removed forever?" The same word, *erets*, is used as in Psalm 78:69. Ecclesiastes 1:4: "One generation passeth away, and another generation cometh, but the earth (#776) abideth forever."

We would add a note to Anderson's comments. The Hebrew word *olam*, translated as "forever" does not, admittedly, always mean "without end" as the modern reader automatically assumes. It can indicate a period of limited time. For instance, the cultic practices of Old Testament Israel, including the sacrifices (Exodus 29:27f), the priesthood (Exodus 40:15), the ceremonial washings, (Exodus 30:19-21), ordinances concerning slavery (Exodus 21:6), and a host of other Old Covenant mandates were all said to be *"olam"* i.e. forever.[76] However, the New Testament is clear that all of those ordinances were only temporary "imposed until the time of reformation" (Hebrews 9:10). Thus, "forever" did not always mean *forever*.

However, you will note that in some of the references offered by Anderson that it says creation would "never be moved." Ecclesiastes 1:4 draws a direct contrast between things that do come and go, and the earth "that abides forever." These kinds of contrasts are significant. If the earth passes away just like generations of men pass away, then the contrast would be meaningless. The enduring nature of creation is the point.

Furthermore, for the scriptures to affirm that the earth and creation "will never pass away" is one of the strongest expressions for the eternal nature of creation that can be found. Notice that the same thing is said of the earth and creation as is stated in regard to the kingdom of Christ. Psalms 93:1 says the earth is established forever "that it should not be moved." Likewise, Daniel describes the kingdom of Christ as a kingdom that can never pass away or be destroyed (Daniel 2:44; 7:13-14), and the writer of Hebrews describes the body of Christ as the kingdom "that cannot be moved" (Hebrews 12:28).

Isaiah affirms, in regard to Christ's Messianic kingdom "of the increase of his government and peace, there shall be no end" (Isaiah 9:7.) The throne of David, on which Messiah would sit, would be established as firmly as the sun, moon and stars (Psalms 89:34-37). Now, if Christ's kingdom has no end, and it was to endure as long as the sun and moon, then does it not follow that the sun and moon will never pass away?

In Psalms 148, the writer extols the wonders of creation. This marvelous Psalm has given rise to the song, "Praise the Lord." In verse 6, it speaks of creation: "He has established them forever, even forever and ever: He has

76

made an ordinance, and it shall never pass away." The LXX shows that the Greek heaps up the "forever" nature of creation, by saying that it is established *"eis ton aiona, kai eis ton aiona tou aionos."* It is "forever, even forever and ever!" This is one of the strongest expressions for unendingness found in the Greek language. Furthermore, the text affirms that God's decree concerning the "foreverness" of the creation is by a decree that shall never pass away (*kai ou pareleusetai*). The word *pareleusetai* is from *parerchomai* and means to pass away.[77] With the negative *ou* added, it means literally, the creation would not pass away.

R. H. Charles, in Mayor, says "the view that prevails" in ancient Jewish sources was that the earth would never pass away. Based on Psalms 104:5, 148, and other passages. Mayor himself tries to counter this because in his view Isaiah 65 predicts the destruction of creation.[78] As we have shown however, Isaiah does not in fact predict the destruction of literal creation. The point is that ancient Jewish sources themselves did not anticipate the end of time and the physical elements. As we have noted earlier, there is a growing awareness of this in the scholarly world.

Gould, commenting on the language of the destruction of "heaven and earth" in Mark 13 says, "this darkening and falling of the heavenly bodies is so common an accompaniment of OT prophecy, and its place is so definitely and certainly fixed there, as belonging to the Apocalyptic imagery of prophecy, and not to the prediction of events, that it presents no difficulty whatever, and does not even create the presumption in favor of the view that this is a prophecy of the final catastrophe."[79] Gould is saying the language of the Day of the Lord is simply not indicative of the actual, literal destruction of the physical cosmos. He continues: "It is needless to minimize these words into eclipses, earthquakes, or meteoric showers, or to magnify them into actual destruction of sun and moon and stars. They are not events but imaginative portrayal of what it means for God to intervene in the history of nations." (p. 250).

Likewise, Milton Terry, author of the respected *Biblical Hermeneutics*, says: "When the leading OT prophet makes use of such language (the destruction of creation, DKP), in foretelling the desolation of Edom, with what reason or propriety can we insist on the literal import of such passages as Matthew 24:29 and 2 Peter 3:10?"[80]

Our point is that Peter's prediction of the passing of "the earth and the elements therein" is typical apocalyptic imagery predictive of a dramatic in-breaking of God into human history. It has nothing to do with the end of human history. The scriptures are too emphatic that the current Christian age and the physical cosmos is an age without end.

In Ephesians 3:20-21, the writer speaks of the church, the body of Christ and extols its unending nature: Unto Him be glory in the church by Jesus Christ, throughout all ages, age without end." The fact that he speaks of the church, as an institution *established among men*, for the proclamation of the gospel to men, as an age without end is definitive. The church age has no end.[81] Yet, the church was established on earth to minister to man, and to glorify God.

So, the consistent story from the Old Testament to the New is that the Old Covenant world –the "heaven and earth" of Israel--had to end, in order to bring in the endless new world of the Messiah. The old world was characterized by words like darkness, sin, and death. That is why those under that old age longed for "the age about to come." They knew that in the new age of the Messiah, they could have eternal life, and fellowship with the Father in a way that could never be under the Old Law (see Hebrews 9:6-10). These are the blessings that are now a reality in Christ, because he did sweep away the old world in the destruction of the Temple and Jerusalem in A.D. 70.

# CHAPTER 7

# GOD AND CHRONOLOGY
## ONE DAY IS WITH THE LORD AS A THOUSAND YEARS

**"But, Beloved, Be Not Ignorant of this One Thing, That One Day Is with the Lord as a Thousand Years, and a Thousand Years as One Day."** (2 Peter 3:8)

Without controversy 2 Peter 3:8 is used more often to explain why God has not operated within clearly defined time limitations than any other Bible text. On a straightforward reading of the Bible the Day of the Lord was *supposed* to occur in the first century. Yet it did not happen according to most students. To explain this failure of fulfillment of the literal expectation it is devoutly stated, "Just remember, 'One day is with the Lord a thousand years and a thousand years is as a day.'" What is meant by this is that while scripture may say something is at hand or must happen very soon, since God does not see time as man does He is under no constraint to operate soon. When God says something is at hand it might not be for thousands of years.

Non-millennialists have seen the fallacy and danger of this type of verbal gymnastics, at least in discussions of the kingdom of God. They have quoted from Mark 1:15 and inspiration's promise, "The time is fulfilled, the kingdom of heaven is at hand." While our dispensational friends have appealed to 2 Peter 3:8, amillennialists and postmillennialists alike have correctly replied, "At hand does not mean 2000 years or more. If at hand does not mean at hand then Bible language is hopelessly un-interpretable." Strangely however, when it comes to the Day of the Lord, matters change. A preterist points out that the same Bible that says, "The kingdom of heaven is at hand," also says, "Behold, I come quickly!, and what happens? All of a sudden the non-millennialists start quoting 2 Peter 3:8![82] Who was it that said, "Ah, consistency, thou art a jewel so rare"?

It is refreshing, although problematic for his paradigm, that Mathison correctly notes that the attempts to use 2 Peter 3:8 to negate the eschatological temporal statements of scripture are misguided:

"This passage of scripture has often been used in an attempt to prove that something God says will come to pass within a certain amount of time may not come to pass for many centuries or millennia. While it is true that the Old Testament prophets do sometimes speak of an event as 'near' that we now know to have been fulfilled many centuries later, this does not seem to be the main point of 2 Peter 3:8-

9. Rather, the main point seems to be that the passage of a long delay is actually a demonstration of God's mercy. The fact that God made a promise long ago that has yet to be fulfilled does not mean that the promise will not be fulfilled." (*WSTTB*, 204)

So, Mathison correctly notes that Peter was not saying "at hand" does not mean near. However, as we have shown, this demands that 2 Peter 3 was to be fulfilled soon from Peter's perspective because: **1.)** Peter said the end of all things had drawn near, **2.)** The judgment of 2 Peter 3 is the same as the judgment of 2 Peter 2, and Peter said that judgment was now coming quickly. Thus, Mathison's admission that the eschatological time statements are not mitigated by 2 Peter 3:8-9, is destructive to his idea that the parousia of 2 Peter 3 is far off.

The amillennialist believes the premillennialist is inconsistent for failing to see this issue. They preach long and loud about how scripture said the kingdom would be set up in the days of the Roman empire (Daniel 2). The premillennialist says it was postponed. Amillennialists say this would mean God's promise failed, because in Psalms 89 Jehovah promised not to alter His promise. *To postpone the kingdom by 2000 years is an alteration!* But again, when it comes to the Day of the Lord, equivocation is the order of the day. It is insisted that "will come" means "*could* come." 2 Peter 3:8 is cited, yet this feeble rationalization does just as grave injustice to the faithfulness of God's promises as those of the premillennial camp.

How is God to communicate with mankind? Granted that God's thoughts are not ours because they are so much higher (Isaiah 55). How then is Jehovah to communicate with His creation? Will He use His words that are beyond comprehension or will He use our words? Suffice it to say that God uses, of necessity, man's words to communicate with us. See I Corinthians 2, Ephesians 3:1-6. God wants all men to come to knowledge of the truth (I Timothy 2:4). God has the ability to cause that truth to be communicated in ways for the common man to understand. Did not the common people hear Jesus gladly? Was not the Bible written in the language of the people? What does *koine* mean anyway?[83] All this means that God chose man's language for purposes of communicating His word.

The foreword of Vines Theological Dictionary is *apropos*, "New Testament Greek is not the Attic of the Classics, nor is it 'a language of the Holy Ghost' as one scholar called it, but it is the ordinary vernacular of Greek of that period, the language of everyday life, as it was spoken and written by the ordinary men and women of the day, tradesmen, soldiers, schoolboys, lovers, clerks, and so on, that is, the *koine*, or 'Common' Greek of the great Graeco- Roman world."[84]

It is incredible to read the commentators who seek to mitigate the first century imminence of the parousia. Few stop to realize the implications of their interpretation of 2 Peter 3:8. What they are saying is that even if God says something is at hand it might be a thousand years away from fulfillment. However, if He says something is a long time that has to mean it is millennia away! Engelsma claims: "The nearness of Christ's coming in the N. T. teaching is not proximity according to the standard of human clock-time and calendar time. The Spirit of inspiration did not mean that Jesus' return was a few years off, or possibly at any moment. Fact is, that in close connection with the assertion that Jesus' coming is near, Scripture indicates that this coming is quite distant as regards clock and calendar time. According to human notions of time, the coming is a long way off. Indeed, it seems to the waiting church that He delays His coming."[85]

So, what we are to believe is that statements of imminence do not mean time, but statements of delay do mean time. If something was said to be at hand, this did not refer to the calendar. However, if it was said to be far off, this *did* refer to the calendar. Let's be candid, this is bad logic.

Are we not back to a discussion of the faithfulness of God, His ability and willingness to communicate? Let us see how this argument will stand the test of Bible. In Numbers 24:17 Balaam the prophet made a prophecy of the coming of Messiah. He said, "I see him, *But not now; I behold him, but not near.*" (emphasis mine). Now should the Israelites have gotten all excited in the belief Messiah was soon to come? It was going to be centuries before he actually came, but since God doesn't think of time like you and I, perhaps what Balaam could have said without any trouble at all was, "I see him coming very, very soon!" Would that not have been deceptive of Jehovah to lead them on like that?

Daniel 8 gives us another example of God and chronological language. Daniel sees a vision concerning the Grecian empire. The vision extends from the third year of king Belshazzar of Babylon to the fall of Antiochus Epiphanes. The period of time covered is 550 B.C. to 164 B.C. (McGuiggan[86]). The entire period is 386 years. Listen to God's message to Daniel in 8:26: "The vision of the evenings and mornings is true; Therefore seal up the vision, for it refers to many days in the future."

Did you catch it? God, talking to man about events in man's world tells Daniel it would be a long time before the vision was fulfilled. It would be less than 400 years, but that is a long time for man, therefore God calls it

81

a long time. This is important then when we read New Covenant statements of imminence. For instance, how could the fulfillment of Revelation extend even to the fall of Rome, (A. D. 476), even if the book was written in A.D. 95, when that would entail a period of almost 400 years? Is 400 years a "long time" in Daniel, but a "little while" in Revelation?

Consider the issue of false prophets and the temporal statements concerning the parousia. In Deuteronomy 18 is the well known "test of a prophet." Simply stated, Jehovah said if a prophet predicted something, and it did not come true, the man was a false prophet. It seems not to have dawned on modern exegetes who seek to negate the temporal statements of scripture that their arguments completely negate that test.

Pratt makes the amazing claim that: "We will argue that Biblical prophecies are seldom fulfilled exactly as they are given. Therefore, even if Scriptures did predict Jesus' return would take place within a few years, his return could still be in our future, even two thousand years later."[87] In that same work, Strimple claims that the time statements of scripture are only examples of "alleged imminency." So there you have it. Even though the Bible might have predicted events to occur within a specific time frame, that does not mean one single thing.

As we have seen, this position negates the possibility of testing the prophets. It negates Jesus' words in Luke 21.8. After all, just because the false teachers would say "the end has drawn near" before the end had drawn near, means nothing! How could the apostles, how could *anyone*, reject them as false teachers, if their time statements could not be tested?

Consider Jeremiah 29:10. Jehovah said Judah was to endure seventy years of Babylonian captivity. The people and other prophets rejected this word, and claimed, "The vessels of the Lord's house will now shortly be brought back from Babylon" (Jeremiah 27:16). So, the Lord said the captivity would be "long" (Jeremiah 29:28), but the people said it would be *short*; they even identified that "short" time as two years (Jeremiah 28:2f). Jeremiah's response was that if the prediction of his adversary, the prophet Hananiah, came true, and the vessels were restored "shortly" then he, Jeremiah, was a false prophet. However, if after two years the vessels were not returned, Hananiah was to die! (Jeremiah 28:10-16) Hananiah died in two years.

The test of the prophet was not only whether *what* he said came true, but the *timing* of the fulfillment his prediction. If the time element of his prediction failed, he was a false prophet.

All attempts to negate the prophetic time statements about the *parousia* nullify God's test of a prophet. But if time statements mean nothing, *why did God condemn prophets for making false time statements?* When God talks to man He uses man's language. This is perhaps no where better illustrated than in Ezekiel 12. The prophet had predicted the coming of the Day of the Lord, see chapter 7, and said it was at hand. The people did not listen. They scoffed at the very idea of Jerusalem falling. God's response to their ridicule is found in verses 21f.

"Son of Man, what is this proverb, that you people have about the land of Israel which says, 'The days are prolonged and every vision fails?' Tell them, I will lay this proverb to rest and they shall no more use it as a proverb... But say to them, 'The days are at hand and the fulfillment of every vision.' For I am the Lord, I speak and the word which I speak will come to pass it will no more be postponed; for in your days, O rebellious house, I will say the word and perform it."

Be sure to read all verses 21-28. God's principle when He speaks in chronological terms is unequivocal. When He said something is at hand, *it was at hand. It did refer to the calendar after all.* It would happen in the lifetime of those to whom it was spoken. When He said something was near He did not intend for man to twist it to mean long time.

Ezekiel 12 gives us direct insight into how God not only communicates with man in regard to time, but how He expects man to understand Him. Just like in Jeremiah, when man tried to make a long time, mean a short time, and God condemned them, in Ezekiel, God said it was near, and man tried to say it was not near. God condemned man for perverting His time statements. And what is so significant, is that man was responding to God's words as if they were to be understood in the normal parameters of language. They did not try to argue that a long time with God is actually a short time; they simply denied that what God said was true. They did not elasticize the words into the oblivion of subjectivity. *They knew what God's words meant,* they just denied them!

Another O. T. example is helpful, because it is similar to Peter's prediction. In Amos 8:12 the prophet told Israel: "The end has come upon my people Israel: I will not pass them by anymore. And the Songs of the temple shall be songs of wailing in that day" (Amos 8.2). So, Amos declared that the Day of the Lord (5.18f) was near. What was the people's response? In Isaiah 56.12, Amos' contemporary recorded the peoples' response to the message of impending judgment: "Come," one says, "I will bring wine, and we will fill ourselves with intoxicating drink. Tomorrow will be as today, and much more abundant." The parallels between the days of Isaiah and Amos, with Peter are clear.

Amos and Isaiah foretold the Day of the Lord. Peter foretold the Day of the Lord.[88] Amos and Isaiah said the Day of the Lord was near. Peter said the end of all things had drawn near. Amos' contemporaries scoffed at the idea that judgment was near. Peter said scoffers were denying the impending judgment. The scoffers of Isaiah's day were claiming, "all things continue" i.e., "Tomorrow shall be as today." The scoffers in 2 Peter 3 were saying, "All things continue as they were."

So, what was God's response to those in Amos' day who scoffed at the warnings of the soon coming judgment? Just like in Jeremiah's day, centuries later, God condemned man for denying the objective reality of His time statements. In Amos 6.3, Jehovah said: "Woe to you who put far off the day of doom." *God condemned them for denying the objective nature of His time warnings.*

Thus, in direct opposition to the claim that, "Time is relative with God" (Jackson, *Isaiah*, 101), there was nothing subjective, or elastic about God's warnings of imminent judgment. And, when man tried to deny the objective nature of those time warnings, they perished.

The significance of this should not be lost in our study of 2 Peter 3. It cannot be denied that Peter affirmed the nearness of the end, as we have seen. Lamentably, modern exegetes basically side with the scoffers by saying Peter's inspired affirmations were not to be taken seriously because time supposedly means nothing with God. Yet, Peter stood in the long line of prophets who proclaimed God's judgments, and as we have seen, when God spoke of events that were near, He expected, no, He *demanded*, that man take His time statements seriously. He even condemned those who refused to honor those time statements.

All of this is significant in studying 2 Peter 3:8. This forces us to reexamine the arguments about the "elastic" nature of prophetic time. How can we insist on God's faithfulness, His desire for men to know the truth, and His revelation of that truth to man, if we then turn around and say that God communicates in ways that call His faithfulness into question?

Peter's purpose in 2 Peter 3:8 is not to imply that God is not honest in his usage of chronological language. His purpose is to reassure his readers that whether God promises something is imminent or in the misty future, He keeps his promises. *God is faithful!* He does not deceive His creation when He speaks to them. What He promises, He will perform, no matter how difficult the task, or the time involved to perform it.

# A FINAL THOUGHT:
## 2 PETER 3:8 AND GOD'S FAITHFULNESS TO *ISRAEL*

We want to take a closer look at Peter's statement. What did Peter mean when he quoted Psalms 90:4? Why did he use that verse? Was he, as many scholars believe, citing Psalms to explain the delayed or failed promises of Christ to return? Did he mean to say that when God speaks to man in chronological terms we are not to pay any attention, since God does not reckon time like man? Was Peter saying time words spoken by God are worthless even when spoken to man? Was He implying that God cannot express himself accurately to man? When it comes to communicating time concepts and time words, are words spoken by Jehovah without objective significance? These are weighty matters that must be addressed when one posits Peter as saying God and time do not mix.

Peter was affirming God's ability to fulfill his promises no matter how little or how much time passes. Time does not affect God's ability to fulfill his promises. It is God's *faithfulness* at stake here, not His ability to communicate. It is not God's use of ambiguous words.[89] It is His unshakable ability to keep His word. But would it not be a serious question of the faithfulness of Jesus for Him to promise, "I come quickly," and that he would return in the lifetime of many of his disciples (Matthew 16;27-28, 24:34), to judge the living and the dead (Matthew 23:33f, cf. I Peter 4:5), *and then not keep his word*? How does it confirm the faithfulness of God to say on the one hand that He is faithful, and on the other hand, affirm that you cannot take His promises seriously as to when He was going to do something? Part of the faithfulness of God is to do, not only *what* He said He would do, but to do it *when* He said He would.

But there is more to be found in Peter's citation of Psalms 90, and it is very vital. It is important to be reminded of the Jewish practice that when one part of a prophecy or scripture was quoted, the Jewish mind thought of the entire context of that prophecy, not just an isolated quotation (Holland, 27). And when we examine the context of Psalms 90, what we find is that the reference to the timelessness of God is set within a discussion of the enemies of God resisting His purposes, but the affirmation of God's faithfulness to Israel to complete her salvation.

This is critical. Psalms 90 is about Israel's reliance on God, her sin and her punishment, but her prayer that Jehovah would not turn His back on the promises He had made to her. The Psalmist sings of Israel's long reliance on God and the Lord's eternal nature (v. 1-4). Let me emphasize that *this is a song about God's relationship with Israel*, and His faithfulness to her.

85

In verses 7-12, the Psalmist recounts Jehovah's just punishments of Israel for her violation of the covenant: "by your wrath we are terrified" (v. 7). We cannot lose sight that for the author, God's wrath was to be seen within the context of *Covenant Wrath*. Israel violated the covenant, God brought the provisions of His covenant with her into action and punished her. Again, this is all about God's dealings with His covenant people. To apply the discussion of wrath here, which must be tied in with the judgment of the ungodly in 2 Peter 3:7, to the material creation, is to miss the point of the text. In Psalms 90 the author discusses the righteousness and glory of God to punish the wicked who had violated His covenant. And that discussion is focused on Jehovah's punishment of *Israel* for violating the covenant. Peter cites Psalms 90 and discusses the impending judgment of the ungodly. This means Peter was anticipating the judgment of Judah for violating the covenant.

In verses 13-17, the Psalmist cries out to the Lord not to forget them, that is, *not to forget Israel*, His chosen people, but, "Let your work appear to your servants...and establish the work of Your hands for us." To understand this prayer as a prayer of an individual, for an individual, outside of the confines of God's covenantal dealings with Israel would be a fatal exegetical mistake.

What is the significance of seeing Psalms 90 within the context of God's covenant dealings with Israel? It means that when Peter quotes the passage in 2 Peter 3, he was refuting the scoffers by reminding them of God's faithfulness to Israel.

> **Peter's use of Psalms 90 proves that he is concerned with the fulfillment of *God's promises to Israel*. He is refuting the scoffers by reminding them of God's covenant faithfulness to His covenant people–and as he had written in 1 Peter, *the time had come!***

Peter was not concerned therefore, with the fate of material creation. He was focused on the fulfillment of God's promises to His covenant people. The scoffers realized that the promises had been in place for many years. But where was the fulfillment? By citing Psalms 90, Peter was reminding the scoffers of Israel's long covenant history. God is faithful.

Remember that in 1 Peter 1:10 Peter said God's promises in the O. T. were not near for the Old Covenant saints, but were now near when he wrote. What had once been far off had drawn near. While Peter affirmed that the time for the consummation of the Old Covenant promises had arrived, the scoffers said "all things continue as they were." When we compare 1 Peter 1:10 and the context of Psalms 90 we can begin to see that Peter's citation of Psalms is *exactly the opposite* of what modern commentators suggest. It is not a case of "cognitive dissonance"[90] on Peter's part, as he struggled to understand why his Lord had not kept his promise. *His citation of Psalms is an affirmation that God would be faithful to His promises to Israel, and the time had come.*

So, while the eternal nature of God is certainly a part of Peter's argument and appeal to Psalms, we must see his citation of Psalms, not as a means of *mitigating* the promises concerning the imminent parousia, but as a means of confirming those promises, because God is faithful, faithful to *Israel*. As we have noted above, all of this places Peter's discourse, and the scoffers, firmly within a discussion of Israel's last days, Israel's covenant, and God's faithfulness to her.

This means that since Peter's citation is a reminder of God's covenant faithfulness to Israel, then Peter's prediction of the Day of the Lord must be seen as the climax of Israel's Aeon. It has nothing to do with the end of the Christian age. Unless one can prove that the fulfillment of Israel's covenant promises are linked with the destruction of the planet earth, then one cannot construe 2 Peter 3 as a prediction of such a catastrophe. As a citation of Psalms 90, 2 Peter 3:8 is a reminder of, and prayer for, the consummation of God's covenant dealings with Israel. That Day would be when the old world was swept away, and the New Covenant world stood triumphant. This is when God would reveal His work in Israel. This is when He would establish the work of His hands, and the True Israel, the remnant, would enter into the realization of God's salvation.

87

# CHAPTER 8
# THE DAY OF THE LORD WILL COME

**"But the Day of the Lord Will Come as a Thief in the Night; in the Which the Heavens Shall Pass Away with a Great Noise, and the Elements Shall Melt with Fervent Heat, the Earth Also and the Works That Are Therein Shall Be Burned Up."** ( 2 Peter 3:10)

Exactly what is the Day of the Lord? If you are like most you got your ideas listening to well intentioned preachers speak forcefully about when the universe will be burned to a crisp. But as with most, this was certainly true with those ministers around whom I was raised, their concept of the Day of the Lord did not spring from a comprehensive study of the Bible. Their concepts sprang strictly from studying the New Covenant and literalizing all eschatological references. I am convinced had they been better students of the Bible such narrow views of eschatology would not have been so prevalent.

How do we determine usage of terms and words? Do we not study precedent, context and repetitive usage? We can determine the lexical definition if it is a single word. We then go to scripture and see how it is utilized. By examining context and repeated uses of the word we have established precedent and rule. If we encounter an instance where the normal definition of the word seems incongruous we can then seek an alternate definition. But until we have strong reason for doing so we must maintain the definitions established by previous usage.

When it comes to terms and defining them we must rely on context. And when it comes to defining the term "the Day of the Lord" there is no paucity of material for research. As a matter of fact, there is no way to examine all of the Old Covenant occurrences of the term. Most assuredly the Old Covenant is where the term is introduced and is, therefore, the source to which the investigator must go to begin the quest for definition.

We will list several of the texts, give the *object* of the prophecy, list any *chronological reference*, take note of the *language* used to describe the Day, and give the approximate time of fulfillment.

Here is an important point before we proceed. As we note several times in this work, the New Testament writers tells us repeatedly that their eschatological hopes are nothing but that foretold by the prophets of old. Paul's doctrine of the resurrection was from "Moses and all the prophets" (Acts 24.13f; 26.21f, etc.) Peter anticipated the "restoration of all things" in fulfillment of "all that the prophets, all who have ever spoken, from

Samuel forward" (Acts 3.19f), and this restoration would be finalized at the parousia of Christ.

Our point is that the New Testament writers were trained in the Old Covenant concept of the Day of the Lord. So, if we are going to properly interpret and define the Day of the Lord we are going to have to get inside the Hebraic mind set. If we set out to interpret a piece of French literature from the 14th century, we have to know the thought of the French society of the time. If we are going to interpret German literature of the 10th century, or English from the 16th century, we have to get inside the world of the people to whom that literature was written. And so it is with the Bible. If we are going to properly interpret the Bible, we have to get inside the Hebraic world view, and understand what they meant, what they thought, when they read about the Day of the Lord.

As we will see, God had manifested himself often. He had come on the clouds many times. He had come in flaming fire, with the sound of a trumpet, and heaven and earth had been shaken and removed. Yet, not one time had Jehovah ever appeared visibly, bodily, literally. The Day of the Lord in the Old Testament was invariably a "historical" event, that manifested the Sovereignty of Jehovah to the discerning: "When your judgments are in the earth, the inhabitants of the world will learn righteousness. Let grace be shown to the wicked and he will not learn righteousness...and will not behold the majesty of the Lord." Go back and read the discussion of Isaiah 64-65 again.

What Isaiah was saying here is highly significant. He was predicting the Day of the Lord, when Jehovah would come out of heaven, and He would "punish the earth" (Isaiah 26.21). The essential thing to see here is that the righteous would see that judgment and know God had come. The wicked on the other hand would witness the identical events and not have a clue that it was Jehovah at work. They would see, but not *see*.

If the Day of the Lord is an earth burning, time ending event, when Jesus literally appears in a flesh and blood body, descending out of heaven on a cumulus cloud, would it be possible for even the most hardened atheist to not know what was going on? It would be impossible! Yet, Isaiah is affirming that the Day he is predicting would be the Day of the Lord when both righteous and unrighteous alike would witness the same identical events. The righteous would see those events and *see in those events* the presence (πρωσοπων, face) of God. On the other hand, the wicked would see those events and say, "I don't get it! This is 'just' the invasion of an army. There is nothing 'divine' going on here."[91] The prophet was saying the Lord was coming, and heaven and earth was going to be destroyed. The skeptics would respond, "My eyes are not seeing what my ears are hearing; it can't be true!" But because they would refuse to see, with the eyes of faith, did not mean Jehovah had not come.

Not only do we have examples of the Day of the Lord, and not one of them is an example of a visible, bodily coming of Jehovah, but Jesus predicted that his own parousia was to be "in the glory of the Father" (Matthew 16.27-28). This means Jesus was to come just like the Father had come many times before. Furthermore, in John 5.19f, Jesus said the Father had committed all judgment to him, so that all men might honor him as they honor the Father. He said he would only do, i.e. in judgment, what he had seen the Father do.

So, Jesus said his coming in judgment would be like he had seen his Father judge. If Jesus had never seen his Father come bodily, literally, out of heaven on literal clouds, but Jesus said his coming in the Day of the Lord was to be in the same manner as the Father had come, then this is *prima facie* proof that the Day of the Lord in 2 Peter 3 was not to be a literal, bodily, visible coming of Christ out of heaven. See my book *Like Father Like Son, On Clouds of Glory*, for a fuller discussion of Christ's coming as the Father had come.

Let us investigate the Old Testament definition of The Day of the Lord.

**1.) Isaiah 13**

This Day would be against Babylon (v. 1-2). It is called the Day of the Lord, and was at hand (v. 6). The sun, moon and stars would be darkened. Heaven and earth would be shaken out of their place (v. 10f). Babylon was sacked in B. C. 689 within a few short years of this prediction.[92] There is no question that this prophecy was about a "historical" Day of the Lord and not about any so-called end of time event.

Interestingly, Gibbs offers the following argument. In Matthew 24:29-31 Jesus directly echoes the language of Isaiah 13. The language of Isaiah 13 is demonstrably, "theophanic, eschatological language to refer to an act of divine judgment upon an earthly nation within the course of history."[93] Therefore, Gibbs argues, the "implied reader" of Matthew 24:29-31 would understand that since Jesus was using the metaphoric language of prophecy to describe the destruction of Jerusalem, then the language of Matthew 24 is likewise metaphoric language to describe the actions of God within history, not to bring history to an end.

This is good logic. However, the problem is that Gibbs, like so many others, fail to see that in 2 Peter 3, Peter is also directly quoting O. T.

90

prophetic metaphoric language of the Day of the Lord. If therefore, we are to interpret Matthew 24 as an "in history" Day of the Lord because of its citation of apocalyptic language, then why is that not true in 2 Peter 3?

**2.) Isaiah 19-20**

The prophecy is against ancient Egypt. Jehovah would ride on a swift cloud into Egypt (19:1f). That nation would be decimated. The Nile would dry up, the crops would fail. This is dramatic language of the coming of Jehovah. The time of the prophecy was approximately B. C. 712. Watts argues that this was fulfilled by the Ethiopian ruler Shabaka, in an alliance with the Assyrians and Sargon (chapter 20), in approximately B. C. 701.[94]

**3.) Isaiah 30-31**

This prophecy is two-fold. It is against Assyria, and it is for Israel. The time of the prophecy was approximately 712-710 B.C. Some date this prophecy in B. C. 704.[95] The Lord said He was coming to save Jerusalem from the Assyrians. He promised that if Israel would trust in Him, they would not suffer defeat. However, if they relied on Egypt and refused to submit to Him: "one thousand shall flee at the threat of one, and at the threat of five you shall flee." (Isaiah 30:17). He promised that if they would trust Him "you shall weep no more" and that, "there will be on every high mountain and on every high hill rivers and streams of water" (30:25f). The light of the moon would be as bright as the sun, and the sun would be seven times brighter than normal.

On Assyria however, Jehovah said He was coming from heaven, with a shout, in flaming fire. There would be a tempest and hailstones, (30:30f), and, "The Lord of Hosts will come down to fight for Mount Zion and for its hill, as birds flying about will the Lord of Hosts defend Jerusalem" (31:4f). Assyria would fall, but not by normal human means (31:8f)

The prophecy was fulfilled in approximately B. C. 701, when the Lord destroyed 185,000 of Sennacherib's army. He went home in disgrace and was later killed by his own sons (Isaiah 37:36f)

The language is graphic, and sounds like the "end of the world." It is "apocalyptic" language that speaks of the destruction of Assyria. However, the language was not fulfilled literally. God never created streams on tops of the mountains when Assyria was destroyed, and did not make the light of the sun seven times more powerful, *thankfully!* Jehovah did not come out of heaven visibly, bodily, or literally with flaming fire and an audible shout.

91

There was no hail storm. There could hardly be a clearer example of the metaphoric nature of the Day of the Lord language.

### 4.) Isaiah 34

This is a prophecy against Edom and "all nations" (v. 2, 8). The prophecy contains some of the most graphic language in all of the Old Testament. It is called "the Day." The mountains would melt with blood. The host of heaven would be dissolved, the heavens rolled up, the stars fall from the sky, earth would flow with blood, the streams would burn with pitch, even the dust would burn. Thorns would grow everywhere. Yet, this is a prediction of the fall of Edom (v. 5-8).

Watts dates this prophecy to the period of Jeremiah 25 and Obadiah, the time, in other words, of the Babylonian invasion of Judah in B. C. 587-586. (*Isaiah*, 9+). At that time, the Edomites supported the Chaldeans, and plundered the Jews seeking to escape that invasion, according to Obadiah. McGuiggan disagrees stating instead that he believes the Edomites joined with the Assyrians in their siege of Jerusalem in the 8th century (*Isaiah* 175). This would be the same siege as described just above, in Isaiah 30f.

I essentially agree with McGuiggan, and on that basis suggest that it is important to follow the time chart of this prediction and its fulfillment.

Isaiah never said this prediction was near to fulfillment. However, over 130+ years later, Jeremiah reiterated the prophecy of the destruction of Edom and "all the nations" (Jeremiah 25).[96] This time however, Jeremiah tells us that Nebuchadnezzar of Babylon would fulfill the prophecy. Ezekiel, Jeremiah's contemporary, also foretold the destruction of Edom and "all the nations" (Ezekiel 35), at the hands of the Chaldeans. Then, the book of Obadiah, written immediately after the fall of Jerusalem, says the fall of Edom and the nations was near (Obadiah 15). *Babylon destroyed Edom within three years of the writing of Obadiah.*[97] The book of Malachi (1:2f) looks back on the destruction of Edom as a historical reality.

So, what we have is a prediction of the Day of the Lord's vengeance, when "heaven and earth" would be destroyed. The mountains would melt, the stars would fall from the sky. Patently, none of this happened literally. Yet, Malachi looked back on the destruction of Edom as an accomplished fact, and even used the language of Isaiah. There is no question that Malachi considered the prophecy to be fulfilled. Once again, we have an compelling example of the metaphoric language of the Day of the Lord.

**5.) Ezekiel 29-30, 32**

This is the Day of the Lord (30:1f). It is the Day of the Lord against Egypt (v. 3-4). Egypt would be destroyed and burn (v. 8f). Egypt's multitudes would be destroyed (v. 10). This Day of the Lord was near when Ezekiel wrote (30:3). Jehovah said: "When I blot you out, I will cover the heavens, and make their stars dark; I will cover the sun with a cloud, and the moon will not give its light. All the bright lights of heaven will I make dark over you, and put darkness upon your land, says the Lord God" (Ezekiel 32:1-16, RSV). This prophecy was uttered in approximately B. C. 587. This Day of the Lord was to be brought about by Nebuchadnezzar, king of Babylon (29:19; 30:10f). Egypt was destroyed by Babylon in approximately B. C. 580. (See Josephus Antiquities 10:9:7).

So, we have the prediction, in graphic language, of the Day of the Lord. That Day was near, and fulfillment came within seven years. Egypt fell to Nebuchadnezzar just as foretold. Clearly though, this was not an end of time event. As Gibbs says: "In context, the language of Ezekiel 32:7-8 shows itself to be figurative." (*Jerusalem*, 193). The Day of the Lord was when Jehovah, in His sovereignty, used Babylon to accomplish His purposes and manifest His glory. When He used the Babylonians to judge Egypt, He said, "Then they will know that I am the Lord, when I have set a fire in Egypt" (30:8).[98]

**6.) Joel 1:15,2:10;3:14f**

Joel foretold the Day of the Lord against Jerusalem and Zion (2:1f). The Day of the Lord was at hand (2:1). The sun, moon and stars were to be darkened (2:2f). The earth would quake and the heavens would tremble. The trumpet would sound and the people would be gathered (2:15f). This Day was fulfilled by a locust plague sometime after B.C. 830. It is possible however, that it could have been a prediction of the fall of Jerusalem in B. C. 586. The dating of Joel is difficult. However, whether one applies it to the ninth century locust invasion or the 6th century Babylonian invasion, the fact remains that this is not an "end of time judgment." The language is clearly hyperbolic and metaphoric. Jehovah was acting by "natural" agency to accomplish His purposes.

**7.) Micah 1:3f**

This prophecy was against Samaria and Jerusalem (Micah 1:2f). The graphic language describes Jehovah coming out of the heavens and walking on the tops of the mountains, and as a result the earth burns up. The valleys split open, and creation is destroyed. The prophecy was fulfilled between 721-712 B.C. when Assyria took the 10 northern tribes into captivity. The language is simply a graphic description of the end of Israel's *world*. Jehovah did not literally come down out of heaven and did not bodily appear at all. Yet, this is the Day of the Lord against Samaria. Time did not end, the earth was not consumed, yet, Jehovah came.

**8.) Zephaniah 1:7,14f**
This Day of the Lord was to come against Jerusalem at the hands of the Chaldeans under Nebuchadnezzar. The prophecy was written circa B. C. 630-625 (Nelson Open Bible). The Day of the Lord is "at hand" (1:7, 14). It was to be the Day of the Lord's presence (*prosopon*, literally His *face*, 1:7). Creation would be destroyed (1:2f). Man and beast alike would perish, even the fish of the sea. It would be the time of the sounding of the Trumpet, a day of darkness and devastation (1:15f). This Day was to be the time of judgment of Jerusalem for worshiping Baal (1:4f). That was fulfilled in B. C. 586 at the hands of Babylon.

So, the language of Zephaniah, like the language of Isaiah, Ezekiel and the other prophets who spoke of the Day of the Lord, cannot be taken literally, to refer to a bodily, visible appearing of God out of heaven. There was no literal destruction of the entire created order. The Lord did come. His *presence* was with them. However, as Isaiah 26 indicated, you would have to be able to "see" with the eyes of faith to know that Jehovah was present.

Note the similarities between Zephaniah and 2 Peter 3. Both passages foretold the Day of the Lord. Both predicted the destruction of the *earth, by fire* (Zephaniah 1:18; 3:8). Both foretold the judgment of the wicked, and both foretold the resulting "righteousness" after the Day of the Lord (cf. Zephaniah 3:12f/ 2 Peter 3:13f). These similarities suggest that Peter *may* actually have had Zephaniah in mind, although that cannot be proven.

Our point is that if Zephaniah could use such hyperbolic, metaphoric language to describe the fall of Jerusalem in B. C. 586, then it clearly cannot be argued that Peter could not do likewise in 2 Peter 3.

**9.) Zephaniah 3:8f**
We list this additional passage in Zephaniah because many dispensationalists insist that it is being fulfilled in our present generation. This text was written in circa B. C. 630-620. It foretold the time when God would arise in anger, and, "My determination is to gather the nations to the

94

assembly of kingdoms, to pour out My indignation, all my fierce anger; all the earth shall be devoured with the fire of my jealousy." This is a prediction, matching that of Ezekiel 35 and Jeremiah 25, of the impending destruction of Jerusalem and the surrounding nations at the hand of Nebuchadnezzar. This was accomplished within a fairly short period of time, in B. C. 606-586.

Current dispensationalism is a good example of how *not* to interpret the Day of the Lord prophecies. Grant Jeffrey, in a book written to refute preterism, cites Zephaniah 3:9 and the prediction: "I will restore to the peoples a pure language." Jeffrey tells of how Israel is once again speaking ancient Hebrew, and says, "The restoration of the ancient tongue of the prophets certainly qualifies as one of the most extraordinary miracles and unique biblical predictions ever fulfilled."[99] However, a closer look at Zephaniah will show the folly of this suggestion.

Notice in verse 8 God said He was going to gather the nations. It was to be the time of His fierce anger, and "all the earth shall be devoured." So, we have the Day of the Lord, when creation is destroyed. It would be *"then"* (v. 9), that God would, "restore to the peoples a pure language." Now, if, as Jeffrey claims, the restoration of Hebrew in modern Israel is the fulfillment of Zephaniah, then we have every right to ask when all the earth was devoured by the fire of God's wrath? Jehovah said that *when earth was devoured*, that the language would be restored. He did not say He would restore the language and *then destroy the earth*. He would first destroy the land and *then* restore the language. So, just exactly *when was the whole earth consumed* before the restoration of the ancient Hebrew language in modern Israel?

The millennial view of Zephaniah will not stand a literal interpretation. The language is metaphoric, never intended to be taken literally.

**10.) Zechariah 14:1f**
This prediction was against Jerusalem (v. 1f). Jerusalem would be taken and ransacked. It is called the coming of the Lord with His saints (14:4-5). The Lord would come down and walk on the Mt. of Olives. (Remember Micah 1? There the Lord *came down* as well, but not literally or bodily.) The mountains would split, and there would be no clear light. There is little doubt that the destruction of Jerusalem in A.D. 70 is in view.

Other examples could be cited. Do your own study. Get out the concordance and research the "Day of the Lord." You will discover that God came with 10,000 saints at Sinai (Deuteronomy 33). You will hear the prophets say they saw the entire earth destroyed (Jeremiah 4).[100] As seen above, you will read of the earth's destruction by fire at the coming of El Shaddai. You will even read David's wonderful description of how God had delivered him from his enemies (Psalms 18, 2 Samuel 22). David tells how God had descended from heaven on the clouds, the earth shook and the very foundations of earth were exposed. God had smoke coming from his nostrils as He rode the clouds and sent hailstones and coals of fire to David's rescue. Fire went before the Lord and lightning and thunder were attendant as Elohim came in the clouds with darkness under His feet.

In Isaiah 29 we find the judgment against Ariel (Jerusalem). Desolation is everywhere. The specific danger is the Assyrian invasion by Sennacherib. In chapter 30 the Lord promises Israel that if they will submit to him He will bless them and, "the light of the moon will be as the light of the sun. And the light of the sun will be sevenfold, as the light of seven days." This is highly exaggerated language. This was language of *blessing*, yet, if God magnified the brightness of the sun seven times the earth would be incinerated immediately. On the other hand, in other prophecies of blessings there is the promise that there would be *no need for the sun or moon* (Isaiah 60:19f).

Whereas when God was going to judge a nation their sun, moon and stars would fall or be darkened, (Study Daniel 8:8f for an excellent example), when the Lord was going to bless a nation, the creation is depicted as being super-abundant, flourishing, or strongly established.

In all these passages one meets a common theme, the Day of the Lord. Although the Day is always described in graphic language that sounds as if the very creation itself was coming apart, this was simply God's way of emphasizing that the *world* of those He was about to judge was about to come crashing down around their ears. He did not intend for the language to be taken literally.

The Day of the Lord was, to put it simply, a time when Jehovah acted. He might use a locust plague to punish Judah, as in Joel. He might use the Assyrians to punish Samaria as in the book of Isaiah, or the Assyrians to destroy Egypt as in Isaiah 19. The Day of the Lord was when the Babylonians destroyed the Edomites (Obadiah), and on and on. The point is, while these texts describe God as coming out of heaven, on the clouds, with fire, with angels, with the trumpets, for the purpose of judging the world, destroying the earth with fire, causing the sun, moon and stars to turn black or fall from the sky, *none of this literally happened.* The nations against whom the prophecies were uttered have fallen as predicted. The prophecies stand fulfilled, but the physical creation remains.

What can we learn from this? We should first of all be cognizant of the fact that the New Covenant writers were Jews steeped in this Old Covenant thought. They lived, ate, thought, and were consumed by that Old Covenant. The Old Covenant is the well-spring of the New Covenant. The New Covenant writers did not suddenly develop a new vocabulary nor a new way of expressing thought. The Holy Spirit utilized their training, thoughts, and words to express New Covenant realities.

When the New Covenant writers, therefore, used the term Day of the Lord, what should we automatically realize they had in mind? Was it a time-ending, universe destroying, cosmic catastrophe? They had never heard that idea before. They *did know* how God had judged the nations and *came* before. Would they not, when they were informed of the coming Day of the Lord, as foretold by Peter, need to be instructed, if, in fact, *this* Day was going to be the end of time and creation?

## ISAIAH 64-66 AND PETER'S
## ANTICIPATED DAY OF THE LORD

In fact, we know for sure that when Israel anticipated the future Day of the Lord, *the time of the coming of the new heavens and earth*, they were expecting Him to act, to *come, as He had come before*. Notice Isaiah 64:1f:

"Oh that thou would rend the heavens, that thou would come down, that the mountains might flow down at thy presence, As when the melting fire burns, the fire causes the waters to boil, to make thy name known to thine adversaries, that the nations may tremble at thy presence! When thou did terrible things which we looked not for, You came down, the mountains flowed down at Your presence."

In this passage, leading to the promise of the new creation (65:17f; 66:15f), Israel longed for her salvation. She prayed for Jehovah to come! She prayed for El Shaddai to reveal Himself by rending the heavens and melting the mountains. Remember the previous passages in which Jehovah came down and the mountains melted?

Now notice, Israel was praying for Jehovah to come *as He had come in the past*. "*When you came down*, the mountains flowed at your presence!" Here is a clear-cut demonstration that the Day of the Lord language was metaphoric and never intended to be taken literally. Jehovah had come in the past. Israel wanted God to come again, as He had come in the past.

97

Therefore, since Jehovah had never literally, bodily, visibly come in the past, Israel was not asking God to come literally, visibly, bodily.

This is significant for our study of 2 Peter 3. Remember that Isaiah 64-66 is the promise of the new creation. Most commentators are agreed that Isaiah is the source for Peter's anticipation of the new creation: "According to His promise, we look for a new heavens and earth" (2 Peter 3:13).

Peter's Day of the Lord is the Day foretold by Isaiah. Yet, the Day of the Lord of Isaiah 64-66 was to be a Day of the Lord like those that had occurred before, i.e. a non-visible, non-literal, historical Day of the Lord, i.e. Jehovah did not literally, visibly descend from heaven on a cloud. Therefore, the Day of the Lord being anticipated by Peter was a non-visible, non-literal, historical Day of the Lord. This argument is *unassailable* unless one can overcome a few insurmountable issues:

**First**, since the Day being anticipated by Isaiah 64 was a Day like previous Days, one would have to prove that there had been a visible, bodily coming before. Very clearly this cannot be done. Jehovah had never come bodily, visibly out of heaven to destroy the entire created order.

**Second**, being unable to prove the first point, one would have to prove that whereas the Day being prayed for in Isaiah 64 was not a visible, literal, bodily coming, Peter was nonetheless anticipating a literal, visible bodily coming. If that is so, where is the evidence that Peter completely changes the definition of the Day of the Lord? Instead of changing hermeneutics, Peter simply affirms that His anticipated Day was what Isaiah foretold.

Since neither one of these obstacles can be overcome, we reiterate our argument:

**The Day of the Lord anticipated by Peter in 2 Peter 3 is the Day of the Lord foretold by Isaiah 64-66.**

**But the Day of the Lord in Isaiah 64-66 was a Day of the Lord of the same nature and kind that had occurred prior to Isaiah 64-66.**

**Therefore, the Day of the Lord being anticipated in 2 Peter 3 was a Day of the Lord of the same nature and kind that had occurred prior to Isaiah 64-66.**

We follow that with this:

**The Day of the Lord being anticipated in 2 Peter 3 was a Day of the Lord of the same nature and kind that had occurred prior to Isaiah 64-66.**

**But the Day of the Lord of the same nature and kind that had occurred prior to Isaiah 64-66 was a non-literal, non-visible, non-bodily coming of the Lord.**

**Therefore, the Day of the Lord being anticipated in 2 Peter 3 was a non-literal, non-visible, non-bodily coming of the Lord.**

Unless one can sever the link between the Day of the Lord in Isaiah and 2 Peter 3, this argument stands. It demonstrates that the language of the Day of the Lord was never to be interpreted literally of the end of the time-space world, as most students have done.

Minear comments on the N. T. use of the Day of the Lord language:

"As one recalls Old Testament passages like these, one is forced to conclude that every constituent essential feature in the New Testament prophecies was an echo of these. No Christian prophet tried to explain the meaning of these references to solar disasters, a fact that suggests that the audience was expected to understand the language. Modern readers, therefore, must compare this idiom not with modern views of the cosmos, but with an ancient outlook within which an intelligible message was conveyed without undue difficulty."[101]

Following the thought of Minear, France says, "The unwary reader is in danger of assuming a note of finality in the future hope of the Old Testament that is in fact foreign to it. The "eschatology" of the Old Testament prophets was not concerned with the end of the world, but with the decisive act of God which will bring to an end the existing order of things in the world, and inaugurate a new era of blessing, of a totally different order."[102] Brown, commenting on the language of Christ's coming in Matthew 24:29f, concurs that this language is from the O.T., and that there is no justification for taking it literally. It is metaphoric language to describe Jehovah's powerful intervention into history, not to end history.[103]

N. T. Wright agrees that Jesus' use of the *Day of the Lord* language does not predict the end of creation. Instead, after an extensive review of the language he concludes, "It is crass literalism, in view of the many prophetic passages in which this language denotes socio-political and military catastrophe, to insist that this time (in the teaching of Jesus, DKP), the words must refer to the physical collapse of the space-time world."[104]

Finally, Ladd, while maintaining a futuristic, literal cosmic catastrophe, nonetheless posed some pertinent questions in light of the persistent use of the metaphoric *Day of the Lord* language,

"Does this not give us the reason to interpret all such language about the eschatological shaking of the world, collapse of the heavens, etc. as the poetical language used to depict the indescribable glory of the final theophany? The importance of this question can be seen by the fact that this terminology provides the conceptual material for the 'apocalyptic' of the New Testament eschatology with its view of a cosmic catastrophe bringing this age to a close and introducing the age to come. Is such language anything more than traditional language of Old Testament poetry used to describe the majesty of God?"[105]

Wright is correct, it would amount to "crass literalism" to take the language of the *Day of the Lord*, so well attested in the Old Testament, literally, when found on the lips of Jesus. And, Ladd's question is pertinent. If the constant use of the Day of the Lord language in the O. T. was metaphoric, and it clearly was since the physical creation had never been destroyed, then when the New Testament writers use that identical language without any indication of a change in usage, we should not impose a literalistic interpretation on that language.

The Old Testament concept of the Day of the Lord is solidly attested. We see there the pattern of definition for the term "Day of the Lord." We should therefore, think of the Day of the Lord, not as a time ending event, but as a time when God acted in history, by "natural" means, to judge His enemies. If the New Covenant uses the term in a new way should we not find clear delineation from the Old Covenant usage?

Where in the New Testament do the writers contrast the O. T. concept with what they are predicting? Instead of any such contrast, the New Covenant authors take it for granted their readers know what they are referring to when they use the term.

It cannot be maintained that 2 Peter 3 is such a contrast. Instead, the writers tell their readers that they were looking for what the O. T. prophets foretold. As we have seen from Isaiah 64, that cannot be construed to be a visible, time ending event.

Instead of contrasting the nature of his anticipated Day, Peter says that just like it was in Noah's day when the world was destroyed, so it would be when the Day of the Lord came by fire. The only contrast is between fire and water. There is no contrast in concepts of the Day of the Lord. Both events were the Day of the Lord. Neither destroyed the physical creation or ended time. Both events destroyed *worlds*.

A word here about similarity of language. McGuiggan, in his debate with King castigated King for going to the concordance and seeing the term Day of the Lord used in several texts, all referring to "natural" judgments of God on His enemies, and concluding that the term should be used in this way in all passages. Just because God used similar language to figuratively describe the destruction of Babylon, Israel, Edom, Tyre, and other nations and cities does not mean we can take this language and apply it to all uses of the term Day of the Lord, McGuiggan urges. In other words it is *possible* it can be used to describe a literal time ending event. And he is correct. However, McGuiggan has several problems.

**First**, he fails to see that the N. T. writers affirm that their eschatology is the eschatology of the O. T. prophets. Thus, McGuiggan would have to prove that the O. T. prophets predicted the end of time, since the N. T. eschatology is drawn from the O. T.. He cannot prove that.

**Second**, McGuiggan would have to show that God moved from the historical "spiritual" comings in the Old Testament to a "physical" coming of Christ at the end of history. This violates the fact that Paul said the natural is first, and then the spiritual (1 Corinthians 15:46). God has never moved from the spiritual to the physical.

**Third**, related to point #1, is the fact that the N. T. writers tell us they were anticipating the Day of the Lord foretold by the Old Covenant prophets. So, unless an O. T. prophet delineated between an in history Day of the Lord, and the metaphoric language used to describe it, and a Day of the Lord to put an end to time, then there would be no way to determine the difference.

**Fourth**, McGuiggan would have to find a prediction of the Day of the Lord that said it was not near in the first century. He cannot do that.

**Fifth**, and related to points #1 and 3, is *the consistency of language*.[106] The Old Covenant language defines the nature of the Day of the Lord. Now, since the Day of the Lord is never a literal, visible end of time event in the O. T. and since the N. T. writers never seek to explain what they mean by their use of the language, then this is strong evidence that, as Minear suggests, they expected their audiences to know what the language meant from its former use in the O. T..

Jesus and all of the New Testament writers refer to the Day of the Lord in the typical O. T. manner, without any indication that the meaning, nature, or definition of that Day had changed. The only changes in regard to the Day were that the *consummative* Day was now near (Matthew 24:29f; I Corinthians 1:4-8; James 5:7f; I Peter 4:5,7,17; Revelation 1,6,14,22) and that it was *Christ* that was coming in fulfillment of those prophecies.[107] This means it was not a time ending cataclysm they had in mind. This is demonstrated in 2 Thessalonians 2:1-2.

Paul had to write those brethren to warn them not to be deceived into believing the Day of the Lord *had already come*. (The King James translation of "at hand" is incorrect[108]) Ask yourself this question: If the Thessalonians believed the Day of the Lord was a time ending, universe destroying event, how could anyone convince them it had *already happened?* The idea is ludicrous. The only conceivable way for them to be convinced the Day had already come was for them to believe in the Old Covenant concept of the Day of the Lord. But if that was not what Paul was predicting, he should have corrected them. However, Paul did not correct their concept of the nature of the Day of God. He only told them what had to happen before it came. Since Paul did not correct the Thessalonian's concept of the Day, we must conclude their views were correct. If their views were correct it is patent the modern view is incorrect.

What we have seen then is that when we study the Old Covenant we find an established usage of the term Day of the Lord. The term never included universal destruction of creation. It always meant God acting in history to judge His enemies by means of various instruments, whether locust plague, army, hailstorm, etc.. We have shown that since the New Covenant writers were Jews thoroughly trained and conversant in such tenets they would naturally utilize these ideas to express the actions of God in their day. Further, we have suggested that unless the New Covenant writers clearly delineate for us that they are departing from the historical usage of the term, we would have no chance of discerning the change. Since it is clear that Jesus and the apostles did incorporate the Old Covenant view of the Day of the Lord in their teaching and writing, this is strong evidence that Peter did not have an earth burning, time ending coming of the Lord in mind in 2 Peter 3.

## CHAPTER 9
## AS A THIEF IN THE NIGHT

**"For the Day of the Lord Will Come as a Thief in the Night"**

One of the most common objections to the view that Peter speaks of the destruction of Jerusalem goes something like this: Peter says the Day of the Lord would come as a thief in the night.[109] This means without warning, without signs. However, Jesus gave signs whereby the disciples could know the general time of the destruction of Jerusalem. Since there are no signs of a thief's coming, then the thief coming must be the final coming, distinct from the coming against Jerusalem. This is an erroneous understanding of what Jesus and Peter had in mind.

It is true Jesus gave signs to discern the general time of the destruction (Matthew 24:15-35). He also gave a specific sign of the nearness of the end, the completion of the Great Commission (Matthew 24:14). Without question that sign was fulfilled in the first century (Romans 10:18; Colossians 1:5, 23).[110] What is *not true* is the claim that Jesus said there would be no signs of a different coming, in Matthew 24:36f. There is no such contrast in the text.

As noted above, the argument is often made that in Matthew 24 when Jesus used the personal pronouns "you,"[111] he was referring to events to transpire in the lifetime of his disciples; when he spoke of "they," or "them," he referred to his distant future. Notice then in Matthew 24:42-44 what he says,

"Watch therefore for you do not know what hour your Lord is coming. But know this, that if the master of the house had known what hour the thief would come, he would have watched and not allowed his house to be broken into. Therefore you also be ready for the Son of Man is coming at an hour when you do not expect him."

Jesus used the pronoun "you," in speaking to his disciples, three times. Of course, futurists generally deny that Jesus was actually speaking about those disciples. Ice claims that Peter, James and John, actually represent believing Israel during the yet future Tribulation period.[112] One can only wonder how the disciples knew this. Jesus did not tell them that the events he foretold were far off, or that they would not personally see those events. He did not tell them that they represented a far removed generation of believers. He was speaking to living, breathing human beings and told them "you will see." How much clearer could language be?

Will the advocates of the "you-them" argument be consistent and allow this to mean that the predicted event, the coming of the Son of Man, would occur in the lifetime of the disciples? (We should point out that "you" is actually present more than three times. "Watch therefore," could properly be translated, "You watch therefore.")

Jesus speaking of an event, his return, to occur in the lifetime of his disciples, but he tells them it will come *as a thief.* Actually, to use the imagery of the thief to refer to something in the vague, misty future, is to completely miss the point of Jesus' warning.

We do not worry about a thief coming in the distant future. We worry about a thief coming *in our lifetime.* We do not take precautions against thieves who may come in two thousand years.

There is strong evidence that the Lord's "thief coming" in Matthew 24 was a reference to the destruction of Jerusalem.

Based upon the *assumption* that Jesus in Matthew 24:36 changed the subject from the Jewish catastrophe to his final return at the end of time, it is argued that Jesus could come *at any time.* No one knows the day or hour, therefore, he could come at any moment. But *stop and think.*

If there is another coming beyond that of A.D. 70, then in a positive way Jesus certainly did tell his followers that his final coming would not occur in their lifetime; it could not be at any moment. Follow me here:

☞Jesus predicted his coming in the fall of Jerusalem.

☞Jesus predicted another "final coming" at the end of history, we are told.

☞Jesus said that his coming in the fall of Jerusalem would positively be in that first century generation.

☞If Jesus' coming in the fall of Jerusalem was unconditionally to be in that generation, this proves *beyond doubt* that his "final" coming could not occur before the fall of Jerusalem.

☞If Jesus' "final coming" was to positively be at some indeterminate future time *after the fall of Jerusalem,* then any exhortations and warnings to the first generation Christians to *prepare themselves* for the "final" coming would be illogical. They would know, without doubt, that the fall of Jerusalem had to occur first.

☞Based on the foregoing, since Jesus urged his living disciples to be ready and to watch for his coming in Matthew 24:42-44, then he could not have been warning them to watch for an event that they knew, without doubt, *would not be in their lifetime!* They would not have to "Watch." for his coming, since they knew (supposedly), that he was not coming until after the judgment of Israel. Since Jesus patently was telling them to "Watch,"

104

to be *ready*, and not allow that Day to overcome *them*, this proves that he was not discussing an event far beyond the fall of Jerusalem. We are told that beginning in Acts 3 and throughout the epistles, the disciples began preparing the church for Christ's final coming, telling them that the world might end at any moment. This is patently false if the "two-coming" view of Matthew 24 is maintained. *How do you convince anyone that the world might end at any moment, if you tell them at the same that the world cannot end until Jesus first comes in judgment of Old Covenant Jerusalem?* In light of the predetermined A. D. 70 parousia, all N. T. warnings to get ready for a supposed "end of time" coming of the Lord would be easily discounted and rejected.

When one studies I Thessalonians 5 and the allusion to the coming of the Lord as a thief in the night, he is faced with the same kind of difficulties. Instead of saying the predicted event was in the far off, uncertain future, the writer warns them in such a way that one can only conclude that the event was to be in their lifetime.

Observe that what Paul says in 1 Thessalonians 5 is exactly what Jesus said in Matthew 24. Jesus said that prior to the Judean calamity people would be going about their business as usual. They would be marrying and giving in marriage. No threat of impending disaster would find credence in them. They would feel secure. Just so, Paul said that prior to the coming of the Lord, the people would be saying, "Peace and safety!"

Jesus said that holocaust would come like a thief. Paul said the same. Jesus said he was coming in the disciples' lifetime (Matthew 24:29-34). The Thessalonians would live to see it (I Thessalonians 4:15,17).

Further, closer examination of Paul's illustration in I Thessalonians 5:1-3 reveals that one cannot press the imagery of the thief too far. The apostle said the parousia would be like a thief. But, he also said it would be like *labor pains upon a pregnant woman*. Now if the *epiphany* was to be like a woman in travail how can it be argued there would be no signs of its coming like a thief? Does not a pregnant woman know she will give birth? Now, she does not know the day or the hour, but she most assuredly knows it will be in her lifetime! She is not concerned about the distant future in regard to giving birth. It will definitely happen in her lifetime. And so, Paul told the Thessalonians they must be prepared: "But you, brethren, are not in darkness, so that this day should overtake you as a thief."

If the imagery of the thief in the night is pressed to mean there is absolutely no way of knowing the event was to be in their lifetime, the imagery comes into conflict with the imagery of the woman with child.

This was not Paul's intent. He simply meant to speak of the suddenness (v.3), and the uncertainty of the exact time (vs 1-2). The Thessalonians knew enough about the time and seasons of the parousia (v. 1-2), so that even though they knew it would come suddenly like a thief, they would be able to escape. They would not be overtaken.

Paul's emphatic usage of *you* certainly indicates that the event was coming in their lifetime. If not, why such urgent warnings? As we have shown, if Jesus spoke of two comings in Matthew 24, he all but assured his followers that they would see him coming to destroy Jerusalem. This of necessity meant that his so-called final coming could not be before then. Urgent warnings for the Thessalonian Christians to be prepared for the "final" parousia were therefore, vain since they had no fear of being alive anyway.

It is only if the imagery of the thief is allowed its natural force, that is, a danger for his contemporary generation, that Paul's warning in I Thessalonians makes sense.

The exact pattern of thought found in Matthew 24 and I Thessalonians 5 is in 2 Peter 3. In Matthew, Jesus said the unbelievers would be eating, drinking, and going about their normal business. Paul said the scoffers, (can we doubt they were scoffers?), would have no concern for the impending destruction and thought, "Peace and safety!"; in Peter the scoffers said, "All things continue as they were since the creation." In all three passages the thought is the same. The Lord was coming like a thief, but, he was coming in the lifetime of the first century brethren See Luke 21:34-36 also.

In Revelation 3:1f we find reference to Jesus coming like a thief. And in this text there is unequivocal proof of a contemporary application. The *KURIOS* warned the church at Sardis: "Remember therefore, how you have received and heard; hold fast and repent. Therefore if you will not watch, I will come upon you as a thief, and you will not know what hour I will come upon you."

Jesus was speaking specifically to the first century church at Sardis. He warned that he would come as a thief against *them*. They would not know the day or hour he was coming, but he would nonetheless come on *them*. He did not say they would die and stand before him in judgment. See the similar positive declaration of Jesus in Revelation 2:25, "But hold fast what you have until I come." Thus, although he was coming in the lifetime of those saints, he was coming like a thief.

If the Lord could come as a thief against the Sardisians, and that coming would definitely be in the first century, then you cannot rule out that possibility in 2 Peter 3.

There is another "thief coming" in scripture that has a direct bearing on the identity of the parousia of 2 Peter 3. In Revelation 16:14-16 we find the gathering for the Great Day of God, *Armageddon*. In describing this coming Jesus said: "Behold, I am coming as a thief, blessed is the one that watches, and keeps his garments, lest he should walk naked and they see his shame." (Revelation 16:15).

In my book *Blast From the Past: The Truth About Armageddon*, I prove that the "Great Day of the Lord" is the time of the vindication of the martyrs of God.[113] We present here just a few thoughts from that work.

In Matthew 23:29f, Jesus stood in the temple and chastised Israel for her long history of killing the saints.

"Woe to you, scribes and Pharisees, hypocrites! Because you build the tombs of the prophets and adorn the monuments of the righteous, and say, 'If we had lived in the days of our fathers, we would not have been partakers with them in the blood of the prophets.' Therefore you are witnesses against yourselves that you are sons of those who murdered the prophets. Fill up, then, the measure of your fathers' guilt. Serpents, brood of vipers! How can you escape the condemnation of hell? Therefore, indeed, I send you prophets, wise men, and scribes: some of them you will kill and crucify, and some of them you will scourge in your synagogues and persecute from city to city, that on you may come all the righteous blood shed on the earth, from the blood of righteous Abel to the blood of Zechariah, son of Berechiah, whom you murdered between the temple and the altar. Assuredly, I say to you, all these things will come upon this generation."

Jesus' referent to "this generation" is not to some future generation, as is admitted by virtually all Bible commentators. Israel was judged for all her blood guilt, in the destruction of Jerusalem in A.D. 70. (*It is important to know that Israel is not under any kind of curse today!*)

There is no question, the Bible says Israel was to be judged, in her last days, for shedding innocent blood. How does this relate to Armageddon?

The battle of Armageddon is described by John as "the battle of the Great Day of God" (16.14). Technically, the gathering at Armageddon is under the *Sixth Vial, immediately prior to the Great Day*, while the Day of the Lord against Babylon is under the *Seventh Vial*. Thus, Armageddon is the *gathering for the Great Day of the Lord*, but the judgment on Babylon *is the Great Day*. There is no lapse of time between these two events however, so we are lumping them together for argument sake.

At this juncture it is important to note that in Revelation, the "Great Day of the Lord" is not only God's judgment of "Babylon," *it is also the time when the martyrs were vindicated (Revelation 6:9-17)*. So, *Armageddon is the gathering for the Great Day of the Lord* when He would avenge the blood of His martyred saints! Here is our argument.

The gathering at Armageddon (Revelation 16.14f),would occur immediately before (Sixth Vial), the Great Day of the Lord (Seventh Vial).

But, the Great Day of the Lord is the time when the martyrs of God would be vindicated (Revelation 6.9-17; 16.6-7).

Therefore, the gathering at Armageddon would be immediately before the time when the martyrs of God would be vindicated.

To follow up on this we would argue:

The gathering at Armageddon (Sixth Vial), would be immediately before the time when the martyrs of God would be vindicated. (Seventh Vial).

But the time when the martyrs of God would be vindicated would be in the judgment of Jerusalem in A.D. 70 (Matthew 23.34-36).

Therefore, the gathering at Armageddon would be immediately before (Sixth Vial) the judgment of Jerusalem in A.D. 70 (Seventh Vial).

There is no evidence to suggest that John (Revelation 6, 16), predicted a different time, a different occasion, and different martyrs from that foretold by Jesus in Matthew 23.[114] So, how does this relate to the coming as a thief?

The coming of the Day of the Lord is the time of the vindication of the martyrs as just seen. And, the time of the vindication of the martyrs is the judgment of Old Covenant Israel. *However, the Day of the Lord is the coming of Christ as a thief!* Therefore, Christ's coming as a thief was his coming against Old Covenant Israel for shedding the blood of God's saints.

It is widely considered that "the war" of Revelation 16 is the final conflict at the end of human history. In other words, *it is the Day of the Lord of 2 Peter 3*. Kistemaker insists that "the war" of Revelation 16 is the consummative war at the end of the current Christian age, "when cosmic time will come to an end" (*WSTTB*, 244+). However, if the Day of the Lord of Revelation 16 is the time of the vindication of the martyrs, and if the time of the vindication of the martyrs was in A.D. 70, then, at the risk of being redundant, this means that the thief coming of Revelation 16 was in A.D. 70. However, if the thief coming of Revelation 16 was the A.D. 70

*parousia* of Christ, and if Revelation 16 is the same coming of 2 Peter 3, then clearly, the thief coming of Christ in 2 Peter 3 was in A.D. 70.

We are constantly told that the meaning of the thief imagery is of suddenness, or perhaps to say that the "day and hour" of the coming is not known. And the later concept is found in Revelation 3, and Christ's warnings to the Sardisians. However, there is perhaps another thought present that is never mentioned, and that is that *the Lord's coming as a thief would be unseen*. More on that in a moment. For now, there are some other issues about Christ's coming as a thief that we need to investigate.

In regard to the coming as a thief, it cannot be argued, especially in Revelation 16, that there are no signs presaging that event. A central tenet in millennialism is the belief that there are two future comings of the Lord. There is the Rapture, and then, approximately 7 years later, the Second Coming of Christ. One reason for believing that the "thief coming" of Christ is the Rapture is because millennialists claim that the Rapture is without signs, and a thief coming is without signs. The thief coming therefore, must be the Rapture.[115] This will not work in Revelation 16.

Christ's *parousia* at Armageddon is supposed to be bodily, visible and physical, totally opposite the Rapture coming seven years earlier. However, in describing his Armageddon coming, Christ said, "Behold I come as a thief" (Revelation 16:15). Further, the Armageddon coming of Christ is everything but "sign-less" according to the millennial view of things.

Remember that according to the millennialist Armageddon is at the climax of the Seventieth Week of Daniel 9. It comes after the treaty with Israel and the Man of Sin has been signed and then broken. It comes after the destruction of the Tribulation Temple, and after the appearance of the Two Witnesses. It comes after the institution of the "Mark of the Beast." It comes after the fulfillment of the Great Commission by the 144,000 "Super Evangelists." It comes after the Great Tribulation in which 3/5ths of the earth's population, and 2/3rds of all Jews are killed. Do you get the point? The point is that the Second Coming of Christ in Revelation 16, *Armageddon*, is, in the millennial paradigm, preceded by a multitude of unmistakable signs. And not only is it preceded by signs, but its very "day and hour" could be calculated. Consider the following.

The millennial paradigm simply will not fit the Biblical datum. Here is what we mean. The millennialists hold to the following ideas:
**1.)** Matthew 24 is about the events of the Tribulation period, following the Rapture. This means that the coming of Christ in Matthew 24:29f is the Second Coming of Christ seven years after the Rapture.[116]

109

**2.)** They believe that the Rapture is a "sign-less event."

**3.)** They believe that the coming of Christ in Matthew 24, the final coming, is preceded by all of the signs enumerated just above.

**4.)** They believe that the coming of Christ in Matthew 24 and the coming of Christ in Revelation 16:14f are the same coming, at the end of the Tribulation period.

**5.)** They believe that the Thief Coming, is a sign-less event, thus, *it has to be the Rapture.* This is where it gets difficult for the millennial view.

The coming of the Lord in Matthew 24 is patently the thief coming of Christ (Matthew 24:42f). The coming of the Lord in Revelation 16 is undeniably the thief coming, and occurs at the end of the Tribulation period. Yet, as just seen, *every sign of the Tribulation period precedes the thief coming of Revelation 16.* Thus, while the coming of Revelation 16 is the thief coming, it is not the Rapture, and it is a "sign-full" event. This is a serious contradiction of the millennial view.

The Rapture of the church is supposed to be Christ's thief coming, because there are no signs of the Rapture, i.e. the thief coming. Note that LaHaye says: "While no one knows the day or the hour of Jesus' rapture of the church, *we do know when the glorious appearing will occur* (*Charting,* 111). Furthermore, Ice says Matthew 24 is the second coming (*Fast,* 116)

This position is a blatant contradiction of what Jesus said. Note their argument: The coming of the Lord of Matthew 24 is Christ's second or final coming at the end of the Tribulation period (LaHaye/Ice). "No one can know the day and the hour of Christ's rapture of the church, but, we do know when the glorious appearing will occur," "As soon as anti-christ and Israel sign a peace treaty, which he breaks in the middle of the tribulation, there will be seven years until the coming of Christ."

Do you see the problem? In Matthew 24, according the millennialists, *Jesus is not discussing the Rapture.* He is discussing his "final coming" at the end of the Tribulation period. It is the coming of Matthew 24 that Jesus was speaking about when he said, "no man knows the day or the hour." Yet, *in direct contradiction to Jesus' words*, LaHaye and Ice claim: "we do know when the glorious appearing will occur." According to the millennial paradigm, the faithful will be able to calculate the very day and hour, yea, even to the precise *minute* the Lord's Second Coming, because, as LaHaye and Ice affirm: "As soon as Antichrist (sic) and Israel sign a peace treaty, which he breaks in the middle of the tribulation, there will be seven years until the coming of Christ."(*Charting,* 37) So,

"We can know the time of the glorious appearing of Christ," the coming of Christ at the end of the Tribulation period, i.e. the coming of Christ in Matthew 24:29f and Revelation 16:14f (LaHaye/Ice).

But, the coming of Christ in Matthew 24:29f and Revelation 16:14f is the thief coming of Christ (Matthew 24:42f; Revelation 16:15).

*Therefore, we can know the day and the hour of the thief coming of Christ.*

So, on the one hand, the millennialists claim that Christ's coming as a thief means there are no signs of that event whatsoever, and then they tell us that we can actually determine the exact day and hour of its occurrence, because it comes at the climax of a series of signs.

LaHaye/Ice have turned Jesus' words upside down. They have taken his statement in Matthew 24:36, and applied it to an event that, according to them, he was not even discussing. Then, they have taken what he said, and completely contradicted it by claiming that we can know the very thing he said could not be known, the day and hour of his second coming.

---

LaHaye and Ice apply Jesus' words to something he was not discussing, and then, make him say the *exact opposite* of what he actually said! This is a perversion of the scriptures!

---

The amillennial school has many of the same problems. Many believe that the thief coming of Revelation 16 is the same coming as 2 Peter 3. There are not supposed to be any signs of Christ's thief coming. Yet, in Revelation 16 the coming of Christ is preceded by a *host* of signs. This means that the coming of 2 Peter 3 must be preceded by those signs. And this contradicts one of the fundamental tenets of the amillennial view: There were signs of Christ's A.D. 70 *parousia*, but there are no signs of his final coming. Yet, again, if Revelation 16 is the "final coming" of Christ, then this argument falls to the ground since there are many signs preceding the thief coming of Revelation 16.

To argue that the coming of 2 Peter 3 must be a yet future event, for which there are no signs, is misguided. If the *parousia* of 2 Peter 3 is the same parousia as in the rest of the N. T., then there are clearly signs of its appearance, and, significantly, as we have seen, other passages undeniably posit the thief coming of Christ at the time of the judgment of Israel in A.D.

111

70. Indeed, if we accept the harmony and unity of the rest of the N. T. in regard to the thief coming, we must see Peter's prediction as a reference to Christ's coming against the Old Covenant world of Israel. It has nothing to do with the "end of time." Now to return to a point just made.

Could it be that the referent to the coming as a thief meant that Christ's coming was to be *unseen*, and therefore, if they did not watch for the signs leading up to the judgment, that the *parousia* would catch them off guard? This certainly seems to be the case in 1 Thessalonians 5. Paul said that the Day of the Lord would come as a thief on those who were saying "peace and safety" and were not watching. However, he said, "but you brethren are not in darkness that that Day should overtake you." You see, the coming itself would not be a visible event. However, there would be very real events signifying its reality, and there would be signs leading up to the Day, that if watchful, they could escape (cf. Hebrews 10:25). Now, if they could watch, and through watchfulness *escape* the Day, does that not demand that there were signs of the Day, and if there were signs of the Day, then the normal arguments concerning no signs of the Day fall to the ground. None of these things fits an end of time, earth burning event. (How could anyone escape that?) The warnings do fit nicely Jesus' warnings concerning his coming in judgment at the end of the Old Covenant age of Israel.

# CHAPTER 10

# HASTENING THE DAY OF GOD

## "Looking for and Hastening unto the Coming of the Day of God" (2 Peter 3:12)

One of the most ignored verses in 2 Peter 3 is verse 12. Why is it ignored? Because it has implications for the chronological understanding of those brethren in regard to the parousia. It is difficult to maintain the modern view of the *epiphany* and do justice to this verse. Therefore the common practice is to just ignore it and concentrate on other things. But this verse will not go away.

When we read the passage it tells us the brethren were "eagerly looking" forward to the day of the Lord, or as it is called here, the Day of God. It is the parousia (presence) of the day of God. Not only were they eagerly anticipating the day, they were hastening its coming. A couple of things strike us about this.

**First**, undeniably the first century church lived in very earnest expectation of the imminent return of Jesus. This is admitted by virtually everyone, even the adversaries of Covenant Eschatology. John MacArthur in his attempt to refute preterism, freely admits: "James, Peter, John and Paul, and the writer of Hebrews all believed Christ's return was very near-'at the door' (James 5:9); 'at hand' (Philippians 4:5; 1 Peter 4:7); 'approaching' (Hebrews 10:25); 'coming quickly' (Revelation 3:11; 22:7)."[117] Ice concurs, "A survey of the New Testament enables one to realize that there is an expectancy regarding the return of Christ and the consummation of His plan not found in the Old Testament."[118]

In spite of these admissions, commentators then set about to mitigate that imminence, and claim that all of these statements meant essentially nothing. After all, time means nothing to God, so even if God tells man that something is near, it may not occur for millennia! As we have seen however, this is misguided.

In Matthew 10:22f as the Lord sent out his disciples to preach, he promised that they would be persecuted and chased from city to city. Yet, he promised: "You will not have gone over the cities of Israel until the Son of Man be come." This was a promise of Christ's parousia in vindication and relief from persecution for his disciples. The parousia would occur in their lifetime, as they preached the gospel and were chased from city to city.

In Matthew16:27-28 Jesus promised that some of those standing there would not die until they saw him coming to judge every man. In Matthew 24:29-34 he plainly said he would return in that generation. Paul in I Corinthians 1:4-8 said the Corinthians had miraculous gifts. The gifts had confirmed them, and the gifts would continue to confirm them until the Day of the Lord. And see the impassioned plea of I Corinthians 16:22, "O Lord, Come!" See also 1 Corinthians 7:28-31; 13:8-13; 10:11; 15:51.

Paul, in Philippians 3:20-4:5, spoke of the coming of Jesus to change "our vile body," and said, "The Lord is at hand." James said, "Be patient, until the coming of the Lord," and, "The coming of the Lord is at hand," plus, "The judge standeth at the door." Incidentally, we have heard preachers insist that the technical word for the final coming of Jesus is *parousia*, and insist this term is not used of the judgment of Jerusalem.[119] But in James 5:8 it says, "the parousia of the Lord has drawn near!"

The Hebrew writer, in terms expressing great expectancy said, "In a very little while, he that will come, will come, and will not tarry" (10:37). And of course Peter said Jesus was, "ready to judge the living and the dead," and, "the end of all things is at hand" (I Peter 4:5,7). John reminded his readers of the prophecies of the events of the last times, said those events were around them even as he wrote, and concluded, "You know it is the last hour" (I John 2:18). Jesus in the Apocalypse said, "Behold, I come quickly" (Revelation 22:6f).

With these passages before the reader, and there are others, how can one accept statements such as the following, "Nowhere does the New Testament teach the imminency of the coming of the Lord. Rather, the New Testament teaches that we are to live *as if* (emphasis his, DKP) the Lord will come in our day (James 5:7-8)."[120] Did James say Jesus *could be at the door*? Did James say the coming of the Lord *might be at hand*? Did he say live your lives patiently *as if* the Lord *could come*, or did he say be patient *until the coming of the Lord*?

Before closing this section we would consider an objection. It is maintained that if Paul or the apostles taught that the parousia was imminent they would be in contradiction with Jesus. Jesus said in Mark 13:32 that neither he nor the angels knew the time of his return, we are reminded. So, it is argued that if Paul taught that Jesus was to return in his generation, "Paul's debate would have been with Jesus Himself, if he had taught that Christ would come in his generation." (Workman, 368).

Consider the problems inherent in such statements. First, it fails to recognize that in Mark 13 the so-called "final coming" of Jesus is not even in the passage. Read verses 1-4. The disciples remark on the exceptional beauty of the temple complex. Jesus predicts the final overthrow of the temple (v. 2). The incredulous disciples respond by asking, "Tell us when will these things be? And what will be the sign when all these things will be fulfilled?" Upon what hermeneutical principle can one interject a discussion of the end of time into their queries, or Jesus' answers? The subject is exclusively the fall of the theocracy.

**Secondly**, when it is argued that Paul and the other disciples would contradict Jesus if they taught that his return was to be in that generation, it overlooks Jesus' express statements in Matthew 16:27-28. He said some of that generation would live to see his return. And when one turns to Matthew 26:64 we see Jesus promising the Sanhedrin, "hereafter you shall see the Son of Man sitting at the right hand of the Power, and coming on the clouds of heaven." Now, if someone were to tell you that you would see them coming, would you not expect them in your lifetime? And remember that Paul said the same thing in I Corinthians 15:51-52, "We shall not all sleep." This is an emphatic declaration that the Corinthians would not all die before the coming of Jesus at the resurrection.

This may be hard to comprehend if you hold to the traditional futurist view, as I once did, but it agrees with Jesus' declaration in Matthew 5:17-18, that the Old Covenant had to be fulfilled before it could pass away, and Paul's statement in Acts 24:14-15 that the Old Covenant Law and Prophets foretold the resurrection.

The Old Covenant could not pass away until it all was fulfilled. The resurrection was a part of the Old Covenant, as Paul expressly says. Therefore, unless the resurrection has happened, the Old Law has not yet been taken away.[121] (This certainly means we have to rethink the idea of physical graves being opened, does it not? Yet even this is more in line with the clearly spiritual resurrection Paul had in mind in I Corinthians 15:35-56.) This indisputably places the time frame for the parousia and their expectation of it, in the first century.

**Third**, and perhaps most importantly, just how would it contradict Jesus if Paul taught that Jesus was to return in that generation? Granting, for argument sake, the use of Mark 13:32 as applicable to the "final coming" there would still be no contradiction whatsoever. Jesus said he was coming in that generation (Mark 13:26,30). In Mark 13:32 he said no man knew the *day or the hour*. Now, is it not possible for a person to know the general time without knowing the specific day and hour?

Let me illustrate this. A young man overhears his parents planning a trip to his cousin's house. All of the conversation he hears says something about "next month." The young man calls his cousin and says, "Hey, guess what? We are coming to visit you!" His cousin asks, "When are you coming?" The boy responds, "I do not know what day, but it will be sometime next month!" Now the father knows what day it will be, but the boy and his cousin, while they know it will be some time "next month" do not know the exact day.

The illustration shows the fallacy of saying things such as the following by Stafford North:

"Of the second coming and final judgment, Jesus says no one knows when it will be. He had told the disciples, on the contrary, precisely when the destruction of Jerusalem would be: during their lifetime and they could read the sign of the approaching army so closely that they could escape it. But of His coming, no one knows when it will be-- neither man, nor angels, nor Jesus Himself. Only the Father knows (v.36)."[122]

Did Jesus tell his disciples *precisely* when the destruction would come? Precisely means specifically, "with no variation, minutely exact." (Webster's New Twentieth Century Unabridged Dictionary). Patently Jesus did no such thing. He told them they could see the signs and know it was near, but they could not know the day or the hour (Mark 13:28-34).

The contention that if the disciples taught that Jesus' return was near they would be contradicting him, is erroneous. Jesus said his return was to be in their generation. They taught the same (James 5:7-9). Jesus said they could not know the day or hour, and they never presumed to set a specific time. He told them they could know by signs when the time was near, and John, among others, appealing to some of those signs said, "You know it is the last hour!" (I John 2:18; Jude 16-19 also).

To listen to some commentators, since Jesus did not know the time of his coming while he was on earth, then he must still be ignorant of the time even now. In other words, Jesus was ignorant of the time of His Second Coming when he spoke the words recorded by Mark, and He is *still* ignorant of the time of His Second Coming 2000 years after returning to the Father. One adversary of the views in this book has stated that because of Mark 13:32, it is not possible for the disciples to have asserted the actual nearness of the parousia. If Jesus did not know the time of his coming, then surely the inspired writers could not know either.[123] Therefore, when the New Testament writers wrote that Jesus' coming was to be "in a very little while" (Hebrews 10:37) they were mistaken. They could have no knowledge of the time because Jesus had no knowledge of the time. Claims such as these are guilty of a *hermeneutic of anachronism*. They are guilty of applying something that was *true at one time* to a time when it was no longer true. They believe that because Jesus was once ignorant of the time of his coming he will always be ignorant. Further, this view assumes that even after Jesus' ascension the Father would not, or could not, reveal to Jesus what he had not known earlier during His incarnation.

The New Testament writers all wrote *after* Jesus uttered the words found in Mark and after the outpouring of the Spirit. The Spirit was given to guide them into all truth and "reveal things to come" (John 16:13). Here is a question for those espousing the "perpetual ignorance" theory of Mark 13:32: Was it *possible* that after Jesus uttered the words of Mark 13:32 that the Father, in sending the Spirit to the apostles to reveal things to come (John 16:13) could have revealed the time of the parousia? If it was *not possible* for the Father, by the sending of the Spirit, to reveal the time of Jesus' parousia what prevented the Father from making that revelation.

## THE FATHER, JESUS, THE SPIRIT, AND THINGS TO COME

In John, Jesus spoke of the coming of the Spirit from the Father. Jesus said, "I will pray to the Father, and He will give you another Helper... even the Spirit of truth" (John 14:16). The Father would send the Spirit and, "He will teach you all things" (John 14:26; cf. also John 15:26).

Not only would the Father send the Spirit, the Spirit, "will tell you of things to come" (John 16:13). Thus, Jesus said that the Father would send the Spirit to the disciples to reveal future events. The purpose of the Spirit was not to testify of His ignorance or of the continuing ignorance of Jesus. *Where is the epistolary text that affirms the ignorance of the writers about the imminence of the parousia?* Where is the NT writer, writing after the sending of the Spirit, who tells us that no man could know if the parousia was far off or near? Where is the N. T. text that even appeals to Jesus' words about not knowing the time of the parousia? There is none.

It cannot be over-emphasized that the Father would send the Spirit. It was not Jesus in His ignorance. It was the *Father* that would send the Spirit to guide the disciples into "all truth" (John 16:13), and to show them *"things to come"* (John 16:7, 13). What truth did the Father keep from the disciples? Did He keep the time of the coming a secret? Did He lie to the disciples--through the Spirit--when He had the Spirit reveal to them that "the parousia has drawn near" (James 5:8)? *Whatever the Spirit revealed to the disciples about the Lord's coming was revealed by the Father.* If the disciples were wrong, the Spirit was wrong. If the Spirit was wrong, He did not guide the disciples into "all truth." He did not teach them "all things." If the Spirit was wrong, the Father was wrong, for the Father gave the Spirit the things to reveal to the apostles.

---

**Jesus may not have known the time of his parousia when he was still on earth, but the Father sent the Spirit to guide the apostles into all truth and to "shew you things to come." Therefore, if the disciples were wrong to assert the nearness of the end, it was the Father's own fault, for He is the one that revealed those things!**

---

Clearly, the "once ignorant, always ignorant" idea concerning Jesus' knowledge of his coming is wrong. The Bible testifies that the chain of revelation concerning "things to come" was, from the Father to the Spirit. There is no justification for claiming that the Spirit-inspired disciples continued to be ignorant of the time of Jesus' coming after they received the Spirit from the Father.

## A MATTER OF INSPIRATION

Could the disciples of Jesus have been so wrong about the time of the parousia? The issue here is inspiration. Liberal skeptics and unbelievers have long denied the inspiration of scripture for the simple fact that the New Testament writers said the parousia was imminent in the first century, but that it failed. Infallible inspiration is therefore, called a myth.

Today however, *Bible believers* are actually averring that the writers of the New Testament were wrong about the time of the parousia. This claim is based upon their view of Mark 13:32.

The Bible doctrine of inspiration can be found in 2 Peter 1:20-21. The Bible says that the prophets did not write of their own volition but they were "moved by the Holy Spirit." This means that the personal views of the writers were excluded and only what the Spirit revealed was given.

The New Testament writers affirmed that the Old Testament writers did not know the time or manner of Christ's coming. However they affirmed that *it was now revealed to them by the Spirit* (1 Peter 1:10-12). In light of the fact that the Spirit only revealed what the Father gave Him, it is therefore, a matter of the gravest importance to charge the New Testament writers with error in regard to the time of the Lord's coming. They said, through the revelatory Spirit, that what was once far off, was now near. If the N. T. writers were mistaken about the time of the parousia could they not be mistaken about other things as well? This is not to say that the *actions* of the writers were perfect. It is however, to say clearly that the *doctrine* of the New Testament was revealed by the Spirit as the Father directed. If the statements of the authors about the time of the Lord's revelation were erroneous, therefore, the blame has to be placed squarely on the Father. The error cannot be dismissed as misguided enthusiasm, simple hope or personal opinion of the Bible writers. It must be admitted to be a failure of the Father to reveal the truth through the Spirit. If the New Testament writers were wrong about the time of the parousia, then the reliability of Scripture, the deity of Christ and the very existence of the God of the Bible is called into question. This is a serious issue indeed.

## THE REVELATION OF JESUS CHRIST

To maintain that even after his ascension Jesus continued to be ignorant of the time of his coming is a direct contradiction of scripture. Read Revelation 1:1: "The revelation of Jesus Christ, which God gave Him to show His servants--things which must shortly take place. And He sent and signified it by His angel to His servant John."

The chain of revelation is undeniable, the subject is undeniable. The Father was giving the Son the revelation concerning him. The Son was then inspiring John to reveal what the Father had revealed to him. Jesus was not testifying in his incarnate "ignorance." *The Apocalypse is emphatically the Father's revelation to the Son about the parousia.*

What did the Father reveal to the Son for the Son to reveal to John? The Father revealed to the Son, to tell John: "Behold, I am coming quickly, and My reward is with me" (Revelation 22:12). The subject is the coming of the Lord in both Mark 13:32 and Revelation. What Jesus said only the Father knew in Mark, he now says the Father has revealed to him in Revelation. In Revelation we find no ignorance, *we find affirmation of revelation.*

Those who deny the objective imminence of the parousia in Revelation, based upon a misguided application of Mark 13:32, must realize that they are denying the very thing that scripture affirms--*that the Father revealed the time of the parousia to the Son and the Son revealed it to John.*

To say that Jesus remained ignorant of the time of His coming after His ascension and the sending of the Spirit from the Father is a misuse of scripture and a denial of Jesus' teaching in John 14-16. Any attempt to

119

apply Mark 13:32 to the time indicators about Jesus' parousia in the epistles is inappropriate. *Jesus did not remain "ignorant" of the time of his parousia after his ascension.* The Father revealed it to him by the Spirit. He sent the Spirit to reveal the things to come to the disciples. The things revealed included the inspired truth that "the end of all things has drawn near," and, "the time has come for the judgment to begin" (1 Peter 4:7, 17). If the disciples were wrong about the nearness of the end *the Father misled them.* God forbid that any would accept such a view.

## LOOKING FOR THE DAY

The fact that the first century brethren eagerly longed for, and expected the parousia is seen in some of the words used in reference to the parousia in the New Testament. One of the words is translated "wait," and appears in Romans 8:19,23,25 and in four other places. It is the word *apekdechomai* (Strong's #553), and is rendered as "eagerly wait" in many translations. (NKJV, NASV, and other versions). The word appears in I Corinthians 1:7, Galatians 5:5, Philippians 3:20, and Hebrews 9:28. Every passage refers to the parousia. The waiting at issue is the, on the edge of the seat, "I just can't wait," kind of waiting. It is not the, "Ho hum, it will get here one of these days," kind. There was an intensity to their waiting which was so fervent that while the inspired writers encouraged this they also had to inject some patience into it. (Romans 8:25.)

As noted earlier, MacArthur would have us believe that the New Testament writers purposely–through the Spirit–gave a sense of imminence in their writings, in order to keep the church through the ages "on the tiptoe of expectation" (*Coming*, 206). In other words, God purposely intended to convey a real sense of the nearness of the end, all the while knowing that the end was not truly near. He just wanted the church to *think* the end is near. This is nothing less than a Divine Deception if this is true. God cannot lie (Hebrews 6:18). If He said that the end was near, with the intent to keep man on the tiptoe of expectation, all the while knowing that the end was not truly near, that is dishonesty. Let's take a look at some of the words that the Spirit used to convey the nearness of the end in the New Testament.

One word worthy of study is *mello*. The lexicons give the primary definition as "to be about to, on the point of."[124] "To be on the point of, be about to."[125] And Thayer (p.396), "to be about to do anything."

There are some who contend that the word simply means "will be," as in expressing simple future without any idea of imminency. However, Gentry says: "Certainly it is true that the word *mello* can indicate simply

120

"destined," or it can be employed in a weakened sense as a periphrasis for the future tense. Nevertheless, when used with the aorist infinitive-- the word's preponderate usage is: 'be on the point of, be about to.' The same is true when the word is used with the present infinitive. The basic meaning in both Thayer and Abbott-Smith is: 'to be about to.' Indeed, '*Mellein*' with the infinitive expresses imminence (like the future)."[126]

This assessment is confirmed by the Blass-DeBrunner Greek Grammar, "*mellein* with the infinitive expresses imminence."[127] Wuest comments on *mello* with the infinitive: "The Greek of 'shall be' is not the verb of being in the future tense, but the verb *mello* is used with an infinitive. It is a device the Greek writer uses when he wishes to indicate that a thing predicted will come to pass very soon, an idea that the simple future does not carry."[128] These comments from the Greek sources could be multiplied.

*Mello* appears 111 times in the New Testament. A few of the passages where it occurs supply food for thought:

**1.)** Matthew 3:7- "flee from the wrath to come." There is no doubt that John expected this wrath in his generation. The axe was already at the root!

**2.)** Matthew 16:27- "The Son of Man shall come" This coming was to be in Jesus' generation according to verse 28, thus, *mello* indicated imminence.

**3.)** Acts 17:31- "In which he will judge the world."

**4.)** Acts 24:15- "there shall be a resurrection,"

**5.)** Acts 24:25- "and judgment to come."

**6.)** Romans 8:18- "the glory which shall be revealed." See our discussion of Romans 8 below. There are other words of imminence in Romans 8 that all but demand that we take *mello* as "about to be."

**7.)** 2 Timothy 4:1- "who shall judge the quick and dead." Note that in 1 Peter 4:5 Peter affirmed that Christ was "ready to judge the living and the dead." So, here is an emphatic declaration of the nearness of the judgment in 2 Timothy 4. Thus, *mello* should be understood as "about to be."

**8.)** Hebrews 10:27- "looking for of fiery indignation which shall consume the adversaries." Note that in Hebrews 10:37 the writer affirms that the coming of Christ, in judgment, would occur "in a very, very little while."

**9.)** I Peter 5:1- "partakers of the glory that shall be revealed." Notice the tremendous imminence in the context. In 4:5 Christ was "ready to judge the living and the dead." In verse 7 Peter affirmed, "the end of all things has drawn near." In verse 17 he says, "the time has come for the judgment to begin." Thus, with all of these statements of imminence linked with *mello*, we suggest that the imminence that inheres in *mello* is emphasized.

**10.)** Revelation 1:19- "things which shall be hereafter."

I must confess a degree of chagrin. When one studies *mello* in the translations of the N. T. he finds a confusing situation. In non-eschatological texts the translators *often* render the word as *about to be*, indicating imminence. See Matthew 17:22, "The Son of Man is about to be betrayed." (NKJV). Matthew 20:22, "The cup I am about to drink." Luke 7:2, "Was sick and ready to die." Luke 9:31, "Which he was about to accomplish." Acts 3:3, "Peter and John were about to go into the temple." The translators had no problem translating *mello* as indicative of imminence in these and other passages. In the eschatological texts however, the translators often render *mello* as a simple future. We have a right to ask how much theological bias is at work here?

A statistical study of *mello* has been done by Albert Pigeon.[129] He examined 60 Bible translations to determine how they rendered *mello* in both eschatological and non-eschatological texts. His findings are revealing. Fifty eschatological texts use *mello*, and 61 non-eschatological passages. The study shows that *virtually without exception, mello* is rendered as "about to be" far more often in non-eschatological passages than in eschatological texts. In some translations the disparity of percentage is extremely high. In other words, in the non-eschatological texts, translators rendered *mello* as "about to be" with regularity, but in the eschatological texts they hardly rendered it that way at all.

What is revealing about this is that imminence is expressed in some of these texts in straightforward ways so that there should have been no question about the propriety of rendering *mello* as "about to be." So, the translators rendered *mello* as "about to be" in non-eschatological texts to indicate the imminence of "mundane" matters. In eschatological passages where imminence is emphasized by a variety of words, the translators virtually ignore *mello* as contributing to that imminence. This is puzzling.

Could it be that the embarrassment of a failed eschatology among many modern day scholars has influenced translators to tone down the imminence in *mello*?

*Mello* is used some ten, perhaps twelve times in which it *might* be argued that imminence is not at issue. (cf. Matthew 11:14; Galatians 3:23; Hebrews 10:1; 11:8,20, etc).[130] I am not personally convinced that these truly are exceptions, but merely list them as possibilities. Yet exceptions do not negate the norm. They are just that, *exceptions*. One cannot say that because there are exceptions that the norm no longer applies. *Mello* has a primary significance of imminence that cannot be ignored or denied. See the Greek commentators who do not hesitate to render *mello* as "about to be," and recognize the imminence factor. Alford, Lenski, Nicholl, are just a few. When one admits to the imminence of *mello*, then the nearness of the end in the N.T. passages becomes almost overwhelming.

Another word which gives insight into the fervent, expectant, longing for the parousia by the first century Christians is *prosdokao* (Strong's #4328), also the related word, *prosdekomai*. See Kittel's.[131] The idea present in *prosdokao* is *expectation*. This is the word used by the disciples of John when they asked Jesus if he was the one they looked for or if they should look for another (Matthew 11:3). It is the word used when Zecharias delayed his exit from the temple and the people *waited* for him (Luke 1:21). It is the word used when the people were in *expectation* about John whether he was the Messiah (Luke 3:15). See also Acts 3:5; 10:24; 28:6.

Peter uses this word three times in our present text (v. 12, 13, 14). And each verse says the brethren to whom he was writing were *expecting* the Day of God and the new creation. They believed these things would happen in their lifetime. It was their blessed hope (Titus 2:13). If it did not happen, their eager longing and expectation was disappointed. And we cannot help but be reminded of Proverbs 13:12, "Hope deferred makes the heart sick."

This fervency of expectation is also detected when one follows the chronological development of the New Testament writings. Even the early books express the nearness of the end (e.g. Galatians 5:5). However, the closer to the end of that generation the writers came the more urgent their sense of expectancy. See again Hebrews 10:37, "In a very, very little while he that will come will come!" Witness I John 2:18, "It is the last hour!" And Jesus' warning, "I come quickly!" in Revelation 22:12.

## HASTENING THE DAY?

In Acts 17:30-31 Paul told the Athenians that God had appointed a day in the which he would (literally "is about to" from *mello*), judge the world." How then could the brethren to whom Peter wrote hasten the day? If the day was set, how could anyone hasten its coming?

First, it should be observed that the word rendered "hasten" can be either hasten or "to desire with earnestness." But without question there were some things that had to transpire before the fateful day could come.

In Matthew 24:14 Jesus said the gospel had to be preached in all nations before the end could come. That world mission was indeed fulfilled, and by the early 60s. And, as the early church perceived that the world mission was being fulfilled, they had a sense of the nearness of the

123

end. In Titus 2:13f Paul said the gospel had been made known to all men, and as a result they were looking (*prosdekao*, expecting) for the appearing of the Lord. Thus, as the fulfillment of Jesus' mandate was fulfilled this "hastened" the Day. Gentry even claims "The way in which we 'hasten the coming of the day of God' (3:12) is by evangelistic endeavor." (*Dominion*, 304). This is a problem for Gentry's postmillennialism, however.

Keep in mind that Jesus said, "This gospel of the kingdom must be preached in all the world, as a witness to the nations, then comes the end." As we have just seen, the fulfillment of the Great Commission was a sign of the nearness of the end, and the N. T. writers point to the fulfillment of that commission as proof that the end was indeed near. To use Gentry's idea, the early church's "evangelistic endeavor" in fulfilling that commission was what was "hastening the Day." There is no justification for removing that "evangelistic endeavor" that was hastening the Day *in the first century*, from its historical context and extrapolating it two millennia into the future from Peter.

Paul, in 2 Thessalonians 2:2f, said the Man of Sin and the apostasy had to come to pass before the *epiphany*. Writing in the early 50s he said the Man of Sin was "already at work," but not yet revealed.[132] He was being restrained, but was not yet revealed. This language definitely indicates that the end was near, and they were hastening to it.

The very fact that the New Testament writers are emphatic that they were in the last days, that the end was near, proves that they were indeed "hastening the day of the Lord." It was that first century generation that was seeing prophecy fulfilled before their eyes and in the events of their world.

Peter affirms this in Acts 3:19-21. Peter urged his listeners to repent, "so that times of refreshing may come from the presence of the Lord, and that he may send Jesus." (emphasis mine, DKP). He continued to say that all of the prophets "from Samuel forward, yea as many as have spoken, have spoken of these days." To say that they were living in the time spoken of by the prophets meant they were in the last days. The Day truly was "hastening"! They were experiencing the time of consummation. And of course if *they* were, that means that you and I today are *not*.

A final point about things that had to happen before the end, and that is the filling up of the measure of suffering. Paul said he was filling up in his body what was lacking in the sufferings of Christ (Colossians 1:24f), and this means that there was a measure of suffering on the part of the saints, decreed by God, that Paul in his ministry was in the process of fulfilling. This is what Jesus taught in Matthew 23. There was a measure of suffering

124

on the part of the saints, and a corollary measure of sin on the part of the persecutors, that was being filled up, in the first century, and when it was full, the Day of the Lord would come. This is significant in Peter because he wrote in his first epistle that they were enduring persecution as they longed for the revelation of Christ. However, the promise was that they would only have to suffer "for a little while" until they received their reward (1 Peter 1:3-7). Just as Jesus had promised that they must suffer until the measure of suffering and sin was fulfilled, the church in the first century was filling up the measure of suffering. What cannot be missed is that the suffering must be seen in the context of persecution by the Jews. Read Matthew 23:29f carefully, and then go through the book of Acts, and you will see that the Jews were the movers and shakers of the persecutions there.

This theme is carried out in Revelation as well. In chapter 6:9f when the martyrs prayed for relief they were told to rest for a little season until the number of their fellow-saints who should be slain as they were was fulfilled. The Apocalypse is about the enigmatic city Babylon, which is "where the Lord was slain" (Revelation 11:8), and that was guilty of shedding all the innocent blood shed on the earth (Revelation 18:20, 24).[133] Her cup of sin, for shedding that innocent blood of God's saints was now full (Revelation 17:1-6), and her judgment was at hand (Revelation 22:6, 10-12, etc.) The correlation with Matthew 23 and the rest of the Biblical testimony is perfect.

In other words, there were some things which had to happen before vindication at the Great Day of God could come. Each event that transpired hastened the day.

The point should be clear. Peter says it, and all the other writers of the New Covenant do as well. There was an eschatological scheme foretold by Jesus and the prophets, and they were living in the days of the fulfillment of that Plan. Peter's emphatic declaration for instance, that the events of Pentecost were the beginning of the fulfillment of Joel 2 is powerful, "This is that which was spoken by the prophet Joel." (Acts 2:15f)[134] And, again, his statement that all of the prophets had foretold the events of his day cannot be lightly dismissed (Acts 3). This informs us that the inspired writers believed and taught that they were living in the eschaton. After all, Paul did say "the end of the ages has come upon us" (1 Corinthians 10:11). They eagerly awaited, expected, and *hastened* the coming of the day of the Lord. Should we not therefore, be extremely cautious before we insist that

125

their great expectation was never intended to occur in their lifetime, indeed, it was not to happen for at least 2000 years?

Consider again Luke 21:8. Jesus warned against making or believing premature declarations of the end. However, he gave signs that would signify that the end was "nigh, even at the door" (Matthew 24:32). The completion of the World Mission, the filling up of the measure of suffering, the appearance of the anti-christ's (1 John 2:18), were all signs that the end was near.

Consider again then, that Peter, who heard first hand of the danger of making premature declarations of the end, but knew of the signs that would presage the nearness of the end, affirmed that the salvation that was foretold by the prophets was now "ready to be revealed" (1 Peter 1:5). What was once far off was now near (1 Peter 1:10f). The judgment of the living and the dead was now ready to take place (1 Peter 4:5), and "the end of all things has drawn nigh"; "the appointed time for the judgment had come (1 Peter 4:5,7, 17). Peter *knew* the danger of making premature predictions of the end. Yet, he unabashedly affirmed that the Day was hastening on; it was near.

## PROTRACTED PAROUSIA?

It is often argued that Jesus did teach that his coming could be delayed for a great length of time. A representative of those who teach this is Burton Coffman in his commentary on Luke 19. Amillennialist David Engelsma makes the same argument. (*Defense*, 16+)

Coffman examines the parable of the pounds and makes the following comments: "The very fact of Jesus prophesying the destruction of Jerusalem as he undeniably did, an event forty years future from his crucifixion, and making that to be a type of the final judgment, as the overwhelming number of Bible scholars agree, shows that the holy Savior fully knew, and revealed it beforehand, that centuries were involved in the progress of his kingdom to the final judgment."[135] Beale suggests that, "The events of A.D. 70 point typologically to the events at the very end of the world."[136] Gibbs likewise argues that all of the metaphoric references to the Day of the Lord are in fact indicative of a yet future, literal destruction of the space-time creation (*Jerusalem*, 192, 195+, etc.).

But, *where in the text does Jesus make the destruction of Jerusalem a type of final judgment?* We have heard that argument for years, and have even made it, but have yet to see Bible *proof* for such an assertion.

126

Are we not living in the age of the "reality" versus the "shadow?" The *Old Law* was a shadow of good things to come (Hebrews 10:1f). The Sabbath and the new moon feasts and festivals were all shadows (Colossians 2:14f). But Jesus is the *reality*, the church is the true tabernacle not pitched with hands (Hebrews 8-9). If the destruction of Jerusalem was only a type or shadow of coming final destruction, are we not bound to at least suspect there are other things not yet fulfilled? Is it true that we are still living in the time of types and antitypes?

If the destruction of Jerusalem is a type of coming final cosmic cataclysm, could it be that Jesus' sacrifice was only a type of a yet future greater, more perfect sacrifice? "No!" it will be rejoined, "because He died once for all time and there is no more sacrifice for sin." True. It is also true that the writers of the New Covenant posit the destruction of Jerusalem as the "end of all things" (I Peter 4:7).[137] It was the time for the judgment of the living and the dead (I Peter 4:5). It was the time when all the dead, all the way back to creation would be judged (Matthew 23:35f).

The fall of Jerusalem was to be the greatest tribulation that had ever occurred, or ever would occur (Matthew 24:21). If the fall of Jerusalem was the greatest thing to ever occur, how can anyone contemplate the end of material creation? Jesus was speaking *covenantally* when he said this. That is, the fall of Jerusalem was the greatest event in all of history because it brought a *covenant world* that had stood for 1500 years to an end. *Nothing like that had ever happened.* And furthermore Jesus said it would never happen again (Matthew 24:35). However, if the Christian age, the age of the New Covenant ends, this falsifies Jesus' promise. And if the Christian age did end that would not only be as great as the fall of the old world, it would be far worse, since it would involve the termination of the better, perfect covenant of grace.

Would not the cosmic catastrophe posited by all futurist eschatologies be exponentially greater than the destruction of Jerusalem? There is some sense in which Jesus said that the demise of Jerusalem was to be the greatest event of all time.[138] However, let me repeat that in *all futurist paradigms*, the cosmic catastrophe drawn from the (erroneous) interpretation of 2 Peter 3 would make the fall of Jerusalem pale in significance. If our view of 2 Peter 3 violates Jesus' statement in Matthew 24, our view of 2 Peter must be false.

The importance of the fall of Jerusalem has been virtually lost in the modern gospel message. Yet, for several centuries the early church used the fall of Jerusalem as a positive proof of the Deity of Jesus. The fourth century Roman emperor, Julian the Apostate, attempted to rebuild the Jerusalem temple in order to counter the success of the Christian message, but he was foiled in his attempt.[139] Tragically, the modern church has either lost or abandoned what was historically one of its most effective evangelistic messages. Instead, it is not uncommon to hear ministers disparage the significance of that event, as if it were nothing.

The fall of Jerusalem cannot foreshadow the end of the Christian age because the end of the Christian age would be greater than the end of the Jewish age. Further, the Christian age has no end (Ephesians 3:20-21). *You cannot bring to an end that which scripture affirms to be endless.*

Where is there a hint that the first century believers viewed the fall of Jerusalem as typical of some coming greater reality? There is not a single New Testament passage that says anything resembling, "As the fall of Jerusalem will be, so also will be the end of the world." Instead of Jesus saying something like, "As it will happen to Jerusalem so shall it be at the end of time," Jesus simply told how it would be when he returned in the lifetime of those disciples.

Whereas, as Hays points out, Paul said that the people and events of the O. T. were "types of us"[140] (i.e. the first century church and events), no N. T. writer ever says that the first century people or events are "types of them," referring to future times. And when Paul says that "the end of the ages has come upon us" (v. 11), this means that his generation was the goal, the destiny of all that had been pre-figured. That generation did not foreshadow or prefigure another eschatological generation to come.

It should be noted that in the parable of the pounds the nobleman gave talents to his servants. He left to receive his kingdom. While he was gone some of those he left behind rebelled refusing to submit to his rule. After receiving his kingdom the ruler returned, *in the lifetime of those servants to whom he had given talents and in the lifetime of his enemies.* If Jesus had wanted to indicate an interim of centuries between his ascension and return, why did he not indicate that his return would be *after the death of his disciples?* Instead, his parables always depict the return of the master as occurring in the lifetime of the subjects in the parable.

Luke 12:35-48 is another story used by those who insist Jesus taught his return would not be for centuries. Jesus tells of the good and evil, the knowing and the ignorant servants. The evil servant said, "My Lord delays his coming," and became corrupt. Coffman finds in this parable, "a definite hint...that the Second Advent will be delayed far beyond the expectations of that generation, and so it has proved to be." (Coffmann, 1976, 279). He fails to see that while the master did delay his coming in the parable, the "long delay" was only "long" in regard to the lifetime of those in the parable. It was not depicted as a long time in the history of the world. The master did not return in the lifetime of future generations of servants; he came in the lifetime of the servants he left behind. And so it is with all the parables which are used to teach that Jesus taught his return would be delayed for many years.

It may be rejoined that there is a parable which disproves the contention just noted. In Matthew 21, (par. Luke 20), Jesus told the parable of the man who let out his vineyard to husbandmen. Luke says he "went into a far country for a long time." At the time of harvest, he sent his servants to collect the fruit. The husbandmen beat them. The master sent other servants who were similarly mistreated. Finally, he sent his son but the wicked workers killed him. Judgment then was meted out to the husbandmen by the master. The obvious application of the parable applies to the history of Israel in their rejection, and martyrdom of God's prophets. Finally they killed the Father's son and were judged.

The first point is the one just mentioned. This parable has to do with *the history of Israel.* It is not a parable about the history of the world. This parable is no different from that of Luke 19, and that is unequivocally related to the Jews rejection of Jesus during his absence.

Coffman claims that history shows that centuries have been involved in the Lord's absence, "we are therefore justified in interpreting the other parables which use the term "long time" in reference to the return of the Lord as meaning it would be centuries." This is faulty reasoning, and fails to consider the emphatic declarations of Jesus as to the time of his return, as noted above. Since Jesus positively posited his return for that generation, yet left the specific time uncertain, it could still be a "long time" in relationship to that generation yet still happen within it. In other words when Jesus made his prediction it was still almost 40 years until it would happen. That, in the span of a life, is a "long time." You cannot make "this generation" or, "some standing here" to mean 2000 years!

The fact that Peter's audience was hastening the Day of the Lord is a clear-cut refutation of the futurist interpretation of 2 Peter 3. We must honor the fact that Jesus and all of the New Testament writers–including 2 Peter 3- taught that the end was near, and coming in their generation.

# CHAPTER 11

# NEW HEAVENS AND NEW EARTH

## "Nevertheless, According to His Promise, We Look for a New Heavens and a New Earth, Wherein Dwells Righteousness." (2 Peter 3:13)

There is perhaps no better proof that Peter had in mind a first century fulfillment than his assertion that he and his readers were looking, (i.e., *expecting*, see above on "looking"), for the *promised* new heavens and new earth. The question is natural to ask as Owens did:

"What is that promise? Where may we find it? Why, we have it in the very words and letter, Isaiah 65:17. Now, when shall this be that God will create these 'new heavens and earth, wherein dwells righteousness'? Saith Peter, 'It shall be after the coming of the Lord, after that judgment and destruction of ungodly men, who obey not the gospel, that I foretell.' But now, it is evident, from this place of Isaiah, with chapter 66:21-22, that this is a prophecy of Gospel times only; and that the planting of these new heavens is nothing but the creation of God's ordinances, to endure forever."[141]

While most commentators give lip service to Isaiah as the source of 2 Peter 3, they give no serious investigation to what Isaiah really says. This is true of the dispensationalists, the amillennialists[142] and postmillennialists.[143] What is fascinating is that, as of this writing, I have not found one writer that denies that Isaiah 65-66 is the source for Peter's prediction of the new creation. Yet, while this is widely admitted, the force of this link is, for all practical purposes, ignored or distorted.

## THE "NEW" HEAVEN AND EARTH

The apostle tells us they expected the "new" heaven and earth. It is worth investigating the word "new" which he used. There are two words translated as new in the New Testament, *neos* and *kainos*. *Neos* is new in time. It is that which has never been before, or that which has recently come into existence. On the other hand *kainos* means new in quality, not time. It means new in contrast to what has "seen service, the outworn, the effete, or marred through age."[144] In 2 Peter 3:13 Peter uses *kainos*.

As we have already seen, Peter in his first letter speaks of the end of all things as at hand (4:7). He saw the passing of an old system. This comports well with Hebrews 8 where inspiration says the old system of Judaism was in the process of vanishing away (8:13). The heavens and earth of that old world was being shaken to usher in the new heaven and earth of the unshakable kingdom of heaven (12:22-28).

Who could doubt that the new creation of Christ's kingdom could be aptly described as *kainos* in comparison to the old system. We have a new (*kainos*) covenant (Hebrews 8). The Christian is a new (*kainos*) creation (2 Corinthians 5:17). The church is the new Jerusalem (Hebrews 12:22, Revelation 21:2). And, while *kainos* is not specifically used, we have a new sacrifice, a new priesthood, temple, nation and song. We are a new creation! All of these stand in stark contrast to the old system which passed away. It is this very contrast, the old system versus the New, that is the heart of Peter's expectation of the "new" heavens and earth.

## ACCORDING TO HIS PROMISE
## WE LOOK FOR THE NEW HEAVENS AND EARTH

There is little scholarly disagreement that the source of Peter's referent to the new creation is Isaiah 65-66. However, some do attempt to delineate between the promise of Isaiah 65 and that of 2 Peter 3. Gentry for instance affirms that Isaiah 65 foretold the new creation of Christ in the church, but that, "The key passage for the consummative new heavens and new earth is found in 2 Peter 3." (*Dominion*, 301).

This is done, it seems to me, to avoid arriving at the consistency of Covenant Eschatology. If Peter was drawing on Isaiah there can be no doubt that Peter was not anticipating the "end of the time-space creation" but, the end of the Old Covenant world of Israel in A.D. 70.

So, while most scholars agree that Isaiah serves as Peter's source, it is interesting that both postmillennialists and premillennialists seek to distinguish between Isaiah's promise, that of Peter, and that in Revelation 21. Let us examine the arguments and dispel them.

While Gentry says that 2 Peter 3 is "the key passage for the consummative new heavens" that is, for a "literal" new creation at the end of time, he acknowledges that other noted scholars, both postmillennialists and amillennialists alike, differ with this position. Noted scholar John Owen applied 2 Peter 3 to the fall of Jerusalem.[145] Roderick Campbell,[146] Cornelius Vanderwaal (amillennlialist), (cf. Gentry, *Dominion*, 301, n. 104), and others have applied Peter's prophecy to the end of the Old Covenant world of Israel in A.D. 70.

The ramifications for the fact that Peter does have the promise of Isaiah 64-66 in mind are great. We refer you to the first part of this work and the study of Matthew 5: 17-18 and Luke 21:22. Jesus said all Old Covenant prophecies would be fulfilled by the fall of Jerusalem. Jesus said not one iota of the Old Covenant could pass until it was all fulfilled. Isaiah 64-66 is part of the Old Law. Therefore, not one iota of the Old Law could pass until Isaiah 64-66 was fulfilled. The promise of the new heavens and earth is an O. T. promise. Therefore, the promise of the new creation must have been fulfilled by the fall of Jerusalem in 70 AD. We turn then, to examine the promised new creation.

## ISAIAH 65
The prediction of Isaiah 65 is critical for any study of the new order. We want now to develop our argument, set forth briefly earlier. In my research, I have not found anyone that has presented the following argumentation.[147] While virtually all commentators admit, to varying degrees, that Isaiah 65-66 serves as the source of Peter's prophecy, *I have not, at the time of this writing, found a single source that investigated the relationship between the new creation of Isaiah 65, and the coming of the Lord anticipated in Isaiah 64.*[148] This is a *critical* oversight. The coming of the Lord to establish the new creation, and the time of judgment (66:15f), *is the Day of the Lord that Isaiah 64 anticipated.* This being true, this is *prima facie* proof that, since Isaiah is the source for 2 Peter 3, then Peter could not have been predicting a literal, bodily, visible coming of Christ to put an end to human history and the material creation.

To properly understand the prophecy of the new creation, one must go all the way back to chapter 63 (at least), and set the context.

♦ **Isaiah 63: 1f**: "Who is this that comes from Edom, with dyed garments from Bozrah, this one who is glorious in His apparel, traveling in the greatness of His strength?"

While the Babylonians pillaged Jerusalem, the Edomites sat back and did nothing. More, they actually cheered at the plight of their cousins, and still more, they even participated. See Psalms 137; Ezekiel 35. So, just as Jehovah had foretold in Isaiah 34, see our discussion above, the Lord had a "Day of vengeance and wrath" (Isaiah 63:4), determined. Edom was about to be destroyed in the Day of the Lord. As we have seen, the Babylonians did not stop at their destruction of Jerusalem. They proceeded to go to Edom and they destroyed Bozrah and the Edomite kingdom, in approximately B. C. 583 (Cf. Malachi 1:2). The point is that Isaiah 63 depicts the Day of the Lord. It is the coming of the Lord. Yet, it was not a literal, visible coming of Jehovah. This is important as we proceed.

♦ **Isaiah 63:9f:** The prophet recounts how in the past, Jehovah had acted to save Israel at different times. The "Angel of His Presence" had worked on their behalf when they were humble before the Lord. The Angel of His Presence, did save Israel at different times, such as at Gibeon and Perizim (Isaiah 28: 21, see 1 Chronicles 14 and 1 Samuel 5:20). However, to reiterate, while Jehovah had come in defense of Israel in the past, not one of those Days included a visible manifestation of the person of Jehovah. He invariably worked through "natural" means, even unseen armies, to accomplish His purpose.

♦ **Isaiah 64:1f:** Israel in her grief looked back on her glorious history, when Jehovah had acted on her behalf, and although she was not truly repentant, she prayed: "Oh that you would rend the heavens! That you would come down! That the mountains might shake at Your presence as fire burns brushwood and fire causes water to boil, to make Your name known to Your adversaries, that the nations may tremble at Your presence." *Israel wanted Jehovah to come–in their defense naturally– as He had come in the past.* The importance of this cannot be over-emphasized. How had Jehovah come in the past? Notice that the people were praying for Jehovah to come, again, *as He had come in the past*, when He had made His name known among the nations. When had Jehovah "come" and made His name known among the nations?

**A.) Exodus 9:14f--** He had come through the plagues of Egypt to deliver His people from bondage, that the nations might know Him.

**B.) Isaiah 37:18f–** The Lord, i.e. the Angel of the Lord's presence, came in judgment of the Assyrian army, killing 185,000 of them, and this was done, "that all the kingdoms of the earth may know that You are the Lord."

**C.) Ezekiel 29-30–** The Lord used Nebuchadnezzar as the "Sword in my hand" to destroy Egypt, and He did this so that "all the inhabitants of Egypt shall know that I am the Lord" (Ezekiel 29:6f).

See our earlier discussion of the Day of the Lord for more examples. The point is that in Isaiah 63-66, the prophet looks back and rehearses examples of the coming of the Lord. And, he records Israel's cry for Jehovah to come *as He had come in the past*. The trouble is that in Isaiah, the people were not truly repentant. They were not humble. They only reluctantly admitted that they had done anything wrong, but, they wanted Jehovah to come on their behalf anyway.

133

There is no way, contextually, to find in Isaiah a prediction of an end of time, earth burning coming of Jehovah. For Israel to pray for, and expect Jehovah to come, *as He had come in the past*, is rock solid, irrefutable proof that they were not expecting a visible, bodily coming of Jehovah. Furthermore, there is not one word to indicate that Jehovah's response would be: "Well, you want me to manifest myself in the same way I have before, but I am going to surprise you and put an end to time, by destroying the entire universe, when I come literally, visibly, bodily out of heaven!"

The only "difference" between what the people were praying for, and what Jehovah was going to do was that they wanted Jehovah to come and *rescue* them. But Jehovah said He was going to come and destroy them, due to their failure to repent. He was going to do a "strange work." At least it would be strange in their eyes![149] We come now to chapter 65.

♦ **Isaiah 65:1f–** As Israel cried out to the Lord, complaining that He seemed to be keeping silent at their plight (64:12), and asking Him to come as He had come in the past, Jehovah "explained" the reason for His "silence," and His promise that the time was coming when He would no longer keep silence. He was going to act, but they were not going to like it when He acted! He was coming, but, His coming was going to be in judgment, not deliverance.

Notice in Isaiah 65:1f the Lord charged Israel with her failure to repent and to respond to his pleadings: "I have stretched out my hands all day long to a rebellious people, who walk in a way that is not good." In Romans 10:21 Paul applies this passage *to Israel of his day*. Thus, in the prophecy of the new creation that serves as the basis for Peter's prediction, another apostle quotes from the prophecy and applies it to Israel of his day. This is highly significant, since, as we shall see, Peter says that Paul's eschatology was the same as his. So, both Paul and Peter draw from Isaiah's prophecy of the new creation, and Paul informs us in no uncertain terms, that Isaiah applied to the judgment that was about to fall on Israel in A.D. 70.

In Isaiah 65:8f Jehovah promised that although He was bringing judgment on Israel, that He would not destroy them absolutely. He would save a remnant. The righteous remnant would inherit God's promises and blessings, but those who were guilty of rebellion would suffer destruction: "You shall leave your name for a curse to my chosen; For the Lord God shall slay you, and call His servants by another name" (Isaiah 65:15).

Notice now, that it is following this judgment, following the destruction of the rebellious nation, that God then gives the promise of the new creation: "For, behold, I create a new heavens and a new earth" (Isaiah 65:17). Notice quickly the constituent elements of the prophecy:

**1.)** The destruction of God's enemies (v. 1-7, 11-12). This is not a prediction of a judgment on the material creation. It is a judgment on Old Covenant Israel for her rebellion against Jehovah (Isaiah 65:11f).

**2.)** The salvation of a remnant, (vs. 8-10). As we have seen, the doctrine of the salvation of the remnant is one of Paul's favorite themes. It is important to see the salvation of the remnant in the context of the judgment of the whole, however. *The whole is not saved. The majority perish, while the righteous remnant is saved.*[150]

**3.)** The making of a new people (v. 13-16). In Psalms 102:18 Jehovah again promised a new creation, when "the heavens and earth" would perish. At the time of this judgment "a people yet to be created" (Psalms 102:18), would be formed to praise the Lord.[151]

**4.)** The giving of a new name (v. 15).

**5.)** A new heavens and new earth (v. 17).

**6.)** A new Jerusalem is indicated (v. 18-19).

**7.)** The "former things" will no longer be *"remembered"* (v. 17). This is a critical issue that places the judgment and the resulting new creation strictly within the confines of God's covenantal relationship with Israel. When God "remembered" someone, or something, He did so in light of His covenant with them. Thus, the old creation was a creation that God had a covenant with, but that covenant bond would be dissolved, and no longer remembered. See Jeremiah 3:14f where God predicted that when the kingdom was established, men would no longer "remember" the Ark of the Covenant. In Jesus' words of John 4:20f we find the imminent fulfillment of that promise. The time had arrived when the Old Covenant world was about to be "forgotten."

**8.)** In this new creation, there would be peace and prosperity (v. 20-25).

The question of course is, has Isaiah 65 been fulfilled. Consider the following:

**A New People:** Can it denied that God has created *a new people?* Paul calls the church the Israel of God (Galatians 6:16). In I Peter 2:9 Peter cites Hosea's prediction of the time when God would grant life and recognition to those once rejected. He exults that the prophecy is fulfilled. In Ephesians 2 Paul tells how God has combined Jew and Gentile into one new body. And John says the church is a kingdom of priests (Revelation 1:5-6). Yes, God has made a new people.

135

**A New Name!** It is a name better than sons and daughters (Isaiah 56:5).[152] What better name can one have than Christian? Peter urged his readers to glorify God in this name (I Peter 4:16). This is a God-given name as a word study of the word translated "called" in Acts 11:26 shows. God's new people have the promised new name.

**The New Jerusalem?** Few Bible students would deny that the church is the new city of God. One has but to read Galatians 4:22f and Hebrews 12:18f to find that the church is "the heavenly Jerusalem, the church of the living God."

If God has a new people, with a new name, a new city, *where does this city and this people sit? Do we not* dwell in the new creation (2 Corinthians 5:17), the new heavens and earth? This is vindicated by examination of the conditions in the new heavens and earth.

Isaiah 65 says that in the new creation there would be peace, "The wolf and the lamb shall feed together, the lion shall eat straw like the ox, the dust shall be the serpent's food. They shall not hurt nor destroy in all my holy mountain, says the Lord" (v. 25). In Isaiah 11:6-9 He describes those same conditions existing, *when the ensign would be raised*, and God would restore Israel, and then call the nations to Him.

We know the ensign has been raised because Paul says so in Romans 15:12f. God has restored Israel, because *Paul's ministry was to call the nations to God,* and again, that would only be done when Israel was restored. Now, Isaiah 11 says peace would be when the kingdom was fully established and God had gathered His people to the Messiah. In chapter 65 He said peace would be in the new heavens and new earth. Both passages speak of the same time but approach it from slightly different perspectives. The new creation is not something different in time from the kingdom. Isaiah 11 was fulfilled in the work of Messiah in the first century, as declared by Paul in Romans 15.[153] Since Isaiah 11 and Isaiah 65 foretold the same events, how can we logically deny the new heavens and earth were established as well?

Let us summarize what we have said to this point.

2 Peter 3 anticipated the fulfillment of Isaiah 63-65, the prophecy of the new heavens and earth that would be fully established at the Day of the Lord.

The prophecy of Isaiah 63-66[154] anticipated the coming of the Lord out of heaven when the mountains would melt under His feet (Isaiah 64:1f), and His name would be made manifest to the nations.

The coming of the Lord foretold in Isaiah 63-66, to bring in the new creation, was to be the same as when the Lord had come before "when you came down, the mountains shook at your presence" (Isaiah 64:1-4). The previous Days of the Lord were non-literal, non-bodily, descents of the Lord out of heaven. Literal heaven and earth never perished before. Jehovah came by means of historical events under His sovereign control. Since the Day of the Lord of Isaiah 63-66 was to be of the same non-literal, non-bodily, non-visible coming as previous Days of the Lord, and since the Day of the Lord of 2 Peter 3 was to be the fulfillment of the prediction of Isaiah 63-66, *it therefore follows that the Day of the Lord of 2 Peter 3 was to be a non-literal, non-bodily, non-visible Day of the Lord.*

> **The Day of the Lord of Isaiah cannot be a bodily, visible coming of the Lord, at the end of time.**
> **But, Peter was looking for the fulfillment of Isaiah's prediction of the Day of the Lord.**
> **Therefore, the Day of the Lord anticipated by Peter cannot be a bodily, visible coming of the Lord at the end of time.**

There is something else here: the millennialists seem confused about where to place the destruction of the old world as foretold by Isaiah 65 and 2 Peter 3. LaHaye and Ice insist that, "two more destructions are predicted in the Bible. One will come by fire, after which God will restore all things (2 Peter 3:4-14; see also Isaiah 65:17-20). The other destruction is described in Revelation 21:1)."[155] So, Isaiah 65 and 2 Peter 3 supposedly describe what will happen at Christ's Second Coming, "producing a refurbished earth *to begin the millennium*." (My emphasis) Revelation 21 describes what happens at the end of the millennium.

LaHaye and Ice say that there are "serious problems" to link Isaiah and Peter with Revelation 21 as most scholars do. To LaHaye and Ice, Isaiah and 2 Peter 3 refer to Christ's parousia *to begin the millennium*, at the end of the seven year tribulation period. Revelation 21 occurs at the end of the millennium.

While LaHaye and Ice say it is a "serious problem" to place 2 Peter 3 at the end of the millennium, on page 42 and 127, *of the same book*, (*Charting*), they place the judgment of 2 Peter 3 *at the end of the millennium!* Speaking of the "Day of the Lord" in 2 Peter 3:10-12, they say:

"Isaiah 34 gives more detail, but this 'day of the Lord' signals that time when, at the end of the Millennial kingdom, God will destroy this old sin-cursed world." (*Charting*, 42). So, the same authors tell us on one page that it is a "serious error" to link 2 Peter 3 with the end of the millennium and Revelation 21, and yet, they tell us on another page that 2 Peter 3 occurs "at the end of the millennial kingdom." This is rank contradiction.

Apart from the fact that the millennialists present a confusing paradigm in regard to Isaiah and 2 Peter 3, is the fact that virtually no eschatological paradigm fully deals with what Isaiah 65 undeniably teaches, and that is that the new creation would only come with the destruction of Old Covenant Israel.

Notice in Isaiah 65:11f Jehovah accused Israel of being full of sin. In verses 13f He said that as a direct result of that sin, "The Lord God shall slay you, and call His people by a new name." Notice then, "for behold, I create a new heavens and a new earth, and the former shall not be remembered or come to mind." (v. 17). What is the point? The point is that the old creation would be destroyed because of Israel's sin, and the new creation would only follow the destruction of Old Covenant Israel.

Does the millennial paradigm allow for such a destruction? No. If the millennialist places Isaiah 65 at the end of the seven year tribulation, at the parousia, then of necessity, at the end of the Tribulation period, in order to initiate the millennial kingdom, *God will destroy Israel and create a new people*, with a new name! Millennialism teaches no such doctrine.

---

**If the new creation of Isaiah 65 has not come, then in order for it to arrive, Israel must be destroyed, (again), and God must create a New People, with a New Name! (Again!)**

---

It does not help to posit the fulfillment of Isaiah 65 at the end of the millennium either, for this means that at the end of Israel's millennial kingdom, *God destroys her* and creates a new people with a new name. Does millennialism allow for this? No.

The problem is equally serious for the amillennialist and postmillennialists.[156] The amillennialists especially believe that the new creation arrives at the end of the time/space creation. More specifically, the new creation arrives at the end of the Christian age. There is no room at all

138

in amillennial eschatology for the destruction of the material creation at the end of the Christian age, *as a result of Old Covenant Israel's sin.*

To the amillennialists, God was through with Israel at the Cross, perhaps in A.D. 70. There are no Biblical prophecies relating to Israel that are yet to be fulfilled.[157] However, if Isaiah 63-66 is the source of Peter's prophecy (2 Peter 3:1-2, 13), and 2 Peter is not fulfilled, then this demands that Isaiah stands unfulfilled today. But, if 2 Peter 3, and thus Isaiah 63-66 is unfulfilled then at some point in the future Israel has to once again be destroyed, and God has to once again create a new people with a new name. You simply cannot admit that 2 Peter 3 is reliant on Isaiah 63-66 without allowing the elements of Isaiah to be present in 2 Peter. But, if those elements are present, then 2 Peter 3 is about the judgment of Israel, and not the destruction of the time world we live in.

Interestingly, Gentry never definitively answers the question, "what promise of the new heavens is Peter referring to?" He acknowledges that Peter, "obviously employs the terminology of Isaiah 65:17 (which speaks of a spiritual event). Yet as an inspired apostle he expands on that truth, looking to the ultimate out-come of the spiritual new heavens and earth in the eternal new creation." (*Dominion*, 305). This is assertion without proof. Where does Peter tell his readers that he was not looking for the fulfillment of Isaiah, but that he was in fact "expanding" on Isaiah's prophecy to speak of something totally unrelated to what Isaiah foretold? Where does Gentry get from Peter's words, "according to his promise we look for a new heavens and earth," that Peter was *actually* looking for something far different in nature and time, from what Isaiah foretold?

> **Where does Gentry get from Peter's words "according to his promise we look for a new heavens and earth," that Peter was *actually* looking for something far different in *nature, purpose* and *time*, from what Isaiah foretold?**

One cannot help but reflect on how Gentry and the late Greg Bahnsen dealt with the millennial use/abuse of New Testament language. They comment on,"how dispensational interpreters struggle with Peter's appeal to Joel 2:28 in his Pentecost address (Acts 2:16:21). Contrary to Peter's interpretation–viz., that Pentecost fulfilled Joel's prophecy ('this is that which was spoken by the prophet Joel')–dispensationalists insist on holding to their own interpretation of Joel in isolation from the control of the New Testament...Peter thus only meant that Pentecost was a foreshadowing of the millennium."[158]

So, dispensationalists lamentably refuse to allow the N. T. to interpret the Old. They say that when the N. T. writers said they were fulfilling, or looking for fulfillment of the Old Testament prophets that they were only speaking of a foreshadowing of what the O. T. prophets foretold. This is bad hermeneutics, says Gentry. Yet, Gentry tells us that although Peter said they were looking for *what was promised*, they were not actually looking for what was promised, because Peter "expanded" on what Isaiah foretold to speak of something far greater! What was promised was actually only a foreshadowing of what they were looking for.

As DeMar has noted, Ice inserts words into the text of Acts 2:15f to make it read: "This is (like) that which was spoken by the prophet Joel."[159] Gentry rightly castigates Ice for this perversion of the text. However, Gentry then comes to 2 Peter 3, and says that although Peter says, "according to his promise we look for a new heavens and earth," that Peter actually meant we are *not* looking for what Isaiah foretold, we are looking for something unrelated to what Isaiah foretold! Just how much different is Gentry from Ice? Both Ice and Gentry deny that Peter really meant to say that what was predicted in the respective verses was being fulfilled, or was being anticipated. Both insist that what the respective prophets foretold was not truly in the mind of Peter.

Gentry's position on the new creation is confused at best. He tells us, "There is a 'now' aspect of the new creation (2 Corinthians 5: 17), and there is a 'not yet' future to it (2 Peter 3: 13)." (*Dominion*, 299) He does not tell his readers that he believes that the not yet came, in some degree, in A. D. 70 (Revelation 21). So, Gentry believes that the "not yet" of the new creation arrived in A.D. 70, but that there is still a "not yet" aspect of the new creation. Exactly where Gentry gets two "not yets" of the new creation, he never tells us. What Gentry also fails to reveal is that the "not yet" of the new creation is invariably posited in the N. T. as coming soon. We are *never* told that part of the "not yet" would arrive in A.D. 70, but that the rest of the "not yet" would arrive tens of thousands of years later.

Peter wrote shortly before the fall of Jerusalem. Gentry admits this. Why is this significant? Because Gentry believes that John's description of the passing of the "heavens and earth" and the new creation that follows is the description of, "the bride of Christ that came down from God to replace the earthly Jerusalem (Rev. 21:2-5) in the first century (Rev. 1:1; 22:6, 10).

140

With the shaking and destruction of the Old Jerusalem in A.D. 70, the heavenly (re-created) Jerusalem replaced her" (*Dominion*, 363).

So, according to Gentry's own chronology and interpretation, Peter was standing on the very cusp of the shaking of the "heaven and earth" of the Old Covenant world of Israel that would occur in the fall of Israel. With the destruction of that old world, the new heavens and earth of Christ would come down from God out of heaven. Furthermore, the fulfillment of that promise was very near when John, and thus Peter, wrote.

So, according to Gentry, we are supposed to focus on and *emphasize* John's expectation of the imminent fulfillment of Isaiah 65, but we are to *ignore* Peter's temporal standing i.e. just before the destruction of the heaven and earth of Old Covenant Israel. We are to ignore the imminent fulfillment of Isaiah 65, being anticipated by John, although Peter says he was looking for what Isaiah foretold. We are to ignore the fact that Peter, "obviously employs the terminology of Isaiah 65:17f," and look far, far beyond what Isaiah foretold to the end of human history as we know it–something not envisioned by the prophecy of Isaiah 65. And *why* are we supposed to accept this?

Gentry offers five reasons why, in his view, 2 Peter 3 is the consummation of human history, and should be delineated from Isaiah and Revelation 21. We want to examine these five reasons.

**Reason #1: "The thrust of the book seems to promote spiritual perseverance in anticipation of the historical long run–a long run that ends up in the eternal new creation" (*Dominion*, 302).**

This statement is a prime example of *petitio principii*. It assumes so many things, without informing the reader of the basic assumptions, that it would demand too much space to expose. For brevity, let it be noted however, that this statement assumes that because Peter calls for perseverance, that this demands a long period of time, perhaps millennia. This is very bad logic. In Mark 13:13, which Gentry applies to the events leading up to and consummating in the judgment of Israel in A.D. 70, Jesus urged his listeners, "The one who endures (from *hupomeinas*) to the end shall be saved." In Luke 18–that Gentry applies to A.D. 70 (*Dominion*, 481)-- Jesus called on his disciples to endure persecution in light of the fact that Christ was going to avenge them speedily. Many other N. T. passages called on the first century saints to persevere, and promised them relief at the parousia of Christ (2 Thessalonians 1), yet, Gentry does not believe that these "patience passages" indicated the passing of millennia.

141

Furthermore, to claim that the "long term" perseverance demands the passing of millennia is misguided. Can one not speak of events to take place within one generation, and yet, at the same time speak of those events taking a "long time?"

The problem for Gentry is that there is no indication of a long term delay in Peter. He says that Peter expected to die soon, "apparently not expecting a rapture of the church in A.D. 70 (as per radical preterists)." (*Dominion*, 302). Well, Peter expected to die soon, but he nonetheless said, "the end of all things has drawn near," and, "the time has come for the judgment to begin" (1 Peter 4:7, 17). He even wrote to the brethren experiencing persecution urging them to faithfulness in light of Christ's parousia (1 Peter 1:5f). Did he expect to die before the fulfillment of his own words? *It is irrelevant whether he did or not.* He did say the end was near, and Gentry's attempt to negate that fact is specious.

**Reason #2: "The mockers scoff at the promised second advent of Christ due to the long await associated with it (2 Peter 3:3-4) ...Peter even suggests that it might be thousands of years before Christ's return, in that delay is based on God's time rather than man's."** (*Dominion*, 303).

These statements are patently false. The scoffers were not scoffing at the parousia because there was a *long time* associated with it. They were asking, *"Where is it?"* If they knew it was supposed to be 20-30,000 years away, as per the postmillennial view, they would never be asking, "Where is the promise of His coming?" Only if the scoffers believed that they were living in, or at the climax of the time foretold for the parousia, could they legitimately ask, "Where is the promise of His coming?" A postmillennial posit would never cause a scoffer to ask this! The postmillennialist would have to respond, "What do you mean, where is it? We have been telling you it is not near, but a long time off! So, stop your scoffing and go about your business. The end of all things is not at hand!"

If Peter taught that Christ's *epiphany* might be tens of thousands of years away, as the postmillennialists do, what right would the scoffers have to scoff? The ridicule would take a totally different form from, "Where is it?' The scoffers could say, "Well, you are predicting something so far removed in time that one cannot know if it will ever occur or not! It is so distant as to be irrelevant!" That is patently not what they were saying.

Gentry fails to honor Peter's appeal to Psalms 90 as well. See our discussion above, and be reminded that the scoffers, and Peter's appeal to

Psalms, must be seen in the light of *God's promises to Israel*, not in the light of a modern cosmology. The scoffers were denying the fulfillment of God's promises to Israel, Peter was affirming God's faithfulness to Israel. Gentry's failure, along with most other commentators, to honor this connection has led to the complete misapplication of 2 Peter 3.

Gentry and the postmillennialists have no place in their scheme for a future Day of the Lord based on God's promises to Israel. Yet, as we have seen repeatedly in this work, Peter's eschatology was based exclusively on God's promises to Israel. Gentry *does* posit a yet future restoration of Israel, yet, that supposedly occurs *at the end of the Christian age, not at the end of Israel's age*. Further, Gentry does not teach a future destruction of creation as a result of Israel's disobedience to the Law, yet, that is the context of the prophecy of the new creation in Isaiah *65–and the source of Peter's prediction*. Gentry's eschatology is for all practical purposes New Testament eschatology, divorced from Israel.

We have already addressed the issue of whether God sees time as man does. God can tell time perfectly well and knows how to communicate as well. See our comments again.

Gentry 's argument here has to be troubling to him. In his writings he emphasizes the need to honor God's time statements. For instance, read his guiding principles for the interpretation of Revelation:

"Another detriment to the strained interpretations listed above is that John was writing to historical churches existing in his own day (Rev. 1:4). He and they are presently suffering "tribulation' (Rev. 1:9a). John's message (ultimately from Christ 1:1) calls upon each to give careful, spiritual attention to his words (2:7 etc). John is deeply concerned with the expectant cry of the martyrs and the divine promise of their soon vindication (6:10; cp. 5:3-5). He (John, dkp) would be cruelly mocking their circumstances (while committing a 'verbal scam' according to Mounce were he telling them that when help comes it will come with swiftness–even though it many not come until two or three thousand years later."[160]

In his wonderful work on Revelation, Gentry argues, "One of the most helpful interpretive clues in Revelation is at the same time both one of the most generally overlooked among lay students of scripture and one of the most radically reinterpreted by evangelical scholars. This clue is the contemporary expectation of the author regarding the fulfillment of the prophecies. John clearly expects the soon fulfillment of his prophecy."[161]

Gentry responds to those, like Swete and Morris, who claim that the time statements in Revelation must be seen, "as a measure of God's time, not man's." Gentry says that this argument, "is destroyed by the very fact that John repeats and varies his terms as if to dispel any confusion." (*Beast*, 27). So, one cannot interpret Revelation as futuristic because God said its fulfillment was near. And, "the most radically reinterpreted key to understanding Revelation" is the temporal indicators of its soon fulfillment.

Does Peter not express the nearness of the end? He does. Gentry says that the many different words used by John proves objective nearness. Why is the same not true in Peter? Gentry rejects the, "God's time versus man's time" argument in Revelation. Yet, *he makes that very argument in 2 Peter 3*. Should we accept Gentry on 2 Peter 3 when he says that there is God's time versus man's time, or should we accept Gentry when he tells us that we must honor the time statements of scripture as God's divine truth?

Gentry cannot have it both ways. Either God communicates truthfully about time, as Gentry argues when discussing Revelation, or, God's time and man's time are so different that we cannot understand what God means when He talks time. If Gentry maintains the position taken in *Beast* and *Before Jerusalem Fell*, he must abandon his argument of a protracted parousia in 2 Peter 3. If he maintains his argument about God's time versus man's time in 2 Peter 3, he must surrender his position on Revelation.

> **Should we accept Gentry on 2 Peter 3 when he says there is God's time versus man's time, or should we accept Gentry when he says that we must honor God's time statements about the nearness of the events in Revelation?**

**Reason #3: "The longsuffering of the Lord is due to a process that is necessarily age long: 'The Lord is not slack concerning His promise'...The process of calling the 'all' to repentance unto salvation is one that spans the entire inter-advental era and is still continuing today."**

More assertions without proof. Furthermore, Gentry believes that the call to repentance of the Great Commission is directly related to the hastening of the Day of the Lord. He says, "The way that we 'hasten the coming of the Day of the Lord' is by evangelistic endeavor" (*Dominion*, 304). Gentry is guilty of several false assumptions.

**First**, Gentry believes in two Great Commissions. He believes there was a great commission, and then a Great Commission, or perhaps we should call it the *Greater Commission*. He believes that Matthew 24:14, the *great commission*, was fulfilled in the first century, and signified the nearness of the end of the Old Covenant age at the fall of Jerusalem in A.D. 70. He affirmed this in his debate with Thomas Ice (*Tribulation*, 44). He then believes that Matthew 28:18f is the *Greater Commission*.

**Second**, Gentry *assumes* that Peter has in mind the "second" or the Greater Commission, and not the commission of Matthew 24:14. This alone is rather odd. Peter was fully aware that the fulfillment of the Great Commission was to be a sign of the end of the age (Matthew 24:3, 14). He was also fully aware that Paul had already affirmed the fulfillment of that Commission (Colossians 1:5, 23). Consequently, there can be no serious doubt that he fully felt the nearness of the end.

According to Gentry, we are to ignore the relationship between Matthew 24:14 and Peter's temporal standing. We are to assume that Peter was also ignoring those issues, to speak of a different Great Commission–one that would truly only begin with the fulfillment of the first one–a different time of the end, and a coming of the Lord different in nature and purpose from that which was about to occur in Peter's day.

**Third**, if "evangelistic fervor" hastened the Day of the Lord, then surely, Peter's awareness of the first century fulfillment of the Great Commission must impact our understanding of Peter's statement that *they*, *not we*, were "hastening the Day of the Lord." Here is what we mean.

Postmillennialists, as a rule, do not believe that the Day of the Lord of 2 Peter 3 was near in the first century. *It was not hastening!* According to some postmillennial calculations, the consummative Day is still 35-38,000 years away![162] Was Peter supposed to know that? Of course he was, *if he was a postmillennialist.*

Gentry is right to affirm that the fulfillment of the World Mission was an eschatological sign and hastened the Day of the Lord. But, given the postmillennial view of things there is no way for Peter to be affirming that his first century audience was hastening the final Day of the Lord. However, since Peter patently did believe that he and his audience was "hastening the Day of the Lord," then it must be true that the Day they were hastening was the Day of the Lord that was just at hand. It was the coming of the Lord after the first century fulfillment of the Great Commission. It was the coming of the Lord at the end of the age in A.D. 70.

145

Gentry's own position on the relationship between evangelism and eschatology effectively destroys his futuristic application of 2 Peter 3.

**Reason #4: "The reference to the unraveling and conflagration of the heavens and the earth is expressly tied to the material creation. Hence, it seems clearly to refer to the consummation, and not to A.D. 70, despite certain similarities."**

More unproven assumptions. Peter is very clear that it was the "world" of the wicked, not the literal heavens and earth that was destroyed in the flood (2 Peter 3:6). If Gentry were consistent, he would argue that since Peter affirms that the *world* (*kosmos*, the order of society, not material creation) was destroyed in the flood, that Peter was affirming a future event in which the world (the order of society, not material creation), would be destroyed. Yet, Gentry abandons Peter's actual argument to say that Peter was affirming the annihilation of the material universe.

Furthermore, in the examples we have examined, the writers use almost the identical language employed by Peter to describe the historical Days of the Lord in the O. T.. Gentry tells us that we must not look for a literal fulfillment of that language. Then why so in Peter?

Peter was affirming the fulfillment of the O. T. predictions of the Day of the Lord. Those prophecies were invariably predictions of historical events, not end of time events. Gentry must explain why he abandons this hermeneutic to make Peter refer to an end of time event. Nothing like that had ever occurred and was never contemplated in any of the O. T. texts from which Peter draws. *Gentry even admits that Isaiah 65-66, the source of 2 Peter 3, is not about the destruction of material creation.* So, as a matter of hermeneutic, Gentry must show that Peter has abandoned and radically altered the definition of the Day of the Lord, making it into something unknown in the O. T. prophets from which he draws.

**Reason #5: "The strong detailed language of the destruction of the heavens and earth seem to go beyond apocalyptic imagery, referring to actual consummation."**

This is a *bad* argument. If Peter is taking his prediction from Isaiah 65-66, as Gentry admits, then how can Gentry claim that the language of 2 Peter 3 is not found in the O. T. use of apocalyptic imagery? The verses that the Holy Spirit draws from are metaphoric, apocalyptic imagery. Apocalyptic language lends itself to hyperbole, to expansion. But, that hyperbole certainly gives no justification for literalization.

146

To suggest that the "detailed language" of 2 Peter 3 is not found in O. T. historic Days of the Lord is false. There is hardly a prediction more graphic, more detailed, than the prediction of the fall of Edom in Isaiah 34. Yet, Gentry has no problem believing, indeed insisting, that the language is metaphoric. He even argues that, "In scripture, prophets often express national catastrophes in terms of cosmic destruction" (*Tribulation*, 55). He lists Isaiah 34 as a prime example. When discussing Matthew 24:29f and the language of "cosmic disturbances" Gentry even says, "Here, we encounter remarkable disturbances that seem too catastrophic for applying to A.D. 70. But as with the previous apocalyptic verses, so here this portrays historical divine judgment under the dramatic imagery of universal catastrophe" (*Tribulation*, 55).

So, when debating against dispensationalism, Gentry correctly notes that the language of "cosmic destruction," and "universal destruction," need not, indeed should not, be taken literally, because of the well attested O. T. use of metaphoric language describing the coming of the Lord. However, when we come to 2 Peter 3, since Peter uses the language of universal catastrophe and cosmic destruction, we are to believe that Peter is totally, radically redefining the language of the Day of the Lord into something unknown in the O. T. source of his prediction.

We have now examined each of Gentry's five reasons why 2 Peter 3 should be taken as a prediction of the end of time, and not as a prediction of the fall of Jerusalem in A. D. 70. We have shown that Gentry's arguments are a violation of the well attested O. T. definition of the Day of the Lord. We have shown that Gentry's arguments are illogical, self contradictory, and self-defeating. There is no good reason for interpreting Peter's prediction as a prophecy of a yet future cosmic catastrophe.

Other commentators argue that 2 Peter 3 is indeed predictive of the judgment of A.D. 70. Seriah says, "We, of course, acknowledge that Peter in 2 Peter interprets Isaiah 65:17f as the coming of a new order of 'heaven and earth'' in A.D. 70. If, however, Paul uses the idea of a new creation in reference to a past event in Corinthians, the pantelist[163] is hard pressed to prove that Paul is changing his usage in Romans 8 to fit with 2 Peter 3 rather than remaining consistent with his own usage elsewhere. Because Peter chooses to use an image to describe A.D. 70 does not mean Paul (in an earlier letter) is pressed to abide by the same image (especially if he clearly considers the image in a different way in 2 Cor. 5)."[164] So, what we have here are two representatives of the postmillennial world. One, Gentry, says that 2 Peter 3 is "the key passage" for proving a future end of time. On the other hand, the other representative says "of course" 2 Peter 3 refers to A.D. 70 and not the end of time.

Seeking to justify a yet future eschaton, Seriah appeals to Romans 8, and the anticipated liberation of "the creation" from futility, and says, "The 'heaven and earth' of Judaism that passed away in the first century (2 Peter 3:10; Revelation 21:1) were 'obsolete and growing old'(Hebrews 8:13); they were not 'futile.' How could any Christian consider the Old Covenant that 'came with glory' (2 Corinthians 3:7) to be futile?" (*TEOAT*, *54*)

Finally, Seriah says, "I acknowledge that most of the passages in the New Testament that are prophetic refer to the coming of Christ against the apostate Jews in the first century (specifically the passages that have 'near' time references). We do not, however, agree that a 'near' time reference can be inserted into every prophetic passage in the N. T." (*TEOAT*, 183).

Frankly, Seriah's logic is so convoluted, that one wonders if he gave serious thought before he wrote. Let's take a look at his arguments.

**First**, Seriah applies the "big three" new creation passages, Isaiah 65, 2 Peter 3, and Revelation 21 to the A.D. 70 judgment. This is more consistent than Gentry.

**Second**, Seriah argues that since Paul in 2 Corinthians 5:17 speaks of the new creation as a present reality, that he could not be looking for that same new creation in the future, in Romans 8. This is an egregious oversight. His argument is that what was present in Corinthians cannot have been future in Romans.

This ignores the fact that in the New Testament there is the "already-but-not-yet" of the new creation, and Christ's work. We dare say that Seriah teaches this truth. In other words, the New Testament says that the early saints had been saved, but were looking for salvation (Ephesians 2:8-9/ Hebrews 9:28). They were redeemed, but were looking for redemption (Ephesians 1:7f/ 4:32). They had been adopted, but were eagerly awaiting the adoption (Romans 8:14/ v. 23). Not only is there the "already-but-not-yet" issue, in the N.T., there is also the immaturity-v-maturity issue.

There is no doubt that the New Testament writers affirm that the body of Christ came into existence on Pentecost. Yet, that body, that Temple, was not completed.[165] There was a period of growth and maturing to occur. Notice the already-but-not-yet aspect of the building of the Temple of God (Ephesians 2:19; 1 Peter 2:5f and then see Hebrews 8:1f). They were anticipating the arrival of "that which is perfect" and the "measure of the stature of the fullness of Christ" (1 Corinthians 13:8/ Ephesians 4:8f). In

148

other words, the new creation had begun, but they were longing for its full arrival. And, *this is exactly what Seriah believes!*

Seriah argues that since 2 Corinthians 5 says the new creation was present, but Romans says the new creation was future, that this demands two different eschatons, two *different "creations."* However, Seriah believes that the new creation of 2 Corinthians 5:17 and the new creation of 2 Peter 3 and Revelation 21 *are the same entity.* Yet, Paul said that new creation was *present* in Corinthians, and Peter and John said it was *future* in Peter and Revelation. Do you see the contradiction? It is a serious one, and cannot be lightly dismissed.

If the "new creation" in 2 Corinthians 5, 2 Peter 3 and Revelation 21 can be the same, then most assuredly it can be the same new creation in 2 Corinthians 5 and Romans 8. In other words, Paul affirmed the "already" of the new creation in Corinthians, but, he, Peter and John affirmed the "not yet" of that same new creation in 2 Peter 3 and Revelation 21. It is an arbitrary exegesis, guided by theology instead of text, that seeks to drive a wedge between these eschatological texts.

**Third,** Seriah makes an incredible statement, "The 'heaven and earth' of Judaism that passed away in the first century (2 Peter 3:10; Revelation 21:1) was 'obsolete and growing old' (Hebrews 8:13); they were not 'futile.' How could any Christian consider the Old Covenant that 'came with glory' (2 Corinthians 3:7) to be futile?" So, according to Seriah, the Old Covenant was not a creation of futility, because it came in glory. One wonders if Seriah has ever even read what the New Testament writers, *all Jews who lived under that old creation,* had to say about it.

**1.)** Peter said that the old creation of the Law, was, "a yoke that neither we nor our fathers were able to bear" (Acts 15:10). Does that not convey the idea of futility?

**2.)** It was life under the Law that Paul describes when he cries out, "O wretched man that I am, who shall deliver me from the body of this death?" (Romans 7:24). Does that not sound like futility?

**3.)** Paul said, "by the works of the Law shall no flesh be justified" (Galatians 2:16). He said all those under the Law "are under (the) curse" (Galatians 3:10). He said the Law could not give life and righteousness (Galatians 3:20-21). He said to live under the Law was to be in bondage (Galatians 5:1f).

**4.)** Paul called the Law "the ministration of (the) death" (2 Corinthians 3:7). Compared to the New Covenant of Christ, the O. T paled in glory.

**5.)** Hebrews 8, a passage to which Seriah refers, says the reason for the promise of the New Covenant was because Jehovah found fault with the first covenant (Hebrews 8:6). The Law could never take away sin (Hebrews 10:1-4). It could never bring man into the presence of God, but was instead a constant reminder of that separation (Hebrews 9:6-10).

Now, if you lived under a law that could not offer forgiveness, that could not make you righteous, but only made you acutely aware of your sinfulness and lostness (Romans 7:6f), would you consider that Law a law of futility or not? The Law was added to make sin–the awareness of sin–abound, and yet, not deliver from that sin (Romans 5:21). So, no matter how many sacrifices, no matter how many pilgrimages one made, there was only, "a remembrance made of sin every year" (Hebrews 10:1-3). And Seriah says the Old Law was not a law of futility. If any one word *epitomized* life under that Law, that one word would be *futility!*

For Seriah to argue that Romans 8 must be a future eschaton because the creation could not be longing to be free from the *futility of the Old Covenant* is therefore, misguided.

**Fourth**, Seriah admits that when statements of imminence are used in a N. T. text that it refers to the A.D. 70 judgment of Christ. However, he then argues, "We do not, however, agree that a 'near' time reference can be inserted into every prophetic passage in the N. T." (*TEOAT*, 183).

Consider this: 2 Peter 3 does not contain an explicit "at hand," "Behold, I come quickly," or, "these things must shortly come to pass" statement. Yet, Seriah has no problem stating, "We, of course, acknowledge that Peter in 2 Peter interprets Isaiah 65:17f as the coming of a new order of 'heaven and earth' in A. D. 70." *So, even without an explicit time statement, he is able to see the impending A.D. 70 judgment in 2 Peter 3.* Yet, when he goes to Romans 8 he ignores *three strong words of imminence,* and refuses to see that it applies to the same judgment as 2 Peter 3.

As we have seen above, in Romans 8, Paul speaks of the "glory that is about to be revealed in us" (v. 18, New Revised Standard). Paul uses the word *mello,* with the infinitive, to indicate the nearness of the coming glory. Second, Paul speaks of the "earnest expectation" of the creation. The word translated "earnest expectation" is *apokaradokeo,* (Strong's #603), and means to await with the neck outstretched. It is a word that indicates a strong element of imminence. The third word is *apekdekomai* (Strongs #553), and means expectant waiting. See our earlier discussion for fuller details.

150

The point is that Seriah agrees that when temporal indicators speak of an event as imminent it refers to the A.D. 70 judgment. Well, Romans 8 contains *three strong indicators of imminence, yet* Seriah rejects them and applies them to a different eschaton from 2 Peter 3. This is inconsistent. On a slightly different note, Seriah admits that we must honor the time statements of imminence in the N. T., but then says, "We do not, however, agree that a 'near' time reference can be inserted into every prophetic passage in the N. T." (*TEOAT*, 183). But wait, 2 Peter 3 does not contain an explicit, "The coming of the Lord has drawn near" statement. However, Seriah believes that Peter's statements in 1 Peter 4:7, 17 can be safely "inserted" into 2 Peter 3. Well, if the time statement of 1 Peter 4 can be imported into the text of 2 Peter 3, why do those time statements not apply equally well to 1 Corinthians 15 and 1 Thessalonians 4? It is not hermeneutics, but Seriah's *theology* that forbids it.

A final point. Seriah sees that 2 Peter 3 is based on the O. T. promise of Isaiah 65 and that it applies to Israel's eschaton. Yet, he fails to see that *Romans 8 is also based on the O. T. promises of Israel's eschaton.*

Isaiah 26, part of what is known as the "little apocalypse" of Isaiah, contains the prophecy that serves as the fountain for Paul's eschatology in Romans 8. Isaiah spoke eloquently of Israel's longing, her struggling for righteousness and salvation, but not finding it (Isaiah 26:18). Isaiah even uses the imagery of Israel being in the pangs of child-birth longing to bring forth that deliverance, but failing (v. 17). That is the "futility" of the Law under which she struggled. Furthermore, Isaiah foretold the time when "Your dead shall live" (v. 19), and this would be in the Day when, "the Lord comes out of his place to punish the inhabitants of the earth" (v. 21). Significantly, this would also be the time when the innocent blood of God's saints would be disclosed and vindicated (v. 21).

Jesus foretold the time when all of the blood of all the righteous martyrs would be vindicated and judged. It would be in the judgment of Israel, in A. D. 70. See Jesus' emphatic words in Matthew 23, "That upon you may come all the righteous blood shed on the earth, from righteous Abel, to Zecharias, son of Berachias, whom you slew between the temple and the altar. Verily I say unto you, all these things shall come upon this generation" (Matthew 23:35-36). Words could not be plainer.

So, Paul, in Romans 8 draws upon Isaiah 26 for his doctrine of the resurrection. But Isaiah 26 foretold the time when the blood of the martyrs would be vindicated in the Day of the Lord. Jesus said that all of the blood of all the righteous shed on the earth would be judged in his generation, in the judgment of Israel. Therefore, the time of the resurrection of Isaiah 26 / Romans 8 would be at the Day of the Lord in the judgment of Israel in A.D. 70. Seriah cannot posit Romans 8 in the future without denying what Jesus said about the time of the vindication of the martyrs. The time of the vindication of the martyrs in Isaiah 26 is the Day of the Lord of 2 Peter 3. The Day of the Lord of 2 Peter 3 would reveal the new creation of Christ, and bring about the "manifestation of the sons of God" promised in Romans 8. Seriah seeks to divorce these texts from one another, when they are actually wonderfully united in theme, content and focus.

Other commentators, e.g. Jay Adams, claim that while Peter is basing his prophecy on Isaiah 65-66, that all new creation prophecies apply only to "the perfect eternal state."[166] Adams insists that Isaiah 65-66, 2 Peter 3 and Revelation 21 all refer to that state, after the end of time. Gentry opposes this, insisting, "There is no reason, neither is there 'substantial evidence'...for identifying (Isaiah 65:17f) with the perfect eternal state." (*Dominion*, 363). The problem for Adams is that according to Isaiah, *the new creation would only come as a direct result of the destruction of Old Covenant Israel, and the creation of a new people, with a new name.*

Does Adams believe that Israel will be destroyed, and a new people created, with a new name, at the end of time? No. Does he believe that the church, the body of Christ, will be destroyed, and another new people, with another new name, will be created at the end of time? No.

Now since Adams sees an inseparable link between Isaiah, 2 Peter and Revelation, this means that you cannot posit 2 Peter 3 or Revelation within a different context from that demanded by Isaiah. This means that for the new creation to come, Old Covenant Israel must be destroyed at the end of the current Christian age, and God must create another new people at the end of the Christian age. But, if God destroys Israel–not the church–in order to create a new people with a new name, what happens to the church?

You cannot admit that Isaiah, Peter and Revelation all speak of the same future time and events, without thereby demanding a yet future total destruction of Israel. Yet, neither the amillennial, postmillennial, or premillennial eschatologies have a place for what Isaiah emphatically predicted. Only Covenant Eschatology allows for the destruction of Old Covenant Israel, and the creation of a new people with a new name, in the proper historical context. That is at the fall of Jerusalem in A.D. 70. It was at that time that the old people was destroyed, and God identified, vindicated, and glorified His new people, wearing the name of His Son.

> Most eschatologies place fulfillment of Isaiah 65 in the future. Yet, *not one* of the futurist eschatologies have room for what Isaiah emphatically predicts, the destruction of Old Covenant Israel, and the creation of a new people. If your eschatology does not provide for what Isaiah predicted, your eschatology is wrong. Only Covenant Eschatology posits the fulfillment of Isaiah in the proper context, the destruction of Jerusalem in A.D. 70.

In order to avoid some of these problems, some commentators seek to delineate between the various prophecies of Isaiah, Peter, and Revelation 21. Gentry argues that since Isaiah 65 speaks of death in the new creation, and Revelation 21 says there would be no death that these must be two different predictions of two different times and realities. McClish argues that in Isaiah 65, "'the new heavens and a new earth' of verse 17 is a figurative description of the Christian age in which we have the glorious church of Christ with all of the blessings common to it."[167] However, he seeks to delineate between Isaiah, Peter and Revelation by arguing,

> While both Isaiah and John's prophecies say that weeping will cease in the new universe (Isaiah 65:19/Revelation 21:4), there will **still be** death and sin in Isaiah's model (Isaiah 65:19-20). But in the model given by Peter and John absolute life and righteousness will prevail because sin and death and all sinners and sin will be forever banished (2 Peter 3:13; Rev. 20:15; 21:4b, 8, 27; 22:4, 15, 19). I am unable to see how Isaiah could have been referring to Heaven as a place where sin and death exist. (McClish, 1996, 348, his emphasis)

McClish and Gentry make several blunders and false assumptions.

**First**, they overlook the indisputable fact that Peter tells us that his anticipated new creation was foretold by the O. T. prophets. McClish acts as if Peter were receiving a new revelation of a new creation different from that foretold in the O. T.. Peter is patently drawing from the O. T. prophets however. In public debates I have called on my amillennial opponents to produce the O. T. prophecies that they believe Peter was citing, and to then prove that those prophets did predict the end of time. I am still waiting for a response from those debate opponents.

**Second**, the reason McClish delineates between Isaiah, Peter and Revelation is because of his underlying amillennial assumptions. McClish believes that all of the Old Testament, that is, all of God's promises to Israel, were fulfilled absolutely no later than A. D. 70. Most amillennialists in McClish's fellowship believe that God was through with Israel at the Cross, and that the entirety of the O. T. was abrogated there. If therefore, God was through with Israel at the Cross, or A.D. 70 at the latest, then, under no circumstances can McClish admit that 2 Peter 3 or Revelation 21 are related to God's O. T. promises made to Israel.

The amillennial paradigm is false. God was not through with Israel at the Cross as proven by Paul himself in Romans 11:1f, "Has God cast off His people whom He foreknew? God forbid!" Furthermore, Paul's eschatology, Peter's eschatology, and John's eschatology was nothing but that spoken by the prophets, and promised to Israel (see Acts 3:19f; Acts 24:14f; 26:6f; 28:20f). The promise of the resurrection for instance, the core of Paul's gospel, belonged to Israel "after the flesh" (Romans 8:23-9:5). So, McClish's attempt to divorce 2 Peter 3 and Revelation 21 from the O. T. promises made to Israel is misguided.

As just noted certain commentators insist that since there are different elements present, or not present, in given passages that this means the respective passages must be speaking of different times and events. However, this is not necessarily the case.

Bales shows that some prophecies, though they clearly predict the same time and event *seem* to contradict each other and do contradict each other if interpreted literally.[168]

Notice that in Isaiah 34, a prophecy noted earlier, the prophet forecast the utter desolation of Edom, in fact the entire created order! When Edom fell, the very dust of her cities would be turned into pitch. Her streams would catch on fire, and the smoke of her destruction would ascend forever. That is a very graphic scene. Yet, the prophet then describes how the birds, the foxes, and the wild animals would live in the ruins of Edom. Remember now, he had just said that the city would burn "forever and ever." Yet animals would live in the midst of that eternal fire? Was the Lord going to create fire proof animals to live in the flames of Edom?

Taken *literally*, there is an internal and serious contradiction in the text of Isaiah. As McGuiggan says, this kind of language cannot be taken literally, "You can hardly have animals and nettles existing in a lake of quenchless fire, and you can hardly have the earth remaining when the sky has been abolished" (*Isaiah*, 176). If one were to apply the logic of McClish, Jackson,[169] and others, he would have to conclude that Isaiah 34 is speaking of two different times and events since he says things that contrast with each other. This is untenable, however.

Even in Messianic prophecies, there are disparate elements, that if one applied the principles of McClish, Jackson, DeMar and others, you would have to conclude that the respective prophecies speak of different times and events. Yet, these commentators do not make those distinctions.

In Isaiah 11, a prophecy applied to the current blessings of the church by McClish, Jackson, and DeMar, we are told that the lion would eat straw like an ox. However, in Isaiah 35, a Messianic prophecy also applied to the blessings in the Christian age, it says there would be *no lions* in the kingdom. Are we to conclude that Isaiah 11 speaks of a different kingdom or time from Isaiah 35? Not according to these men. They affirm that the prophecies speak of the same time and events.

In Isaiah 2:3f, it speaks of men traveling to Jerusalem to be taught God's Word. Jerusalem is the center of the world. Yet, in Jeremiah 3:15f, Jeremiah foretold the time when men would *no longer travel to Jerusalem* to worship because that would no longer be done, nor even *remembered*.[170]

Finally, as we have noted above, in some prophecies of the Day of the Lord, the sun and moon are magnified in their light (Isaiah 30-31). On the other hand, in other prophecies of blessing at the Day of the Lord, we are told there is no need of the sun or the moon (Isaiah 60:19f).

Thus, to argue that because there are disparate elements in Isaiah and Revelation, i.e. death versus no death, that Revelation could not have been anticipating the imminent fulfillment of Isaiah is to ignore the nature of prophetic language. We should never seek for a wooden literalism of the language of prophecy. It is the language of mental images, word pictures, of graphic imagery. It is not intended to convey precise mathematical detail, or perfect harmony of detail.

What we see then is that the attempt to delineate and divorce Isaiah and 2 Peter 3 and Revelation is misguided. It ignores the nature of prophetic language. It ignores the fact that both 2 Peter and Revelation are concerned with the fulfillment of God's promises to Israel. There is no contrast between Isaiah, Peter and Revelation. They all foretold the same time and the same event, the passing of the old creation of Israel, and the full manifestation of the New Covenant glory of Jesus the Messiah.

155

## Summary of Isaiah 65

We have spent a good bit of time on Isaiah 65, but it is essential to do so. Commentators who do not see that Isaiah lies behind 2 Peter 3 are essentially doomed to a wrong interpretation of 2 Peter 3.

Those who see the connection, but who fail to see that the coming of the Lord in 2 Peter 3 is the coming foretold in Isaiah 64:1f–and at the time of this writing I have not found a single commentator who mentions the connection–tend to make Christ's coming in 2 Peter 3 to be a literal end of time event. Seriah for instance, makes no mention of the fact that the coming of Isaiah 64 is determinative for defining the nature of the parousia of 2 Peter 3, but nonetheless freely admits that Peter was predicting Christ's A.D. 70 parousia.

We have shown that commentators try various ways to either make Isaiah a prediction of the end of time (Adams), or admit that it is predictive of Christ's present kingdom (Gentry, McClish, et. al.), yet insist that Peter and John had something different in mind. We have shown that none of the futurist paradigms fully embrace what Isaiah foretold: the destruction of O. T. Israel and the creation of a new people in the new creation.

What we have done in this section then is to show the importance of:

**1.)** *Acknowledging* that the O. T. is the source of Peter's prophecy.

**2.)** *Identifying* Isaiah 63-65 as the key source of Peter's prophecy.

**3.)** *Understanding* that Isaiah did not predict the end of time.

Isaiah is the source of Peter's prophecy of the Day of the Lord. Isaiah in no way foretold the end of time or a literal, visible, bodily return of Christ. It is therefore *prima facie* evident that 2 Peter 3 is not a prediction of the end of time or of a literal, bodily, visible coming of Jesus Christ.

## THE NEW HEAVENS AND EARTH
## AND THE RESTORATION OF ALL THINGS

Before proceeding to consider Isaiah 66 we need to consider the connection between Peter's anticipated new creation, and the prophesied "restoration of all things" that the same apostle foretold in Acts 3.

As Peter and John entered the Temple area, the crippled man implored them for alms (Acts 3). Unable to give that, they gave him a far greater gift, his health. The excitement generated by this miracle gave rise to one of the most stirring promises, and theologically significant sermons, in scripture.

"Repent, therefore, and be converted, that your sins may be blotted out, so that times of refreshing may come from the presence of the Lord, and that He may send Jesus Christ, who was preached to you before, whom heaven must receive until the times of restoration of all things, which God has spoken by the mouth of all His holy prophets since the world began."

## THE RESTORATION OF ALL THINGS:
## THE HOPE OF ISRAEL

Proper interpretation of Acts 3 clearly depends on the determination of what was to be, or will be, depending on a person's view, restored. The word *apokatastasis* (restoration, Strong's #605) means to restore, to set back to the correct position.[171] Thayer's says it is, "the restoration not only of the true theocracy, but also of that more perfect state of (even physical) things that existed before the fall."[172]

The focus of restoration in Acts 3 was Israel, and through Israel, the restoration of man, not material creation. This is the theme of Acts.[173]

### RESTORATION AND THE PASSING OF THE OLD COVENANT

Peter says the *parousia* –which would bring in the new creation of 2 Peter 3--could not occur until the prophetic declarations of restoration had been fulfilled. Just as 2 Peter 3 said the Day of the Lord would fulfill the prophecies of the Old Covenant prophets, he here says that the restoration of all things would fulfill the *Old Covenant* prophets, Moses, "and all those who have spoken, from Samuel forward." Peter is emphatic about the divine necessity for the yet future *to him*, fulfillment of the Old Covenant. This is acknowledged by commentators who fail to grasp the significance of their own comments. McGarvey says of the O.T. prophecies referred to by Peter, "Not till all are fulfilled will Christ come again."[174]

But, while it is indisputably true that Peter was anticipating the fulfillment of Israel's Old Covenant prophecies, this fact belies most of futurist eschatology. The eminent postmillennialist, Lorraine Boettner claimed: "For information concerning the first coming of Christ, we go to the Old Testament. He came exactly as predicted, and all those prophecies were fulfilled or were forfeited through disobedience. But for information concerning his Second Coming and what future developments will be, we go only to the New Testament."[175] To varying degrees, this view is held by amillennialists and postmillennialists alike, but, it is patently mistaken.

In Matthew 5:17-18, Jesus stated, "not one jot nor one tittle shall pass from the Law until it is all fulfilled." Most amillennialists (e.g. McGarvey, 259), believe the Old Testament was removed at the Cross. Yet, they then assert that the Old Testament prophecies will be valid until the *parousia*.

157

How could the Old Law have been removed at the Cross, and yet mankind be awaiting its fulfillment at Christ's coming? This is a *major* contradiction. As we have shown, the Old Law could not pass until it was all fulfilled (Matthew 5:17-18).[176] All of the Old Covenant would be fulfilled at the *parousia* of Jesus (Acts 3:21). Therefore, the Old Covenant could not pass until the *parousia* of Jesus.

The Old Covenant would remain valid until it was all fulfilled (Matthew 5:17-18). The Old Covenant system was symbolic (prophetic) of coming things, and would remain valid until the time of reformation (i.e. the time of fulfillment, Hebrews 9:6-10). The Old Covenant system was still *unfulfilled* when Hebrews was written (Hebrews 9:9; circa A. D. 60+). Therefore, the Old Covenant system was still valid when Hebrews was written (A.D. 60+).

The Old Covenant Law could not pass until it was all fulfilled (Matthew 5:17-18). All of the Old Covenant would be fulfilled by the time of, and in the events of the fall of Jerusalem in A.D. 70 (Luke 21:22). Therefore the Old Covenant Law and system could not pass, until the time of and in the events of the fall of Jerusalem in A.D. 70.

To affirm that the Old Testament ended at the Cross, and that Christ gave a new set of eschatological predictions, is to deny what Peter says. Peter's hope of the *parousia* was tied inextricably to the fulfillment of the O. T prophets.[177] The *parousia* would fulfill those prophets.

If the Old Covenant has been fulfilled and removed, then *the restoration of all things* has been fulfilled, *Christ must have come.* The Day of the Lord of 2 Peter 3 is fulfilled. The new creation is a reality in Christ. The *parousia* was to be the crowning act of fulfillment and restoration. Any attempt to posit the revelation of Christ into the future, implicitly re-establishes the Old Covenant and Israel as the Covenant people awaiting her promises.

## RESTORATION AND THE *PAROUSIA*

The word that Peter used to speak of the new creation at the *parousia* is translated as restoration. It is the word *apokatastasis* (Strong's #605). *Apokatastasis* means, "to put back into the original condition."[178] This is a distinctive word used by the prophets to speak of the restoration of Israel. Malachi 4:6 said that the coming Elijah would turn (verbal form of *apokatastasis*), the hearts of the children to the fathers. The disciples used a verbal form of the word when they asked Jesus if he was about to "restore the kingdom to Israel" (Acts 1:6). This word represented their Messianic kingdom hopes.

We want also to take note of another word *diorthosis* (Strong's #1357). This word also means to "restore something to its natural and normal condition."[179] In Isaiah 62:7 Jehovah promised to "establish" Jerusalem at the coming of the Lord in judgment (v.11-12) Thus, the Old Covenant prophets, in speaking of the restoration of Israel, used *apokatastasis* and *diorthosis* as synonyms. Ellingworth says that *apokatastasis* and *diorthosis* convey the same ideas, and speak of the eschatological consummation.[180]

So, what we have is that the O. T. prophets use these two words (in the LXX, the Greek translation of the Hebrew) synonymously. Further, the lexicons define the two words the same. And, commentators on the Greek tell us that the two words are synonymous.

This is significant when we compare Acts 3 with Hebrews 9:6-10. Like *apokatastasis*, *diorthosis* is used to speak of the fulfillment of Israel's Messianic hope. In Hebrews 9, the writer speaks of the symbolic (prophetic) significance of the Old Testament cultus. Specifically, his focus is on the high priest and his service on the Day of Atonement, and then the wider application of the entire liturgical system that stood in, "foods and drinks, various washings, and fleshly ordinances until the time of *reformation*"(*diorthosis*, 9:10).

It is imperative to honor the author's temporal perspective. When he spoke of the O.T. system he says, "which is symbolic for the present time" (v. 9). The "present time" was *his first century time*, not our present day. Otherwise, the Old Covenant cultus still stands as a type and shadow of the "good things to come" (Hebrews 10:1-4).

The writer emphasizes that as long as the Old Covenant cultus had[181] validity[182] there could be no access to the Presence of God (v. 8). This means man could not be restored to the Garden. He shows that Christ sacrificed himself and entered into the Most Holy to prepare it for man (v.23-24), and that he was to return "for salvation" to those who, "eagerly await Him" (v. 28). Christ would appear (the *parousia*) to bring man into the Presence of God, back to the Garden, where the Old Covenant could never bring him. The coming of Christ would bring in the new creation of 2 Peter 3.

The writer's point is that the Old Covenant worship signified (prophesied) the coming of better things. As long as the Old Covenant stood *unfulfilled*, there was no access to the Father. Those Mosaic institutions were imposed until the time of their fulfillment, the time of "reformation" (v. 10). Through fulfillment, the typological significance of the old system would pass, and man would be brought into the Presence of the Father, at the *parousia* (Hebrews 9:24-28). Man could enter the Presence because of the

New Covenant relationship of *righteousness* in Christ, as opposed to being separated by the old veil and Torah. Notice the correlation with Acts 3.

Peter says Christ would come when all that the Old Covenant prophets predicted, was fulfilled. (Don't forget that the Day of the Lord in 2 Peter 3 would be in fulfillment of the O. T. prophets). Hebrews says the Old Testament was typological, intended to stand only until what it foretold was fulfilled. Peter anticipated the *"restoration* of all things"–and the new heavens and earth. Hebrews anticipated the "time of *reformation."* The eschatological significance of this correlation cannot be over-emphasized.

The Greek words *apokatastasis* (*restoration,* Acts 3:21) and *diorthosis* (*reformation,* Hebrews 9:10), are synonymous, referring to the same time and event.

Jesus' parousia –to consummate the restoration of all things– was to occur at the time of the *apokatastasis* (Acts 3:21).

Therefore, Jesus' Second Coming was to occur at the time of the *diorthosis* (reformation, Hebrews 9:10, 28), when man would be brought into the Presence of God (Hebrews 9:28).

Jesus was to come at the time of restoration/reformation, (Acts 3; Hebrews 9:10, 28).

But the time of reformation (*diorthosis*) was *to come at the end of the Old Covenant age* (Hebrews 9:10).

Therefore, *Jesus' parousia would occur at the end of Old Covenant age.*

*This argument shows conclusively that Christ's coming was not, and is not to occur at the end of the Christian age.* Notice what this means for the interpretation of 2 Peter 3.

**The coming of Christ of Acts 3 is the same coming of Christ in 2 Peter 3.**

**But the coming of Christ of Acts 3, the time of the *apokatastasis/diorthosis*, would be at the end of the Old Covenant age of Israel (Hebrews 9:10-28).**

**Therefore, the coming of Christ in 2 Peter 3 would be at the end of the Old Covenant age of Israel.**

The covenantal framework of 2 Peter 3 and the *parousia* is established. Unless one can prove that the "restoration of all things" in Acts 3 is referent to something different from the new creation "wherein dwells righteousness" of 2 Peter 3, then this argument stands. Unless one can prove that the *apokatastasis* and the *diorthosis* refer to two totally different hopes of Israel–two totally different "setting things right" -- then our argument stands. Biblical eschatology is *Covenantal,* and not Historical.

160

Peter's affirmation, in both Acts 3 and 2 Peter 3, of the absolute necessity for the fulfillment of the O. T. prophetic hopes, culminating in the *parousia*, shows that the Old Covenant would remain valid until the *parousia*. This is confirmed by Matthew 5:17-18, where, as you will remember, Jesus said that not one single crossing of the "t" or dotting of the "i" would pass from the Old Law until it was *all* fulfilled.

The correlation of Acts 3, with Hebrews 9, and 2 Peter 3 is remarkable. All three texts anticipated the fulfillment of the Old Testament promises made to Israel. All three texts anticipated the arrival of the new world, the world of righteousness, the new creation. Unless 2 Peter 3 was anticipating a different salvation, a different new creation, a different restoration of all things, a different eschatology, a different *parousia* from Acts and Hebrews, then the vision of the new creation, in 2 Peter 3 is a vision of the New Covenant world of Christ.

In Hebrews, man would be brought into the presence of God in the, "heavenly Jerusalem" (Hebrews 12:21f), because the Old Jerusalem was not to abide (13:14). The old system, the old heaven and earth, was even then "nigh unto passing away," giving way to the "unmovable" kingdom (Hebrews 8:13; 12:25-28). In 2 Peter 3, man would be brought into the new heavens and earth at the *parousia* of the Lord (2 Peter 3:10-13).

Israel and her covenant, via the veil in the Temple, epitomized separation from God. The Old Law had become the, "ministration of death" (2 Corinthians 3:6f), and thus exacerbated the problem of sin and death introduced by Adam (Romans 5-8). The Law could not give life, but it promised the coming of life (John 5:39). The Law was only given to prepare man for the arrival of the "second Adam" (Romans 5/ 1 Corinthians 15), who would restore man. The new creation promises to Israel are the promises of that restoration.

If the "restoration of all things"and the new creation remains unfulfilled, the Old Covenant remains valid today. Israel has not received her salvation. If this is the case, salvation for the nations still awaits fulfillment. Praise God that He kept His promises to Israel, and as a result salvation is now available to all of every nation! Man has access, in Christ, to the River of Life and the Tree of Life. The restoration of all things has occurred.

## ISAIAH 66

Since we have spent so much time on Isaiah 65, we will only briefly survey Isaiah 66. In this set of verses, which promised the new heavens and earth, there is more than a passing similarity with 2 Peter 3. The relevant aspects of this passage, vs.14-24, are as follows:

**1.)** The coming of the Lord in fire (v.15-16).

**2.)** Destruction of God's enemies (v.15-16).

**3.)** Raising of an ensign for the nations (v. 19).

**4.)** Evangelism (v. 19).

**5.)** Evangelism among the Gentiles (v.19).

**6.)** Worship in Jerusalem (v.20).

**7.)** New order of priests to be ministers (v. 21).

**8.)** New heavens and earth in which worship, service and evangelism to occur (v.22f).

The prophet uses typical prophetic language when he says the Lord would come with fire and chariots to judge his enemies. Furthermore, we cannot overemphasize what we have already shown, and that is that this coming of the Lord, is the coming of the Lord of Isaiah 64. The Lord was going to come from heaven, rend the earth, and make the mountains tremble at His presence *as He had come in the past!* This means without any doubt that the coming of the Lord in Isaiah 66 cannot be referent to a literal end of time coming of Jehovah, or Jesus, out of heaven. See again the section above on the Day of the Lord. The idea is that God would act. And any time God acted to punish his enemies it is called the coming of the Lord, the Day of the Lord, the day of visitation, or some similar term.

The priestly prophet said that in the new creation God would raise an ensign among the nations. This is an allusion to the coming of Jesus and Paul is emphatic that Christ, the ensign foretold by Isaiah had been raised (Romans 15:8f). Now if Paul believed that he was living in the time of the raising of the ensign, then he believed that he was living in the time for the coming of the Lord foretold by Isaiah.

But the prophet says in the new heavens and earth, after the coming of the Lord, after the judging of his enemies, the remnant, "them who escape," would be sent to the nations. Why would they be sent? To preach the word of God and gather God's people, "they shall bring all your brethren for an offering to the Lord" (v. 20). Is this not also the very thing Jesus said would happen, in Matthew 24? He foretold the calamities of Jerusalem's demise and said, "Immediately after the tribulation of those days the sun will be darkened and the moon will not give its light, the stars will fall from heaven and the powers of the heavens will be shaken. Then the sign of the Son of Man will appear in the heaven and then all the tribes of the earth will mourn and they will see the Son of Man coming on the clouds of heaven with

162

power and great glory. And He will send His angels with a great sound of a trumpet, and they will gather together his elect from the four winds, from one end of heaven to the other" (vs 29-31).

Here you have Jesus coming in the clouds to judge his enemies (cf. Isaiah 66:15), and the gathering of God's elect. It will not do to argue that the Gentiles were brought in prior to the fall of Jerusalem, therefore the passages in Isaiah and Matthew are different. Jesus realized this would happen when he made his statements in Matthew 24. Yet he declared all of that would happen in his generation. He, nor Isaiah, were excluding any Gentile evangelism prior to or after the coming of the Lord, they were simply focused on the Day of the Lord itself.

Isaiah said there would be evangelism in the new creation. This fits the picture of Revelation 21-22 quite well, since the nations of the earth come into the City for healing. The new heavens and new earth cannot be an existence after the end of time and destruction of earth. Evangelism implies telling the good news of salvation, but salvation from what? From *sin*. Will there be sin in heaven? How then can we interpret Isaiah's prophecy to speak of the glories of heaven? Remember, Peter says in the new creation which they looked for, righteousness would dwell. Righteousness involves the keeping of the will of God. Heaven is the *reward* for living righteously while here on earth. But this is not all.

Isaiah said this evangelism would take place among the nations that did not know God, as well as among the Jews. Does this not demand a Messianic fulfillment? This evangelism would occur *after the coming of the Lord in fire to judge the wicked*. The coming of the Lord in view then, cannot be the incarnation and personal ministry of Jesus. That coming was the coming of the gentle servant of Isaiah 42. The coming in view here is the same as envisioned by Malachi, the coming of the Great and Terrible Day of the Lord (Malachi 4:5). This is the day the Immerser warned his listeners to beware of in Matthew 3 when he said Jesus would baptize with fire, his fan was already in his hand, and the axe was already at the root. The only scenario which fits this prophecy is that described by Jesus in Matthew 24.

This interpretation receives further corroboration from Isaiah's prediction of a new order of priests. The prophecy says of those gathered from the nations, and that would include both Jew and "pagan," that God would, "take some of them for priests and Levites" (v.21). He did not say He would pick the Levites out from those that had been converted. He said He would take of those who had been brought, and remember this included Jew and non-Jew, *to be Levites*. The old Levitical requirements would no longer be effective. *God would make a new order of priests.*

Due to the work of Jesus, there is now a new priesthood. The old has been changed (Hebrews 7:12-19), removed with the demise of the temple in A.D. 70. We are now a kingdom of priests (Revelation 1:5-6). There are now new sacrifices to be offered (Romans 12:1-2; Hebrews 13:15-16; I Peter 2:5f).

In summation:

➡ Peter's prediction of the new creation is from the O. T..

➡ The specific O. T. prediction of the new creation is Isaiah 63-66.

➡ Isaiah 65-66 foretold the new creation at the time of the destruction of Old Covenant Israel.

➡ This means that Peter's prediction of the new creation would be fulfilled at the time of the destruction of Old Covenant Israel.

In addition:

✔ Peter's prediction of the new creation is from the O.T.

✔ Jesus said that none of the O. T. could pass until it was all fulfilled.

✔ Therefore, if 2 Peter 3 is not fulfilled, *then none of the O. T. has passed away.*

We need now to define the term "the heavens and earth," as used by Peter and other Biblical writers.

## WHAT HEAVEN AND EARTH?

Peter did not have the physical universe, the physical heavens and earth, in mind when he spoke of the dissolution of the heavens and earth. The study done early in this book on the Day of the Lord should help the reader understand that in prophetic language when God speaks of the fall of a *world* He puts it in terms which sound like He means the earth or creation.

We do not suggest that the Bible never uses the term "heavens and earth" in a literal way. It does. However, what we are suggesting, is that in apocalyptic, prophetic language of *the Day of the Lord*, the term heavens and earth bears a metaphoric definition. Not only that, but in Jewish writings of the first century, the term "heaven and earth" was used to speak of the Temple itself, "The proportion of the measurement of the Tabernacle proved to be an imitation of the system of the world; for that third part thereof which was within the four pillars, to which the priests were admitted, is, as it were, a Heaven peculiar to God; but the space of the twenty cubics, is, as it were, sea and land, on which men live, and so this is peculiar to the priests only." (Josephus, *Antiquities*, Bk. 3:6:4; cf. 3:7:7)

164

It is lamentable that some commentators are so desperate to avoid the metaphoric nature of Biblical language that they are willing to make astounding claims, claims that are so patently false, that one wonders at the frame of mind of those who make them.

Ice appeals to Matthew 24.35 to show that "heaven and earth" cannot be used metaphorically.[183] I contend that in Matthew 24.35 Jesus was referring to the Old Covenant Temple as heaven and earth. Ice argues, "This passage clearly states that, 'heaven and earth *will* pass away' one day, but in contrast to that Christ's words 'shall not pass away.' In order to strengthen the emphasis upon the absolute impossibility of His words passing away, Christ uses not one, but two Greek words that mean "not," (grouped together), to say that something will not happen.[184] 'The double negative *ou me* with the subjunctive is the usual form for the emphatic negation,' notes Randolph Yeager.[185] Lenski agrees and says that *ou me* is used 'all-inclusively' and calls it 'the strongest negation.'"[186] Furthermore, Arnold Fruchtenbaum, oft cited by Ice, says "The law of Christ will never be rendered inoperable."[187] About all I can say to this is, Amen!

Ice's appeal to this text destroys his own theological paradigm. In the millennial view, Matthew 24:29f is the second coming of Christ, to *initiate* the millennial reign. However, v. 35 is the summary statement, reiterating and summarizing v. 29-31. The problem is that in the millennial view, the heaven and earth is not destroyed until *the end of the millennium*. So, if v. 35 is the summary of v. 29f, and if v. 29f is referent to the parousia of Christ to initiate the millennium, then literal heaven and earth are destroyed at Christ's second coming, i.e. at the beginning of the millennium. You cannot insert a 1000 year gap between v. 29f and v. 35. Thus, by appealing to Matthew 24:35 as proof of the passing of literal creation, Ice has created a problem of epic proportions for the millennial view of things.

As Ice insists, Jesus was emphatically telling his disciples that his word will never pass away. That could not be clearer, and *that is precisely what I affirm*. However, *what is the word of Christ?* Is it not the gospel of Jesus Christ? Would *anyone* deny that? Follow closely.

The word of Christ will never pass away (Matthew 24.35, Ice /Fruchtenbaum). The word of Christ *is the current gospel, the Covenant of Grace preached by the church among men for salvation*. Therefore, the gospel of Jesus Christ–the current Covenant of Grace preached among men for salvation *will never pass away*. Does this not demand that the "heaven and earth" that Jesus was speaking of was a metaphoric reference to the Old Covenant world of Israel? But there is more.

165

The gospel of Christ will never be inoperable (Ice/Fruchtenbaum). But, the gospel of Christ condemns physical circumcision as a religious act, negates temple worship, in Jerusalem, with the offering of animal sacrifices. Therefore, the gospel of Christ will always condemn physical circumcision as a religious act, will always negate temple worship, in Jerusalem, with the offering of animal sacrifices. This means, *prima facie*, that the millennial doctrine of the restoration of Israel is totally falsified by the fact that the gospel will never pass away. There is *still more*.

Millennialists tell us that the rapture brings the church age to an end. Yet, it is the gospel that created and sustains, is the heart and core of the church age. *The church age is the gospel age. You cannot bring the church age to an end without thereby nullifying the gospel itself!* This being true, notice the argument:

The gospel will never pass away, and will never be rendered inoperable (Ice/Fruchtenbaum). But, the millennial rapture doctrine demands the termination of the gospel age, and the suspension or negation of the gospel doctrines that condemn physical circumcision as a religious act, negates temple worship, in Jerusalem, with the offering of animal sacrifices. Now, how can it be true that the gospel will never be rendered inoperable, and yet, the things that it condemns be restored in the millennial kingdom? The millennial concession that the gospel will never pass away, or be rendered inoperable, forces us to see Matthew 24:35 as referent to a metaphoric "heaven and earth." As just seen, Josephus helps us with that identification.

To the Jewish mind, the Temple was a symbolic "heaven and earth." As Fletcher-Louis says, "The temple was far more than the point at which heaven and earth met. Rather, it was thought to correspond to, represent, or in some sense, to be 'heaven and earth' in its totality."[188] In Matthew 24, the topic was the destruction of that temple (Matthew 24:2-3). Jesus describes the destruction of that incredibly significant covenantal edifice, and contrasts it with his own covenant creation. The old heaven and earth of the Temple would pass. Jesus' new heaven and earth of the new creation, will never pass away. See our longer discussion of the Jewish concept of the temple as the "heaven and earth" in chapter 12 below

The point is that Jesus did affirm that his word, the gospel which is concerned not only with the "salvation of the soul," but with teaching men how to live in time, on earth, among men, will never pass away. And this presents a daunting challenge to the idea that v. 35 is talking about the collapse of the time-space world. As Fletcher-Louis says, "If there is here, a promise that Jesus' teaching as a whole will endure the collapse of the space-time universe, then one has to wonder what role it will have beyond the end of history when His teaching quite clearly prescribes the lifestyle of the people of God *within* history." (*Destruction*, 49)

Another central text to corroborate this contention is Matthew 5:17-18. Jesus said, "*Till* heaven and earth pass away one jot or one tittle will by no means pass from the law *till* all is fulfilled." Please observe that the word "till" occurs not once, but twice. And it is the first "till" that is so often ignored. Many commentators simply pass over the verse by trying to make the words apply to the words of Jesus. That is, they have Jesus saying the word of God would not pass away. Physical creation would pass away, but not the word of God. *This is not what Jesus said.*

Jesus tells his listeners he did not come to destroy the law and prophets. The law and prophets were the *Mosaic Covenant*. He reassures his audience that *until heaven and earth passed* not one iota of the law would pass. He tells them *it would pass when it was fulfilled.*

Now if Jesus was asserting, as some suggest, the eternality of the Word, then he was asserting the unending nature *of the Mosaic Covenant.* Jesus was not referring to the gospel. He was referring to the Law of Moses. If he was referring to the physical heavens and earth, he was saying the Old Law would not pass *until the physical creation passed.* But scriptures are too emphatic in declaring the Old Covenant was on the verge of passing away in the first century (Hebrews 8:13; 12:25f).[189]

Notice the dilemma for Ice. He claims that the term "heaven and earth" is never used metaphorically in the Bible. However, Jesus said "until heaven and earth" pass away, *the Mosaic Law–and that includes the sacrificial system--would not pass.* Therefore, since "heaven and earth" is never used metaphorically, per Ice, this means that the Mosaic Law–including the sacrificial system-- will not pass until the literal heaven and earth passes. Of course, Ice contradicts himself, since he affirms that the Mosaic Law, "has forever been fulfilled and discontinued through Christ." (*Prophecy*, 258) So, on the one hand Ice says that "heaven and earth" is never used metaphorically, but then he takes a position that demands that "heaven and earth" was used metaphorically. If the Law has passed, the "heaven and earth" have passed.

Jesus said until the law was *fulfilled* it would not pass away. He said *when it was fulfilled it would pass away.* Now if the law has passed away, *then heaven and earth has passed away.* And if the "heavens and earth" have not passed away, *then the Old Covenant has not been fulfilled and passed away.* Jesus said the passing of the Old Law was dependent on two things, the passing away of heaven and earth, and the fulfillment of the law. Since Jesus patently declared that heaven and earth must pass before the Old Law could pass, this necessarily means that the heaven and earth he had in mind is not the physical creation. Let's look at some other key texts.

### Hebrews 12:25f

The Hebrew writer presents many contrasts between the new, better way of Jesus, and the old way. In the verses before us he presents what may be considered one of the finest pieces of logical argument to be found in Holy Writ. Unfortunately many commentators, Milligan, Fudge, Interpreters Bible, Lenski, Pulpit, etc. view this as a prophecy of the destruction of the physical universe. This position is untenable.

Notice the author's line of thought. He alludes to the giving of the Law at Sinai and the One who spoke from earth. He says that Voice then shook the earth (v. 26). He then quotes the prophecy of Haggai 2:6f in which God promised, "Once more I will shake heaven and earth." The explanation given by Hebrews 12:27 of Haggai 2:6 is that God, when He promised to shake not only earth but heaven also, meant to remove "the heaven and earth." To shake something, the writer tells us, is to remove it.

Why was God going to shake the heavens and earth? The writer informs us that God was going to remove heaven and earth, *so that*, that which cannot be shaken might remain (v. 27). In other words, the unshakable would not come *until* the heaven and earth had been removed. Now if heaven and earth had to be removed so that the unshakable could come, then if the unshakable was at the time *being given*, it must be true that heaven and earth either had, or was in the process of passing away.

Is it not tragic that we so often quote verses for years and never really know the verses which come before and after? This is the case with Hebrews 12:28. In debates with millennialists, amillennialists have shown that the everlasting kingdom prophesied by Daniel 2:44 was, at the very time Hebrews was written, being given. Daniel foretold the establishment of the kingdom that can never be moved, Hebrews speaks of them currently receiving the kingdom that cannot be moved. That proves it is not to come in 2000 years. It was a reality in the first century. What has been missed is the fact that if they were receiving the unshakable kingdom, then this means that *"heaven and earth" was passing away.* Not the material creation to be sure, but the heavens and earth of the Jewish *aion*.

If heaven and earth had to pass away so that the unshakable could remain, and if the unshakable was being given, then it must be true that the heavens and earth were passing away. Put another way, the unshakable could not come until the passing of the heavens and the earth (v. 27). *But, the unshakable was being received at the time of Hebrews.* Therefore, the heavens and earth were passing away. Obviously the heavens and earth in view cannot be the material creation. This should not surprise us.

Hebrews presents over and over the contrast of the glory of Jesus and the new creation over the old. Jesus is better than angels, Moses, the prophets, the Levitical priests, animal sacrifices, the temple, the law, or anything else. It is he that is in control of "the world to come" (2:5f). It is because of his New Covenant that the old is "ready to vanish away" (8:13). That old tabernacle was only to stand until the time of reformation (9:8-10). Jesus sits on the right hand of the Father waiting until his enemies are made his footstool (10:12-13). The book of Hebrews is vibrant with anticipation of the coming new order, yet somber with the sense of a dying old world. The fiery judgment awaits the disobedient (10:27f). And the one coming will come very soon (10:37). Is it any wonder then that the writer in chapter 12 summarizes the passing of the old order under the imagery of the heavens and earth? The entire world of the Jews was about to crumble around their heads under the inexorable march of the everlasting kingdom of God!

Lane takes note of the fact that many commentators apply Hebrews 12 to the dissolution of the material creation. However, as he notes, "The explicit association of 'the earth' with Sinai and the Old Covenant (vv. 25b, 26a) implies that the 'heaven' is to be associated with the New Covenant (v. 25ac). 'Earth' and 'heaven' are symbols of the revelation at Sinai and of the New Covenant revelation to the writer's generation, respectively."[190] The old heaven and earth of Israel was about to pass away. The unending new creation of Messiah was about to be fully revealed.

While Hebrews 12 does not use the *specific term* "new heavens and earth" this is the import of the text. And since the passage is not talking of the dissolution of the natural creation, rather, the passing of the old world of Judaism it sheds light on 2 Peter 3. It helps us see how the Jewish mind thought. We should therefore, be hesitant to discard these concepts just because we are not familiar with them. On the contrary, we must, if we would be good Bible students, learn to think as much like them as possible.

## YOU HAVE COME TO MOUNT ZION!

There is something else to consider to help us determine that the heavens and earth that were to pass in Hebrews 12 must be seen as a metaphoric referent to the Old Covenant world of Israel. The writer contrasts Mt. Sinai with Mt. Zion, "you have come to Mt. Zion, and to the city of the Living God" (Hebrews 12:22). In Jewish eschatological thought, there is nothing more central than *Zion*.

In what is known as the "little apocalypse" (Isaiah 24-29), Isaiah described Israel's future--her judgment and her salvation. In Isaiah 24:1-3 we find the destruction of creation. Verse 5 tells us the reason, "they have broken the everlasting covenant." *This is a judgment determined because Israel broke her Old Covenant with Jehovah.* This would be a judgment of fire (v. 6), and earthquake (v. 19) when, "the earth is violently broken, the earth is split open, the earth is shaken exceedingly...it will fall and not rise again" (v. 19-20). Here is the destruction of "heaven and earth" in the context of judgment on Israel.

In Isaiah 24:21-23 the Lord judges the wicked and in verse 23 He reigns, "For the Lord of hosts will reign on Mount Zion and in Jerusalem and before His elders gloriously." See Revelation 5.

Chapter 25 continues the Messianic predictions. In verse 6 we find the removal of the veil/curse mentioned in 24:4-6. The Lord prepares a great banquet "in this mountain, (Zion! DKP) the Lord of hosts will make for all people a feast of choice pieces." This is the Messianic Banquet so central to Jesus' public teaching. See Matthew 8:11; Matthew 22; Luke 14:14; Luke 22:29f; Revelation 19, etc.

In verse 8 God promises to destroy death and take away all tears from the eyes. In verse 9 we find *the climax of Israel's prophetic history,* "Behold, this is our God; We have waited for Him and He will save us. This is the Lord; We have waited for Him we will be glad and rejoice in His salvation." Hebrews 12 is a clear affirmation that the zenith of Israel's hopes was near. Since Hebrews 12 and 2 Peter 3 are parallel, this means, once again, that we must view 2 Peter 3 within the confines of God's promises to Israel. It is not about the end of human history.

---

**For the writer of Hebrews to say, "You have come to Mt. Zion" was an affirmation that the time for the passing of "heaven and earth" had come. The time for the resurrection had come. The time for the Messianic Banquet had come. The time for God's rule had arrived! The climax of *Israel's history* was near.**

---

170

The point is that Isaiah posited salvation in Zion, after death and "heaven and earth" were destroyed. When this happened, the Messianic feast would be prepared and enjoyed on Zion, where Jehovah would reign.

Patently, if Isaiah was predicting the destruction of literal heaven and earth, that it would be impossible for Jehovah to reign on earth, in Zion, and for the saints to rule with Him in Zion, and enjoy the Messianic Banquet there. Literal Zion would no longer exist, if "heaven and earth" were destroyed. The destruction of creation has to be taken metaphorically, and, in Isaiah we get a taste of the centrality of Zion in Israel's Messianic hope.

So, for the writer of Hebrews to affirm "you have come to Mt. Zion," was an incredible statement. Wrapped up in the word "Zion" are all of the eschatological and soteriological motifs that one could imagine. It said that the time of the resurrection, the Messianic Banquet, the judgment and destruction of those who had "violated the everlasting covenant" had come. *The climax of Israel's history had arrived.*

All of this means of course, that in Hebrews 12, the author was not anticipating the passing of literal heaven and earth when he spoke of the shaking of the heavens and earth. He was anticipating the removal of the heavens and earth foretold by Isaiah. It was Old Covenant Israel that was about to be shaken and removed.

Since the prophets used the term the heavens and the earth to refer to the world of Judaism, is it strange then, if Peter, that devout Jew, describes the demise of that glorious and beloved system in the words of the prophets? If Isaiah called that system the heavens and earth, if Jesus did, if the writer of Hebrews did, why is it hard to believe that Peter does the same in 2 Peter 3? He would simply be following the style of the earlier prophets and using words and thoughts familiar to all.

A common problem facing the modern student of the Bible is the disposition to look at scriptures from a Greek, occidental, world view, instead of the Hebraic world view. Holland cautions against imposing our Greek mind-set on the Hebrew scriptures, "While the vocabulary of the N.T. could be found throughout the Hellenistic world, it did not have the same meaning when it was used in the religious sense within the Jewish community."[191] He notes that when a N.T. writer wrote in Greek it was, "Hebrew in its mind-set and essential meaning." (*Contours*, 52). Wilson likewise urges the modern Bible student to understand that proper Bible interpretation begins with an understanding of the Hebraic world view. The challenge is to become intimately familiar with how the Hebrew scriptures used the terms.[192] Yet, few Bible students today seem to be aware of the vast

171

difference between the Hebraic mind-set and the Hellenistic. The old cliche "The Bible says what it means and means what it says," is naively cited as a sort of mantra, without any concern for proper hermeneutic.

Peter did in fact, use the term new heavens and earth in the same way as did the prophets. Since we have shown that what the earlier promises meant was the Messianic kingdom established on earth, (although not an "earthly kingdom"), the conclusion is inescapable that the new heavens and earth which Peter anticipated was the consummated kingdom of Christ triumphant over her persecuting foe, Judaism. The heavens and earth that was about to perish was that old decaying heaven and earth of Judaism.

For space considerations we will confine our study of the new heavens and earth to one further passage. The priestly prophet wrote:

"But I am the Lord your God, who divided the sea whose waves roared- The Lord of Hosts is his name. And I have put my word in your mouth, I have covered you with the shadow of my hand, That I may plant the heavens, Lay the foundation of the earth, And say to Zion, 'You are my people.'" (Isaiah 51:15-16, New King James)

The NIV renders this, instead of "to plant the heavens," as, "I who planted the heavens." But the KJV, NKJV, ASV, NASV, all concur in the above rendition. McGuiggan says the KJV is based on the Masoretic text and comments on such translations as the NIV, "Perhaps this is the way we should go but it doesn't always help to dismiss the more difficult reading because we think it doesn't 'make sense.'"[193] The noted commentators Keil and Delitzsch, as well as Leupold, Barnes, and Clark concur with the KJV rendering, although they *interpret* it as advert to the millennium.

Take note that God says to Israel that He gave them His word, an allusion to the Mosaic Covenant, *to plant the heavens, lay the foundations of the earth, and establish them as His people.* God is not saying that He established the natural creation for Israel to occupy. He said He gave them the Old Law to establish the heavens and earth! Now the material creation existed long before God gave Torah to Israel, but He says He gave the Law to them to establish heaven and earth. He not only gave Torah to them to establish heaven and earth, He gave it to them that they may be His covenant people. This places the law in view as the Sinaiatic covenant. If this is true, it is inescapable that that is also when and where the heavens and earth He has in mind was established.

God gave His word to Israel to establish their world. Their world was spoken of here as the heavens and earth. This is confirmed when Jehovah says He gave the Word to Israel, not only to establish the heavens and earth

172

but *to make them His people*. Isaiah places the establishing of the heavens and earth, and the entering into covenantal relationship as when God gave His law to Israel. This was at Sinai. Therefore, in the eyes of God and Israel, the heavens and earth were established at Sinai. Obviously not the physical creation, but the world of Israel.

## THE WORLD TO COME

Consistent with the view presented above, that the new heavens and earth for which Peter longed was the predicted kingdom of God, is the fact that the New Testament also looked for "the world to come." More accurately, they looked for "the *age* to come." The "age to come" was nothing less than the new creation.

We want to present three facts about the first century belief concerning "this age" and "the age to come." Simply stated, the Jews, and more importantly Jesus and the N. T. authors, believed the following:

**1.)** They believed in only two ages, what they called "this age" and "the age to come."

**2.)** They believed that "this age" was the age of Moses and the Law. The "age to Come" was to be the age of Messiah and the New Covenant.

**3.)** The age of Moses and the Law, "this age," was to end. However, "the age to come" *would never end*. Reiser has done a good job of not only delineating these beliefs, but of showing, as Wright, McKnight and others have done, that Jewish eschatology was not about the end of time, or the destruction of material creation, but of a dramatic intervention of Jehovah into history, to bring man, still living on earth, into His presence.[194]

In light of these beliefs, one has to ask, If the age to come was to never end, and if the current Christian age is the age to come, then when we interpret 2 Peter 3, it cannot mean the end of the current Christian age. This is critical, and yet, the fundamental fact that the current age of Christ has no end (Ephesians 3:20-21), is one of the most ignored facts in scripture.

> How can 2 Peter 3 be the end of the current Christian age at the end of time if the Bible teaches, repeatedly, that the current Christian age has no end? This is a major contradiction that is ignored by virtually all commentators!

With these facts in mind, let us turn now to examine what the New Testament has to say about "the age to come."

## MATTHEW 12:31-32

When Jesus was speaking of the sin against the Holy Spirit he maintained that blasphemy against the Holy Spirit, "will not be forgiven him, either in this age or in the age to come."

Barnes says Jesus meant to say that the one blaspheming the Spirit "can never obtain forgiveness."[195] Nicoll says Jesus meant the one guilty of this sin could not be forgiven either before death or after.[196] Lenski says the term "neither in this age nor the age to come," simply means the person could receive no forgiveness "neither in time nor in eternity." These interpretations will not stand close scrutiny.

When Jesus spoke of the age to come he was using an idiom of the Jewish world of his day. Schurer tells how deep seated the belief was of the coming new world of the Messiah.[197] It was believed that after a period of intense suffering, called "the time of Messiah's trouble," and the "birth-pangs of Messiah" (cf. Matthew 24:8), the Messiah would usher in "the age to come" at his coming. From the New Testament perspective, this new age was about to dawn (1 John 2:8; 2 Peter 1:16f).

The kingdom had been established in infancy at Pentecost, it would be perfected, the "age to come" would be finally realized after the troublesome time of the passing away of "this present age," the antiquated Mosaic World. Matthew 12 demands that "the age to come" be understood not as timeless eternity after the destruction of material creation, not as heaven, but as the now present age of Messiah.

Ask yourself a simple question: In what age was Jesus living while on earth? Galatians 4:4 contains the definitive answer. He was born under the law of Moses. By *any standard*, the Old Law did not pass until the cross, even though properly, the Law did not actually pass at the cross as many contend. Thus another question should be self answering, Under what age, under what law was Jesus living when he said that blasphemy of the Spirit would not be forgiven "in this age, or the age to come"? Since Jesus was patently living under the Mosaic Age, does it not follow that "this age" of which he spoke was the Mosaic Age? Since "this age" was the Mosaic Age, does it not follow that "the age to come" is referent to the Messianic or Christian age? This has Jesus saying that blasphemy of the Holy Spirit would not be forgiven either in the Mosaic Age or in the Christian age. This is the only interpretation that does not engage the interpreter in extreme difficulties.

Jesus is speaking of the forgiveness of sin. He said that every sin, even blasphemy against him, would be forgiven "in this age." But blasphemy of the Spirit would not be forgiven "in this age" or "the age to come." Now if the age to come is heaven as many expositors suggest, then it is most assuredly true that there will be the possibility of blasphemy in heaven.

Coffman says, "One should avoid reading into this passage any hope that some sins will be forgiven in the world to come which remain unforgiven now."[198] But one *cannot avoid* seeing in this passage such hope if in fact Coffman and others are correct in their interpretation. Jesus is manifestly talking about what sins would or would not be forgiven, and in what "ages," they would be forgiven. He said there would be one sin that would be unforgivable in "the age to come," the blasphemy of the Spirit.

If the "age to come" refers to heaven after the "end of time" when no sin exists, Jesus' words lose their force. If there would be no sin in the age to come, why did Jesus mention an "unforgivable sin" in the age to come? Why not just say there will be *no sin* in the age to come?

Jesus is patently speaking of forgiveness of sins in the age to come. He is thereby implying the possibility of sinning in the age to come. Why talk about forgiveness in eternity if the time for sinning is over? Jesus is not speaking about the forgiveness of sins committed in this life and not forgiven after death. *He is speaking of sins committed in the age to come.* He is speaking about sins which a man "may commit," not about sins he had committed and carried with him. So we say again that Jesus' discussion of the possibility, or lack thereof, of forgiveness of sins in the age to come, raises the possibility of sinning in the age to come. If therefore, the age to come is heaven there must be the possibility of sinning in heaven.

We concur with Clarke's assessment of Jesus' words, "Though I follow the common translation, yet I am fully satisfied the meaning of the words is, 'neither in this dispensation, (viz, the Jewish,) nor in that which is to come,' viz. the Christian."[199]

## Mark 10:29-30

After the rich young ruler came to Jesus inquiring about what he must do to have life, he left, disappointed because he was unwilling to do what was told him. The disciples were amazed that a wealthy, not to mention influential, man would be turned away. They could not fathom a kingdom in which the wealthy did not have the same position of prominence and favor as the one in which they then existed. Jesus told them not only was this so, but it would be easier for a camel to pass through the eye of a needle than to enter the kingdom. Astounded, the disciples then asked what profit it was for them to have forsaken all they had to follow him. The Lord reassures them by saying, "Assuredly, I say to you, there is no one who has left house or brothers or sisters or father or mother or wife or children or lands, for my sake and the gospel's, who shall not receive a hundredfold now in this time--houses and brothers and sister and mothers and children and lands, with persecutions--and in the age to come, eternal life."

McGuiggan blundered in his debate with Max King,[200] insisting that what Jesus meant was, "Jesus was telling them they would be a part of a family *in this life* (emphasis his) and enjoy the material blessing of each other (see for example Acts 2:44) and then, in the next age, 'eternal life.'" His comments make us wonder if he forgot what he had written elsewhere about the parallel passage to Mark 10.

In his *The Reign of God*, McGuiggan comments on Matthew 19:28: "Whatever one holds about the passage, all are forced to agree that the apostolic group join Christ in reigning and judging. The questions as to when they do this and who it is they will judge are much debated. I'm satisfied at this moment that the time issue is settled (perhaps I'm too optimistic or naive)---it's to occur in 'the regeneration.' The regeneration is the period of time during which regeneration takes place (see Titus 3:5). It is the present age in which Christ sums up all things in himself (Ephesians 1:10."[201]

It is evident then, that to McGuiggan, the regeneration is the Christian age. The problem for McGuiggan is, the Christian age was also, from Jesus' perspective in Mark 10:30, *the age to come*. The reference to the regeneration in Matthew 19:28 is parallel to the age to come in Mark 10:30. If the *regeneration* is the Christian age then the *age to come* is the Christian age as well. Further proof is the fact that as was the case in Matthew 12 when he spoke about the coming age, Jesus was living in the Mosaic age anticipating the coming of the new age.

Still stronger confirmation of this is found when we examine another passage parallel to Matthew 19:28. In Luke 22:30 Jesus promised the disciples the same thing as he did in Matthew 19:28 only with added perspective. He said, "I bestow on you a kingdom, just as my Father bestowed one upon me, that you may eat and drink at my table in My kingdom, and sit on thrones judging the twelve tribes of Israel."

Now according to Matthew 19:28 the disciples were to sit and judge Israel *in the regeneration*. In Luke they sit on thrones *in the kingdom*. In Matthew the regeneration is equivalent to *the age to come* in Mark 10:30. The disciples were to sit and judge Israel *in the kingdom* (Luke 22), but the disciples were to sit and judge Israel *in the regeneration* Therefore, the regeneration is the kingdom. Since the regeneration is the same as the age to come (Matthew 19:28-Mark 10:30), then the age to come is the same as the kingdom. And since the regeneration is the Christian age (Titus 3:4-5), it therefore follows that the kingdom is also in the Christian age, (see Colossians 1:13). This means that "the age to come" being anticipated by the New Testament writers was/is the Christian age.

## Luke 20:27-36

As the Sadducees tempted Jesus with their hypothetical situation of the woman, the number of her husbands, and whose wife she would be in the resurrection, Jesus responded, "The sons of this age marry and are given in marriage but those who are counted worthy to attain that age, and the resurrection from the dead, neither marry nor are given in marriage."

It is not our purpose to enter into a discussion of the resurrection.[202] It is our purpose to demonstrate the identity of the age to come. However, we should note that scholars are awaking to the fact that Jesus was not predicting the end of the Christian age. Those who oppose Covenant Eschatology, the views set forth in the book, argue, "In the age to come, Jesus said there will be no marrying and giving in marriage. Preterists are married, therefore, we are not in the age to come."[203] However, Wright has correctly noted, "The point is that the Levirate law of marriage, on which the Sadducees' apparent *reductio ad adsurdum* is based, only applies when the people of YHWH are constituted by marriage and begetting. Jesus was announcing that dawn of a new age, the time of the resurrection, in which this would not be the case."[204]

Once again we must ask the question, *in what age was Jesus living* when he alluded to "this age" and "that age?" To interpret the passage to be a reference to the Christian age and eternity following the destruction of the physical creation and cessation of time, one must do several things:

1.) Completely ignore the age/world in which Jesus was living.

2.) Assume that the dissolution of the age in which Jesus was then living, i.e. the Mosaic age, was of virtually no significance.

3.) Posit Jesus as actually living in the as yet to be established kingdom age.

177

**4.)** Have him contemplating the coming of the end of the Christian Era. This simply will not do.

This interpretation also implies a contradiction with what the scriptures say about the duration of the Christian age, *it will never end.* It is true that the words forever, everlasting, perpetual, etc., especially in the Old Testament, do not always mean what the western oriented Bible student would normally understand. The original Hebrew word, *olam,* meant age-lasting. It meant that what ever was under consideration was to last as long as God intended. The Old Testament priesthood, temple, sacrifices and law were all said to be perpetual, eternal, everlasting, they were also predicted to end. See Jeremiah 31.

But when the Bible said something was *never to end* this was another matter. And this is where the above interpretation runs counter to the Bible statements about the church. In Daniel 2:44, Jehovah promised that the kingdom would be set up in the last days and *it would never be destroyed.* In Daniel 7:13-14 we are informed that the kingdom of Messiah would have *no end.* In Isaiah 9:6-7 we are told that Messiah would rule in his kingdom *without end.* In Luke 1:33 the angel tells Mary that her son would rule over the kingdom of David and there would be *no end* of that kingdom.

It must be kept in mind that these are prophecies of the establishment of the kingdom *on earth.* (Not an *earthly kingdom,* but the establishment on earth nonetheless.) None of these predictions contemplate the end of the church age or a transformation of the church age at the end of time. What they unequivocally assert is the unending nature of the church age.

But if one interprets Luke 20:27f as speaking of the end of the Christian age or the end of time he is thereby asserting the end of what inspiration declares would not end. It is far more consistent, although admittedly contrary to tradition, to admit the force of language in Luke 20. Jesus was alive in the Mosaic Age. He called it "this age." He anticipated the coming of "that age," and this can only be the coming of the new world or Messianic Age, the age in which we are now living.

### Ephesians 1:21

This passage ascribes to Jesus universal dominion. The words of F. F. Bruce, are insightful, "Whatever differences in administration may appear between this age and the coming age, they will involve no diminution of the sovereignty of Christ."[205] It is evident that Bruce holds the view of McGuiggan, Coffman and others that "this age" is the Christian Era and the "age to come" is the eternal age after the dissolution of this material creation. But if this be the correct view in Ephesians it poses a problem for the traditional construction of I Corinthians 15:24f which maintains that Jesus will one day lay down the sovereign rule over the kingdom of God. Here in Ephesians it insists that Jesus' sovereignty is unending. If the age to come is the "age" after the end of time, Paul here manifestly asserts the continuation of Jesus' sovereignty after the cessation of time.

An objection could be raised here that while the references to the age to come in Matthew and Mark can best be understood as advert to the coming Christian age, in Ephesians 1 we are dealing with a time subsequent to the establishment of the Christian age on Pentecost. At first blush this sounds plausible. It fails however, to consider what we have noted elsewhere in this book that while the church/kingdom was established on Pentecost it was only a nascent kingdom. It was not yet perfected (Ephesians 4:13f). It would not be completed until the old system from which the kingdom sprang was taken out of the way. This maturation process was still on-going when Paul wrote Ephesians. The age to come, the perfected, matured kingdom was not yet fully come. It was still the age to come. Just as the early Christians were sons, but were longing for *the manifestation of sons* (Romans 8), just as they had been redeemed, but were looking for redemption (Luke 21), just as they had been saved, but were looking for salvation (I Peter 1), just so it was that the age to come had been ushered in at Pentecost, but was not yet completed. It was still the age to come because it was to be perfected, shortly, at the coming of Jesus.

This scenario allows the passage in Ephesians to stand in it's own light without the difficulties of the amillennial construct. Paul's "this age" was the antiquated old world of Judaism. It was passing away, and the coming age was being ushered in. Jesus had been declared Lord and Master not only over that old world, but the Messianic world as well.

That one will experience difficulties by identifying references to "this age" in post-Pentecost passages is well exemplified in Galatians 1:4. The inspired writer says Christ, "gave himself for our sins, that he might deliver us from this present evil age." If we understand "this age" as advert to the Christian age, in post-Pentecost texts, then Paul here characterizes the Christian age as "evil," and says that Jesus died to deliver us from "this evil Christian age." Is that *really* what Paul was saying?

### Hebrews 2:5
Certainly one of the most fascinating passages dealing with the world to come is found in Hebrews 2:5. One of the questions surrounding the

179

interpretation is whether the "man" of the context, the one to whom all things have been subjected, is mankind in general or Jesus specifically. This writer takes the later position. For a commentator who holds that mankind is the subject, see Fudge.[206]

One thing to note is that the passages cited above use the word "aion," properly translated as age. The word here is *oikoumene*. This word means *the inhabited world*. (Thayer, Vines, etc).

The writer tells us that he speaks of the world to come. The *New English Bible's* translation suggests that for the Hebrew writer the age to come was the "theme" of his discourse. And a study of Hebrews shows that the writer was not longing for a world after death, but the consummation of the long awaited unshakable kingdom of God.

In chapter 1 he contrasts the Old Covenant prophets and the Son of God. Here in chapter 2 he contrasts the two worlds. This contrast is just a continuation of his earlier contrast between the ministry of angels and that of the Son (1:8-2:1-4). There was the old world with its prophets as spokesmen and the law delivered by angels (2:2). But there was a coming new world not ruled by nor delivered by angels, but the Son (2:5). The Hebrews are told to hold fast unto the end in 3:6, 14, and 6:11. This end is not the end of their life. That is not indicated anywhere in the context. The end is not subjective, but an objective coming reality. It is the predicted end of the (then) present age. In chapter 4 the writer urges his readers to enter into the promised rest that remains. In chapter 6 he speaks again of the world to come. In chapter 7 he discusses the superiority of the priesthood of Jesus, and in chapter 8 he speaks of the Old Law which is in the process of vanishing away because of the establishment of the promised New Covenant (v. 6-13). In chapter 9 he tells of Jesus appearing at the end of the age and anticipates his return a second time. In chapter 10 we are told Jesus sat down at the right hand of Jehovah, "henceforth expecting until his enemies are made his footstool." He speaks of "the day approaching" (v. 25), stating that the promised return would be in a "very, very little while," and it would be judgment for some and salvation for others (10:26-37).

Chapter 11 tells of the great men and women of faith and how they longed to receive their promised inheritance. The writer tells us they could not do so "without us" (11:40). In chapter 12 he urges his readers, based on the fact that all those worthies were gathered around in anticipation, to not become slack, but to endure the persecution. They now stand before Zion, which means that the "age to come" was about to be realized!

He tells them of God's promise to "once again shake not only the earth, but heaven also" (12:26), and He said He would shake them in order to produce the unshakable. He then reminds them they were, at that very moment, receiving that unshakable kingdom, therefore they must hold fast. Finally, he urges them to spurn the altar of the present Temple and remember that they have an altar which the then present priests had no right to partake. Therefore, he urges them to remember and look for the continuing city, "the one about to come" (13:14).

In this brief overview then, we can see how the writer of Hebrews anticipated the arrival of the world to come (and that the Hebrews had already tasted of its glory (6:5), but were eagerly anticipating it's consummation). He saw it in the form of the perfected New Covenant world. He saw it in the imagery of Sabbath rest. He anticipated it in Jesus' return and promised it would be very, very soon. He saw it as the final fulfillment of the promises to the old world worthies, and he saw it as the passing of the heavens and earth of that old world. In none of these did he anticipate the destruction of physical creation or the cessation of time. He saw only the final passing of that old age with its inferior prophets, law, priesthood, sacrifices, temple, hope and promises. He saw in their place the new temple, the priesthood, the new altar, the new city, the New Covenant, the better sacrifice that had been once for all time given, he saw the new heavens and earth of Christ the Messiah.

The Hebrew writer insists, "He has not put the world to come in subjection to angels" (Hebrews 2:5) Why would he say such a thing? It is to contrast the "age to come" with the then present age which had been "subjected to angels." Bruce, has some excellent comments on the background of the idea of the subjection of the world to angels. It seems though, that he is somewhat confused on Hebrews 2:5, "To angelic beings the present world has been entrusted for administration, but not the world to come."[207] This is opposed to what the Hebrew writer says.

The Christian age, the age of Christ, is not the age put in submission to angels. Hebrews gives us positive identification of the age which was subjected to angels. In chapter one he *contrasts* the role of angels with that of the Son (v. 5-13). Jesus, not any angel, is the Son of God (v. 5). Angels must worship the Son (v. 6). Angels were the ministers to serve, Jesus is God on the throne of the kingdom (v. 7-9). Jesus is the creator, the angels are the created ones (v. 10-13). Because of Jesus' obvious preeminence then, "We ought to give the more earnest heed to the things we have heard

181

lest we let them drift away. For if the word spoken by angels proved steadfast" (2:1).

The contrast then is between the Old Covenant world and law "given by the direction of angels" (Acts 7:53), "appointed through angels by the hand of a mediator" (Galatians 3:19). The world to come is the New Covenant age which Jesus inaugurated when he, "ascended up on high and led captivity captive" (Ephesians 4), but which he consummated by his return to sweep away the last vestiges of the world which had been subjected to angels. Bruce correctly states that the age to come is, "the new world-order inaugurated by the enthronement of Christ at the right hand of God, the world order over which he reigns from that place of exaltation, the world of reality which replaces the preceding world of shadows" (Bruce. 1978, 33).

We concur with Pate, "Thus, the point of Hebrews 1:5-2:4 is that the angelic mediation of the law attests to the indirect divine origin of the Torah contrasted to the direct revelation from God of Christ's gospel."[208] The "world to come" was not the timelessness of heaven after some proposed "end of time," but the unending New Covenant kingdom.

## THE AGE TO COME AND THE END OF THE AGE

There is a manifest relationship between the "end of the age" and "the age to come." The New Testament scriptures are replete with references to the end of the age and the age to come. For too long the inter-relationship of these concepts has either been overlooked, obfuscated, or over-reached chronologically. As we have seen, the normal interpretation of the age to come passages is to see in them either an allusion to the so-called millennium or to eternity. This ignores the fact that Jesus, in the Synoptics, was alive *under the Old Law*. The traditional interpretations regard the old world as if it was already past. They act as if Jesus was living in the still not existent new age, anticipating the end of time. This is done while virtually ignoring the passing of the world which had stood for over 1500 years as if it was of no consequence whatsoever.

To help visualize the fact that what was being anticipated by the N. T. writers was not the passing of the Christian age and the institution of eternity, one needs to consider the passages mentioning the end of the age, or the end, in conjunction with the passages on the coming age. This will help illustrate that in the New Testament there was only one "end" anticipated, the end of the Jewish World, and there was only one "coming age," the perfected Christian age. To illustrate this we list below references to the end of the age and the end, with brief comment.

## The End of the Age

**1.) Matthew 13:39**–Harvest is at "the end of this age." Matthew 13 cannot refer to the end of the Christian age. Here is why.

☞ Matthew 13:43 says that the end of the age Jesus was predicting would be when the righteous would shine like the sun. This is a direct reference to Daniel 12:3.

☞ Daniel 12 foretold the end of the age, the time of the resurrection (Daniel 12:4).

☞ Daniel 12:7 says that "all of these things," which includes the resurrection and the end of the age, would be fulfilled, "When the power of the holy people is completely shattered." (Daniel 12:7).

☞ Since Matthew 13:39-43 predicted the end of the age foretold by Daniel 12, and since the end of the age foretold by Daniel 12 was the end of the Old Covenant age of Israel, it follows that the end of the age of Matthew 13 was the end of the Old Covenant age of Israel.

**2.) Matthew. 24:3** -- "What shall be the sign of the end of the age?" In this great chapter, the end is mentioned two times (vs 6,14). Jesus is patently answering the question about the end of the age, and says it will happen in that generation (v. 34). The same distinctive Greek term used in Matthew 13 is used in Matthew 24:3. Unless one can prove that the end of the age of Matthew 24 is a different end of the age from Matthew 13, then the end of the age of Matthew 24 is the end of the Old Covenant age.

Most commentators assume, without proof, that the disciples were asking about the end of the cosmological world, i.e. the universe. In my debate with Engelsma, he appealed to Matthew 24 as proof of a yet future end of time. But, this idea comes mostly through a mistranslation of the Greek term *sunteleias tou aionos* (consummation of the age).

The fact is that the disciples were asking about the end of the age that the Temple represented. And what age did that Temple represent? Did that Temple represent the Christian age? No. That temple represented one age, and only one age, *the Old Covenant age of Israel.*

The disciples pointed out the stones of the Temple. Jesus predicted the destruction of that Temple. The disciples asked about the end of the age. There is no doubt that in their mind, *the fall of the Temple and the end of the age were inextricably linked.* And contrary to the majority of

183

commentators who suggest that the disciples were confused, it is clear that they are not the ones that are confused. To suggest that the disciples were asking about the end of an age that had no connection with the Temple is illogical, and violates the text and context.

Calvin claimed that the disciples, "did not suppose that while the building of this world stood, the temple could fall to ruins."[209] The disciples were therefore mistaken in their questions. Really? Why? Consider this:

*The disciples knew* that the Temple had been destroyed by the Chaldeans.

*The disciples knew* that physical creation did not end at that time.

*The disciples knew* that Jehovah had come in that event, although He had not come visibly.

Now, since the disciples knew these things, what is the basis for saying they could not imagine the destruction of the Temple foretold by Jesus without thinking of the end of time and a visible coming of Christ? Jesus had already told them that he was coming "in the glory of the Father" before all of them died (Matthew 16:27-28). This means that the disciples had every right to associate the coming of Christ and the end of the age with the destruction of the Old Covenant Temple in A.D. 70. North is certainly correct, "The destruction of Jerusalem was the means by which the Lord marked the end of the age of His dealings with the Jews as His special chosen people...with the destruction of Jerusalem and the Temple by Titus in A.D. 70, the Jewish Age came to a complete and final end." (*Armageddon Again,* 42).

**3.) Matthew 28:20** -- Jesus promised his disciples, as he sent them out on the Great Commission, "Lo, I am with you alway, even unto the end of the age." A comparison of this verse with Mark 16:15-20 will reveal that Jesus' promise to be "with" the apostles was nothing less than the promise of the miraculous gifts of the Holy Spirit, given to confirm the word they were sent to preach. This verse is an implicit statement concerning the duration of miraculous gifts. They were to last until the end of the Jewish Age. See I Corinthians 1:4-8.

**4.) I Corinthians 10:11**--The inspired apostle wrote to the Corinthians and said the "ends of the ages" had come on them. It cannot be suggested that the consummation of the age had come on them, yet now, two millennia later, it has not yet arrived. But there is more here.

When Paul said "the end of the ages has come upon us," he was in reality saying that *the goal of all the previous ages had arrived*, and the implications of this are profound. The word "end" is from *telos* (Strong's # 5056), and means "the point aimed at." In other words, it means the *goal*. Now, *telos* can and does often have a "terminal" meaning, but, the idea of the word is that of "goal, destiny, target." Furthermore, Paul says that the goal of all the previous ages "has come upon us." This is from the word *katantao* (Strong's #2658), and means arrived. The meaning is clear. Paul says that the goal of all the previous ages had arrived. (It is clear of course, that the full end of the age had not arrived; the full arrival of that anticipated goal was not completed, but, Paul speaks proleptically, since he stands on the very cusp of that fulfillment).

Paul's statement is devastating to the millennial view that says the Christian age was totally unknown in the O. T. prophecies. Supposedly, the church is "Plan B" while the establishment of Israel's earthly kingdom remains "Plan A." For Paul however, the church was no interim plan. It was in fact *the goal of all previous ages*. This repudiates the suggestion that the church will one day be raptured out of the world, and out of the *way*, so that God can resume His dealings with Israel. If the church of Jesus Christ was the "goal of the previous ages" as Paul affirms, then it is dangerous to affirm that God will one day remove her, to resume His dealings with a nation that was a mere *shadow* of the "goal of all the ages."

**5.) Hebrews 9:26** --The writer tells us that Jesus appeared, "now once, in the end of the ages." In what age did Jesus appear? Read Galatians 4:4, Jesus appeared under the Old Covenant age of Moses and the Law. He appeared in the last days of that age (Hebrews 1:1-2). Thus, the "end of the age" being anticipated was the end of the Old Covenant age.

As we have seen from Matthew 24:2-3, Jesus' prediction of the fall of Jerusalem prompted the disciples to ask "when shall these things be, and what shall be the sign of your coming and the end of the age?" They undeniably linked the two events. Were they confused to link the judgment on Israel with the end of the age? Most modern commentators believe they were confused. Ice says the disciples definitely linked the end of the age and the fall of Jerusalem, but that *they were wrong. (End Times*, 155)

**However, this is not accurate.** Take a look at Matthew 13 again. After emphatically linking the end of the age with the fulfillment of Daniel 12, and the time of the destruction of Israel, Jesus asked his disciples, "Do you understand?" What was their response? Did they tell the Lord that they did not understand about the end of the age? Did they indicate that they did not comprehend the link between the destruction of Israel and the end of the age? No, they responded "Yes, Lord." (Matthew 13:51)

Did the disciples lie to Jesus? Were they actually confused, but just did not want to admit it? To suggest either of these is to contradict their words. Furthermore, Matthew does not tell us that they were actually confused but refused to say so. He does not write, *post facto*, that in fact they did not understand until after Pentecost and the sending of the Spirit, that what they thought they understood was wrong. So, *the disciples did understand the link between the end of the age and the destruction of Israel.* They were not confused, and they were not wrong to make that connection. It is the modern commentators who exhibit such arrogance as to continually ascribe confusion to the disciples that are in fact the ones that are confused.

Since the disciples were patently not confused to link the fall of Jerusalem with the end of the age, this means that they were not asking about the end of the material world, or a literal bodily coming of Christ. They were asking for a sign, "when the power of the holy people is completely shattered." They were not concerned with the fate of the material cosmos, and thus, all attempts to introduce that idea into Matthew 24 are misguided and falsified.

In addition to the references to the end of the age, the New Covenant contains many allusions to "the end." As a fine golden thread, references to "the end" are inextricably woven into the tapestry of New Covenant eschatological thought. And invariably, the references to the end are couched in language of imminence. We want now to examine some of those predictions of "the end."

**1.) Matthew 10:22-23** -- Jesus warned his living disciples that they would be the object of unbridled animosity. He promised the ones that endured *to the end* that they would be saved. Verse 23 continues his warnings, but contains promise of deliverance at his coming. When would that be? *Before those disciples died.* This passage presents no little problem for all futurist paradigms. Jesus was not promising to "meet them in Capernaum," or saying that the world mission would barely be fulfilled before he came. Jesus was warning his disciples that as they preached, they would be persecuted. He told them to flee from city to city, but promised that before they had fled through Israel that he would come. *This coming is in vindication of the suffering of his first century saints.*[210] When was Jesus to come in vindication of their suffering? Jesus promised that the vindication of all the blood of all the righteous would occur in the judgment of Israel in his generation (Matthew 23:29f). That was the time of "the end."

**2.) Matthew 24: 6, 13-14** -- Jesus had been asked about the end of the age (v. 3). He answers that the end would not be when they saw the "signs" of wars, famine, etc. He warns about persecution and repeats the promise of Matthew 10:22. In verse 14 he says the end would come when they had completed their world-wide evangelism. In Matthew 24:34 he says the end would be in that generation.

As we have just shown, the disciples knew that the end of the age and the fall of Jerusalem were the same. There are not two "ends" discussed in the chapter. The completion of the World Mission was to be the sign of the end of the age about which they asked. There is no justification to insert another end beyond the destruction of Jerusalem into the text.

**3.) I Corinthians 1:4-8** -- Paul assures the Corinthians that they would have the miraculous gifts of the Spirit to continue the work of confirmation "until the end...the day of our Lord Jesus Christ." Unless the Corinthians are still alive, or unless Paul's inspired promise failed, the Day of the Lord Jesus Christ has arrived and miracles have ceased. If the Day of Christ has not come miracles are still operative. But if that Day of Christ has not come those Corinthians are still alive![211]

**4.) I Corinthians 15:24**-- The apostle said the end would come when Jesus had put all things under his feet. The last enemy to be destroyed is death (v. 26). But in verse 50-51 he unequivocally promised the Corinthians that not all of them would die before the coming of the Lord. (It will not do to speak of an "editorial we" far removed in time from his contemporaries. "Editorial wes" are, in the vast majority of cases, spoken to and of contemporaries, not timeless unknowns. An adherence to the basic rules of hermeneutics would limit Paul's "we" to the Corinthians unless there was overwhelming contextual reason for so dramatically altering the obvious meaning of his words. This means that Paul affirmed that the resurrection and "the end" would occur in the lifetime of the Corinthians.

Paul's "we shall not all sleep" is directly parallel to Jesus' promise "there are some standing here who shall not taste death" promise in Matthew 16:27-28. In both passages, entrance into the kingdom, at the parousia, is promised to living humans before they die.

187

It is clear in Corinthians that Paul was definitely expecting the end in his generation. As just noted, he said the Corinthians would possess the charismata until the end. He said that the days had been shortened, and that the "form of this world is passing away" (7:26-29). He said that the end of the ages had arrived. All of these references to the end are parallel with 1 Corinthians 15:24, and it is undeniably clear that the end was near.

**5.) Hebrews 3:6, 14, 6:11**-- In these verses the writer urges his readers to be firm and steadfast "unto the end." It is obvious he has some *objective* not *subjective* end in view. The end for which he looked was the "day approaching" of 10:25 when the one who was to come "in a very, very little while" would come (10:37). This was when the heaven and earth would be removed and the unshakable kingdom which they were in the process of receiving at that very time would be consummated (12:25-28.).

**6.) I Peter 4:7** -- "The end of all things is at hand." The verse literally reads "the end of all things has drawn near." The nearness of the end is undeniable. This is the same imminent end as in the verses cited above. In addition, in verse 5 the writer said that Christ was "*ready* to judge the living and the dead." The Greek word he uses, as noticed elsewhere, is *hetoimos*, and conveys the idea of imminence. Furthermore, in verse 17 the writer affirmed "the time has come for the judgment to begin."

Jeremy Lile has pointed me to the use of the *anaphoric article*.[212] Simply stated, this means that sometimes an article is not used early on, but is used later in the text. When the article is then used, it points back to the previous referent. In this case, 1 Peter 4:5 refers to the judgment of the living and the dead. In verse 17, Peter uses the article to point us back to the judgment already mentioned, the judgment of the living and the dead. He affirms that the time for the judgment had arrived. This then, is a powerful declaration that the time of the resurrection had arrived.

Interestingly, Gentry, perhaps in an unguarded moment, actually lists 1 Peter 4:5 as a passage indicating the A.D. 70 parousia of Christ, "Similar notes of temporal proximity of divinely governed crises abound in the NT: Matthew 26:64; Acts 2:16-20, 40; Romans 13:11, 12; 16:20; 1 Corinthians7: 29-31; Colossians 3:6; 1 Thessalonians 2:16; Hebrews 10:25, 37; James 5:8,9, and *1 Peter 4:5, 7.*[213] (My emphasis) It is remarkable that Gentry includes 1 Peter 4:5 in his list of passages supporting a 1st century parousia, because the text speaks of the *resurrection*. Christ was "ready to judge the living and the dead." For Gentry to list 1 Peter 4:5 as indicative

188

of a 1$^{st}$ century eschatological event posits the resurrection in the 1$^{st}$ century. How could the New Testament express nearness more clearly?

It is easily seen from the above that the inspired writers wrote often of the impending end. The end was not some vague concept of the far off future. It was an earnest expectation of imminent realization. The Biblical writers clearly saw themselves and their readers as living in the last times.

In James 5:3 the writer speaks of contemporary events perpetrated in "the last days" by the rich. The events were not, as suggested by LaHaye and Ice (*Charting*, 120), predictions of things to come in the future, they were present realities as he spoke.

In I Peter 1:5 the former fisherman spoke of the salvation ready to be revealed in the last times. This salvation was to come at Christ's parousia, and had been foretold by the O. T. prophets (7-10). What should not be missed is that Peter said the prophets knew that they were not predicting events for their time,[214] but Peter affirms that they prophesied of his day. In other words, what was once far off was now near. In verse 20 he said he was living in the last times. In his second epistle he warned of the coming of scoffers in the last days. And in Jude the author reminds his readers of this prediction, and says the very ones predicted were alive and troubling the assembly even then.

The favorite apostle of the Lord wrote, "Little children it is the last hour. As you have heard that anti-christ should come, even now there are many anti-christs, whereby you know that it is the last hour"(I John 2:18). It is important to note here that John uses the term "last hour" or "hour" in reference to the hour of the resurrection more than any other writer. Thus, when he says, "It is the last hour," we must see that in the context of the eschatological hour. The time of the end had arrived. See also the references to the last times in I Timothy 4:1 and 2 Timothy 3:1.

The observant student cannot fail to see the correlation between the end of the age, the end, and the last days. (We would also note John's use of "the last day" in 6:39,40,44,54, and 11:24). Nor can we fail to see the time statements, the positive declarations of inspiration that the last days were present, and the end was coming soon.

So, what have we done in this chapter? We have shown the harmony in Peter's teaching on the passing of the world of Noah, the passing of his, Peter's, world, and the New Covenant teaching about "the world to come." We have seen that when Jesus spoke of the age to come he was alive in the Mosaic World anticipating the coming of what we call today the Christian age. We have seen that the scriptures portray a consistent picture of the early church which saw itself living in the waning days of the old world, eagerly anticipating the consummation of the new age. From Matthew to Revelation there is an indivisible thread of eagerness, of *expectation* of the imminent coming of the new heavens and earth wherein dwelleth righteousness. And in full accord with the coming of this new world was the passing of the old. Not just a part of the old was to pass, the very foundations upon which it was based and which sustained it must perish. The very *elements* of that world had to be dissolved.

**"The Heavens Shall Pass Away with a Great Noise, and the Earth and the Elements Therein Shall Be Burned Up." (2 Peter 3:10)**

One of the arguments often made to prove that Peter had the material creation in mind for destruction is that he says the "elements" would melt, or be burned up. Winkler, says "in the passage being studied, (2 Peter 3, DKP) the word (*elements*, DKP) no doubt refers to the rudimental portions of the earth's system, the atoms, etc."[215] Let us take a closer look at this word "elements," for there is *considerable doubt* that Peter had the building blocks of physical creation in mind.

Elements is from the Greek word *stoicheia* (Strong's #4747). It, "primarily signifies any first things from which others in a series, or a composite whole, take their rise."[216] In pre-Christian times, and to some extent in the Christian era, it had reference to the four basic elements of the world as perceived at that time, earth, wind, fire, water. The word also had to do with other rudimentary concepts, fundamental doctrines or concepts as well, having nothing to do with physical creation. *And this is how the Bible uses the word.*

*Stoicheia* appears seven times in the New Testament. Examination of these texts will reveal how the Spirit utilizes the word.

In Galatians 4:3,9 Paul uses the word twice. The context is manifestly his discussion of the relationship of the Jews under the Old Law (vss. 1-7). In verses 8-9 he continues that discussion reminding his readers how they were once held in bondage to the "elements of the world" when they observed "day, weeks, months, and years." This refers to observance of the Old Law. The Jews were held in bondage to the Old Law, the fundamental laws and regulations of the *Torah* that constituted "the *stoicheia* of the world (*kosmos*)." Paul's reference is to the *system of* the Torah in which his readers had served, not to the material elements of creation. Yet it is called the "elements of the world."

The apostle also used the word twice in his letter to the Colossian church (Colossian 2: 8, 20). In verse 8 he pleads with them not to allow anyone to cheat them by way of philosophy, or traditions of men according to the elements of the world. Patently, what he has in mind are any *teachings* which would detract them from serving the Lord. He was not concerned with atoms, protons, and neutrons. In the context of the book the danger was Judaistic activities (Colossians 2:14-17). Vines says Paul refers to, "the delusive speculation of Gentile cults and of Jewish theories, treated as elementary principles, 'the rudiments of the world.'" (ibid). We personally reject the "Gentile" aspect of Paul's concern, but, the point is, once again, the reference is not to material creation, but to doctrines or systems.

It should be noted that Paul not only affirms that the *stoicheia* of the world was the enslaving power, he also affirmed that those elements were ready to pass away. Notice the parallels between Colossians and 2 Peter 3.

| Colossians 2 | 2 Peter 3 |
|---|---|
| Discussion of the passing of the elements (*stoicheia*, v. 20) | Discussion of the passing of the elements (*stoicheia, v. 10*) |
| "elements" were to pass away (2:20) | "elements" were to pass away (3:10) |
| The *world* (*cosmos*) was to pass (v. 20f) | The *world* (*cosmos*) was to pass (v. 4f) |
| The call to righteousness in light of the passing of the *elements* (v. 20-22) | The call to righteousness in light of the passing of the *elements* (v. 13) |
| The elements were the basic doctrines of Old Covenant Israel | Peter said his doctrine of the elements was what Paul taught |

When you couple these parallels with the fact that both Paul and Peter affirmed repeatedly that their eschatological hope was "the hope of Israel," and was found in "Moses and the prophets," then it becomes apparent that the elements in view are not the elements of physical creation. The elements were the fundamental aspects of the Old Covenant world.

The fifth time the word *stoicheia* is used is in Hebrews 5:12 when the writer laments the fact that the Hebrew brethren had not grown in Christ as they should. He says they have need for someone to teach them again the "first principles" of Christ. These first principles of Christ are the fundamental doctrines of the Old Covenant that had led them to Christ.[217] Once again, *stoicheia* is used of the teaching or the system under consideration, not to atoms or earth, wind, fire, or water. And what is more, the author makes sure to tell them to *leave behind (aphentes, Strong's*

*#863),*[218] those "elements," because the "heaven and earth" of that old world was even then in the process of passing away (Hebrews 8:13; 12:25f).

The other two times *stoicheia* is used is in 2 Peter 3:10,12. In both verses he says the elements would melt. Now, it is *possible* that Peter could be using the word differently from Paul does in these other passages. However, *Peter affirms that he was saying the same thing in his eschatology that Paul taught "in all his epistles."* (2 Peter 3:15f)

The consistent definition of *stoicheia* as the fundamental doctrines of the Jewish system, should make us very cautious before rejecting that inspired precedent and usage. Since we have already shown that Peter is not focused on the destruction of this physical world, then his claim to use *stoicheia* as Paul does demands that the "elements" which were to melt, were the same "heaven and earth" of Judaism which were about to pass in the conflagration of A.D. 70.

One of the eminent hermeneutical authorities, Milton Terry, made some pertinent observations in regard to the language of 2 Peter 3:

"We might fill volumes with extracts showing how exegetes and writers on New Testament doctrine assume as a principle not to be questioned that such highly wrought language of Matthew 24:29f; 1 Thessalonians 4:16; 2 Peter 3:10, 12, taken almost *verbatim* from Old Testament prophecies of judgment on nations and kingdoms which long ago perished, must be understood literally. Too little study of Old Testament ideas of judgment, and apocalyptic language and style, would seem to be the main reason for this one sided exegesis. It will require more than assertion to convince thoughtful men that the figurative language of Isaiah, and Daniel, admitted on all hands to be such in those ancient prophets, is to be literally interpreted when used by Jesus and Paul."[219]

Likewise, John Lightfoot, says of the elements of 2 Peter 3, "The destruction of Jerusalem and the whole Jewish state is described as if the whole frame of this world were to be dissolved."[220] And this view is supported, perhaps inadvertently, by Kraftchick when he notes:

"The participle 'dissolved' that modifies 'all things' is in the present tense, and while the NRSV's 'are to be dissolved' is acceptable since in Koine Greek, present tense participles often take future meanings (e.g. *kolazomenous* 'under punishment' 2:9), a better translation is, 'are being dissolved.' The present tense indicates that the dissolution of creation is already under way, and, therefore, that the coming of the Lord could not be far off. The verb form emphasizes the author's exhortations because it emphasizes that God is, even now, altering the world in preparing for the day of judgment."[221]

Moo also notes the present tense, "Peter may have chosen this tense to suggest that the destruction of 'everything' is even now in process."[222]

Kraftchick believes that the author of 2 Peter was mistakenly anticipating the end of the material creation, and in 2 Peter 3 was struggling to explain to his audience the failure or delay in Christ's return. Moo, somewhat similarly, believes that Peter is defending the end of time parousia of Christ against those who "were scoffing at the idea of a history ending parousia" (Moo, 1996, 196). This low view of inspiration is not necessary, however,[223] when it is understood that Peter was not defending a failed Savior. He was not feeding *cognitive dissonance*. He was not trying to explain why the predictions had failed. He was in fact affirming the faithfulness of God, and the nearness of the end. He was even affirming that the passing of the "elements" was occurring as he wrote. The present tense verb, as Kraftchick and Moo note, is not misguided. As the Hebrew writer expressed it in regard to the Old Covenant system, "that which is growing old is now ready to vanish away" (Hebrews 8:13).

Peter's use of the present tense passing of the elements is not a statement of the Second Law of Thermodynamics. Peter was affirming what the author of Hebrews affirmed. The old world, with its elements "was ready to pass away" (Hebrews 8:13). The heaven and earth was already being shaken, as the unmovable kingdom was being delivered (Hebrews 12:25f). See again my comments there.

It is disturbing that commentators can see that Isaiah 65 serves as the basis for 2 Peter's prediction of the passing of the elements, and then deny that Peter foretold the destruction of the elements of the Old Covenant world. Jackson says that Isaiah 65's prediction of the new heavens and new earth "is merely descriptive of the new realm that will replace the Mosaic period. The 'former things,' i.e. *the elements of the Mosaic system*, will pass away (Isaiah 65:17)."[224] (My emphasis)

If Peter's prediction of the passing of the elements is from Isaiah, and if Isaiah foretold the passing of "the elements of the Mosaic system," then this virtually demands that Peter was predicting the passing of the elements of the Mosaic system, and not the dissolution of the material universe.

The elemental things of Judaism, the priesthood, the temple, the sacrifices, the city, the genealogies, were all swept away in the catastrophe

194

of A.D. 70. The very heart and soul of that world died and it has never been the same. Truly that world, *with its elements*, perished.

## ISRAEL, THE TEMPLE, AND HEAVEN AND EARTH

The modern reader of 2 Peter 3, indeed, of the entire Bible, is confronted with a hermeneutical hurdle that they are perhaps even unaware of, and that is that few modern readers think in the conceptual world of Hebraic thought. By and large, modern Bible readers are Greek in their world view, while the Bible was written from an Oriental/Hebraic world view. What this translates into is that when we pick up the Bible, we don't even realize that we are bringing our Grecian way of thinking, our presuppositions, or prejudices, and our preconceived ideas into the text as we read. Since the Grecian world view is not as mystical, metaphorical or spiritual as the Hebraic, we are often offended at the suggestion that the Bible does not mean what it says.

The fact is that the Bible *does* say what it means, and it *does* mean what it says. *However*, to assume without question that the ancient authors thought exactly like we do today, and expressed themselves as we do today, is a faulty assumption. As Wilson says, "Westerners have often found themselves in the confusing situation of trying to understand a Jewish Book through the eyes of a Greek culture."[225]

We must be careful not to think and interpret in ways that either reject, or distort the Hebraic background of the Biblical text. As Bivin and Blizzard state about the Bible, "The writers were Hebrew, the culture was Hebrew, the religion was Hebrew, the traditions were Hebrew, and the concepts Hebrew."[226] Beale reminds us that, "The Bible was written in very specific circumstances and the better one understands these surrounding circumstances the more rich one's understanding of the Bible may become." (*Temple*, 31) So, while the Bible says what it means, and means what it says, if you and I are not attuned to the matrix from which the Bible springs, *then we don't even really know what it says,* and we have little hope of *knowing what it means.* As already noted, there is, thankfully, a growing awareness of this issue among Bible scholars and students alike.

The importance of understanding the problem of Hebraic thought versus Grecian thought presents itself when we consider how the Jews thought of their holy city Jerusalem and especially the temple. I suggest that because we today are so literalistic in our approach to scripture, that we are fundamentally and presuppositionally prejudiced toward misunderstanding 2 Peter 3.[227] We automatically assume that since Peter is talking about the

195

"earth and the elements therein," that he must have been talking about the material creation. However, we must be careful that we not bring our Grecian literalism into the world of the apocalyptic.

Snyder has noted that the early church, under the influence of Hellenization, misunderstood the apocalyptic nature of eschatology and literalized it, "so that an actual end of time was expected...the chronological misunderstanding resulted in a problem regarding the delay of the parousia to such a point that the community was forced to identify that disjuncture with the baptism or the birth of Jesus rather than to speak of a radical disjuncture yet at hand...in other words, the problem of the delay of the parousia is a problem only in so far as the early community misunderstood and literalized the apocalyptic."[228]

What Snyder is saying (partly) is that due to the Hellenistic world view of things, the early church did not understand the nature of the prophetic language, and as a result, they expected a literal end of time, a literal coming of the Lord. As a result of this literalizaton, and it goes without saying that this same kind of literalization lies at the root of all modern eschatological paradigms, the church was and is forced to deal with the problem of the failure of Christ to come and bring time and history to an end. How do you explain to unbelievers– how do you rationalize your own faith??-- that your Lord failed to come when he said he would, when your concept of his coming is based on a false world view, a false hermeneutic?

There is a great deal more we could say on this. However, what we want to do now is to demonstrate that consistent with what we have presented so far, it is perfectly logical, textual, and contextual to see that in 2 Peter 3 Peter was predicting the end of the Old Covenant world of Israel under the imagery of the passing of the "heaven and earth."

By way of reminder, let me point out what we have seen to this point:
**1.)** We have shown that the purpose of 2 Peter was to defend the doctrine of the parousia against the scoffers. Peter's approach was to appeal to the Transfiguration as a vision of the parousia. As a vision of the parousia, the Transfiguration defines the Lord's coming as the end of the Old Covenant world of Moses and the prophets, and the full establishment of the New Covenant world of the Messiah. This fits the idea that the heaven and earth that was to pass was the city and the temple of Jerusalem since the Jews considered the temple to be "heaven and earth."
**2.)** We have shown that Peter was anticipating the fulfillment of God's promises to bring Israel's salvation hopes to realization. By the very nature of the case, the consummation of Israel's promises would occur at the end

of *her age*, not the end of time. This suggests that the passing of the Old Covenant temple and city would be the signal proof that the shadow world was now passed and the "body" had arrived.

**3.)** We have shown that the language of imminence demands that, unless Peter was mistaken, then he knew that the Day of the Lord he was anticipating was near. This fits the "*sitz em leben*" i.e. the "very specific circumstances" as Beale puts it, of Peter's world, since he was writing just a few years before the fall of the temple.

**4.)** We have shown that Peter's prediction of the new heaven and earth is taken directly from Isaiah 63-66, and that promise is couched in the context of the destruction of Old Israel and the creation of a new people. This fits the historical context of 2 Peter 3 as Peter stood on the very cusp of the sweeping away of the old world.

**5.)** We have seen that not only does Isaiah 63-66 serve as the foundational text for Peter, but that the coming of the Lord predicted in Isaiah 64 could not have been a literal, time ending, earth burning, cosmos destroying event. Isaiah foretold the coming of the Lord *in the same manner as He had come before*. This precludes a visible, bodily parousia in 2 Peter 3. If Isaiah was not predicting a visible coming of God out of heaven, then that is not what Peter was predicting.

**6.)** We have seen that another foundational text lying behind 2 Peter 3 was Daniel 9 and its prediction of the establishment of "everlasting righteousness." Daniel 9, like Isaiah 63-66, posited the climax of Israel's glorious history at the time of the destruction of the old world, which was necessary to reveal the new creation.

Now, we have presented a great deal more information of course, but with these things in mind, we should be able to see that there is virtually no evidence to suggest that Peter had the visible, material creation in mind. He was anticipating the fulfillment of God's promises to Israel. He was predicting the end of Israel's covenant world, her old creation. And this meant that he was predicting the destruction of her "heaven and earth," the temple at Jerusalem.

In what follows, it is our purpose to demonstrate how the Jews thought of the temple as "heaven and earth." As Fletcher-Louis notes, "There is now a clamorous chorus of Old Testament/Hebrew Bible scholars who have welcomed the presence of the belief in the temple-as-microcosm (of the heaven and earth, DKP), throughout Israel's canonical scriptures." (*Destruction*, 157+) By demonstrating that Peter was anticipating the consummation of Israel's Old Covenant world, that was symbolized by the temple, and by showing that the Jews, which of course included Peter, thought and spoke of the temple as "heaven and earth," it is our contention that 2 Peter 3 must be understood as a prediction of the imminent demise of that old creation of Israel. We will draw heavily from the work of Beale, although we will refer to others as well. For brevity, we will list only the key point that we want to make, and urge the reader to do follow up study. **1.)** The Bible uses "creation language" to describe the construction of the temple. Construction of the Solomonic temple and creation are structured around seven acts. Just like Genesis describes creation occurring over a period of seven days, Solomon took seven years to build, dedicated it on the seventh month, during Tabernacles, (feast of seven days), and the dedicatory speech contained seven petitions. God rested on the seventh day, and the tabernacle and temple are called God's resting place (Psalms 132). (Beale, *Temple*, 61)

**2.)** "The seven lamps on the lamp stand may have been associated with the seven light-sources visible to the naked eye (five planets, sun and moon). This identification is pointed out in Genesis 1 which uses the unusual word 'lights' (mĕ'rōt, five times) instead of 'sun' and 'moon', a word that is used throughout the remainder of the Pentateuch (10 times) only for the 'lights' of the tabernacle lamp stand."(Beale, *Temple*, 34)

**3.)** When the High Priest entered the Most Holy Place, he burned incense on his censor to create a cloud of smoke. This cloud of smoke represented the clouds of heaven (Beale, *Temple*, 36).

**4.)** Citing Levenson, Beale notes that "'heaven and earth' in the O.T. may sometimes be a way of referring to Jerusalem or its temple, for which 'Jerusalem' is a metonymy (Isaiah 65)." (Beale, *Temple*, 25 ). We have already seen that according to Josephus, the Most Holy Place was considered to be a type of "heaven" and the Holy Place was called "earth."

**5.)** Even the High Priest's garments and vestments were highly symbolic,[229] "The priests garments represented the temple shape, and the colors and stones represented the stars." (Beale, *Temple*, 39) Likewise, Stevenson cites Philo to the effect that when the High Priest entered the MHP, "the whole universe may enter with him by means of the copies which he bears upon himself: the ankle-length robe being a copy of the air, the pomegranate of water, the flowery border of earth, the scarlet of fire, the ephod of heaven, the circular emeralds...of the two hemispheres according to their form, the twelve stones on the breastplate in four rows of threes a copy of the Zodiac, the logeion (sic), a copy of what holds together and governs everything."[230]

**6.)** According to Stevenson, Philo identifies "the fifty pillars of the tabernacle with the foundation of the creation. The veil represents the four elements of the creation (earth, air, fire, water). The candlestick represents the light of heaven provided by the sun, moon, and stars, while the seven candlesticks symbolize the seven planets. The table on the northern part of the HP represents the winds and the nourishment that comes from the north, while the altar of incense symbolizes the earth." (*Power*, 156).

Take particular note that Philo identifies the veil as the "elements" i.e. earth, wind, fire and water. These are the *stoicheia*, that Peter refers to in 2 Peter 3:10!

When the veil of the temple was torn as Jesus hung on the cross, the astute observers had to know that the entire complex of the temple, i.e. heaven and earth, was now doomed. Allison suggests that the veil, "a Babylonian curtain, embroidered with blue, scarlet, linen thread and purple hung before the main entrance into the sanctuary, at the back of the vestibule, and 'worked into the tapestry was the whole vista of the heavens (excepting the signs of the Zodiac).' Now *if* Mark 15:38 pertains to this particular curtain (an unresolved problem), then the picture conjured up by the verse is a panorama of the heavens splitting."[231] Additionally, Allison notes that, "Several Jewish texts composed before A.D. 70 announce that the old temple will not continue into the new age. God will instead build a new temple." (Allison, *End*, 32) The conflation of 2 Peter 3 and Revelation 21-22 fits this interpretation extremely well.

Fletcher-Louis comments on the symbolism of the veil with the "elements of the world" woven into it, and the implications of the rending of that veil, "If the temple's destruction is symbolized and if the temple embodies heaven and earth, then the Jewish (Christian) reader of the synoptic crucifixion scene would naturally assume that at this point there is insinuated the passing away of heaven and earth." (*Destruction*, 164). We would only demur that the rending of that veil did not mean that heaven and earth *had been destroyed*, but that heaven and earth, i.e. the temple, *was going to be destroyed*. As noted from Allison, this is how many rabbis and Christians interpreted that event.

**7.)** Stevenson cites the Mishnah, "It is stated that the temple sustains the world, occupies the very center, and serves as the foundation point of the world." (*Power*, 155).

It is evident that to the Jewish mind, the temple was the center of their world. It really was their "heaven and earth." Now, if the first century Jews, and the Old Testament prophets, referred to the temple as heaven and earth, and even spoke of the "elements" being represented on the veil, then it cannot be denied that Peter *could* have been using that vernacular to describe the fall of the temple world. And, given the background that we have presented, i.e. that Peter was indeed anticipating the consummation of Israel's age, this identification becomes almost irrefutable.

So, here is what we have.

**1.)** Peter was anticipating the passing of the old creation and the coming of the new creation, in fulfillment of the Old Covenant promises made to Israel (2 Peter 3:1-2, 13). *Everything in 2 Peter 3 is about God's promises to Israel!*

**2.)** Those promises would be fulfilled *in the last days*, and Peter said they were living in the anticipated last days (1 Peter 1:5f, 19f; 4:5, 7, 17; 2 Peter 3:1f).

**3.)** Those Old Testament promises to Israel would be fulfilled at the end of Israel's age (Daniel 12:3-7).

**4.)** Those promises would be fulfilled when "heaven and earth" was destroyed and the new heaven and earth created (Isaiah 64-66).

**5.)** The passing of the old heaven and earth and the coming of the new creation would be *when Old Covenant Israel was destroyed* (Isaiah 65:13f; Daniel 9:24f).

**6.)** The Jews and the Old Covenant clearly called Jerusalem and specifically the temple, the "heaven and earth."

So, in light of the prophetic background, and the social and religious context of 2 Peter 3, there can be little doubt that Peter was concerned, not with the passing of the material creation, but with the passing of the Old Covenant world symbolized and epitomized by the Jerusalem temple.

Consider a final point. In Matthew 23 and 24, Jesus foretold the destruction of the temple (23:37; 24:2). Sitting on Olivet, directly across from the temple, he answers the disciples' questions about that event and says, "Heaven and earth shall pass away, but my word will never pass away" (Matthew 24:35).

It is incredible to me that Beale, after presenting such convincing documentation of how the Jews thought of the temple, *then completely ignores the significance of that for understanding Matthew 24:35.* The verse is not listed in his scriptural index at all. How is it possible to argue so convincingly that the temple was called "heaven and earth," and then not apply that understanding to Jesus' prediction of the destruction of that temple?

Given the "specific historical circumstance" in which Jesus makes that statement, and given the thought world of the temple as heaven and earth, how is it possible to say that he was predicting the dissolution of material creation? He has used typical prophetic language already to predict the fall of the city (v. 29f), and now, he uses the vernacular of the day to describe the fall of the temple and the old creation, the old heaven and earth, that it represented.

As Fletcher-Louis says, "Within the broader sweep of the temple focus throughout this eschatological chapter and the specific time reference of the preceding verse (Mark 13:30; Matthew 24:34), Jesus' promise that 'heaven and earth' will pass away makes best sense, not as a collapse of the space-time universe, as has been so often understood, but as a collapse of a *mythical* space-time universe which is embodied in the Jerusalem temple." (*Destruction*, 162, his emphasis) Jesus was not therefore, predicting the destruction of physical creation. He was contrasting *two covenant worlds*, foretelling the passing of the "earth and the elements therein" of the old world of Judaism, epitomized by Jerusalem and the temple. Just like Revelation is John's expanded version of the Olivet Discourse, 2 Peter 3 is Peter's expanded commentary on Jesus' prediction of the destruction of that old world.

# CHAPTER 13
## WHEREIN DWELLS RIGHTEOUSNESS

**"We Look for a New Heavens and Earth,
Wherein Righteousness Dwells" (2 Peter 3:13)**

Peter tells his readers that righteousness "makes its home" in the new creation. It is often insisted that this constitutes proof that the new creation can only be heaven. This depreciates the value and glory of the church.

Paul tells us in Romans 6:16f that obedience to the law of Jesus constitutes righteousness. One of the great themes of Romans is righteousness. In verse after verse the writer strives to inform us that righteousness is a present reality in Christ. Study chapters 3, 5, and 6 especially. It should not be overlooked that in chapter 14:17 he speaks of what the kingdom (church) is to be. The kingdom *is*, he says, righteousness. This is true because Jesus our Savior and Redeemer is also righteousness (I Corinthians 1:30). The Hebrew writer tells us our king loves righteousness and his is a kingdom of righteousness (Hebrews 1:7f). Righteousness is to be so much the character of the church that in 2 Corinthians 6 Paul contrasts the world and the church by speaking of the world as lawlessness, and the church as righteousness (v. 14). The New Covenant is described by the same writer in 2 Corinthians 3:9f as the ministry of righteousness. When we obey this New Covenant we put off the old man of sin and the new man is created "after righteousness and true holiness" (Ephesians 4:24f).

We could go on, but since the church is a kingdom of righteousness, with a law of righteousness, a king who *is* righteousness, and who loves righteousness, is it not evident that righteousness dwells in the kingdom?

It might be asked then, why did Peter look for the new creation in which righteousness would dwell? We have earlier given the key to this question. *The church was in a transition period in the first century.*

When established on Pentecost the church was an infant. In need of inspired men and miracles to sustain and equip her (Ephesians 4:8f), she struggled to overcome a hostile world. Her chief enemy was the old world of Judaism which denied every claim of Jesus and persecuted his followers. The early church longed for, "the manifestation of the Sons of God" (Romans 8:18f), for confirmation of the word which they preached. The gifts assured them that Christ would finish his work (I Corinthians 1:4f). They longed for vindication for the suffering they endured (Revelation

6:9f). They desired the state of maturity (I Corinthians 13:8f). And that maturity, that time when God would give them the "salvation ready to be revealed in the last time" (I Peter 1:5), was upon them. See I Peter 1:20 and I John 2:18.

The early church had the adoption, but longed for the adoption (Romans 8:15,23). They had grace, but looked forward to grace (Ephesians 2:8-9, cf. I Peter 1:13). They had been redeemed, but looked for redemption (Ephesians 1:7 cf. Luke 21:28). They had the kingdom, but looked forward to its coming (Hebrews 12:28, cf. Luke 21:31). Likewise, they had righteousness, but they longed for the perfected church, wherein righteousness would dwell.

In Galatians 5:5 Paul says, "we through the Spirit eagerly wait for the hope of righteousness by faith." What was it that Paul was waiting for? He was waiting for the new heavens and earth wherein dwells righteousness.

In Galatians 4 the apostle speaks of the two sons and the two mothers. These represented the Old Covenant and Israel, and the New Covenant and new people In Galatians, Paul spoke of the inability of that old world to impute *righteousness*, "If a law could be given that could give life, then verily righteousness would be through the Law" (Galatians 3:21). That old creation of futility, that could not give life and righteousness was at that time "persecuting the seed of promise," and as a result Paul said, "cast out the bondwoman and her son." (Galatians 4:30-31). Contrary to the popular belief that God was through with Israel at the cross, Paul makes it clear that Israel was to be cast out *for persecuting the church*. Unless Israel persecuted the church *prior to the cross*, then Israel was not cast out at the cross.

Not only was Paul anticipating the casting out of the old creation, he was eagerly awaiting the revelation of "the Jerusalem that is above, and is the mother of us all" (Galatians 4:26). This is the "heavenly Jerusalem" of Hebrews 12:21 that the author said was "about to come" (Hebrews 13:14). It is the new Jerusalem that John said was about to "come down from God out of heaven" (Revelation 21:10).

Peter's anticipated "new heavens and earth wherein dwells righteousness," was not a refurbished planet. It was not a destroyed planet. It was a covenant world that in contrast to the Old Covenant creation that could never give righteousness, would make those under that New Covenant righteous in the eyes of God.

The new creation had broken into the old creation. The last days of the old were now in place, but the new day was dawning, "The darkness is passing, and the true light is already shining" (My translation, 1 John 2:8). As Paul said, "The night is far spent, The Day is at hand" (Romans 13:11f). Now if, as many hold, the transition to the new order was completed at the cross, how could these writers say they were still anticipating the arrival of the new order? They were not waiting for the end of time. They were not waiting for the end of the Christian age. They were waiting for the "manifestation of the sons of God" (Romans 8:18f).

Peter has in mind this contrast between the old creation and the new. The failure to see the contrast between covenant worlds, as they related to *righteousness*, is a huge failure in the proper exegesis of 2 Peter 3. Under the old law one was born into a covenant relationship and then taught who he was. He was first born then taught. Son ship was by blood, not by faith, not by choice. Under the new law a man is first taught about God and His covenantal promises. If and when he desires, a person then chooses of his own volition to accept the gracious invitation to become a member of God's family. By faith, a person receives, "the right to become children of God" (John 1:11f). Son ship is now by *grace, not race*. So, whereas the Old Covenant could not offer righteousness and life, the New Covenant world of Christ can and does, "By him all that believe are justified from all things from which you could not be justified by the law of Moses" (Acts 13:39).

If only we could get this point across to every member of the body of Christ. *We are to be holy in the church!* The church is God's instrument and venue for demonstrating the righteousness of Christ (2 Corinthians 5:21). What a shame therefore, when members of Christ's body forget or do not care about who we are. What a shame also that so many believers seem to think that we have to wait for the end of time to, "be made the righteousness of God in him"(2 Corinthians 5:20-21).

When the fisherman says they longed for the new creation where righteousness dwells, there is another Old Covenant prophecy directly at root of his thought. In Daniel 9 inspiration records the angel's words to the prophet. He told Daniel that 70 weeks were determined upon his city and his people. The 70 weeks would bring to a close God's exclusive dealings with the nation and accomplish His redemptive plan. In verse 24 we are informed as to what all God would accomplish within the predicted time. For our purposes let it be noted that within, or at the very least by the time of the completion of, the 70 weeks, God said He would "bring in everlasting righteousness." There are several things to be noted here.

**First**, Daniel's prophecy is concerned with the fate of Israel, and the consummation of God's covenant dealings with her. The prophecy is not about the church *per se*, and is certainly not concerned with the church divorced from Israel. The prophecy is thus about the last days of Israel, not the last days of the Christian age. This is admitted by virtually all scholars.

**Second**, Daniel's prophecy is concerned with the ultimate fulfillment of God's eschatological and soteriological (salvation) promises to Israel. It involved the time when the Messiah would come (v. 26) and bring salvation. And please note that the fulfillment of Daniel would "bring in everlasting righteousness" (v. 24). Here is what Paul said he was eagerly expecting (Galatians 5:5).[232]

Was the world of righteousness that Daniel foretold a different world of righteousness being eagerly longed for by Peter in 2 Peter 3? Remember that Peter twice informs us that his prediction of the new creation was a reiteration of what the Old Covenant prophets foretold. So, the world of righteousness of 2 Peter 3 was foretold by Old Testament prophets. If then Peter was looking for the destruction of planet earth, followed by a new creation wherein dwells righteousness, *what O.T. prophet foretold that kind of destruction and that kind of new order?*

The failure of modern exegetes to see the inextricable link between what Peter was anticipating and the fulfillment of Daniel 9 is an indication of the tragic dichotomy that has been created between the N. T. writers and the O. T. prophecies. We are told that Peter was anticipating the "end of time." However, Peter says his prediction is based squarely on the O. T. prophets. *Any interpretation of 2 Peter 3 that cannot produce the O. T. prophecy that foretold the destruction of planet earth and the end of time is therefore falsified.* Peter is emphatic about the source of his eschatology, i.e. the O. T. prophets. But, here is what is significant, there are no O. T. prophecies of the end of time and destruction of planet earth. As we have shown, the *key* O. T. prophecy of the new creation, Isaiah 63-66 which serves as the foundation and fountain for 2 Peter 3 was a prediction of the destruction of the covenant heaven and earth of Old Covenant Israel, and the New Covenant creation to follow.

---

Any interpretation of 2 Peter 3 that cannot produce the O. T. prophecy, or prophecies, that foretold the destruction of planet earth and the end of time is falsified. Peter is emphatic that his prophecy is a reiteration of what the O.T. prophets foretold.

---

**Third**, the prophecy of Daniel 9 ends with the destruction of Jerusalem. This is seen in verses 26-27. The end of the Seventy Weeks is the fall of Jerusalem that occurred in A. D. 70.[233]

Now, Daniel was not predicting that the end of time would be at the end of the 70 weeks. This is admitted by all. However, he did see the consummation of the scheme of redemption, the bringing in of everlasting righteousness. And Daniel's prophecy terminates with the destruction of Jerusalem. That destruction, with the attendant removal of the covenant that could not give life and righteousness, would signal that all was now completed, all was fulfilled (Luke 21:22), *everlasting righteousness had been brought in!*

The argument then is quite simple. Daniel predicted that 70 weeks had been determined on the nation of Israel– not the church, and not planet earth--for Jehovah to consummate His scheme of redemption. This scheme, this wonderful plan, meant the bringing in of everlasting righteousness (Daniel 9:24). This righteousness was, as we have seen, to spring from Messiah the king of righteousness, and his word, the New Covenant of righteousness (2 Corinthians 3:9). Daniel was informed that the destruction of the city was to be the unmistakable declaration that God's purposes had been accomplished, the prophecy was fulfilled. And, in 2 Peter 3, Peter stood only a few short years away from the fall of the city.

Peter knew well the prophecy of Daniel. He was on Olivet (Mark 13:3), when the Lord predicted the final fall of the city and temple and referred to that very prophet (Mark 13:14). He heard Jesus say that in that cataclysm all prophecy would be fulfilled (Luke 21:22). Peter had the words of Jesus himself, that Daniel's prediction of the bringing in of everlasting righteousness had to be fulfilled by the time of the destruction. How can we fail to see that as the apostle stands on the very brink of that destruction he was eagerly expecting the promised consummation, the "new heavens and new earth, wherein dwelleth righteousness?" He was not longing for the dissolution of material creation. He was anticipating the fulfillment of God's prophetic word, the promise of the Messiah's glorious kingdom standing triumphant and perfected at the sweeping away of the old world (Revelation 11:15f).

Let's present our argument simply:

2 Peter 3 anticipated the arrival of the new creation of righteousness foretold by the O. T. prophets (2 Peter 3:1-2, 13).

Daniel 9:24-27 foretold the coming of the new creation of righteousness.

206

Therefore, 2 Peter 3 anticipated the fulfillment of Daniel 9:24f (among other O. T. prophecies).

Here is what that means:

2 Peter 3 anticipated the fulfillment of Daniel 9:24f.

But, Daniel 9:24f would be completely fulfilled by the time of, and in the destruction of Jerusalem in A.D. 70.

Therefore, 2 Peter 3 would be completely fulfilled by the time of, and in the destruction of Jerusalem in A.D. 70.

Let's put it in a slightly different way:

The world of righteousness of Daniel 9 would come at the end of Old Covenant Israel's history.

Peter was anticipating the arrival of the world of righteousness foretold by Daniel 9.

Therefore, Peter was anticipating the end of Old Covenant Israel's history.

We are told that 2 Peter 3 has not yet been fulfilled. Well, if what Peter was anticipating was the fulfillment of Daniel 9, but that has not yet been fulfilled,[234] then this *demands* that Israel remains God's chosen people, and the Old Covenant remains valid. It means that the pivotal 70th week of Daniel 9 remains unfulfilled.[235]

Put another way, if Peter was predicting the "end of time," and if Peter was anticipating the fulfillment of Daniel 9, then Daniel 9 will not be fulfilled until the "end of time."[236] If Daniel 9 is not yet fulfilled today, then, since Daniel 9 is a covenant promise of God to Israel, then, this means that God's covenant with Old Covenant Israel remains valid, and will remain valid until the fulfillment of Daniel 9 at the "end of time."

The only way to counter these arguments is to prove the following:

**1.)** You must prove that Peter was anticipating a totally different world of righteousness from that foretold by Daniel 9. Yet, Daniel 9 foretold the coming of a new world of righteousness, and Peter said that his prophecy was from the Old Covenant promises.[237]

**2.)** If you maintain that Peter was anticipating the fulfillment of Daniel, but that he was predicting an "end of time fulfillment," then you would have to show that Daniel 9 foretold the end of time. Yet, you cannot extend Daniel beyond the 70 Weeks that terminated in the destruction of the City.

**3.)** You would have to show how, although Peter anticipated the fulfillment of God's promises to Israel, that the fulfillment of Israel's promises belong to the end of the *Christian age*, and not to the climax of her Aeon.

207

**4.)** You would have to show why, that although God's promises to Israel remain valid, that His Theocratic relationship with her is no longer valid. God's relationship with Israel was based on His covenant with her. If His promises to her remain valid, His relationship with her remains valid. Unless you can prove that Daniel 9 was not about the fall of Jerusalem in A. D. 70, or unless you can prove that Daniel has nothing to do with 2 Peter 3, then, this proves that 2 Peter 3 is not predictive of the end of time.

None of these things can be proven. This demands therefore, that since Peter was anticipating the arrival of the new world of righteousness foretold by Daniel 9, that Peter was eagerly expecting the end of the Old Covenant age of Israel that came to its end in A.D. 70.

Yet another prophecy of the coming of everlasting righteousness must be noted before leaving this section. In Daniel 12:1f the prophet was told about a number of things which were to happen. They are listed here:

✔A time of trouble, "such as never was since there was a nation even to the same time" (v. 1). In Matthew 24:21 Jesus alludes directly to this prophecy and leaves no doubt that it would be fulfilled in his generation.

✔ "Many that sleep in the dust shall awake" (v. 2). Here is the promise of the resurrection, and it was to occur at the time of the Great Tribulation.

✔The righteous would shine as the stars forever (v. 3).

✔"Knowledge shall be increased" (v. 4).

✔Daniel's vision was to be sealed until "the time of the end" (v. 4).

✔The abomination of desolation would appear (v. 9f). Once again, Jesus alludes directly to this prophecy (and chapter 9:27), and states emphatically that it would be fulfilled in his generation (Matthew 24:15, 34).

As he continued to watch the unfolding prophecy, Daniel heard one of the "men" who was delivering the prophetic word ask, "How long shall it be to the end of these wonders, and when shall all of these things be fulfilled?" This was clearly for Daniel's sake.

Before we get heaven's infallible interpretation as to the time of the righteous shining forth as the sun, i.e. the resurrection, let's examine Jesus' use of this prophecy.

In Matthew 13:24-30 Jesus told the story of a man with a field. The enemy came and sowed tares in that field. When discovered by the master's servants the question arose as to what to do. The master said to let the tares and wheat grow together until the harvest, then they would be separated.

The disciples came to Jesus inquiring about the interpretation of the parable. He said the field was the world (13:38). The good seed are the "children of the kingdom" (v. 38), the tares are the children of the evil one.

Harvest, said the Lord, "is the end of the world" (v. 39, 40, literally, "at the end of this age"). He said at the harvest the righteous would, "shine forth as the sun in the kingdom of their Father," a direct reference to Daniel 12:3. This parable is almost universally understood to refer to the end of the Christian age. But if one is going to accept inspiration as the final interpreter of scripture he must reject these commentators.

In the first place we note that Jesus did not say harvest is at the end of the "world." He said it would be at the end of the "age," and specifically, he said "harvest is at the end of *this* age." As we have already shown, the original word is *aion*, and a comparison with a number of translations will reveal it is more correctly translated as *age* not world.

It is clear that Jesus taught that harvest was to occur in his generation. Throughout his ministry he referred to the harvest as an imminent event. He said the harvest fields were ripe already (John 4:35). He urged the disciples to pray for workers because the harvest was plentiful but workers few (Matthew 9:37-38). One cannot fail to notice the imagery of harvest in Matthew 3 when the Immerser warned the obdurate Pharisees that Jesus was going to purge his threshing floor and, "his winnowing fork is in his hands" (Matthew 3:11-12). The imagery is graphic and gives one the definite sense of imminence.

In Matthew 24:3 the disciples, in response to the Lord's prediction of Jerusalem's demise, asked about the sign of the end of the age, (again the word is not world but *age*). Jesus told them of the coming tribulation attendant with the destruction. He told them they would "see the Son of Man coming in the clouds" (v. 30). The Son of Man would send forth the angels "to gather together the elect" (v. 31). And he emphatically said this would all happen in that generation (v. 34).

Furthermore, in Revelation 14 the harvest imagery is used to speak of the time of judgment surrounding Babylon, the city "where the Lord was slain" (Revelation 14:6f; 11:8). It is obvious that the end of time cannot be in view. This is proven by his discussion of the 144,000.

Ice and other millennialists claim that during the Great Tribulation, which follows the removal of the church from the earth at the Rapture, 144,000 converted Jews begin to minister to the nation of Israel, to bring them to the Messiah. (*Prophecy*, 193). However, there is no way to extrapolate the appearance of the 144,000 into the future. In Revelation 14:4 it says of the 144,000, "These were redeemed from among men, being first fruits to God and the Lamb."

209

Do you catch that? *The 144,000 were the first generation of Jewish Christians!* They are the *first born*, the first redeemed! They cannot be a yet future generation of Jewish Christians. They *must be* the first generation. James wrote to the "twelve tribes scattered abroad" (James 1:1-2), and said, "Of His own will He brought us forth by the word of truth, that we might be a kind of first fruits of His creatures." (James 1:18). The writer of Hebrews, writing to Jewish Christians, spoke as well of "the church of the first born ones" (Hebrews 12:23). So, the 144,000 were to be the first generation of Christians, and James and Hebrews write to the first generation of Christians.

Now, if the first fruit of the harvest was in the first century, then, without doubt, the harvest, i.e. the resurrection of Daniel 12 and Matthew 13 was to occur in the first century. This is confirmed further by a continuing look at Revelation.

The writer depicts the judgment scene of the great persecuting city and then says, "Blessed are the dead who die in the Lord from now on." 'Yes,' says the Spirit, 'that they may rest from their labors, and their works follow them'" (Revelation 14:13). You will notice that there is *death following this judgment.* Since physical death is a natural part of life on earth it is patently obvious that *after the harvest*, at Christ's coming, life on earth, including physical death, continues.[238] (Revelation 14:14f) It is evident then that the harvest is viewed by the writers of the New Covenant as being a first century reality to take place at the end of the Jewish *aion*.

But the determinative answer to the question of the harvest and when the righteous would shine forth is to be found in the prophecy of Daniel.

Daniel heard the "man" ask when the things forecast would take place, and remember this includes the "shining forth of the righteous." The angel gave heaven's reply, "it shall be for a time, times and a half, and when the power of the holy people has been completely shattered, all these things shall be finished." (NKJV)

Can it be denied for even a moment that the power of the holy people[239] was completely shattered ("finally broken," NIV), in the destruction of A.D. 70? Jesus said harvest would be at the end of the age (Matthew 13:39-40), and that is when the righteous would shine forth. Daniel said the righteous would shine forth at the time of the end (Daniel 12:3-4), which is when the power of the holy people would be completely shattered. Therefore, the time of the end, the end of the age, the time of the harvest, when the righteous would shine forth would be when the power of the holy people would be completely shattered in A.D.70.

As we have seen, Peter stood within a few years of the shattering of the power of the holy people. This would, in the words of Jesus, be a time of unparalleled tribulation (Matthew 24:21), but it would be more. It would be the time when God's marvelous plan for mankind would be consummated. The kingdom, nascent at Pentecost, being fed and nurtured by the living word (I Peter 2:2), and equipped for the ministry by miraculously endowed men (Ephesians 4:8-16), finally arrived at the unity of the faith, to a measure of the stature of the fullness of Christ. Now fully grown and fully equipped by the faith once for all delivered, (and confirmed, DKP), to the saints, the church stood "manifested as the Sons of God" (Romans 8:18f).

The battle would be won. The persecuting city was doomed. The question of who were the Sons of God would be answered in definitive way by Jehovah. As the conflict had raged for years, the question of Son ship had been at heart of the issue. When doom fell on the former city of God it revealed the new city of God, the New Jerusalem. Those who claimed to be Jews were shown to be liars (Revelation 2:9; 3:9). The animal sacrifices which could never take away sin were shown to be futile in contrast to the "one time for all time," perfect sacrifice of the Son of God (Hebrews 9:14f). The Levitical priesthood, weak through the flesh, was abolished by the destruction of the genealogical records. A new priesthood took its place, a priesthood based on the lineage of Jesus the Messiah. The temple would be gone from the city. That marvelous edifice, one of the wonders of the world, would be merely a mountain of overturned stone. In its place, triumphant over the antagonism emanating from that city and temple, would stand the temple of the living God, the everlasting kingdom of Messiah. It would be the temple made of living stone (I Peter 2:5f), built on Jesus Christ as chief cornerstone (Ephesians 2:19f). Truly, in that climate, emerging from the conflict victorious, it can be seen how the wise would "shine as the brightness of the firmament and the righteous as the stars for ever and ever." In the mind of the Christian, righteousness had overcome the Law, this new world was truly one in which righteousness dwelt!

What we see then, is that when Peter says they eagerly awaited the new creation, wherein righteousness dwells, that he was alluding to the soon to come consummation of the kingdom. When all revelation had been given, when the enemy of the church had been defeated, when all prophecy was fulfilled, when the mystery of God was finished, *then* the church would stand triumphant and the righteous would shine forth as the stars of heaven. In this kingdom righteousness would be by faith (Romans 3), and would

211

stem from the righteous king (2 Corinthians 5:21, Romans 5:21). Truly, righteousness does dwell in God's kingdom.

## WHERE RIGHTEOUSNESS MAKES IT'S HOME: THE QUESTION OF ETHICS AND ESCHATOLOGY

A common objection to the views set forth in this work is that if the end came in A.D. 70 then there is no ground for ethical living today.[240] Ice claims that without the promise of a yet future eschatology, there is no basis to urge holy living today.[241] Let's take a closer look.

Ice believes that Jesus would have established the kingdom in the first century. When Jesus said, "The time is fulfilled, the kingdom of heaven is at hand," (Mark 1:15) he, like John the Immerser, called on Israel to, "Repent for the kingdom of heaven is at hand." Now here is the question. Since the kingdom arrives at the parousia[242] (Matthew 16:27-28; 2 Timothy 4:1, etc.), then if the kingdom would have been established in the first century, *would that have negated the ground for ethical conduct?* Ice does not believe so. He believes that the coming of the Lord initiates the millennium, and life in the millennium *demands* moral uprightness.[243]

Furthermore, at *whatever point* the kingdom is finally established, will the fulfillment of the eschatological predictions eliminate the need for moral conduct? If the fulfillment of 2 Peter 3 in A.D. 70 would negate the need for moral living, then the establishment of the kingdom *at whatever point in history*, would/will nullify all demand for righteousness.

The Biblical writers did exhort their readers to holiness in light of the impending judgment. As Moo notes, virtually every N. T. writer uses the coming of the Lord as the ground for ethical conduct (*NIV*, 196). However, because virtually all writers appeal to the impending consummation does not mean that eschatology was the *only* ground for ethical living. As Peter expressed it in the first epistle, "As the one who called you is holy, be ye holy in all of your conduct" (1 Peter 1:15). Thus, the relationship that a person has to God, *and the very nature of God Himself*, is used as a paranesis to holy living. Life in the kingdom, in fellowship with Messiah, is incentive for living for Him in holiness. After all, if one dwells in the presence of the Righteous King, that person should want to reflect the glory of that King, right?

In other words, those who would follow the Lord, should be like the Lord because of what He is. Not from fear of doom, destruction and damnation, but, because we want to be like Him. Now, in the very nature

212

of the case, to be like God means that we love what He loves, and we hate what He hates, we condemn what He condemns.

The question naturally arises, does God no longer hate those things that always were antithetical to His very *nature*, to His very *character*? We are not discussing God's *modus operandi*. We are discussing His *nature*. Or, were the things that Jehovah said He hated, just a bunch of arbitrary "rules" that He made up and said that He hated those things, when in fact, they were okay with Him? If God's very nature abhors certain actions, and rejects them, then to be holy is to hate those things and reject them. Unless the very nature, the very heart of God has changed, then He still abhors immorality, He still rejects dishonesty, He still condemns murder.

This point should be driven home. In the Old Testament, the end of the age was *not near*. It is true that there were "Days of the Lord" in light of which the people were called on to repent, as we have seen, but, those exhortations were a call to Israel to live holy lives, not simply because the Lord was coming, *but because they were the people of God and they had failed to live up to that holy standard.* Their failure to obey the covenant was bringing the Day of the Lord.

The Day of the Lord was to be a cathartic judgment to cause them to live for Him *after that Day.* The call to holiness in light of an impending Day of the Lord in the O. T. did not indicate that after the Day of the Lord came there would be no more ground for ethical living. On the contrary, holiness and morality were demanded after the Day to a greater degree, because they had come to realize their shortcomings and were now attempting, with renewed vigor, to keep the covenant.

Related to this point is the covenantal significance of the Day of the Lord. In the O. T. the Day was a covenantal "wake-up call" for Israel. It was to correct their violations of the covenant, and *bring them back to an obedient heart.* Consider then, that in the N. T. the Day of the Lord was to bring that Old Covenant to its consummation/termination, and to bring perfection and completion the New Covenant. In other words, the time before the Day of the Lord was seen as the time of the revelation of the New Covenant, and the Day of the Lord was to consummate that process. The Day was the perfection of the New Covenant world of Christ and the church, it was not the *termination* of the New Covenant–but of the old.

In the Old Testament, Jehovah promised to make a New Covenant with Israel and Judah (Jeremiah 31). This New Covenant would terminate the Old, and bring the new creation into full bloom. This New Covenant world, the new heavens and earth of 2 Peter 3, would give life and righteousness, where the old creation could never give it (Acts 13:38f; Galatians 3:20-21). The revelatory and confirmatory work of the Spirit in bringing that New Covenant world into existence and maturity was not completed on Pentecost. Paul's own personal ministry, guided and empowered by that revelatory Spirit, was for the purpose of transitioning believers from the old world to the new (2 Corinthians 3:16-4:1-4).

Our point is that the New Covenant world–with its demands for righteousness--was not completed on Pentecost. However, the ethical mandates that would exist after the consummation were being delivered during that transition from the old to the new (e.g. 1 Corinthians 5-6; Galatians 5:19f). The consummation did not nullify the fact God called (calls) on those *in the kingdom* to manifest the works of the Spirit, love, joy, peace, etc. (Galatians 5:22f). For Paul, life in the kingdom is to be characterized by righteousness (Romans 14:17). To argue that this standard of living was to cease at the parousia is to completely misunderstand the very nature of the kingdom itself, and to miss the point of the parousia. The parousia was not to bring life on earth, with the attendant expectations of obedience and humility before God, to an end.

> **The time *before* the Day of the Lord was the time of the revelation and confirmation of the New Covenant. The Day of the Lord was to consummate that revelatory process. The time *after* the Day of the Lord was/is *life in the New Covenant World*.**

We need to emphasize something. Those who make the argument that the arrival of the parousia negates any demand for ethical conduct fail to understand that the time of *the parousia and the arrival of the kingdom are synchronous events*. The kingdom did not come in its full glory until the parousia. (See Matthew 25:31f; Luke 21:28-31; 2 Timothy 4:1f; Revelation 11:15f). So, if it is argued that righteousness would be the order of the day when the kingdom arrived, then one cannot argue that the fulfillment of the parousia negates ethical exhortation. Thus, eschatology is not the only ground for ethical exhortation and moral living. Rather, *the full arrival of the kingdom demands holiness and righteousness*. This presents a major problem, especially for the amillennialists and postmillennialists. Here is what we mean.

214

The amillennialists and postmillennialists believe that the arrival of the kingdom on Pentecost brought about the nascent body of Christ. Attendant with the creation of Christ's church was the demand for ethical living. So, on the one hand, they see and emphasize that *the arrival of the kingdom brought with it the demand for ethical living*. The problem is that those who admit to the laying of the foundation for the kingdom on Pentecost do not stop to think of the implications of that in regards to the question before us.

In my library are numerous debate books between charismatics and non-charismatics. In those debates, the cessationists argue consistently that the church was established in infancy on Pentecost, and that the revelatory and confirmatory work of the Spirit was to bring the church, "to the perfect man, to the measure of the stature of the fullness of Christ" (Ephesians 4:13f). They argue that there was a transitional period of time between the Old Covenant world and the New. They argue that the arrival of "that which is perfect" would complete the New Covenant.[244]

I no longer believe that "that which is perfect" is simply a referent to the completed canon. I do believe however, that the church was established as a new born babe, so to speak, on Pentecost, and was growing toward maturity during the period between Pentecost and the parousia. In other words, I would argue that the New Covenant demands for ethical living were "perfected" at the parousia, not terminated. Take a look at Paul's teaching for just one example.

Paul definitely taught that the new creation was a present reality in Christ (2 Corinthians 5:17). However, he was still anticipating the full arrival of that new creation (Galatians 4:22f; Philippians 3:20-21, and Hebrews 12, if you take the Pauline authorship). Paul believed in *the already, but not yet*, of the new creation. And, for Paul, life in the new creation meant, "there is neither Jew nor Greek, bond or free, etc." (Galatians 3:28). Life in the new creation meant that, "neither circumcision nor uncircumcision avails, but faith that works through love" (Galatians 5:6). He believed, "for in Christ Jesus, neither circumcision nor uncircumcision avails, but the new creation" (Galatians 6:15).

So, for Paul, life in the new creation meant equality in Christ for all men. In light of the "not yet" aspect of the Kingdom, are we to believe that this equality in Christ was to *terminate* at the parousia, or, was it to be fully practiced afterward? So, our point is that the maturity of the church, manifested by the parousia, was not to nullify the demand for ethical living, it was to bring it into full force.

215

To put this another way, Paul rejected circumcision for those in Christ, before Christ's coming. However, he was anticipating the full arrival of the new world. And what was to be the order of the Day in that new creation? It was to be a world in which, "neither circumcision nor uncircumcision avails, but the new creation." In other words, Paul's rejection of circumcision was in force before the parousia, and would be in force after the parousia. So, this means that in the new order, what was true ethically before the parousia would be true after the parousia. Christ's coming would not terminate the command for a certain kind of living, it would put that certain kind of living, a Torah free, grace filled life, in full force.

Let me reiterate something. The parousia and the arrival of the kingdom are synchronous events. That is, the full *manifestation* of the Sons of God, the *vindication* of the Sons of God, and the *glorification* of the Sons of God, are linked with the full arrival of the kingdom at the parousia (See 2 Timothy 4:1f; Revelation 3:13f; 11:15f, etc.).

Now if the church is posited as being in a state of immaturity awaiting the time of maturity, i.e. at the parousia, then surely, when that time of maturity arrived, then the church's constitution, with its call for holy living, did not *cease to exist* then, but instead, came into full force.

Consider the situation that exists in Iraq as I write this (January 2006). The old regime of Saddam Hussein has fallen. A new government has been "set in place." Yet, patently, it has not yet conquered all of its enemies. They are "ruling in the midst of their enemies." While they are combating their foes, they are in the process of drafting a constitution. The idea is that when the new constitution is completed, and their enemies defeated, that Iraq will be a new world totally different from the old Iraq. There is an already-but-not-yet to the new world of Iraq. Will the completion of their constitution, the conquering of their enemies, the installment of the new government, put an end to life in Iraq, or will it bring into full bloom, a "brave new world"?

The arrival of the kingdom, the consummation of the New Covenant, the final destruction of Christ's enemies, are all tied together. Yet, nowhere does the Bible speak of the termination of the New Covenant, the end of the kingdom, and the demand for holiness, at the parousia. The arrival of "the end" was, in the fullest sense, the arrival of "the beginning!" This is why Paul told the Romans to live "as in the Day" (Romans 13:11f). That is, they were to live *as if the Day had fully come.* That exhortation did not mean that ethical conduct would no longer be expected from children of the King. It meant just the opposite.

216

Those who object to Covenant Eschatology based on the misguided claim that a fulfilled parousia negates the demand for moral living, are guilty of misunderstanding the relationship between the full arrival of the kingdom, ethics and eschatology. The consummation of eschatology was not to bring ethical conduct to an end, it was to emphasize the nature of God's holiness, the holiness of His new creation, and the demand for living according to the standard of that new creation, "Seeing then that all these things are to be dissolved, what manner of persons ought we to be?...we look for a new heavens and earth, wherein dwells righteousness" (2 Peter 3:11-13). McKnight has touched the hem of the garment by suggesting, "Until we tie the surviving remnant, the church, into Jesus' predictions about both salvation and judgment, in connection with A. D. 70, his teaching about God, ethics, and kingdom cannot be given their proper historical significance." (1999, 13).

To suggest that the fulfillment of the eschatological promises of the New Testament nullifies the need for ethical living is to completely miss the point of the full arrival of the new creation.

Be sure to see our addendum, on "The New Creation and Universalism." The question of ethics and eschatology is directly related to this topic, and universalism is currently experiencing somewhat of a revival in the evangelical world today.

# CHAPTER 14
# PAUL SAID IT TOO!

**"Our Beloved Brother Paul, According to the Wisdom Given Him, Has Written to You, as Also in All of His Epistles, Speaking in Them of These Things." (2 Peter 3:15-16)**

Peter tells us that the things of which he writes are what Paul had also written. In other words Paul wrote of the Day of the Lord also. Paul had written of God's longsuffering, of the passing of the elements, of the coming new creation. As a matter of fact, Peter says Paul wrote of it "in all his epistles." This tells us something of the importance of eschatology in the N. T.. While prophecy is often ignored and avoided in some fellowships it should be clear that the Spirit did not intend it to be this way. Someone has calculated that the parousia is mentioned or alluded to some 1800 times in the New Testament.[245]

But what is the significance of Peter saying that Paul wrote of the same thing as he does in 2 Peter? Well, if Paul defines the Day of the Lord as a historical event in the same manner as the O. T. Days of the Lord, and says that the Day was near in the first century, then since Peter tells us that his Day of the Lord is the same as predicted by Paul, this would mean that Peter is not predicting an end of time event, and literal coming of Christ.

There is no other book of Paul's which has a fuller discussion of the *epiphany* than Thessalonians. We will not repeat all of the points made earlier in the discussion of whether Paul believed the coming would be in his lifetime. We encourage a closer look at the following facts, however. What we want to do now is to take a quick survey of Thessalonians, both epistles, to see what we can determine about Paul's eschatology.

**1.)** In 1 Thessalonians 1:10 he says the Thessalonians turned to God to serve Him and wait for His Son to come from heaven. Jesus delivered them from the "coming wrath." This "wrath to come" was none other than the "wrath to come" foretold by John the Immerser (Matthew 3).[246] It was what Peter warned his audience to avoid, "save yourselves from this untoward generation" (Acts 2:40). It was the Great Day of God's wrath foretold by John, the Day that would vindicate the martyrs (Revelation 6:9f). The "coming wrath" was the time when God was going to judge Israel, for persecuting the saints. So, at the very outset of Thessalonians, Paul alludes to the impending judgment that was coming on the nation of Israel.

218

**2.)** In 2:15-17 Paul speaks of the wrath that was about to come on the Jews to the uttermost. The sense of imminence here is overwhelming. What is so impressive about this text is that it matches perfectly with Jesus' prediction (Matthew 23:29f). Notice that in Matthew, Jesus said that Israel had killed the prophets. They were going to kill the prophets that Jesus sent, and of course, they were going to kill Jesus (Matthew 21:37; 23:29f). In this persecution, Israel was filling up the measure of her sin, and judgmnet would fall in that generation.

Likewise, in 1 Thessalonians 2:15f, Paul says that the Jews had killed the prophets, they had killed Jesus, and were now killing Jesus' apostles and prophets. In doing so, they were filling up the measure of their sin, and wrath was about to fall on them.

The "wrath to come" here, is none other than the coming of Christ "in flaming fire, taking vengeance" on the persecutors of the Thessalonians (2 Thessalonians 1:7f). Paul says the *parousia* of Christ was for the purpose of bringing vengeance on the persecutors of the saints. The correlation between Matthew 23, 1 Thessalonians 2:15f, and 2 Thessalonians 1 cannot be ignored. And, naturally, the connection with 2 Peter is direct, since the scoffers were persecuting the saints.

**3.)** In 1 Thessalonians 4:15,17 Paul affirmed that some would be alive and remain until the Lord's coming. This is parallel with Matthew 16:27-28, and Jesus' promise to come in judgment in the lifetime of his audience. Corroboration for the posit that the events of Thessalonians were to be in that first century generation is found in comparing Matthew 24 with I Thessalonians 4-5. Canfield[247] lists several parallels between the two texts:

| Matthew 24 | 1 Thessalonians 4:13f-5:1f |
| --- | --- |
| Coming of Christ (v. 30) | Coming of Christ (v. 16) |
| Coming with a shout (v. 30) | Coming with a shout (v. 16) |
| Coming with angels (v. 30) | Coming with angels (v.16) |
| Sound of the Trumpet (v. 31) | Sound of the Trumpet (v. 16) |
| Believers gathered (v. 31) | Believers gathered (v. 17) |
| Coming in clouds (v. 30) | Coming in clouds (v. 17) |

| | |
|---|---|
| Specific time unknown (v. 36) | Specific time unknown (5:1-2) |
| Coming as a thief (v. 43) | Coming as a thief (5:2,4) |
| Unbelievers (not believers) unaware of impending judgment, (24:37-39) | Unbelievers (not believers) unaware of impending judgment (5:3) |
| Judgment as the travail of a woman (v. 37) | Judgment as travail on a woman (5:3) |
| Believers to watch (v. 42) | Believers to watch (5:6) |
| Warning against drunkenness (v. 49) | Warning against drunkenness (5:7) |
| This generation shall not pass away until all these things are fulfilled (v. 34) | Those of us who are alive and remain until the coming of the Lord (v. 15, 17) |

Similarity of language does not always demonstrate identiticality of subject. The similarities here are more than superficial, however.[248] They are exact and substantive. More, they are chronologically synchronous. Very clearly what Jesus foretold was the judgment on Israel. Paul's discourse is identical to Jesus. But, Peter's eschatological doctrine is the same as Paul. Since it is clear that Paul's eschatology in Thessalonians must be confined to the first century, this means that Peter's eschatology is confined to the first century.

**4.)** In 1 Thessalonians 5:1f Paul says they were sufficiently learned about the times and seasons of the parousia as not to be caught unaware by its coming. How could Paul say, "But concerning the times and seasons, you know well"? Contrast this with Acts 1:6f. There, the disciples asked about the establishment of the kingdom. Jesus told them that the "times and the seasons" (*kronous e kairous*) were known only by the Father.

Yet now, in 1 Thessalonians 5, Paul told the Thessalonians that they knew the times and the seasons (*kronon kai ton kairon*), of the Lord's coming so well that they could escape it. *This means that the revelatory Spirit had revealed the times and the seasons to them sufficiently well for them to take action.* The Father had truly revealed "things to come."

220

It is clear from the text that Paul was writing to people that would and could escape the impending Day of the Lord because of their knowledge. But if that Day is without signs, how could they "see the day approaching" (Hebrews 10:25) and escape? It should be noted that his discussion of Christ's coming as a thief cannot be taken as an end of time coming. Just as the coming as a thief on the church at Sardis was definitely to occur in their lifetime (Revelation 3:1f), this coming as a thief contains the same urgent sense of nearness, and cannot be extended two millennia into the Thessalonians' future.

**5.)** In 5:23 he prayed that their *body*, soul, and spirit be blameless at the Day of the Lord. This is a clear-cut affirmation that the Thessalonians were to live until the Day of Christ. Paul prayed that those living breathing Christians would live until Christ's coming. This fits Peter's affirmation that his audience was "hastening the Day of the Lord" very well.

**6.)** 2 Thessalonians 1:4f. Please go back and read again our earlier more extensive comments on this text. Paul speaks to living, breathing human beings, experiencing all too real, very present persecution. He was not speaking of prophetic events for a far away "last days." Paul promised those Christians relief and vindication from that suffering at the coming of Jesus to judge the wicked. To speak of a coming of Christ two millennia removed from those suffering saints would give no "relief" from that persecution *whatsoever*. Paul did not say that the church at some far off distant future, undergoing persecution would then receive relief from that distant persecution. He was writing to suffering saints and promised them relief, "when the Lord Jesus is revealed from heaven."

Paul used two distinctive words to speak of their suffering and the coming vindication. Their suffering was "tribulation" from *thlipsis*, (Strong's #2347), which means pressure. However, Paul promised them "rest," from *anesis (Strong's #425)*. When *thlipsis* and *anesis* are used together, *anesis* is always relief from whatever pressure is in view. It might even be relief from financial pressure (2 Corinthians 8:13). The point is that *anesis* means *relief* from whatever pressure is under consideration. *Anesis* is not *reward*, it is *relief*.

With this in mind, note again that Paul says the Thessalonians, living, breathing humans who lived 2000 years ago, were being persecuted. Paul uses the present tense of *thlipsis* four times. However, Paul also said that the Thessalonians would receive rest, "when the Lord Jesus is revealed

221

from heaven" (v. 7f). The statement is unequivocal and undeniable. Paul was speaking to real, living humans experiencing persecution in the streets of their city. But Paul promised them, by inspiration of the Spirit, that they, not some far distant, unknown generation, but that *they* would receive relief from that persecution when the Lord came. Note that the relief would be "when" the Lord was revealed from heaven. It would not be *before* the Lord was revealed. It would not be when they *died*. Relief would come when and only "when the Lord Jesus is revealed from heaven."

The choices here are simple, but challenging. If the Lord did not come and give relief to the Thessalonians then,

**A.)** Paul lied.

**B.)** Paul's prediction failed.

**C.)** The Thessalonians are still alive being persecuted.

It is important to note that Paul *did not say* that the Thessalonians would die, and then some day the Lord would reward them with heaven. Paul did not say that they would die, go to Hades, and there enjoy a reprieve from their persecution. Paul did not say that *they* would die, and then some day, the Lord would come, and take away the suffering of a *later generation* of Christians. Paul told that group of living, breathing humans, experiencing the travail of persecution, that they would receive relief from that very real life persecution *when the Lord came.*

If the coming of the Lord in 2 Thessalonians 1 is the same Day of the Lord of 2 Peter 3, then it is *prima facie* evident that the Day of the Lord in 2 Peter 3 is referent to the judgment on Old Covenant Israel for persecuting the faithful. And of course, we need to be reminded that Peter does tell us that his eschatology and Paul's eschatology "in all his epistles" was the same. Thus, unless one can delineate between 2 Thessalonians 1 and 2 Peter 3 then the coming of the Lord of these passages is inextricably bound with the judgment of Israel.

There are those who delineate between "comings" in Thessalonians. We have briefly noted DeMar's attempt to see 1 Thessalonians 4 as the "final coming" while positing 2 Thessalonians 2 as A.D. 70. But DeMar is not the only that sees two different comings of the Lord in Thessalonians.

Gentry applies 2 Thessalonians 2 to Christ's judgment coming in A.D. 70 (*Dominion*, 386), but argues that the coming of 2 Thessalonians 1:10 is the Second Advent, since in chapter 1, "Paul even employs a different word for the coming of Christ (*elthe*) from what he does in 2:1 (*parousia*). There the Second Advental judgment brings 'everlasting destruction from the presence of the Lord:' here the temporal judgment makes no mention of these mighty angels (2:1-12)" (*Dominion*, 386).

Gentry's hermeneutic is disturbingly inconsistent.[249] When writing about the proper interpretation of the Apocalypse, Gentry gives four reasons why it is improper to apply it to our future. We have already cited this above, but think it important enough to repeat here:

"Another detriment to the strained interpretations listed above is that John was writing to historical churches existing in his own day (Rev. 1:4). He and they are presently suffering "tribulation' (Rev. 1:9a). John's message (ultimately from Christ 1:1) calls upon each to give careful, spiritual attention to his words (2:7 etc). John is deeply concerned with the expectant cry of the martyrs and the divine promise of their soon vindication (6:10; cp. 5:3-5). He (John, dkp) would be cruelly mocking their circumstances (while committing a 'verbal scam' according to Mounce were he telling them that when help comes it will come with swiftness–even though it many not come until two or three thousand years later" (*Beast*, 27).

We wholeheartedly agree with this hermeneutic. Our question is, why is it not valid in 2 Thessalonians 1? Was Paul addressing a historical church in his day? *Yes.* Was he, and were they suffering persecution? *Yes.* Was Paul concerned with, "the expectant cry of the martyrs and the divine promise of their soon vindication?" *Yes.* Would Paul have been, "cruelly mocking their circumstances were he telling them that when help comes it will come with swiftness–even though it may not come until two or three thousand years later"? *Yes!*

There is no substantive difference between what Paul said and what John wrote to suffering saints. Why then does Gentry not apply his excellent hermeneutic to 2 Thessalonians 1? Because 2 Thessalonians 1 uses the Greek word *elthe* and not *parousia*, as does 2 Thessalonians 2, and because 2 Thessalonians 1 speaks of "everlasting destruction" not a temporal judgment. These arguments are specious at best.

Gentry applies Isaiah 34 to the "temporal" Day of the Lord against Edom. Yet, it was to be an *everlasting judgment* (Isaiah 34:10). Further, the judgment of Babylon of Revelation–and Gentry identifies Babylon as Old Covenant Jerusalem-- was to be an *eternal judgment* (Revelation 14:8-11). Yet, Gentry has no problem believing that the judgment of Babylon was a first century temporal judgment. It is therefore, untenable to suggest a contrast in comings in Thessalonians based on an imagined contrast between a temporal judgment and an everlasting judgment.

Gentry's hermeneutic of division is also suspect when he delineates between 2 Thessalonians 1 and 2 Thessalonians 2 because chapter 2 does not mention *angels* in describing Christ's coming, whereas chapter 1 does (*Dominion*, 386). Should we delineate between passages, and see in them different events because one passage does not include every single tenet mentioned in another text? Let's test that hermeneutic.

1 Corinthians 15 speaks of the resurrection of the dead. Yet, it says not one word about the destruction of the heavens and earth. It does not mention the burning of the elements, as does 2 Peter 3. Yet, Gentry applies both passages to the same time, the end of human history as we know it.

1 Corinthians 15 makes no mention of Christ coming with a shout, on the clouds, or coming with the *angels*, which in 2 Thessalonians 1 is determinative for Gentry in delineating between the final parousia and A.D. 70. While 1 Corinthians *omits these elements*, 1 Thessalonians 4 mentions all of them, and Gentry believes that both passages describe the same event. If Corinthians can omit all mention of the shout, angels and clouds, why cannot 2 Thessalonians 1 be the same coming as 2 Thessalonians 2 even though chapter 2 makes no mention of angels?

Gentry says 1 Thessalonians 4:13f and 2 Thessalonians 1 are the same event, i.e. the Final Advent. But there is a *major* problem here for Gentry. Remember that he delineates between 2 Thessalonians 1 and chapter 2 because of the use of *elthe* in chapter 1 and *parousia* in chapter 2.

*1 Thessalonians 4 and 2 Thessalonians 1 contain the same "different words" as do 2 Thessalonians 1 and 2 Thessalonians 2!* In 1 Thessalonians 4 Paul uses the word *parousia* (v. 15, the same word used in 2 Thessalonians 2:1), to describe the coming of the Lord. However, remember that in 2 Thessalonians 1 Paul uses *elthe*, and Gentry insists that this word indicates a different coming from *parousia*. Why then does he not delineate between 1 Thessalonians 4 and 2 Thessalonians 1? This is inconsistency exemplified.

Here is what Gentry does:

1 Thessalonians 4:15- *parousia* is final coming

2 Thessalonians 1:7f– *elthe*, is final coming.

So, Paul uses *different words* to describe the *same event*, and Gentry has no problem with this.

**However,**

2 Thessalonians 2:1-2– is *parousia,* and is A.D. 70, but,

1 Thessalonians 4:15, 17 is *parousia* and is the "final coming."

224

So, Paul uses *the identical words*, and in both contexts he speaks of the gathering of the saints. But, Gentry insists that these are two totally *different events*, disparate in nature and time.

If the use of different words (*parousia-v-elthe*), does not demand different events in Gentry's application of 1 Thessalonians 4 and 2 Thessalonians 1, then why does the use of those same different words demand two different events in 2 Thessalonians 1 and 2 Thessalonians 2 (*elthe -v-parousia*)? And, if different words can be used describe the same event, then why does not the use of *the identical words* demand the reference to *the same event* (1 Thessalonians 4:15, *parousia* / 2 Thessalonians 2:1-2, *parousia*)?

Again, Gentry sees different comings in 2 Thessalonians 1 and 2 because Paul uses different words. But, if the use or non use of a single word delineates between comings, *why then does a point by point parallel between words and terms not demand the same coming?* We will see the importance of this question momentarily.

DeMar engages in the same inconsistency, *only with different texts, texts that contradict Gentry's distinctions.* DeMar applies 2 Thessalonians 1 to the A.D. 70 parousia (*Madness*, 371). However, he delineates between 1 Thessalonians 4:13f and 2 Thessalonians 2 *because of the use of different words.* This time, DeMar focuses on the word *episunagogee* found in 2 Thessalonians 2:1, and the fact that this word is not used to describe the "gathering" of 1 Thessalonians 4.

Gentry applies 2 Thessalonians 1 and chapter 2 to different events because of the use of different words. DeMar insists that both chapters are the same event, the A.D. 70 parousia, even though different words are used. Yet, he then delineates between 1 Thessalonians 4 and 2 Thessalonians 2 *because of the use of different words.* So, Gentry says you cannot apply 2 Thessalonians 1 and 2 to the same event *because of the use of different words.* Demar denies this, but then, delineates between 1 Thessalonians 4 and 2 Thessalonians 2 *because of the use of different words.*

*Can the same author not use different words to describe the same event?* Note that in Matthew 24:3 the disciples asked about Jesus' *parousia* (Strongs #3952). Gentry and DeMar believe that the parousia of Matthew 24:3 is the A.D. 70 judgment. In answering the disciples' question about the parousia, Jesus used a different Greek word *erchomai* (Strong's #2064, v. 30). Are we to conclude that verses 29f describe a different coming from what the disciples asked about? Not according to Gentry and DeMar, who say the *erchomai* of verses 29f is the A.D. 70 *parousia* of verse 3.

225

(*Madness*, 152+). So, according to Gentry and DeMar, the same writer *can use* different words to speak of the same event. Why is that not true in Thessalonians, or, in Isaiah, Peter and Revelation?

Remember that in 2 Thessalonians 1 Paul uses *elthe,* and Gentry says that this must be different from *parousia* in 2 Thessalonians 2. But why? If Jesus used *parousia* and *erchomai, (from whence elthe comes),* to speak of the same event, why could not Paul do the same?

DeMar is inconsistent in his claim that different words indicate different events. In fact, he actually holds that *the use of identical words does not mean identical comings!* In Matthew 24:3 the disciples asked about Christ's *parousia.* DeMar says that was the A.D. 70 coming of Christ. However, in 1 Thessalonians 4:15 Paul uses the word *parousia,* yet, DeMar insists that it cannot be the same coming as in Matthew. Now, if the use of different words in 2 Thessalonians 2 and 1 Thessalonians 4 demands different comings, then why does not the use of *identical words* in Matthew 24 and 1 Thessalonians 4 demand the identical coming?

This is an important point in light of DeMar's excellent work on the comparison between *Matthew 24 and 2 Thessalonians 2.* DeMar produces *nine parallels,* including *the use of the same words in the two texts,* to show that 2 Thessalonians 2 anticipated the same events as Matthew 24. DeMar says, "There are striking parallels between the Olivet Discourse and 2 Thessalonians 2. The events described in Matthew 24 were fulfilled prior to Jerusalem's destruction in A.D. 70. We should expect the same for 2 Thessalonians 2" (*Madness,* 325). We agree. However, *why does the same principle not apply to the parallels between 1 Thessalonians 4 and the Olivet Discourse?* Take a look again at the point by point parallels between the Olivet Discourse and 1 Thessalonians 4.

| Matthew 24 | 1 Thessalonians 4:13f-5:1f |
|---|---|
| Coming of Christ (v. 30) | Coming of Christ (v. 16) |
| Use of *parousia* (v. 3) | Use of *parousia* (v. 15) |
| Coming with a shout (v. 30) | Coming with a shout (v. 16) |
| Coming with angels (v. 30) | Coming with angels (v. 16) |
| Sound of the Trumpet (v. 31) | Sound of the Trumpet (v. 16) |
| Believers gathered (v. 31) | Believers gathered (v. 17) |

| Coming in clouds (v. 30) | Coming in clouds (v. 17) |
|---|---|
| Specific time unknown (v. 36) | Specific time unknown (5:1-2) |
| This generation shall not pass (v. 34) | We who are alive and remain until the coming of the Lord (v. 15, 17) |

*Here are nine points of perfect correspondence!* Now if the *nine points of comparison* between the Olivet Discourse and 2 Thessalonians 2 demands that we link them, *then why do the nine points of comparison between the Olivet Discourse and 1 Thessalonians 4* not demand that we link the two passages to the same event as well?

Interestingly, what DeMar does *not* note is that the Olivet Discourse uses *episunagogee* and *parousia to describe the same event,* the A.D. 70 coming of the Lord. Yet, DeMar tries to delineate between 1 Thessalonians 4 and 2 Thessalonians 2 because in chapter 2 Paul uses *episunagogee,* and does not use it in 1:4:13f. DeMar omits the fact that in 2 Thessalonians 2:1-2 Paul uses both *parousia* and *episunagogee,* the same two words used by Jesus in Matthew 24, and that DeMar applies to the same event.

We have spent considerable time to show that there is a consistent eschatology in Thessalonians. While some scholars seek to find two different comings of the Lord, thus *two different eschatologies* in Paul's two epistles, we have shown that this is false. There was *only one eschaton* with which Paul and Peter were concerned and that was *Israel's eschaton,* Israel's last days, the coming of Israel's Messiah to bring her salvation to perfection. This cannot be over-emphasized! To overlook or ignore the fact that Paul's doctrine of the resurrection (1 Thessalonians 4), was the promise that was made to and *belonged to Israel* (Acts 24:14f; 26:6f; Romans 8:23-9:4;1 Corinthians 15:54f), and to then posit that event at the end of the (endless) Christian age is misguided at the very least, and dangerous at worst. The resurrection, and thus Biblical eschatology, *belonged to Israel,* and was to occur in her last days.

Most interpretations of 2 Peter 3 assume as unquestionable the idea that Peter was anticipating the end of time and the Christian age. This fundamental fallacy of all futurist eschatologies is imposed on all N. T. prophetic texts, and as a result, prophecies that emphatically anticipate the fulfillment of Israel's O. T. prophecies are cut off from those roots, and made to speak of something totally foreign to their origins. The tragic belief that Israel was cut off at the cross, and that God from Pentecost onward was dealing with the church, divorced from Israel and her last days hopes, is the root of the majority of eschatological confusion today. Biblical eschatology belonged to Israel, and her last days, not the last days of the church.

The admission by noted theologian R. C. Sproul Sr. that, "we must take seriously the redemptive-historical importance of Jerusalem's destruction in A.D. 70,"[250] is encouraging. However, while Sproul has begun to see *some* major significance to that event, he and others still divorce the "final judgment" and the resurrection from Israel's last days, Israel's eschaton. They thereby continue to create two eschatons, demanding that 2 Peter is about the end of the (endless) Christian age, and that Paul in Thessalonians and Corinthians spoke of the resurrection in a context isolated from the hope of Israel. As long as commentators and Bible students continue to view 2 Peter 3, 1 Corinthians 15, and 1 Thessalonians 4, divorced from Israel's promises, it is that long that eschatology will continue to be a source of confusion. It is time to admit and agree with the inspired text: Biblical eschatology was the hope of Israel. We must bring our preconceived ideas into conformity to that truth.

Thus, the attempt to find two comings of the Lord, two eschatons, in Thessalonians is wrong. To admit that Thessalonians does speak of the A.D. 70 coming of Christ at the end of the Old Covenant age of Israel is, in effect, to admit that all Biblical eschatology was fulfilled at that time. However, to admit to the A.D. 70 parousia of Christ, to bring Israel's eschatological and soteriological history to its climax, and to then posit a yet future different parousia is to create an eschaton foreign to scripture.

Of course, the application for our study of 2 Peter 3 should be obvious. There is only one *parousia*, one eschaton in Corinthians, Thessalonians, Peter, and Revelation. That is the A.D. 70 *parousia* of Christ. Since Peter said that Paul's eschatology is the same as his eschatology in 2 Peter 3, this means that the eschatology of 2 Peter 3 was the A.D. 70 *parousia* of Christ. We continue now with our survey of the Thessalonian passages.

**7.)** In 2 Thessalonians 2:2 Paul warned the Thessalonians to not be deceived into thinking the Day of the Lord had *already come*. But if the Day of the Lord ends time and destroys the universe how could they possibly believe it had already happened? Only if they had the Old Covenant concept of the Day, as outlined earlier, would this be possible. Just think of this for a moment.

If the Day of the Lord of 2 Peter 3 is a time ending, cosmos destroying event, as most interpreters suggest, then how in the world could anyone believe it had *already happened*? If someone wrote you a letter and told you that the entire universe had burned up yesterday, would you, *could you*, believe them? If you received a phone call that told you that all of the physically dead who had ever lived came to life yesterday, and that all the grave yards are now empty, would you, *could you* believe them?

Remember, Paul was writing to the church at Thessalonica urging them to reject those who said "the Day of the Lord has already come." So, the Day of the Lord is when the earth burns up and time ends, according to the traditional view of 2 Peter 3. But, some at Thessalonica believed that the Day of the Lord had already come. Therefore, some at Thessalonica believed that the earth had already burned up, and time had already come to an end! Can *anyone* believe such a thing?

To repeat therefore, only if the Thessalonians believed that the Day of the Lord was a historical, in time event, that manifested God's sovereignty, could anyone believe that the Day had already occurred. This means that if the Day of the Lord in 2 Thessalonians 2 and 2 Peter 3 are the same event, that the Day of the Lord in Peter could not have been an earth burning, time ending, bodily appearing of Jesus. It would be the coming of Christ "in the glory of the Father" (Matthew 16:27-28). It would be Christ judging as the Father had judged (John 5:19f), and this precludes a bodily, visible return of Christ.

**8.)** In 2 Thessalonians 2:3f Paul says the Man of Sin was alive, but being restrained at that time.[251] He would be loosed and do his horrible work, but be destroyed at the appearing of Jesus. If the Man of Sin was alive in the first century, but was to be destroyed by the coming of Jesus, it follows that Jesus was to come in the first century.

This is but a sampling of the things that Paul had to say about the Day of the Lord. Undeniably, Paul taught that the Day was to be in that generation. Since Peter said Paul taught the same thing about the Day of the Lord as he did we cannot escape the conclusion that Peter expected the Day to occur in his lifetime.

In addition, remember what we have noted earlier concerning the word *elements*. We have already shown that the word *stoicheia*, is used by Paul to speak *exclusively* of the passing of the Old world of Israel.

Peter said that he and Paul taught the same things about the Day of the Lord, and that includes the passing of the elements. When Paul spoke of the passing of the elements (*stoicheia*), he spoke *exclusively* of the passing of the elements of the Old Covenant world of Israel. Since therefore, Peter said his discussion of the passing of the elements at the Day of the Lord meant the same thing as found in Paul, we conclude that Peter's discussion of the passing of the elements at the Day of the Lord was a discussion of the passing of the elements of the Old Covenant world of Israel.

# CHAPTER 15
# HARD TO UNDERSTAND

**"Consider That the Longsuffering of Our Lord Is Salvation–as Also Our Beloved Brother Paul, According to the Wisdom Given to Him, Has Written to You, as Also in All of His Epistles, Speaking in Them of These Things, in Which Are Some Things Hard to Be Understood."** (2 Peter 3:15-16)

In my early days I would read 2 Peter 3 and believe it to be one of the easiest passages in all of the Bible to understand. Then one day I read verse 16. Peter says Paul wrote of these same things, and then he says these things are hard to understand. I was perplexed. What was so hard about it? It slowly dawned on me that if an inspired apostle says it is hard to understand, then perhaps someone like me should take a closer look. Yet today it is still common to hear preachers expound on this text and say it is too clear to be misunderstood. I have heard ministers, some quite famous, say a person would have to have help to misunderstand what Peter means here. That may be so, but I am not convinced it is.

One of the greatest problems in Bible studies today, and especially the subject of eschatology, is a failure to study the Old Covenant background of the New Covenant. My personal tradition does not encourage the in-depth study of the Old Testament at all. I have personally had church leaders tell me that preachers should not preach from the Old Testament! I am glad to say however, that in places this is changing. But such an attitude robs us of not only the riches of the wisdom of the ages contained in the Old Covenant, but fails to realize that a knowledge of the Old is indispensable to a proper understanding of the New.

Romans 15:4 tells us the Old Testament is to be used for learning. Do we understand why? We know I Corinthians 10:11 says the things of the old were written as ensamples. But do we *study* them as we should? A knowledge of the Old Testament is *essential* to a proper understanding of 2 Peter 3. The usual response however, is, "It says what it means and means what it says!" However, a failure to know the mind-set, the world view of the Hebrew writers and readers automatically lends itself to misapplication and misunderstanding of the scriptures. The failure to acknowledge and honor the O. T. source of 2 Peter 3 is fatal to any proper interpretation. The failure to see that Peter was anticipating the realization of the "hope of Israel" dooms any interpretation of 2 Peter 3.

In this book, I have challenged the prevailing interpretation of 2 Peter 3. It is not always easy to change our convictions. Yet, to borrow the words of Gentry, as he appealed for open minds in regard to his work on Revelation:

"Almost certainly you have been taught a radically different view at some point in your Christian journey. You may even be tempted to scoff at its very suggestion at this point. Nevertheless, I challenge you to bear with me as we wade through the evidence on this matter in Revelation. I am convinced that you will find the flood of evidence becoming a 'river that no man can cross.'" (*Beast*, 18).

Insert the term "2 Peter 3" for "Revelation," and you have my sentiments. Furthermore, in his response to Wayne Gruden, Gentry says, citing the Westminster Confession of Faith, "the supreme judge by which all controversies of religion are to be determined, and all decrees and councils, opinions of ancient writers, doctrines of men, and private spirits, are to be examined, and in whose sentence we are to rest, can be no other but the Holy Spirit speaking in Scripture" (*Gift*, 121). *We fully agree!*

It is admittedly fearful to violate our own traditions, the beliefs received from parents, respected preachers, professors, or perhaps from long cherished creeds. More on this below. However, our call here is *Sola Scriptura!* We are appealing for the reader to have the courage to live up to that lofty principle. As Keith Mathison says, although he personally *violates* what he says, "We must turn to scripture, not Augustine or Calvin, to verify the truthfulness of a doctrine."[252]

This book challenges you to have the mind of the great reformers that have gone before. You are being challenged to study and know what the Bible meant to the people to whom it was written, not to impose a modern Occidental (Greek) interpretation on it. Simply put, you are being challenged to be better students of the Word of God. We never lose by re-examining what the Book says. We only lose when we close our minds to thinking, to study.

We have shown that the river of evidence in regard to 2 Peter 3 flows swift and deep. The evidence for the first century application of 2 Peter 3 is overwhelming, solid and irrefutable.

# CHAPTER 16
## OBJECTIONS CONSIDERED

We come now to consider some objections to the position set forth here. We have already examined some of Gentry's comments, and will include others, along with Winkler's. We will try to address the objections that our adversaries consider the most powerful.

**Objection #1**– Apocalyptic language does not actually speak of the destruction of the universe, only the covering, or darkening of sun, moon, etc. whereas Peter speaks of actual destruction. This is essentially the same objection offered by Gentry and noted above.

**Response**-- This is patently false. Isaiah 24:2f; 19f speaks of earth fading away, and being completely removed, never to rise again. Chapter 34 speaks of *mountains melting*, the host of heaven *dissolving*, the earth *burning*. Micah says the mountains melt at the coming of Jehovah (1:3f). It is a false dichotomy to suggest that apocalyptic language does not speak of the destruction of creation, but that 2 Peter 3 does. In fact, much of the Old Testament language–that cannot in any sense be considered literal– is even more graphic than 2 Peter 3.

**Objection #2** -- Prophetic imagery, i. e. rolling of heavens like a scroll (Hebrews 1, DKP), is "impossible." Peter's language is not. (Winkler)

**Response**-- Interestingly, Winkler applies Hebrews 1:11-12 to "the end of time," yet says that what it predicts is "impossible." The text says the world would be "folded up." This is only impossible when literalized. Winkler would also preach "nothing is impossible with God." He admits this is imagery, but literalizes the language. If it is imagery it is not literal! Why is it possible for the elements of the cosmos to be destroyed, but it is not possible for the creation to be "folded up?" See our response to Gentry's objection #4 earlier in this work as well.

Furthermore, the prophetic context Hebrews 1:10 is Psalms 102:16f and foretold the time when God would create *a new people for a new world* when God destroyed the "heavens and earth," *when He redeemed Zion. Psalms 102 is about the redemption of Israel!* Does Winkler believe that God will destroy one people and create a new people at the "end of time"? No. Does he believe that Israel's salvation hope is unfulfilled? No. The prophetic source of Hebrews 1 is the dissolution of the Old Covenant world and the creation of Christ's New Covenant world.

233

**Objection #3** -- Peter referred to the flood to prove the possibility of earth being destroyed. Again, this objection is similar to that offered by Gentry. Go back and read our comments on page 146f.

**Response**-- Peter did no such thing. He says it was the "world" that perished (v. 6). If Winkler is consistent he must agree Peter is foretelling the end of a "world," not the end of time. Peter writes of three worlds, Noah's, his world, and the coming new world. Peter's world had to be destroyed. *Peter's world was the world of Judaism!* And the "age to come" was the consummated kingdom of Christ (Mark 10:27-30). The fact that Peter says a physical event destroyed "the world of the wicked," should prevent the astute student from arguing for a destruction of material creation. Peter does not say the earth was destroyed, for it was not. It was the "world of the wicked." To suggest that Peter shifts the focus from the world of the wicked to focus on the material creation changes horses in mid-stream, and destroys the continuity of the text.

**Objection #4** – Peter says his Day of the Lord was judgment of ungodly men, therefore, "we can deduct that he has no particular city or nation in mind."

**Response** -- That is assumption, not deduction. Isaiah said the whole creation would suffer. But he spoke against Babylon (Isaiah13-14). In Isaiah 34 he describes "universal" destruction, but it was Idumea and the other nations judged in the Babylonian invasion. Furthermore, Jesus clearly placed the judgment of the un-godly in his generation (Matthew 23:35-36, I Corinthians 15:51-56, I Peter 4:5, 17, Revelation11:18, 22:10-12).

Winkler does like Gentry in his study of Thessalonians. He seeks to delineate between passages because one passage mentions an element that is omitted in another passage. This is a faulty hermeneutic. See our discussion above. It does not matter if Peter specifically named the object of the impending judgment. The fact that the rest of the New Testament unmistakably posits the time of the judgment as the first century, makes that distinction, or lack thereof, immaterial.

**Objection #5** – Peter speaks of a new heavens and earth. This indicates he is speaking of "the day for the final windup of all matters."

**Response**-- There are several problems with this objection.

**First**, it *assumes* that time will end, and that the earth will be literally destroyed. We have shown that the current Christian age has no end.

**Second**, this objection fails completely to consider the Old Testament source of Peter's prophecy. Remember, we have shown there was, per Isaiah 66, to be evangelism in the new creation. This hardly fits the "heavenly" construct of the new heavens and earth after the end of time.

**Third**, we have shown from Isaiah 65, the seminal promise of the new creation, that the new creation would arrive at the time of the judgment of Israel (Isaiah 65:13-17), "The Lord God will slay you, and call His people by new name...I create a new heavens and earth."

Since Peter tells us that the new creation was what was promised by the Old Testament prophets, and since the Old Testament prophets said that the new creation would come when the old creation of Israel was destroyed, then we are safe to conclude that Peter was anticipating the destruction of the old creation of Israel.

**Fourth**, it is interesting that Winkler argues that the term heaven and earth indicates that Peter is speaking of the final wind-up of things. If this is so, then this demands that Isaiah 64-66 was speaking of the final wind-up of things. However, as we have already shown, Isaiah 64-66 foretold the destruction of Old Covenant Israel with the new creation being the direct result. Neither Winkler, Gentry, nor any other commentator with which we are familiar believes that "the final wind of things" occurs as a result of Israel's sin and destruction.

**Objection #6** – 2 Peter 3 can't be speaking of the fall of Jerusalem in A.D. 70 because that was a local event, and Peter refers to a universal event.
**Response**: This objection fails on several accounts

**First**, the universalistic nature of apocalyptic language falsifies this objection. In the O. T. the Day of the Lord is described in universal language almost invariably. The constellations–that is pretty *universal*– would be dissolved. The earth would melt. The heavens and the earth would be removed (Isaiah 13:9f). The earth would be shaken (Isaiah 2:19f). These references are admitted by Gentry, Seriah, Sproul Sr., etc., to be historical Days of the Lord that predicted judgment of "local" cities and kingdoms. If the Lord could and did use universal language to describe temporal Days of the Lord, why could not Peter do that in 2 Peter 3?

**Second**, this objection fails to consider that Jesus said that the destruction of Jerusalem would be the greatest tribulation that the world has ever seen, or ever will see (Matthew 24:21). Is that not "universal?" Did Jesus lie when he said that the fall of Jerusalem would be the greatest event the world had ever seen, or would ever see? One has to seriously consider

235

just how Jesus could describe the fall of Jerusalem in such terms, and still hold to a literalistic interpretation of 2 Peter 3.

**Third**: this objection also fails to see that Jesus used "universal" language to describe the fall of Jerusalem. Note that in Matthew 24:29f: "The sun will be darkened, the moon will not give its light, the stars will fall from the heaven." Is this not universal language? Further, note Luke 21:25f, "There will be signs in the sun, in the moon, and in the stars; on the earth distress of the nations, perplexity, the sea and the waves roaring, men's hearts failing them from fear and expectation of those things which are coming on the earth, for the powers of the heavens will be shaken."

How much more universal could language have been? How much more universal would the language have to be to satisfy the critics?

Many who make this objection do not stop to think of the implications of their argument. In my personal experience, I have been confronted with the, "Jerusalem was a local judgment, but Peter was speaking of a universal judgment" argument. But, consider Revelation for a moment. Some of those who make the "local versus universal" argument believe that Revelation is primarily concerned with the judgment of Rome, or even the Roman Catholic church. That was the belief of my youth, incidentally.

The language of Revelation therefore, applies to the destruction of Rome. However, the destruction of Rome was not a universal destruction. Therefore, the language of universal language demands that Revelation cannot be speaking of the judgment of Rome. Do you see the problem?

What made the destruction of Rome more important than the demise of Jerusalem? Rome was never a covenant city. Rome had never been "the perfection of beauty" (Psalms 50). Rome had never been "the holy land."

**Fourth**, and perhaps most significantly, the contention that the fall of Jerusalem was merely a "localized" event, of no consequence or interest to those in Athens, Corinth, or certainly America[253] is an abject failure to understand the significance of Jerusalem in God's Scheme of Redemption. Thankfully, more thoughtful insight is beginning to come to the surface.

We have already noted the comment of Sproul, "We must take seriously the redemptive-historical importance of Jerusalem's destruction in A.D. 70." (*Last Days,* 26). Wright cites Sanders in regard to the Temple and its place in the mind of Israel, "I think that it is almost impossible to make too much of the Temple in first century Jewish Palestine" (*Victory*, 406ff). Anderson noted that, "No greater cultic calamity could be imagined than the loss of this sacrifice, (the Temple cultus, DKP), since it symbolized the severing of the divine-human relationship (Daniel 8:11)." (Cited in Wright,

*Victory,* 407, n. 133). Stevenson says that to the Jew, "the destruction of the temple could be seen as tantamount to the destruction of the nation." (*Power*, 168) He cites the Talmud where it is said that, "with the destruction of Jerusalem 'an iron wall intervened between Israel and the Father in heaven'" (*Power*, 130). To the Jewish mind, the Holy of Holies was "the garden of Eden" (*Power*, 127, n. 50).

These quotations from various sources demonstrate in a small way the significance of the Temple in Jerusalem to the mind of the Jews. Jerusalem is the place God had chosen to represent Him, to be His dwelling. There was not another city like it in the world. To suggest that the destruction of Jerusalem was therefore a "local event" with little or no eternal spiritual significance betrays a woeful ignorance of the Biblical data, and history.

Does an event have to be of universal scope, to be universally significant. In other words, does an event have to be geographically widespread, and widely known about, to be truly important? Does the distance of an event from a given audience hearing of that event determine whether that event is important? Do people have to really *care* about an event to make it significant? Jackson argues:

"Was the whole world judged in A.D. 70? Were the people in South America judged in A.D. 70? What did the destruction of Jerusalem have to do with them? Not a thing under the sun. By the way, what would the destruction of Jerusalem have meant to those people who were living in Athens, Greece? Paul says, 'Gentlemen, you had better repent.' Why? 'Because Jerusalem, hundreds of miles away is going to be destroyed in A.D. 70.' They likely would have said, 'So what? What does that have to do with us?'" (*Theory*, 67)

The inherent fallacy, we might even suggest the desperation, of such an argument is apparent. Let's just change a word or two in the quote and see if it makes the same sense:

"Was the whole world subjected to Christ at Pentecost? Were the people in South America brought under his reign? And what did the death of Jesus have to do with them? Not a thing under the sun. By the way, what would the death of Jesus have meant to those people who were living in Athens, Greece? Paul says, 'Gentlemen, you had better repent.' Why? 'Because a Jew hundreds of miles away says so!' They likely would have said, 'So what? What does that have to do with us? Who cares if another troublesome Jew has been killed by the Romans. Good riddance!'"

237

You see, the geographical size, or even the scope of the knowledge of an event has no bearing on whether it is universally, spiritually significant. *Fewer people knew of the death of Jesus than knew of the destruction of Jerusalem!* The destruction of Jerusalem would have had a far, far wider impact, socially, economically, militarily than the death of Jesus. Should we then argue that the fall of Jerusalem was more important than his death? Surely not. Should we likewise depreciate the significance of the end of the Old Covenant age because folks in South American did not know it was taking place? Surely not.

It is time that Bible students take note of and admit to the incredible significance of the fall of Jerusalem. As Coffman says, "The destruction of Jerusalem in A. D. 70, only five years after our epistle, (1 Peter, DKP), was the greatest single event of a thousand years, and religiously significant beyond anything else that ever occurred in human history." (1 Peter, 1979, 246).

**Objection #7--** Preterism is opposed to the creeds. Preterism is not found in any of the creeds, therefore, it is wrong. (Gentry, Mathison, etc.)

**Response:** Gentry, Mathison, Sandlin and others reject the full preterist paradigm because it is not creedal. Yet, *it is the height of hypocrisy* for them to condemn full preterists based on its omission from the creeds, for they themselves hold to positions that are either absent from the creeds or explicitly condemned by some of the creeds! As Engelsma states, "Postmillennialism has no basis in the Reformed creeds. Postmillennialism conflicts with the Reformed creeds. Postmillennialism is condemned by the Reformed creeds, explicitly by the Second Helvitic confession of 1566, implicitly by others."[254]

The emphasis, no, *the over-emphasis*, on the creeds is manifested by Mathison. He asks, "Why did the Reformers continue to maintain that Scripture must be interpreted within the boundaries of creedal orthodoxy? If creedal orthodoxy is not maintained as a boundary, biblical interpretation necessarily sinks into the sea of subjectivity and thereby loses claim to absolute authority. it becomes impossible to declare anything to be heresy."[255]

Do you catch what Mathison is saying? As Frost astutely observes, "According to this line of reasoning from Sandlin and Mathison, the Bible is to be interpreted within the boundaries of the creeds. This makes the creeds the standard, and not the Bible."[256]

238

This is tantamount to saying that the drafters of the creeds had divine insight of the scriptures and that their interpretations are the last word. I agree with Frost that, "Mathison, Seraiah, Gentry and Sandlin have it reversed, and I consider this far more dangerous than any eschatological understanding, based on an attempt to be solely Biblical" (*Hope*, 46). Mathison's posit says that following scripture alone leads to heresy! This sounds suspiciously like the early leaders of the Jehovah's Witnesses who claimed that if one failed to read the Watch Tower literature, and read the scriptures alone, that within six months they would go into apostasy. So, according to the Jehovah's Witnesses, a person must follow their "creeds." Failure to do so is dangerous. Of course, Mathison rejects those "creeds," in fact condemning them, but then demands that we submit to the Westminster Confession of Faith, or the earlier creeds of the church.[257]

If one follows Mathison and Gentry's position we no longer need the Bible we need only to read what the creeds have said *about the Bible*. But wait, the creeds, at least some of them, condemn Gentry and Mathison's doctrine! What *will* they do? Will they reject the creeds that condemn their postmillennialism? What right do they have to reject some creeds and demand that we honor others?

As we noted above, Gentry calls on his readers to accept the Biblical evidence even if it contradicts cherished traditions. Gentry even manifests the spirit of his quote *by holding to eschatological views that violate the creeds*. According to Engelsma, (see above), Gentry's eschatology is condemned by the creeds. How then can Gentry condemn preterists for holding to an eschatology that is contrary to the creeds?

The bottom line is that the *creeds are not the last word for doctrine*. We should never be intimidated by what the creeds say and teach. Should we not respect, even admire in many cases, what the creeds say? Surely! But, the creeds do not, as Mathison claims, set the boundaries for scriptural truth. *Scripture sets the boundaries for the creeds.* The creeds are the mere work of men, good men to be sure, but still *uninspired* men.

An appeal to history, tradition, and creeds would condemn all progress, whether social, technological, or theological. An appeal to tradition and history would have, even *tried*, to destroy the Reformation Movement.

We don't honestly think that everyone gladly accepted Luther's "radical," "controversial," and "new" doctrines do we? Luther was considered a trouble making rabble rouser– a *heretic*!-- who was upsetting the hallowed traditions of the fathers. Was Luther guilty of *heterodoxy*? Was he in violation of "the creeds?"According to his enemies he was!

How did Luther's enemies *know* he was wrong? Read the words of the Roman Emperor Charles V, "For it is certain that a single brother is in error if he stands against the opinion of the whole of Christendom, as otherwise Christendom would have erred for a thousand years or more."[258] That sounds amazingly close to, "Why if this doctrine is true we have been wrong all these years! This doctrine violates the creeds!" It sounds like "The creeds set the boundaries of orthodoxy." It sounds like, "Preterism is false because it is not in the creeds."

Creeds do not determine the boundaries of orthodoxy for those who *truly* believe in *Sola Scriptura*. We have presented the evidence for our views concerning 2 Peter 3, and have done so based on the inspired text of scripture. We are not concerned that the creeds do not agree with this view, and, we might note, there are many Reformed theologians that have and do agree with our view of 2 Peter 3.

In the words of Luther at the Diet of Worms in 1521, "I rejoice that the Gospel is now, as in former times, a cause of trouble and dissension. This is the character--this is the destiny of the Word of God. 'I came not to send peace on earth but a sword, said Jesus Christ.'...I cannot submit my faith either to the pope or to the councils, because it is clear as the day that they have frequently erred and contradicted one another. Unless therefore I am convinced by the testimony of scriptures, or by the clearest reasoning--unless I am persuaded of the passages I have quoted--and unless they thus render my conscience bound by the Word of God, I cannot and will not retract, for it is unsafe for a Christian to speak against his conscience. Here I stand, I can do no other; May God help Me! Amen!"[259]

We have examined some of the chief objections to the view that 2 Peter 3 speaks of the passing of the Judaic world. They are untenable objections springing from a lack, not of honesty or integrity, but of genuine study of Peter's text and the Old Covenant fountain from which it springs.

## SUMMARY

We come now to the conclusion of this work. And what have we seen? We have demonstrated the irrefutable fact that 2 Peter 3, whatever it teaches, it anticipated the fulfillment of the Old Covenant promises made to Israel. The key source prophecies of 2 Peter 3 are Deuteronomy 32, Isaiah 28, Isaiah 63-66, and Daniel 9. *Not one* of those texts can be construed to predict a yet future destruction of material creation. In fact, since what Peter was anticipating was the fulfillment of these prophecies, and these prophecies dealt with the end of the Old Covenant age of Israel, this is *prima facie* demonstration that 2 Peter 3 is not a prediction of the end of time. Peter's reliance on the Old Covenant prophecies proves beyond dispute that he was anticipating the fulfillment of God's promises to Israel, not the fulfillment of a brand new set of "church promises" divorced from Israel.

Peter offers the Transfiguration as proof of the parousia. The Transfiguration was a vision of the coming of Christ being denied by the scoffers. However, the Transfiguration was a vision of the passing of the Old Covenant age of Moses, not a vision of the end of the Christian age. This means that 2 Peter 3 anticipated the end of Israel's last days.

We have shown that 2 Peter 3 is a reiteration of Peter's first epistle, and that in the first epistle he stated repeatedly and emphatically that the day of salvation foretold by the Old Testament prophets was now near.

We have shown that Peter, based upon prophecies of the Old Testament, speaks of the last days prior to the *parousia*. The last days are reference to the last days of the Jewish Dispensation. The term "the last days" is not a referent to the Christian age or the end of the Christian age.

We have proven that appeals to 2 Peter 3:8 to mitigate the time statements concerning the nearness of Christ's coming are misguided. Peter was not trying to explain a delayed parousia by saying that his own words of its nearness are meaningless! He was drawing on Psalms 90 to reprove the wicked, by promising that God would fulfill His promises and bring Israel's salvation to its goal.

We have shown that Peter's description of the passing of the heavens and the earth is to be viewed as an apocalyptic prediction of the fall of the world of Judaism. Prophetic language often used the terms heaven and earth and spoke of the destruction of same when speaking of the fall of different nations. The passing of the old system heralded and cleared the way for the consummation of the kingdom of God. With the passing of the old the new stood identified, confirmed, vindicated, mature. The predicted

241

kingdom of the Old Covenant worthies, the everlasting kingdom of heaven, was about to be ushered in. Peter and his readers eagerly expected, longed for, and hastened that day. That kingdom is to be a kingdom of righteousness. Everlasting life is to be found there. Today that kingdom does exist. It is the glorious church of Jesus in which we are to live and magnify his name.

We have shown that Peter's promise of the new heavens and earth is, by virtual unanimous consent, a direct reference to Isaiah 65. Yet, the new creation of Isaiah 65 would come at the Day of the Lord foretold in Isaiah 64. That Day would be a Day like previous Days of the Lord, and this is irrefutable proof that the Day of the Lord in 2 Peter was not to be a literal, visible, bodily coming of Christ.

Peter's promise of the new heavens and earth is drawn directly from Isaiah 65. Yet, Isaiah emphatically teaches that the new creation would only come with the dissolution of the old creation of Israel.

We have shown that Peter's prediction of the destruction of the "elements" must be a reference to the destruction of the elemental world of Old Covenant Judaism. Peter says that Paul taught the same thing on the passing of the elements as he did. But Paul, when discussing the passing of the elements, invariably speaks of the passing of the Old Covenant system.

We have shown that Peter's anticipated new creation "wherein dwells righteousness" echoes and reflects the Seventy Week prophecy of Daniel 9. Daniel's prophecy was concerned only with the consummation of Israel's salvation history, and would terminate in the destruction of the holy city. Unless it can be proven beyond doubt that Peter was anticipating a totally different world of righteousness from that foretold by Daniel, then this is *prima facia* proof that 2 Peter 3 was predictive of the full end of the Old Covenant world of Israel in A.D. 70.

We have shown that the temple was the center of Israel's world and they even referred to it as "heaven and earth." They thought in these metaphoric ways and it is the responsibility of the modern reader of 2 Peter 3 to at least to consider that world view when attempting to interpret 2 Peter 3.

2 Peter 3 says not one word about a cosmic catastrophe that ends time. Instead, it was a divine prediction of the Jewish cataclysm that occurred in 70 AD when Jehovah swept away the last vestiges of the old world of Judaism and consummated His glorious Scheme of Redemption. Having accomplished His purpose He now reigns forever over the new heavens and new earth wherein dwelleth righteousness, His everlasting kingdom.

# ADDENDUM
## THE NEW CREATION AND UNIVERSALISM

A final point needs to be addressed in relationship to the issue of universalism. A growing number of preterists and non-preterists alike are adopting, the doctrine of universalism.[260]

I read about the "Death of Death," and I read that God will give the opportunity of repentance to those who die physically and find themselves in danger, a revival and revision of H. B. Wilson's views expounded in 1860 (*Salvation*, 209). Thus, this "second chance" or a temporary punishment with the opportunity for repentance in the afterlife results in the ultimate salvation of all. On one universalist Internet site, it was affirmed that *faith is totally unnecessary for salvation!* I read of those outside of Christ are actually "in Christ" and other claims. I read of historical Universalism, and of Christian Universalism, and frankly, it is a bit bewildering, since much of it seems based more on *ad hominem* arguments or emotionalism, rather than solid exegesis.

This is not to lightly dismiss the issue. Very clearly, sincere believers through the ages have differed on this issue. There is no doubt "universalistic" language is found in the N. T., and any serious student must confront these issues candidly. However, in my experience, those who appeal to those "universalistic" passages are not themselves giving full weight to the "limited" salvation texts, and seeking instead to simply deny, ignore, or mitigate those statements. There must be a synthesis of both the *universal* and the *limited* texts. And this is not as simple as some, on either side of the aisle, would suggest.

I cannot address this issue comprehensively. I realize that I will be accused of being simplistic, and of not addressing all of the issues. Some will probably say, "I answered that on my website, or in my article." Perhaps. But, this book is not a treatise on Universalism *per se*. So, I cannot address every article, every book, every blog. I want to briefly address a few issues that seem to me to be overlooked, or ignored.

243

# ETHICS AND ESCHATOLOGY
# ETHICS AND UNIVERSALISM

One thing that is undeniable is the fact that from the prophetic perspective, the key characteristic of the new creation was/is to be "righteousness." As Peter anticipated the arrival of the new world, he wrote "according to His promise, we look for a new heavens and earth, wherein dwells righteousness" (2 Peter 3:13). The exact meaning of this is, naturally, somewhat controversial. Is man made righteous solely through the Fiat act of God, irrespective of any participation on man's part, or is man counted righteous, as Abraham was, through his faith in the work of God? Some preterists say that since A.D. 70, there is no such thing as sin. Some preterists even say that man is not saved by faith in Christ!

Patently, the issue of universalism is currently a matter of widespread discussion in preterist circles. It seems to me that many have gone beyond the scriptural testimony in their understanding of the new creation, failing to understand that Biblically, the new creation demands that we live holy lives, and that we condemn sin today. I consider it a dangerous error to take the position that there is no such thing as sin today, and that all men, regardless of their faith in Christ or lack thereof, are destined to receive the blessings of his atonement. I want to approach this topic from a slightly different perspective from what I have seen presented so far. My focus here is on ethics and eschatology, and on ethics and universalism.

I want to emphasize two things: **First**, I am not ascribing to all preterist universalists (hereafter PU), the logical implications of their doctrine. It is easy to take a position without fully understanding the implications of that doctrine. This is clear from 1 Corinthians 15. Some seemingly devout believers in Corinth took a position concerning "the dead ones," but they did not think through their position. Therefore, Paul began by showing them the implications of their doctrine. Paul did not say that they believed what he presented. He said that if they believed what they taught, then, logically, their doctrine led to other conclusions that they themselves rejected. For Paul, to accept one was to lead to the other. He did not charge them with the implications of their doctrine. But, he held them accountable for *leading the way* to the logical end of what they taught.

So, I am concerned to show that the *logical implications* of saying that all men are saved regardless of faith, and that there is no such thing as sin or wickedness, no such thing as a moral standard of right and wrong to which men must submit today, is to say that all men are free to live lives of profligacy and indulgence. Now, to be sure, *thankfully*, I have not heard or read any PU openly *espouse* such a lifestyle. However, I do have in my files, but will not divulge names, an Internet exchange in which a *PU* said that since A.D. 70 there is no such thing as right and wrong, no sin, no law of morality. The church cannot therefore, condemn fornication, adultery, homosexuality, or any other kind of actions. The church, the body of Christ, has no standard to proclaim, except, "God's grace is great! You are saved!" My point is that you cannot teach a doctrine without implications. And if the implications are dangerous, then the doctrine is dangerous.[261]

**Second**, if one takes the position being espoused by some PUs, then the logical implication of that doctrine is the very *antinomianism condemned by the inspired N. T. authors.* You might not personally espouse or accept the implications, but if you teach that doctrine, and others accept and act on the implications, then Biblically, that is a very dangerous thing.

## ETHICS AND MORALITY *BEFORE THE END*

Since I am addressing universalism as it is being manifested in the preterist world, I am not concerned with proving that Christ came in A.D. 70, revealing the new creation. I want to ask two questions at this point.

*Do the N. T. authors demand ethical moral living on the part of the first century, pre-parousia saints?* This is easily and irrefutably answered in the affirmative. Of course the N. T. writers demanded moral living. Paul and the rest of the inspired writers *demanded* that Christians, *as members of the new creation*, live lives of holiness. This is critical, for the inspired writers believed that the new creation had begun, and was awaiting consummation. So, the fact that the inspired writers demanded holiness of the new creation, is highly significant and informative.

*Did the N. T. writers condemn immoral conduct on the part of the pre-parousia saints?* Undeniably. Paul is emphatic that if those members of the *new creation* were to abandon their faith, and enter once again into profligacy, they could not inherit the kingdom (1 Corinthians 6:9f). He did not believe, nor did he teach, that they had been sanctified and justified in order to have the freedom to commit the sins of the flesh. On the contrary, he taught that *as the new creation*, they were expected not to live that life, and he said they would be condemned for living that life. This kind of teaching is of course, repeated in Galatians 5:19f; 2 Peter 2, and one has only to read the letters to the churches of Pergamos and Thyatira to see the identical moral requirements, and warnings being given.

Significantly, these moral mandates, and the condemnation for violation, were present before the parousia, *but were characteristic of the new*

245

*creation.* The New Testament writers were instructing the pre-parousia saints how to conduct themselves in light of the impending consummation, in light of the fact that the consummation meant that what was in place, morally and ethically, was to be the order of the Day. The moral mandates of Christ, pre-parousia, are *nowhere*, in contradistinction to some other elements of the pre-parousia, church, said to only last until the parousia. On the contrary, the moral mandates of the pre-parousia body were preparatory for the consummative body of Christ, post-parousia.

Let me illustrate with a pre-parousia situation. The mystery of God was Jew and Gentile equality in Christ (Ephesians 3:6f). This was Paul's distinctive personal ministry (Colossians 1:24-27). His message was that in Christ "there is neither male or female, Jew nor Greek," and he taught that in Christ, "neither circumcision, nor uncircumcision avails, but faith that works through love" (Galatians 5:6). His gospel was scandalous, revolutionary. Our point is that this equality proclaimed by Paul was a *new creation reality*, "in the making" as it were, but was to be perfected, by Christ, at the parousia. In other words, that equality was an already but not yet reality, and when the parousia occurred, that reality was to be *emphasized*, not terminated. What was "partially true," but demanded of the new creation, pre-parousia, was expected even more, post parousia.

The same is true of ethical conduct, and the condemnation of that which is antithetical to the heart of God. The New Testament writers were fully aware that the new creation had broken into the world, and that this being true, it demanded that they live lives of holiness, rejecting and condemning that which was in violation to the very nature of the new world. They did not believe for one moment that the full arrival of the new world would obliterate the existence, reality and the danger of immorality. They knew it would continue to exist outside the new creation after the end (Revelation 21:27). They did teach that there was a haven and deliverance from that danger, but, that deliverance was in the City, *not outside.*

So, the New Testament writers mandated holy living on the part of the new creation, and condemned immorality on the part of the new creation, *prior to the end.* They taught that the holiness they were proclaiming was the kind of holiness that was befitting children of the King, and the coming new world when it fully arrived. If the current teaching among some preterist universalists is true however, then what Paul condemned among pre-parousia saints can no longer be condemned. It is no longer sin, although it was *sinful and dangerous* for those pre-parousia saints. This raises the question: why would Paul condemn, in pre-parousia saints, those

246

things that could not be condemned in the post-parousia New world? Were the antinomians that Paul condemned simply before their time? Were they simply proclaiming universalism "before its time?" How could the inspired writers condemn the antinomians for preaching what was in fact true?[262]

> Were the antinomians that Paul, Peter, Jude and John so adamantly condemned simply ahead of their time? Were they proclaiming "universal salvation" before it was realized? How could the inspired writers condemn them for preaching what they themselves were preaching?

## PRE-PAROUSIA GRACE AND ETHICS

An answer to the above question might be offered, that at the parousia, God's grace covers all. However, this overlooks the fact that Paul and the rest of the New Covenant writers proclaimed the abundant grace of Christ in the pre-parousia new creation (Ephesians 3:17f). But, while they proclaimed and rejoiced in the abundance of God's grace, at the same time, they warned against "taking advantage" of that grace, by leading profligate lives. In other words, *the inspired writers did not believe that God's grace covered rebellion against God's grace!* After all, it was God's grace that instructed them to live "soberly, righteously, and godly in this present age" (Titus 2:11f). And to return to the point just above, lest it be argued that Paul was saying that they were to live holy lives *in the end of the Mosaic Age,* while this is true, we would also reiterate the point that they were to live those holy lives in anticipation of the new order *where that kind of life was also demanded.* Are we to suppose for even one moment that Paul was saying that Christians were to live holy lives in light of the end of the Old order, only to be set free from those constraints of holiness in the new world of Christ, *the world of righteousness?*

The choices here are relatively few.

*First*, Paul was demanding holiness of New Covenant Christians based on the mandates of the Old Covenant. This is patently false, since Paul never called "Gentiles" into obedience of the Mosaic Mandates.

*Second*: Paul was demanding holiness based on the New Covenant of Christ, but, the demand for that holiness was only temporary, since the end of the age was near. This being the case, one would have to prove

247

conclusively that the moral nature of God and of the Son, from which God's moral laws have always flowed, has changed, dramatically, and that now, in the new creation, that soberness, righteousness and godliness is no longer demanded of new creation saints.

*Third*, The third option is the one I am proposing, and that is that the moral mandates–based on the righteousness of God Himself-- dictated by Paul were given to pre-parousia saints in light of the impending end of the age. That holiness is a permanent part of the very warp and woof of the new creation.

The implication of saying that there is now no sin, no moral standard of right and wrong, is to demand that Paul's moral "legislation" was either temporary, or wrong. I have not seen one scripturally derived or logically based argument to prove either one of these possibilities.

But, again, the argument is made that now, everything is about grace. Grace covers all; it is comprehensive. It is universal! What this overlooks is that *grace was very much at work in the pre-parousia world,* and yet, there was still sin and condemnation for those outside of that grace, and there was still the demand that man respond to that grace through faith! There was even condemnation for perverting and distorting that grace.

I have heard it said that unless we today are preaching grace in such a way that men can misunderstand it and misapply it to mean that "anything goes," then we are not preaching grace like Paul did. And, there is perhaps, *some* merit to that suggestion, although in my opinion it is a bit too strong. It is certainly possible for men to pervert and distort things no matter how clear-cut, no matter how concise, no matter how well we think we have communicated. So, we don't have to teach in such a way that it "allows" misunderstanding and perversion.

Nonetheless, Paul's doctrine of grace was misunderstood (one wonders if it was misunderstanding or just *perversion*, but the result was the same) by those who said one of two things.

*First*, they taught that since grace abounds where sin is, then that means we should, or at least we are free to, indulge in the works of the flesh.

*Second*, Paul was misunderstood, or perverted, to say that because grace abounds, there is no right and wrong, no moral "law" to which Christians are amenable, therefore, licentiousness cannot be condemned.

What was Paul's response to these perceptions of his doctrine of grace? He gives it in Romans 6:1, "What shall we say then, shall we continue in sin, that grace might abound? God forbid!" Now, if PU is correct, Paul was only *temporarily* true. He should have said, "Well, now, you have to

248

understand that my condemnation of immorality is only temporary, and that while I am not suggesting that you actually indulge in immorality after the parousia, I cannot condemn it if you do, because then, there will be no such thing as sin! God's grace will cover you then. If you do decide to become profligate, just wait until the parousia, and things will be different!"²⁶³

So, our point is that in the pre-parousia period, no one taught abundant grace more abundantly than the apostle Paul. Perhaps no one understood grace more than he (1 Corinthians 15:9-10). Yet, in spite of his understanding of the comprehensive nature God's grace, he uncompromisingly *condemned* those who taught and practiced the idea that God's grace allows a life of profligacy. If the one that understood grace better than any of us today demanded lives of self discipline, holiness, and conformity to the will of God, *and condemned in no uncertain terms those who abused his doctrine of grace so as to allow and encourage selfish indulgence*, then it is dangerous today to espouse a doctrine that embraces or permits the very abuse of grace that he condemned.

So, Paul proclaimed the marvelous grace of Christ, and its comprehensive nature prior to the parousia. In full knowledge of the extensive nature of that grace, the apostle said that those who taught that God's grace encourages or allows open profligacy were perverting God's grace. It was such a strong perversion of God's grace that Jude described those who taught unlimited grace as "twice dead," and both Jude and Peter said those who taught that doctrine of unlimited grace would be condemned at the parousia (Jude 14-15). This tells us several things.

**1.)** God's grace does not negate moral law, rather, it emphasizes it (Titus 2:11f).

**2.)** God's grace did not, in the pre-parousia kingdom, extend to open rebellion against God.

**3.)** The doctrine of God's grace that taught, pre-parousia, that God's grace covers open moral transgressions, and negates all moral law, *was a perversion of the truth concerning Christ's grace*. To reiterate, no one taught more about grace than Paul. He taught, "you are not under law, but under grace" (Romans 6:14), but immediately added that being under grace *demanded* that they not, "yield your members as instruments of unrighteousness unto sin; but yield yourselves unto God, as those alive from the dead, and your members as instruments of righteousness unto God" (Romans 6:14f).

Notice that Paul does not say "you are not under *the* law" here, even though he does say that they had died to "the law" in chapter 7. The

249

definite article is missing, and this is not by accident. Paul was saying that they were not under a law system. The PU posit is that since we are not under "the law" today, and not under "law," that therefore, there is no moral law, no such thing as sin. This is a direct violation of Paul's doctrine. He affirms that they are not under "law" as a *system*, but under grace, but nonetheless says that grace *forbids* them (us!), to live lives given over to immorality. Grace *teaches*, grace *demands*, and yes, grace *condemns* that which is contrary to the heart and the nature of the grace giver!

Notice that three times Paul warned the Romans against giving themselves over to becoming the "slaves" of self indulgent immorality. He told them that the "fruit" of doing so was "death." This very fact destroys PU. If universalism is true, then nothing actually, objectively "ends" in death. (Patently, the death in view is not physical death.) If anyone, at any time, was condemned to "*death*" then universalism is falsified. Paul warned the Romans that to abuse God's grace and give oneself to indulgence as a slave of sin would *end* in death. Universalism is falsified.

It cannot be rejoined that Paul was speaking only of the pre-parousia situation. This overlooks what we have noted about Paul delivering the New Covenant in preparation for post parousia life. It also *does not matter* if one speaks of the pre-parousia situation or the post parousia situation here. The fact is that Paul said that the "*end*" of becoming a slave of sin was death. If PU is correct, he should have said, "If you give yourself over to sin, you will be threatened with death, but will never experience it, the *end* will actually be life." For Paul however, the "*end*" of a life of sin was death, and that is irreconcilably and fatally contradictory to PU. If the *end result*, not an *interim* or *temporary* result, but if *the end result* of that kind of life, either pre-parousia or post, was true, PU is falsified.

Notice the contrasts between PU and what Paul taught. Paul taught that the Romans were not under law, but that *grace condemned profligacy*. PU says that we are not under law, and that there is no such thing as sin today. Paul said that to abuse grace and live a life of profligacy produced the fruit of death. PU says there is no such possibility.

If today, the PU posit is true, then Paul's pre-parousia warnings are falsified and nullified. Yet, Paul was delivering *the New Covenant gospel of grace*! Was his doctrine that said that grace forbids and condemns profligacy a 40 year flash in the pan, to take the thrill out of life for that one generation? Are all future generations of New Covenant saints not in fact under the New Covenant constraints that Paul proclaimed? Don't forget, Paul was saying these things about grace and morality to the *new creation*, instructing them how to live in the new creation. He was not imposing Old Covenant law on the new creation.

**4.**) Since the doctrine of grace as taught by Paul was the *New Covenant doctrine of grace*, preparatory of life in the kingdom, post-parousia, then, to suggest that today there is no such thing as moral law, no such thing as sin, is a direct contradiction of what the New Covenant apostles taught about God's grace. To say that today, God's grace does cover those in open moral rebellion is to justify *what Paul's doctrine of grace condemned*. To say that today, there is no moral law, is to teach the very antinomianism condemned by Paul, Peter and Jude.

Let me reiterate that all of the New Testament authors were, naturally, fully conversant in regard to the comprehensive grace of Christ. They knew better than any of us today how broad that grace was, and in light of that knowledge they unequivocally condemned those who applied that grace to the rebellious, the profligate, the unbeliever. In spite of *our* difficulty today with the "universal" nature of God's grace, those who taught it initially, and best, excluded some from that comprehensive grace.

One can discuss the extent of God's atoning work all day long, and that is surely important. However, in the final analysis, if our theology says that since Jesus died for all men, that this means that those who give themselves over to immorality inherit the kingdom *anyway*, then you do thereby *fundamentally distort Paul's proclamations*. He *knew* that Jesus died for all, did he not? He *knew* God's grace was comprehensive, did he not? He *knew* that God is the "savior of all men, and especially those who believe," did he not? Yet, in light of this knowledge, he, and the rest of the N. T. authors, declared that there were some things that would exclude one from the blessings of the grace of Christ, *after Christ finished his work*.

It should, of course, be noted that Paul was not talking simply about "outsiders," saying that those outside of Christ committing such things do not inherit the kingdom. (Of course, in the universalist paradigm, there does not seem to be an objective "inside" versus "outside"). Paul was addressing *Christians—but if it were true of Christians, would it not be doubly true of non-Christians?*-- telling them that if they continued in their profligate ways that they would not inherit the kingdom. So, Paul was saying that Christians engaged in and, *committed* to that lifestyle would be excluded from the kingdom. He was not, of course, addressing the sins of the weakness of the flesh. He was addressing "the sin" of a rebellious life, in the manner of Adam.

Need I say that to be excluded from the kingdom is to be excluded from "all spiritual blessings in Christ"? Will the universalists argue that inheriting the kingdom here amounted to simply temporal blessings? Would they argue that inheriting the kingdom does not have eternal implications, beyond this time and space world? It should not be overlooked that for Paul, there is one kingdom, one family, one body, that not only spans "heaven and earth" but joins them as well (Ephesians 1:10; 3:14f). To be in the kingdom, while on earth, is to be a member of the kingdom beyond earth. It is to be seated "in the heavenly places" (Ephesians 2:6f). To be excluded from the kingdom while on earth means to be excluded from the kingdom beyond earth, does it not? If not, how so?

For universalism to be true, we must stand Paul's words on their head. We must be willing to say that adultery, fornication, homosexuality, drunkenness, etc. *have no consequences*. Yet, they did have consequences, eternal consequences prior to the consummation. And, do not forget, that as we have seen, Paul was laying down the "constitution" of the kingdom, and demanding that Christians live lives of holiness, *in anticipation of the consummation*. And he was doing so because he taught that life in the realized kingdom demanded even more a certain kind of ethical and moral life. *Paul did not ascribe to the view that after the consummation there would be no such thing as sin and that there would be no danger from sin.*[264] Remember, he said "Let us walk honestly, *as in the day*" (Romans 13:13), and this meant, "live as if the day has already arrived and you are living according to its standard!"

## PRE-PAROUSIA DANGERS
## POST PAROUSIA BLESSINGS?

To emphasize what we have just seen, I want to focus on four areas of concern to the N. T. writers even as they expressed their appreciation for God's grace. In other words, the inspired writers affirmed on the one hand that Christ died for all men, and said that God was "not willing that any should perish." They desired that men would understand the vastness of the grace of God. Yet, *at the same time*, they addressed areas of concern, and when they discussed these issues, they undeniably excluded some from the benefits of the wonderful grace of which they spoke.

Now, by the very nature of the case, it seems that for anyone to be excluded from the blessings of the parousia, especially the blessings mentioned by the authors in these discussions, was to be excluded from the spiritual blessings of life and immortality itself. And that of course, negates the very premise of universalism.

## PROFLIGATE IMMORALITY

"Know ye not that the unrighteous shall not inherit the kingdom of God? Be not deceived: neither fornicators, nor idolaters, nor adulterers, nor effeminate, nor abusers of themselves with mankind, Nor thieves, nor covetous, nor drunkards, nor revilers, nor extortioners, shall inherit the kingdom of God. And such were some of you: but ye are washed, but ye are sanctified, but ye are justified in the name of the Lord Jesus, and by the Spirit of our God." (1 Corinthians 6:9f)

"Now the works of the flesh are manifest, which are these; Adultery, fornication, uncleanness, lasciviousness, idolatry, witchcraft, hatred, variance, emulations, wrath, strife, seditions, heresies, envyings, murders, drunkenness, revellings, and such like: of the which I tell you before, as I have also told you in time past, that they which do such things shall not inherit the kingdom of God." (Galatians 5:19f).

Let me reiterate something here that is vitally important. Paul was not addressing the mere weakness of the human nature when he spoke of these problems and dangers. He was addressing the danger of yielding one's body as a *slave* to this manner of life (Romans 6:16f). He was addressing the danger of *open rebellion* against God by giving oneself over to licentiousness. A mistake of weakness is one thing, and Paul is not addressing that issue. He is addressing "the sin" of open rebellion. He is addressing the situation also, just addressed above, that some were saying that God's grace allowed the child of God to live the "fleshly life" and still be covered by God's grace.

Another thing that has to be considered is that Paul was anticipating the arrival of the kingdom, and all concomitant blessings. Needless to say, the arrival of the kingdom is the time of the giving of eternal life and immortality (1 Corinthians 15:50-56). It is the time of the resurrection and judgment (2 Timothy 4:1). To forfeit the blessings of entrance into the kingdom, was to forfeit salvation itself. Thus, Paul, Peter (2 Peter 2), and Jude, specifically say that those who gave themselves over to the life of the flesh would not enter into kingdom blessings, i.e. salvation.

Universalism has to alter Paul's words, or deny them outright. PU has to say that those guilty of those things then, were punished for a while, and then taken to heaven. I have not found one single scriptural, logical argument in support of this, but, it is logically demanded to support the PU posit. Similarly, to support universalism, it would have to be argued that those guilty of those things were, or are, given the opportunity to catch a glimpse of condemnation, after they die, and are then, in light of that vision of horror, given the opportunity to repent and enter heaven. Again, I have not found one sound argument in defense of this, but something like this has to be argued for the PU argument to be tenable. PU has to say that ultimately, those who were or are guilty of the life of the flesh did, and do, after all, *in direct denial of Paul's words*, inherit the kingdom.

To suggest that those things that would exclude one from inheriting the kingdom *at the parousia* (1 Corinthians 6:9f; Galatians 5:19f), will no longer exclude one from the blessings of the kingdom now that it has arrived, demands that there has been a fundamental alteration in the very nature, *not only of God*, but of the New Covenant as well. Paul was expressing New Covenant realities. He was writing to Christians to whom he had proclaimed the abundant grace of God. Yet he warned them that to give themselves over to immorality[265] would result in loss of the kingdom blessings.[266] Since Paul, as proclaimer of the grace of God, was "legislating" New Covenant realities, then, to repeat, if those things that Paul warned about are no longer dangers to the salvation of the body of Christ, there has been a fundamental change in the very nature of the New Covenant. Any way that you want to express it, the view that says God's grace is so all encompassing that there is no longer any such thing as sin, no moral law, is the very kind of perversion of Paul's grace that he unequivocally condemned.

Notice the following:
Paul said that the profligately immoral person would not inherit the kingdom (1 Corinthians 6:9-11).
The kingdom represents fellowship with God, immortality and life (1 Corinthians 15:50f).
The kingdom would fully arrive at the parousia (Revelation 11:15f; 20-22). John said that the immoral remain outside the city, *after the parousia*. That is they remain outside the kingdom wherein is found fellowship with God, immortality and life (Revelation 22:15).

So, Paul–who wrote of the salvation of "all men"-- nonetheless said that *someone*, i.e. the morally profligate, would not inherit the kingdom. The kingdom represents *salvation* (Matthew 25:31f). Therefore, the morally profligate would not inherit salvation. Universalism is falsified if the morally profligate did not, or do not inherit the kingdom/salvation. The morally profligate did not/do not inherit the kingdom. Therefore, universalism is falsified.

## LEGALISM

"Stand fast therefore in the liberty wherewith Christ hath made us free, and be not entangled again with the yoke of bondage. Behold, I Paul say unto you, that if ye be circumcised, Christ shall profit you nothing. For I testify again to every man that is circumcised, that he is a debtor to do the whole law. Christ is become of no effect unto you, whosoever of you are justified by the law; ye are fallen from grace." (Galatians 5:1-4).

Paul is addressing the Judaizing problem. He struggled mightily with these Judaizers, who taught that the Gentiles, "must keep the Law of Moses and be circumcised to be saved" (Acts 15:1-2). These Judaizers were *Christians*. However, for the discussion of universalism, *it does not matter who they were*. The point of fact is that Paul stated emphatically that:
**1.)** Those who submitted to physical circumcision for theological reasons were subject to the entirety of the Old Law.
**2.)** Those who–and of course this is a direct referent to Christians–submitted to circumcision, "Christ shall profit you nothing."
**3.)** He emphatically said that those who sought their justification in Torah and circumcision, "you are fallen from grace."
Question: can a person be saved without the benefit, i.e. the "profit" of Christ? We are not even discussing the Moslem, the Hindu, the atheist, etc.. We are talking about the so-called believer. Paul was speaking to and about Christians, and he said that those who sought their justification through Torah, i.e. legalism, that Christ was of no benefit to them.
The PU has to say that the "benefit" of Christ here is not related to or identified as eternal salvation. Perhaps it is some "temporal" benefit. But where is the suggestion of that in the text? Or, the PU has to simply deny, outright, what Paul said. In other words, the Judaizers, who taught a different gospel from that delivered by Paul, and as a result of that were "*anathema*" (Galatians 1:6-9), ultimately were not *anathema* at all.
Chronologically, it makes no difference where one stands in regard to this text, and its warning. If one takes it in reference strictly to the first century situation, then it does not change the fact that Paul said there were some in that situation that Christ would not benefit. And, if a person today can be guilty of trying to live by "law" and self-justification, then does not Paul's warning still apply? Is the principle of justification by works

255

condemned only for Paul's first century situation, or, is it okay for a person today to seek justification through personal perfection?

How could Paul, who wrote that, "God is the savior of all men, and especially those who believe," harmonize that doctrine with his warnings that Christians seeking justification from the Law would receive no benefit from Christ? How did Paul harmonize his doctrine of the marvelous saving power of grace, with his warnings that those who sought justification through Torah would in fact fall from that saving grace? Paul never tries to explain this tension. It is clearly more of a problem for us than it was for him. Yet, we cannot afford to deny his words of warning, his specific and emphatic declarations that those guilty of "legalism" have no benefit from Christ, and in fact, fall from his saving grace.

The argument is sometimes made that at the parousia, "the law" and "the death" were to be thrown into the lake of fire, and that therefore, sin-death no longer exists as an objective danger. These statements are of course true, but do not fully explicate the situation, nor do they explain the reality of the situation of Paul's day, nor mitigate his warnings. These facts do not take into consideration the pre-parousia world in which Paul wrote.

Paul wrote before the objective passing of "the law." However, he wrote to those who had *died to the Law* through the body of Christ (Romans 7:4), and for whom Christ had, "abolished death, and brought life and immortality to light through the gospel" (2 Timothy 1:10f). True, the objective reality of the post parousia world had not yet arrived, but they were, as already noted above, a part of, and participants in the new creation (2 Corinthians 5:17). Yet, as we have shown, *even for those who had died to the Law,* and been "raised from the dead" (Ephesians 2:1f; Colossians 2:12-13), Paul condemned the profligate life, and he condemned a return to the Law. What was to be true after the parousia– the passing of "the Law and the death"-- *was already at work in the pre-parousia saints in Christ,* and yet, *Paul still condemned profligacy and legalism in those saints.* Is it not dangerous therefore, for modern students to ignore or overlook Paul's' pre-parousia awareness of grace, his awareness of the dying to the Law, his awareness of their raising to life, and yet, his uncompromising condemnation of profligacy? What was demanded of those dead to the Law, but alive to Christ in the pre-parousia period, was in fact the foretaste and preparation for life in Christ post parousia.

Universalism is falsified if anyone would not be, or will not be benefitted by Christ's work. Those who sought (seek) justification through

256

the Law (or *law*), are not benefitted by Christ's work. Therefore, universalism is falsified.

## UNBELIEF, AND OTHER ISSUES

"Who is a liar but he that denieth that Jesus is the Christ? He is antichrist, that denieth the Father and the Son. Whosoever denieth the Son, the same hath not the Father: (but) he that acknowledgeth the Son hath the Father also." (1 John 2:22-23)

"Whosoever transgresseth, and abideth not in the doctrine of Christ, hath not God. He that abideth in the doctrine of Christ, he hath both the Father and the Son." (2 John 9)

"Whosoever hateth his brother is a murderer: and ye know that no murderer hath eternal life abiding in him." (1 John 3:15)

It is highly significant that John wrote some of the more "universal atonement" words in the N. T., "And he is the propitiation for our sins: and not for ours only, but also for the sins of the whole world." (1 John 2:2).Yet, the very one that, like Paul affirmed the "universal" atoning work of Christ, also affirmed that those who reject Christ are "liars," they are "antichrist," and they do not have i.e. possess fellowship with, the Father.

What does it mean to not have either the Son or the Father? Is that a salvific issue? Is that strictly an issue of temporal blessings? The idea is foolish at best. John was not concerned here with temporal blessings. He was concerned with *fellowship, and he said that those who deny Jesus as the Christ do not have either Christ, or the Father.* This sounds suspiciously like, "I am the Way the Truth, and the Life, no man comes to the Father but by me" (John 14:6).

These verses affirm, directly, several things:

**1.)** That salvation is not by the Fiat act of God separate and apart from man's acceptance of Christ.[267]

**2.)** There must be "acceptance" of Christ, by the believer (Cf. John 1:11-12).

**3.)** Those who refuse to accept Christ have no fellowship with the Father.

**4.)** Those who refuse to accept Christ in faith are **liars** in their denial, because the Truth is that Jesus is the Christ, and their unbelief is a denial or rejection of Truth. They are not only *liars*, they are "antichrist" i.e. they stand opposed to Christ.

257

Now, for the PU to posit salvation for those who are "antichrist" they must be able to demonstrate that the enemies of God have ever been rewarded by God. They must be able to prove *with scripture*, not emotionalism, that God ignores unbelief and rebellion, and actually rewards it with salvation. They must be able to prove, with scripture, that what John really meant is that the unbelievers are only temporarily liars and antichrist, but that they will ultimately not be liars and antichrist, because once they realize the awfulness of their condition that they will be taken to heaven. He said no such thing.

At this juncture, it would be good to take note of a situation that Revelation describes, i.e. the post-parousia world. In Revelation 21: 27 we are told that after the end, after the arrival of the new creation when every person who has ever, or will ever live, is supposedly declared justified and redeemed according to PU, that there are still liars *outside* the city. They do not dwell in the presence of the Father and the Son—just as 1 John 2:22f suggests. The Tree of Life is inside; they are outside, and they do not enter the city. In one discussion with a PU, I pointed these things out, and was simply met with a derisive comment that I was "nitpicking." However, it is not nitpicking to honor the words of the inspired text. *What does it mean to be outside the city, in the post parousia world?*

So, John says that those who deny the Son do not have the Father, they are liars. And in the Apocalypse, the picture is *post parousia*. It posits liars as outside the city, outside the blessings of the city. The question is, *how can John depict anybody outside the city, unable to enjoy the blessings of the Father and the Son, if universalism is true?* No hint of a "second chance," no hint of acceptance in unbelief. No suggestion that God's grace is so comprehensive—or compelling--that it brings the unbelieving "liars" under the umbrella of that grace. No hint that God's "desire" that all men would be saved has over ridden man's rejection of His grace.

Just as Jesus said to Jerusalem, "Oh Jerusalem, Jerusalem, thou that killest the prophets, and stones those who are sent to thee! How often I wanted to gather your children together, as a hen gathers her chicks under her wing, but you were not willing!" (Matthew 23:37). Was it Jesus' "will" that Judah come to him in fellowship and obedience? If we accept his words it was. But, *they would not!* And as a result, they were destroyed. Likewise, God "desires" all men to come to His salvation. Yet, clearly, in Revelation, some, i.e. those who work abomination, liars, etc. *would not*, and they are excluded from the city. God did not drag them, kicking and

258

screaming into the City. He offered His Son to invite them in, but they "would not" and as a result of their refusal, they remained outside.

Remember who is writing these things. It is the apostle who said that Christ died for all men. Was John contradicting himself? More importantly, was the Holy Spirit confused? No. It seems that there are only a few possible solutions to this issue:

**1.)** Christ died for all men, and the benefit of his atoning death would be applied to all men whether they believe or do not believe. However, unless John was contradicting himself, this is patently not true in the light of what he says in the verses given above. The liar does not have the Father. The one denying the Son has neither the Son nor the Father. The murderer does not have eternal life. Thus, the atoning benefit is not automatically applied to all men, although Christ died for all men.

**2.)** Christ died for all men (1 John 2:2), but the *benefit* of that atoning death is applied only to those who accept Christ (1 John 2:22-23). By accepting Christ, they are of the Truth, and they have both Father and Son.

John's doctrine of "universal salvation" must be viewed as "all, *except,* " and *"all who."* In other words, Christ died *potentially* for all men. He died *effectively* for all who accept him.

Universalism is falsified if anyone forfeits or fails to obtain the fellowship of the Father and the Son. Those who reject Jesus as the Christ forfeit, or fail to obtain, the fellowship of the Father and the Son (1 John 2:22-23). Therefore, universalism is falsified.

PU is falsified if, after the *parousia* anyone remains outside the parameters of God's city, i.e. of His grace. Revelation 21:27 posits those who remain outside the parameters of God's city, i.e. of His grace. Therefore, universalism is falsified.

We should point out that any proposed "second chance" doctrine must distort John's inspired words. To get universalism, in the PU sense, from John, one must take 1 John 2:2 as the over riding principle that negates and mitigates what John said in 2:22f; 3:15; 2 John 9. Was John so confused as to on the one hand affirm the salvation of all men, regardless of their attitude or belief in Christ, and then affirm that if anyone denies Jesus that they do not have the blessings of Christ? That sort of suggestion would impugn inspiration.

What John should have said, if the PU concept of universalism (at least some advocates), is correct, is, "Those who deny the Son, will be threatened with loss of fellowship with the Father, but when they repent of their unbelief, they will have that fellowship." But he did not say that. If PU

259

is correct, he should have said, "Whoever hates his brother is a murderer, and you know that no murderer has eternal life, until they see their awful danger, repent, and enter life." He did not say that. If universalism is correct, John should have written that those who "transgress and go beyond the doctrine of Christ" would be threatened with loss of the Father and Son, but that threat would not be real, because they will undoubtedly be taken to heaven anyway, because, after all, Jesus died for them. He did not say that.

In fact, John did not say *anything* universalists needed for him to say. He said that Christ did indeed die for all men, but he also said that all men would not enter into the blessings of that atonement. And we cannot emphasize enough that John was fully aware of the incredible grace of God. He knew full well how marvelous, deep and wide it was. Christ's grace could encompass anyone and everyone, no matter what they had done, *if they accepted that grace through faith*. But in full knowledge of that grace and its wonder, he nonetheless said that there were limits to that grace, and one of the limits of that grace was unbelief, and rejection of Christ. This is not the doctrine of universalism.

## APOSTASY

"For it is impossible for those who were once enlightened, and have tasted of the heavenly gift, and were made partakers of the Holy Ghost, And have tasted the good word of God, and the powers of the world to come, If they shall fall away, to renew them again unto repentance; seeing they crucify to themselves the Son of God afresh, and put him to an open shame." (Hebrews 6:4f).

"For if we sin wilfully after that we have received the knowledge of the truth, there remaineth no more sacrifice for sins, But a certain fearful looking for of judgment and fiery indignation, which shall devour the adversaries. He that despised Moses' law died without mercy under two or three witnesses: Of how much sorer punishment, suppose ye, shall he be thought worthy, who hath trodden under foot the Son of God, and hath counted the blood of the covenant, wherewith he was sanctified, an unholy thing, and hath done despite unto the Spirit of grace?"

We could write a book on these verses, but will only make a few observations.

**1.)** In chapter 6, the text does not say "if they shall fall away," it literally speaks of those "falling away." There is no hypothetical situation. The author is considering those who have been partakers of the Spirit, and tasted of the heavenly gift, etc. *These are Christians.* They were apostatizing. And the writer likens them to the thorns and non-productive plants of the field "whose end is to be burned" (6:8). Was the author simply expressing the idea that Christians who went back into Judaism were doomed to die in the city, or does the idea of "rejection" go beyond that?

**2.)** In chapter 10, the author is dealing with those who had been "sanctified" (v. 29), and "enlightened" (v. 32, from *photesthentes*. Robertson, says this is equivalent to "regeneration,"[268]). These are like those in chapter 6 who have tasted of the heavenly gift, and partaken of the Spirit of God. The only difference is that in chapter 6, the writer contemplates those who were falling away, and in chapter 10 he is encouraging the readers not to fall away.

**3.)** In chapter 10 the author is considering those who rebelliously reject Christ, and return to the Law. So, we are dealing with a situation *similar* to that under the "legalism" heading, but, here, we have open apostasy back into the old creation. These had once come to "the full knowledge of the truth" (v. 26– from *epignosko*). This is not just intellectual knowledge, but comprehensive acknowledgment. They had made it theirs. *They had known Christ.* Once again, we are not dealing with the simple human condition of weakness of the flesh. This is open apostasy, open rebellion, open rejection of that once believed, embraced and practiced.

**4.)** Those who had once embraced Christ, and his grace, but were now openly rejecting him and returning to the Law, were guilty of three things: **a.)** They had trodden Christ under foot. They were guilty of crucifying Christ afresh (Hebrews 6:4f). **b.)** They were despising the very blood of Christ, the blood that confirmed the New Covenant of grace, counting it as an unholy thing. **c.)** They were guilty of "doing insult" (from *enubrizo*, a "strong word" per Robertson, p. 414), to the very *spirit of grace* that they had received. *They had known and experienced grace but were now rejecting that grace.* Was God going to impose grace on those who knew of it, but still did not want it?

**5.)** Those who were guilty of these things were subject to a fate worse than those who despised the Law of Moses and died a physical death as a result. Question: *What is worse than physical death?*

It can't be argued that all the writer is expressing is the threat of physical death in the impending Jerusalem holocaust. Those who perished in Jerusalem did perish, without mercy, *for despising the Law of Moses*. Those who rejected Christ were to suffer being "cut off from the people," *because they were in fact being disobedient to the Law*, that testified of Jesus (Acts 3:23f). So, in effect, those who rejected Moses and the Law through rejecting Christ *did suffer the penalty of the Law*. However, those who had accepted Christ, *and then rejected him*, were subject to, and would endure a greater, *worse punishment than that*. So, again, the question is: What punishment is worse than physical death? There can only be one answer, and that is "spiritual death."[269]

In these verses, there is no hint of a second chance. No hint of grace imposed. No suggestion of repentance on the part of the apostate. There was only something worse than physical death for those who had come to rejoice in the crucifixion of Jesus, and had come to despise the New Covenant–the covenant of grace, forgiveness and salvation-- and had come to despise *the very grace they had once received*.

It might be rejoined that no one today can be guilty of that since the Old Law has been removed. This is a *non-sequitor*. Can anyone duplicate precisely, *what those who crucified Jesus did*? No. But, according Hebrews, to once embrace Christ and then to forsake him is *tantamount* to engaging once again in his crucifixion. Can a person today come to agree with those who crucified Jesus? They can, they have, and they do.

Furthermore, can a person today be guilty of involvement in the world, accept Christ, and then abandon Christ and become an unbeliever? Consider a Moslem. Islam rejects Christ's atoning death, and denies his resurrection. He is not the Son of God! Well, if a Moslem abandons Islam by faith in Christ, but then later rejects Christ and once again embraces the former belief that Christ is not the Son of God, did not die for our sins, and is not raised from the dead, just how different, *in principle*, is that from the situation in Hebrews? He has made the transition from unbelief to faith to unbelief. He now counts the blood of the covenant by which he was sanctified an unholy thing. He is now insulting the spirit of grace, is he not? He now denies the Son, does he not? If the rejection of faith and journey to unbelief is still possible, then is not the *danger* of that transition not still valid? After all, what we have threatened in Hebrews 10 (and cf. Hebrews 2, 12 also), was not Old Covenant wrath (only). *It was worse than Old Covenant punishment!*

Let me express it like this. It does not matter, to some degree, who the writer of Hebrews is discussing.

**1.)** If a person takes the Arminian view, then those who were once sanctified and redeemed by the blood of Christ were now apostatizing and were to receive a fate *worse than physical death*.

**2.)** If a person takes the Calvinistic view, then these were never really "saved" in the first place, having only an appearance of salvation. Nonetheless, from the writer's perspective, if, even taking a Calvinistic view, if anyone ever did, or ever will, suffer a fate worse than physical death, then universalism is falsified. And undeniably, in Hebrews, the author was saying that someone was to suffer such a fate.

**3.)** It does not matter how one wishes to delineate between the words atonement, reconciliation, and salvation. The fact is that there was a group under consideration that were to receive *a fate worse than physical death*.

The fact is that in Hebrews we have a group of people who had and were "falling away." They had been partakers of God's grace and gifts. However, they had now rejected Christ as the Messiah, and, per 1 John 2:22f, were now classified as liars because they now rejected Jesus as Messiah. Thus, they no longer had the Father and the Son. They now counted the blood of the covenant, by which they had been sanctified an unholy thing, and were insulting the Spirit of grace. Thus, there awaited them a fate worse then physical death.

Had Christ died for them? Surely, for it is his blood by which they had been sanctified.[270] Christ's blood is a direct referent to his atoning work (Hebrews 9:24-28), and is thus a *salvation* reference. So, we have a reference here to a group of people, and remember that it does not matter if a person takes a Calvinistic perspective or an Armenian, this group of people was to receive a fate worse than physical death. Thus, if this group of people did in fact receive that threat of a fate worse than physical death, then universalism is falsified.

> If anyone suffered a fate worse then physical death, universalism is falsified. Those written about in Hebrews 6, 10 were to receive a fate worse than physical death. Therefore, universalism is falsified.

Universalism is falsified if a person could or can forsake Christ, faith and grace, and suffer a fate worse then physical death. Those in Hebrews

263

6, 10 were forsaking Christ, faith and grace, and were in danger of a fate worse than physical death. Therefore, universalism is falsified.

We have to be reminded again that if the author of Hebrews was Paul, that he was the author of the statements that God desires all men to be saved. He wrote that God wanted all men to come to knowledge of the truth and be saved. He wrote that God is the savior of all men, especially those who believe. Yet, in full recognition of those facts, Paul (or *whoever* wrote Hebrews, it does not matter), was still compelled by the Spirit to say that while God wants all to be saved, there were some who were going to *effectively reject that grace*, that salvation, and *suffer a fate worse than physical death*. I therefore suggest again that the Biblical doctrine of Christ's "universal work" is that "he died for all men *potentially*, but for the believer *effectively*."

## POST PAROUSIA ETHICAL DEMANDS

"And that, knowing the time, that now it is high time to awake out of sleep: for now is our salvation nearer than when we believed. The night is far spent, the day is at hand: let us therefore cast off the works of darkness, and let us put on the armor of light. Let us walk honestly, as in the day; not in rioting and drunkenness, not in chambering and wantonness, not in strife and envying. But put ye on the Lord Jesus Christ, and make not provision for the flesh, to fulfil the lusts thereof." (Romans 13:11f)

I have argued that Paul and the N. T. writers were giving their moral mandates, not based on the old creation, but on the new, preparing and instructing the new creation members for life in the new world. In other words, what was wrong morally, in the pre-parousia new creation, was to be wrong when the New Jerusalem came down from God out of heaven. What was holy, pure and good in the pre-parousia world was to be expected when the new order was fully in place. Paul nor any other inspired writer ever suggests that there would be a time when morality, based on the holiness of God and the New Covenant, would not be demanded of the children of the King. The text above demonstrates this definitively.

Notice that Paul says that the old world of darkness was ready to pass. The Day of the Lord was near, to usher in the glorified new creation. Consequently, the apostle urges his readers to live lives of holiness by putting aside, among other things, "rioting and drunkenness, chambering and wantonness, strife and envying." See also the works of the flesh in 2 Corinthians 6, Galatians 5, 2 Peter 2 , Jude, and Revelation again. And now note, that in putting these things off, and clothing themselves with Christ, they were to live "as in the day." This highly significant term means one thing, "live your lives as if the Day of the new creation had fully arrived." The implications here are undeniable.

**First**, to engage in profligacy was to live in darkness, and it was *wrong*.

**Second**, to put on Christ and live a holy life was *right*.

**Third**, to live a holy life was *demanded*.

**Fourth**, to live a holy life was to live *as if they were already in the Day*, where that kind of life would be the standard. This simple little phrase "as in the Day" belies the contention that eschatology destroys any ground for ethical paranesis post parousia.

**Fifth**, undeniably, to refuse to live the life consistent with the Day would be *wrong*. It would be to refuse to put on Christ.

What these irrefutable facts show us is that in the new world, the world of the Day, that there is a definite standard of right and wrong. Those things listed by Paul, i.e. "rioting, drunkenness, chambering, wantonness, strife and envying," and the other evils listed, are still evil, they are still *sin*, because they are a violation of the very nature and character of the Day.

The fact that Paul sets forth a standard of right and wrong that would, and does, characterize life within the new creation, is totally destructive to claims of some advocates of PU. To say that there is no right or wrong, that grace covers even the most rebellious of unbelievers, flies in the face of Paul's demand for a certain kind of living when the Day arrived.

This same kind of demand of righteous living, and condemnation of immorality is to be found in Peter's famous statement that they were anticipating "a new heavens and earth, wherein dwells righteousness." That world of righteousness, the body of Christ, was not to be a world in which morality has become subjective, unknowable, or non-existent. It is to be a world of righteousness, based on faith in the one who founded and perfected this Aeon. Just like Abraham believed God and it was imputed to him for righteousness, the N T. writers believed that imputed righteousness, *through faith*, was the order of the Day. They knew that there was no righteousness through the Law (Galatians 3:20f). They knew however, that for those who believed, as Abraham did, that they, became "the children of God by faith in Jesus Christ" (Galatians 3:26-29).

The N. T. writers did affirm that Christ died for all, and desires that all men be saved. They affirmed *nonetheless*, uncompromisingly, that salvation is *in* Christ, *only* in Christ, by faith.

265

We have seen that Paul said that "the end" of becoming a slave of immorality was death. The fact that Paul affirms that the *end* of profligacy is death, negates universalism.

We have seen, that in the pre-parousia world, the N. T. writers affirmed that those who lived lives of immorality "will not inherit the kingdom." We have seen that John, in describing the post parousia world, says that the immoral are outside the city. *They have not inherited the kingdom.*

We have seen that John, writing before the parousia, said that those who deny Christ do not have the Father or the Son, and are *liars.* The same author, describing the post parousia world, said that *liars are without the city,* excluded from its blessings.

We have seen that in the pre-parousia world, the blessings of God were to be found "in Christ." In the post parousia world of Revelation blessings are found only "in the city."

These irrefutable facts falsify the doctrine of universalism. An emotional appeal to the "mercy and grace of God" cannot mitigate or falsify these inspired statements and descriptions. We have no authority today to impute to the rebellious unbeliever what the inspired writers promised only to those of faith.

# END NOTES

1. W. Robertson Nicoll, *Expositors Greek Testament*, (Grand Rapids, Eerdmans, 1970, Volume 5)115.

2. S. Lewis Johnson, Jr. "The Transfiguration of Jesus," *Bibliotheca Sacra*, 124 (1967)133.

3. G.H. Boobyer, "St. Mark and the Transfiguration," *Journal of Theological Studies*, London, Vol. 41, (1940)121+.

4. Arthur Michael Ramsey, *The Glory of God and the Transfiguration of Christ*, (Longmans, Green and Co. 1949)114.

5. While Peter uses the future tense in v. 1-2, he is not consistent in the use of the future tense. He also uses the present tense, and this indicates that in his use of the future tense, he is using the O. T. prophetic background as the source of the future tense. In other words, the coming of these false prophets was future from the perspective of the O. T. prophets cited by Peter, but, from Peter's perspective they were present.

6. Richard Bauckham, *Jude and 2 Peter*, Vol 50, (Waco, Word Biblical, 1983)241.

7. Robertson Nicoll, *The Expositor's Greek* Testament, Vol. V, (Grand Rapids, Eerdman's, 1970)134.

8. Henry Alford, *Alford's Greek Testament, Hebrews To Revelation,* Vol. IV, (Grand Rapids, Baker, 1980)403.

9. Keith Mathison, *When Shall These Things Be?: A Reformed Response to Hyper-Preterism*, (Phillipsburg, NJ, 2004)202+. *See House Divided: Bridging the Gap In Reformed Eschatology. A reformed Response to When Shall These Things Be?* Ed. Michael Green, (Ramona, CA. Vision International2009). The book is available from me.

10. Get your concordance and check it out for yourself. The following are but a few of the verses listed. Matthew 2:23, 5:12, 17; 13:17, 22:40. Luke 1:69-70, 16:16, 18:31, 24:25, 27, 44. Acts 3:21,25; 10:43, 13:27,40, 15:15, Hebrews 1:1, James 5:10, I Peter 1:10.

11. Mark Nanos, *The Mystery of Romans*, (Minneapolis, Fortress, 1996)61, n. 70.

12. N. T. Wright, *Jesus and the Victory of God*, (Minneapolis, Fortress, 1996)345.

13. See my formal written debate with Kurt Simmons: *The End of Torah: At the Cross or AD 70?*. The book is available from my websites.

14. While many O. T. prophecies have the new creation in mind, only Isaiah 65-66 use the specific term "new heavens and earth." This is what we mean when we say that only Isaiah 65-66 refer to the new heavens and earth. We are referring to specific language.

15. Dwight Pentecost, *Things to Come*, (Grand Rapids, Zondervan, 1958)67.

16. See my book *Seal Up Vision and Prophecy*, for a full demonstration of this point. There is a widespread consensus that "seal up vision and prophecy" means to "reveal and confirm through fulfillment" the prophetic corpus. This means that all inspired prophecy was to be revealed and confirmed through fulfillment, by the end of the 70th Week, and that period ended with the dissolution of Israel's Aeon in A.D. 70.

17. I have engaged amillennialists in formal public debate, and one of the questions I have asked, repeatedly, is, "Are your eschatological hopes based on the Old Covenant promises made to Israel?" The answer has invariably been "No!" This shows a disturbing ignorance of the source of all NT eschatology, or a presuppositional approach to the topic that blinds the student to what the Biblical actually says.

18. See my *Have Heaven and Earth Passed Away?* for a fuller discussion of the passing of the Old Covenant.

19. 1997 Oklahoma City Prophecy Conference. Tapes of that conference, and Chilton's presentation, are available from our website: www.eschatology.org. Full ownership of that tape belongs to me personally. It is interesting to me that I have been asked on more than one occasion to withdraw the tape from public distribution, since Chilton died not long after that conference. I have been told that the tape would be "embarrassing" to his family, and to all those who learned from him. However, it was my great privilege to visit with Chilton for several month's prior to that presentation, and his dedication and commitment to the full preterist paradigm was complete. Given Chilton's dedication, and courage in the face of certain persecution, I suggest that it would be a greater disservice to his memory to pull the tape than to distribute it. Chilton firmly

believed the full preterist view needed to be told, at all costs.

**20.** I am currently working on a MSS on the cessation of the charismata. Paul's emphatic statement that the miraculous gifts would cease to function when "that which is perfect is come" is, naturally, a hotly debated issue. What the majority of commentators seem to be missing is that the arrival of the "face to face" reality, at which time Paul said the gifts would cease, would be the time of the fulfillment of *God's promises to Israel.* It is somewhat perplexing to me therefore, when I read or hear preterists who affirm that God has kept all of His promises to Israel, and has terminated His relationship with them, and yet, the charismata continue. This is a logical and Biblical contradiction. I have a taped presentation on "That Which Is Perfect: The Destiny of Miracles" that is available for $7.50 postpaid. Contact me through the website.

**21.** Ephesians 4:8f is not speaking of the completion of the revelatory process, but the consummation of "the mystery of God." Paul's referent to "the perfect man" and the "measure of the stature of the fulness of Christ" refers to Paul's ministry to present the Gentiles as an acceptable offering unto God (Romans 15:16f). The mystery of God was Jew/Gentile equality in Christ (Ephesians 3:3f), and this equality was the "mature man" Paul was working toward. He did not have the completion of the revelatory process specifically in mind.

**22.** Kenneth Gentry, *The Charismatic Gift of Prophecy: A Reformed Response to Wayne Gruden,* (Memphis, Footstool Publications, 1989)53+ Gentry argues that the charismata were signs of the impending Day of the Lord in A.D. 70, and that they were to cease with the completed revelation of inspired writ (p. 55). At the same time, Gentry argues that we are in the last days. Well, if the charismata were to be a sign of the last days before the Day of the Lord, Gentry is hard pressed to say the Day of the Lord was in A.D. 70, and yet, turn around and say the *real* Day of the Lord is yet future, but we do not have the charismata. Are we to believe God gave signs of the "minor" day of the Lord in A.D. 70, allowing for time of preparation, but will not give signs of the *real* Day? Where is the delineation between a Day with signs and a Day without signs?

**23.** David Engelsma, "A Defense of (Reformed) Amillennialism." His defense of Reformed amillennialism can be found at: http://www.prca.org/articles/amillennialism.html.

Engelsma is representative of virtually all amillennialists in positing Biblical eschatology at the end of the current Christian age, thus, divorcing God's eschatological promises to Israel from the consummation of her age.

24. The entire dispensational paradigm is built on the concept that Jesus came to fulfill the O. T. promises of the kingdom, but could not do so, due to Jewish unbelief. As a result of that unbelief, God postponed the kingdom, interrupting and stopping the prophetic countdown of the 70 Weeks of Daniel 9:24f. This simply is not true. See my book *Seal Up Vision and Prophecy* for definitive proof that the fulfillment of the 70th Week of Daniel 9 was in A.D. 70. The book can be found at www.eschatology.org.

25. See Kittel's Theological Dictionary, Arndt-Gingrich, Thayer etc.. These sources all confirm the nearness implied in the word *ready (hetoimos)*.

26. In a radio debate with noted author F. LaGard Smith, Smith argued that 2 Peter 3 is a prediction of the end of time. In response, I called attention to the fact that Peter said 2 Peter 3 was the reiteration of 1 Peter, and that the numerous temporal indicators of the nearness of the parousia in 1 Peter demand that 2 Peter 3 was near. Smith responded by saying Peter definitely taught that something was near, but the near events of 1 Peter were types and shadows of the final coming of 2 Peter 3. (This is Mathison's view as well, *When*, 168). The problem is that what Peter foretold in 1 Peter was the revelation of Jesus Christ to bring in the salvation foretold by the Old Testament prophets (1:5-12), the judgment of the living and the dead (4:5), the end of all things (4:7), and "the judgment" (4:17). The Old Testament prophets did not foretell a typological salvation, a typological judgment of the living and dead, a typological end of all things, for the last days. They foresaw one eschaton, and Peter affirmed it was near. Transcripts of my debate with Smith are available from me.

27. See my book *In Flaming Fire, A Revealing Look At the Revelation of Christ*, for demonstration that 2 Thessalonians 1 predicted the A.D. 70 coming of Christ in judgment of Israel.

28. Bauer's, Gingrich and Danker, *Greek English Lexicon*, Second Edition, (Chicago, University of Chicago Press, 1979)65

29. I personally dislike, very much, the "hyper-preterist" label.

The reader needs to understand that the term is not simply being used for convenience sake by Mathison and others. They *intend* it as a pejorative term. Of course, Mathison, Gentry, Sproul Jr. and others insist that they are the "real preterists" while those of us who hold to the consistent preterist paradigm are hyper-preterists. We are radicals, heretics, and false teachers. In reality, Mathison, Gentry and the like are "semi-preterists." They are not consistent, and have not accepted the logical and scriptural implications of their own arguments.

30. Simon Kistemaker, in *When Shall These Thing Be?: A Reformed Response to Hyper-Preterism*, Keith Mathison, Editor, (New Jersey, Phillipsburg, P and R Publishing, 2004)272.

31. I have written a fuller response to Kistemaker that I hope to publish as a small book in the near future.

32. Don K. Preston, *The Last Days: Identified!,* (Ardmore, Ok., JaDon Management Inc. 1405 4$^{th}$ Ave. N. W. #109, Ardmore, Ok. 73401,2004).

33.Thomas Ice and Timothy Demy, *Fast Facts on Bible Prophecy*, (Eugene, Ore, Harvest House, 1997)43.

34. Kenneth Gentry, *He Shall Have Dominion*, (Tyler, Tx, Institute for Christian Economics, 1992)324-328.

35. See David Englesma, "A (Reformed) Defense of Amillennialism." In this series of articles, Engelsma sets forth the Reformed view of amillennialism, that the Christian age is "the last days." The series can be found at: http://www.prca.org/articles/amillennialism.html.

36. A. T. Robertson, *Word Pictures in the New Testament*, Vol VI, (Nashville, Broadman, 1933)143.

37. Many postmillennialists agree that Israel was judged in her last days, in the Day of the Lord, in A.D. 70 (e.g. DeMar, *Madness*). However, they actually apply Isaiah 2-4 to the future! This is anachronistic to be sure. The judgment of Israel in the Day of the Lord is the *climax of the prophecy*. You cannot put the Day of the Lord in the past, but put the events leading up to the Day of the Lord in the future!

38. Larry Spargimino, *The Anti-Prophets, The Challenge of Preterism*, (Oklahoma City, Hearthstone Publishing, 2000)194

**39.** I am convinced the Song of Moses served as the blue-print for Paul's ministry. He saw himself as a last days prophet to Israel, destined to suffer martyrdom, "last of all" in the long march of the prophets sent to, and slain by, Israel. See 1 Corinthians 4:9, Colossians 1:24-26.

**40.** See my book *Who Is this Babylon?*, p. 30f, for a full discussion of this important fact.

**41.** See my book *Have Heaven and Earth Passed Away?* where I show that the Bible predictions of the destruction of "heaven and earth" refer to the destruction of Old Covenant Israel, and not the literal cosmos.

**42.** *Like Father Like Son, On Clouds of Glory* is available from our website: www.eschatology.org, or www.bibleprophecy.com

**43.** Jack Van Impe, *Your Future: An A-Z Index to Prophecy,* (Troy, Michigan, Jack Van Impe Ministries, 1989)67.

**44.** Thomas Ice, "The Seventy Weeks of Daniel 9" found at the website: www.according2prophecy.org/seventy-weeks-pt1.html

**45.** In his written debate with Kenneth Gentry, *(The Great Tribulation*, Grand Rapids, Kregel, 1999)103), Ice, in a desperate attempt to negate Jesus' prediction that the end of the age would be in his generation (Matthew 24:34), argued, "The use of 'this generation' in all other contexts is *historical*, but 24:34 is *prophetic*. In fact, when one compares the historical use of 'this generation' at the beginning of the Olivet Discourse in Matthew 23:36 (which is an undisputed reference to A.D. 70) with the prophetic usage in 24:34, a contrast is obvious." Now, notice that he admits that 23:36 is an undisputed reference to A.D. 70. This means the last days of Israel, per our argument, were undeniably in A.D. 70. Further, Ice's claim that Matthew 23:36 is a historical, and not prophetic reference is patently false. Jesus was *predicting* the events that were 40 years removed from him. To say this is a *historical* text, and not *prophetic*, is desperation exemplified.

**46.** The postmillennialists give mixed signals on the last days, as we have seen. Many affirm the vindication of the martyrs in A.D. 70, and yet, extend the last days far beyond that event. However, the prophets saw that vindication as occurring *at the end of the last days* at the Day of the Lord. So, if the last days ended at the parousia, how can the postmillennialists extend the last days

2000 years beyond that point?

47. William Barclay, *Daily Study Bible, Matthew*, Vol 2,(Philadelphia, Westminster, 1958)334. See also Emile Schurer, *The History of the Jewish People in the Age of Jesus Christ*, Vol II, (Edinburgh, T and T Clark, 1979)514f.

48. In two public formal debates I have affirmed the unending nature of the Christian age. My opponent in both debates, Thomas Thrasher, in a desperate attempt to disprove the emphatic statements of scripture, has rejected the lexical evidence, the translational evidence, and the doctrinal evidence that the Messiah's kingdom was to never end. Audio tapes of both of those public debates are available from our website: www.eschatology.org

49. Ed Wharton, "Premillennialism: True or False?" Ft. Worth Lectureship Book, (Ft. Worth, Winkler Publications, 1978).

50. McGuiggan-King Debate, (Warren, Ohio, The Letter Shop, 1975).

51. E. Earle Ellis, *The Making of the New Testament Documents*, (Boston, Brill, 2002)296. We might quibble over the "gnosticizing" claim by Ellis, but, we do agree that the scoffers were apostates.

52. I am thankful to Jack Scott for pointing Isaiah 28 out to me. He saw the connection between Isaiah 28, 2 Peter 3, and the scoffers, as he was preparing for a public debate. He shared those seminal thoughts with me and that prompted my further study. I presented a lesson "Romancing the Stone,"at the Prophecy Conference in Sparta, N. C., May 12-15, 2005. Copies of that lesson, including a PowerPoint presentation, are available from me.

53. The irony of Jesus' use of Psalms 118 along with Isaiah 8 to speak of himself as the chief cornerstone, and the impending destruction of the old Temple, is profound. Jesus was the chief cornerstone of the new True Temple, while, that Stone, himself, would fall on the old Temple in judgment and sweep it out of existence. See N. T Wright (*Victory*, 498) for further comments.

54. Tom Holland, *Contours in Pauline Theology*, (Geanies House, Fearn, Ross-Shire, IV20 1TW, Scotland, Mentor Imprint, 2004)27.

**55.** O. Palmer Robertson, "Tongues: Sign of Covenantal Curse and Blessing," *Westminster Theological Journal*, Philadelphia, WTS, Vol. 38, (1975), 43-53.

**56.** This is not to suggest there was no paranetic power in tongues. It does suggest however, that the Corinthian insistence that they were for the church and not Israel, was a perversion. The exhortative power of tongues was in the realization that God was about to give the Corinthians and the early church "rest, with us, when the Lord Jesus is revealed from heaven, in flaming fire taking vengeance on those that know not God." (2 Thessalonians 1:7f), for persecuting the church. Those today who insist that tongues are for the church have missed that same truth. Tongues were never a "good sign." They were invariably a sign of imminent judgment.

**57.** We noted earlier how Jesus combined Psalms 118:22 and Isaiah 8, applying that combination to the impending judgment on Israel. Now, Paul cites Psalms 118, and combines it with Isaiah 28. Are we to boldly assert that Paul was changing the application of Psalms 118 by adding Isaiah 28 to it, instead of Isaiah 8? We think not. What would be the justification for that? This shows that the NT writers, and of course Jesus, believed that the "Stone" prophecies all spoke of the same time and events. This will be demonstrated even more as we proceed.

**58.** R. B. Rackham, *Acts of the Apostles*, (London, Metheun and Co., 1947)218.

**59.** Norman Hillyer, *New International Bible Commentary*, 2 Peter, (Peabody, Ma., Hendrickson,1992)212.

**60.** Albert Barnes, *Barnes on the Old Testament*, Isaiah Vol. 1, (Grand Rapids, Baker, 1978).

**61.** John D. W. Watts, *Word Biblical commentary*, Isaiah 1-33, Vol. 24, (Waco, Word, 1985)371.

**62.** R. C. Sproul Jr. article, "To A Thousand Generations," on the website:
http://www.gospelcom.net/hsc/ETC/Volume_Five/Issue_Two/FamilyCircle.php

**63.** It is common for the millennialists to affirm that none of the things foretold by Jesus occurred in the first century. This is patently false. The great commission, one of the chief signs of the nearness of the end, was fulfilled in the first century

(Colossians 1.5-7; v. 23). It is significant that Paul affirmed the completion of the commission in the early 60s and Peter, in approximately 63-64, shortly after Paul's affirmations, proclaimed "the end of all things has drawn near." See my book *Into All the World, Then Comes the End*, for a full examination of the eschatological significance of the World Mission.

**64.** John MacArthur, *The Second Coming*, (Wheaton, Ill, Crossways Publishing, 1999)206).

**65.** LaHaye and Ice equivocate, however. They claim on the one hand that 1948 was the Super Sign of the End, and that no other generation has ever seen as many signs as ours, but then claim "This does not mean that He will, but it certainly means that He could." This is nothing less than "escho-babble." If the signs of the end are present, then the end is definitely near without doubt. No "maybes" "could bes" about it. Jesus did not say, "when you see these things come to pass know that the kingdom might be or could be, but not necessarily is, near!'

**66.** While many amillennialists insist that there are no signs, whatsoever, of the "end of time" other amillennialists are equally adamant that there are signs. David Engelsma, Reformed Amillennialist, is very vocal that there are signs of the end. See his articles: "A Defense of (Reformed) Amillennialism," on the website: http://www.prca.org/articles/amillennialism.html. I had a radio debate with Dr. Engelsma 9-18-05, on The Voice of Reason radio program. My debate with Engelsma is archived at www.theVoiceofReasonlive.com.

**67.** Robertson's comments and a scientists response can be f o u n d a t : http://www.livescience.com/forcesofnature/051010_end_of_w orld.html

**68.** Thomas Ice and Timothy Demy, *Fast Facts on Bible Prophecy*, (Eugene, Or. 1997)45.

**69.** I have written in more detail about the contradictions in the millennial world in regard to signs. When one examines this topic in detail, he soon becomes aware that there is a bewilderingly contradictory array of views among dispensationalists. More importantly, their claims concerning the "signs of the end" contradict the scriptural data. My article can be found on my website: www.eschatology.org

**70.** The paper, "A Review of Max King's, *The Spirit of*

*Prophecy,"* is available from Harding College, Searcy, Arkansas.

71. Richard Bauckham, *Word Biblical Commentary*, Vol. 50, *2 Peter and Jude*, (Waco, Word Publishers, 1983) 290.

72. William Barclay, *The Letters of John and Jude, Daily Bible Study Series*, (Philadelphia, Westminster Press, 1976)56

73. Frank Gaebelein, Expositors Bible Commentary (Zondervan, Regency, 1981)285.

74. Walvoord and Zuck, *Bible Knowledge Commentary*, (Kenneth Gangel), p. 876:

75. Don K. Preston, *The Last Days Identified*, (Ardmore, Ok. JaDon Management Inc. 1405 4th Ave. N. W. Commerce #109, Ardmore, Ok. 73401, 2004).

76. Even God's covenantal wrath against Israel and Jerusalem would burn "forever" (Isaiah 32:14-16; Jeremiah 17:4)! Yet, Isaiah said that wrath would only burn "until" God restored her.

77. Bagster's Arndt and Gringrich (BAG), (Chicago, Chicago Press, 1979) 625

78. Joseph Mayor, *The Epistle of St. Jude and the Second Epistle of St. Peter,* (Eugene, Or., Wipf and Stock Publishers, 1907/ 2004)162, n. 2.

79. Ezra Gould, *International Critical Commentary, Mark*, (Edinburgh, T and T Clark, 1901)250f

80. Milton Terry, *Biblical Hermeneutics*, (Grand Rapids, Zondervan, 1974)446

81. In my radio debate with Prof. David Engelsma, I introduced the point of the unending nature of the church. Engelsma tried to avoid the obvious implications of this truth by arguing that the church itself will never end, but "this present history and present form of creation comes to an end." This is not what the Bible teaches. As we have shown, the Bible affirms the unending nature of creation, and the unending nature of the church, on earth, among men. Engelsma and all futurists must ignore, deny, or distort this truth in order to maintain their doctrine.

82. Keith Mathison is a prime example of the flip-flopping on time statements. When writing against premillennialism, Mathison is forceful in emphasizing that the time statements of the Bible must be honored. However, in *When Shall These*

276

*Things Be?* Mathison's comments on the temporal statements in regard to the parousia are ambiguous, confused and confusing. All of a sudden, the time statements that he used against the millennial paradigm, as "clear" and unmistakable" temporal indicators, have become unclear, vague, and all but timeless language. When commenting on these statements he gives a dizzying array of differing opinions as to what they "might" "could" or "possibly" mean: "Some say this, and some say that" seems to be the mantra about these time statements. It appears that in *WSTTB*, Mathison is purposely trying to cloud the issue as to whether God can tell time.

83. The word *koine*, is the word for the Greek language used in the New Testament, and means common. In other words, the Greek of the Bible is not some esoteric language. It was the everyday common language of the people on the street.

84. W. E. Vine, *Expository Dictionary of New Testament Words*, (Old Tappan, NJ, Fleming H. Revell, 1966) Foreword.

85. Prof. David Engelsma, of the Protestant Reformed Seminary, "The Nearness of Christ's Coming," Internet article, at: www.mountainretreatorg.net/eschatology/nearness.html

86. Jim McGuiggan, *Commentary on Daniel*, (Lubbock, Texas, Montex, now International Biblical Resources, [IBR] 1978)170f..

87. Richard Pratt Jr., in *When Shall These Things Be? A Reformed Response to Hyper-Preterism*, Keith Mathison editor, (Phillipsburg, New Jersey, P & R Publishing, 2004)122.

88. We dare not make the mistake of the millennialists and assume that the Day of the Lord of Amos and Isaiah was the Day of the Lord of Peter. The Day of the Lord anticipated by Amos was the impending judgment of the 10 Northern Tribes of Israel that occurred in B. C. 721. The Day of the Lord anticipated by Peter was the end of the Old Covenant world that occurred in the fall of Jerusalem in A.D. 70. Both were "historical" Days of the Lord.

89. See my *Can God Tell Time?* for a full discussion of the issue of God and time statements. Simply stated, it can be shown conclusively that when God uses time statements, He uses them in ways that man understands them. God can tell time.

90. *Cognitive dissonance* is a term used by scholars for the

phenomenon of when a person knows that their belief system has been proven wrong, but, they continue to defend it anyway. The term is commonly used to describe the later generations of Christians who supposedly know, down deep, that Jesus' promises to return in the first century failed, but they keep believing in him anyway. To be honest, those who maintain the literalistic view of Christ's coming, in light of the multitudinous statements that he was to return in the first century, *are* forced into accepting cognitive dissonance to maintain faith. Modern examples of date setting groups who clearly have adopted *cognitive dissonance* are the Mormons, Jehovah's Witnesses, Adventists, etc. all of whom set dates for the end of the world. All of the dates undeniably *failed*, but the adherents of those groups continue to cling to those falsified systems.

91. In my book *Like Father Like Son, On Clouds of Glory*, I fully demonstrate the "unseen" nature of the parousia of Jehovah in the O. T.. This relates directly to Jesus' promise to come "in the glory of the Father."You can order the book from my website: www.eschatology.org.

92. See *The Bible Knowledge Commentary*, John Walvoord and Roy Zuck, (Ontario, Can, Victor Books, 1985)1059+ for an excellent discussion of the destruction of Babylon. They demonstrate that Babylon was destroyed in 689 B. C. just a few years after the prophecy of Isaiah 13.

93. Jeffrey A. Gibbs, *Jerusalem and Parousia*, (Saint Louis, Concordia Academic Press, 2000)195.

94. John Watts, *Word Biblical Commentary*, Vo. 24, Isaiah, (Waco, Tx. 1985)248+.

95. Frank Klassen, *The Chronological Bible*, (Nashville, Gaddy and Associates, 1977)944+.

96. "All the nations" of Isaiah 34 are "all the nations" of Jeremiah 25 and Ezekiel 35 as well. However, it is clear that while universal language is used, it is not a referent to the US, South America, China, Russia, etc.. "All the nations" are those listed in Jeremiah 25 and Ezekiel 35. It is a serious mistake to ignore the definition given by scripture, and apply a modern day definition to these terms.

97. *New International Standard Bible Encyclopedia,* Revised, Article "Edom," Vol. II, (Grand Rapids, Eerdmans, 1982)20.

98. Invariably, the Day of the Lord, against whoever was the focus of Jehovah's wrath, was said to reveal God as sovereign: "Then shall they know that I am God." This statement is made in regard to the Day of the Lord against Judah, against Tyre, against Egypt, and all others against whom God moved. Ezekiel uses that phraseology seventy four times. Consider then that Jesus said the Father had committed all judgment to him, so that all men might honor him as they honor the Father, and, that he was coming "in the glory of the Father." Jesus was given the sovereign prerogative of judgment to reveal him as King of kings and Lord of lords (Revelation 19).

99. Grant Jeffrey, *The Triumphant Return*, (Toronto, Canada, Frontier Research Foundation, 2001)224.

100. Gibbs, (*Jerusalem*, 192), recognizes that Jeremiah did not predict a literal destruction of creation, even though the language is graphic "The prophet speaks of God's judgment upon Judah and adorns the description of that judgment with the most dramatic language available to him."

101. Paul Minear, *New Testament Apocalyptic,* (Nashville, Abingdon, 1981)52+.

102. R. T. France, *Jesus and the Old Testament*, (Grand Rapids, Baker, 1982)84.

103. Colin Brown, *New International Dictionary of New Testament Theology*, vol. 2, (Grand Rapids, Regency Reference Library, Zondervan, 1986)35f.

104. N. T. Wright, *Jesus and the Victory of God*, (Minneapolis, Fortress, 1996)361.

105. George Eldon Ladd, *The Presence of the Future,* (Grand Rapids, Eerdmans, 1974)62.

106. Mathison appeals to the consistent use of the OT *language of time* to suggest that if we can determine how the OT prophets used time statements, "we will be much closer to understanding the use of such texts in the New Testament." (*When*, 163) We concur with this. However, Mathison incorrectly affirms that the OT prophets often spoke of events as if they were near when they were actually hundreds of years away. This is patently false. See my *Can God Tell Time?* for a fuller explication.

107. In the O. T. the predictions were of the Day of *Jehovah*.

However, Jesus applied those prophecies of the Day of Jehovah to *himself*, and this has tremendous Christological implications. Jesus was not saying that he was the Father. He was saying that he was coming "in the glory of the Father" (Matthew 16:27), to manifest his deity in the identical way his Father had come and manifested His deity. See my book *Like Father Like Son, On Clouds of Glory*, for a full discussion.

108. In my debate with Engelsma he stated that 2 Thessalonians 2 is "critical" to a proper understanding of eschatology, and that Paul was warning the Thessalonians not to believe the Day of the Lord was "at hand." Engelsma insisted that "at hand" is the proper translation of *enesteken*, the perfect active indicative of *enistemi*, and gave 1 Corinthians 7:26 as a proof text. The problem is that in 1 Corinthians 7, the word is *enestosan*, a perfect participle, and is rendered as *present*. This is my point exactly. All lexicons show that *enistemi* in the past tenses (including the perfect), means "has come, present." When I cited several lexical sources, Dr. Engelsma suddenly wanted to talk about Matthew 24.

109. See my book *He Came As A Thief*, for a more in-depth discussion of Jesus' "thief coming." Available from my websites.

110. See my *Into All the world, Then Comes the End*, for proof that the great commission was fulfilled in the first century. The book can be ordered from our website, www.eschatology.org.

111. Mathison, likes to appeal to the use of the personal pronouns of some texts to prove a first century application and fulfillment, in refutation of millennialism (e.g. on Matthew 10:23). However, he *conveniently disregards* the use of pronouns in other critical eschatological texts, (e.g. 1 Corinthians 15, 1 Thessalonians 4, 2 Thessalonians 1), and posits them in our future, even though the personal pronouns in the text are undeniably referent to the first century *setz em leben*. (Life situation, context). Why should we honor the pronouns in Matthew 10 and ignore them in these other texts? This inconsistent hermeneutic is a glaring failure in the postmillennial construct.

112. Thomas Ice and Tim LaHaye, *The End Times Controversy*, (Eugene, Ore. Harvest House, 2003)155.

113. Don K. Preston, *Blast From the Past: The Truth About Armageddon*, (Ardmore, Ok. 73401, JaDon Management Inc.

1405 4<sup>th</sup> Ave. N. W. #109, 2005).

**114.** As I show in *Blast From the Past*, there is a consistent thread that runs throughout scriptures in regard to the martyrdom of God's saints, and the guilt is almost invariably assigned to Old Covenant Israel. This is an incredibly important eschatological theme, but one that is greatly ignored in the literature.

**115.** Cf. Dwight Pentecost, *Things To Come*, (Grand Rapids, Zondervan, 1980)230.

**116.** Ice and other millennialists insist that it is somewhat dangerous to believe that the signs of Matthew 24 belong to our age. Ice particularly holds, contra LaHaye his co-author, that the events of Matthew 24 belong strictly to the Tribulation period. *(End Times,* 167f).

**117.** John MacArthur, *The Second Coming*, (Wheaton, Ill., Crossways, 1999)122.

**118.** *Kenneth Gentry and Thomas Ice, The Great Tribulation, Past or Future,* (Grand Rapids, Kregel, 1999)117.

**119.** Gary Workman, *Denton Lectureship book*, Studies in 1 and 2Thessalonians and Philemon (Denton, Tx, Valid Publications, 1988)419.

**120.** Ed Wharton in *Ft Worth Lectureship Book*, "Premillennialism: True or False?" Wendell Winkler editor, (Ft. Worth, Winkler Publications, 1978)24.

**121.** The force of this argument is logically dynamic, and yet, it is either ignored, or overlooked by many. In my radio debate with Prof. David Engelsma, I appealed to Jesus' statements in Matthew 5, and asserted that since the OT foretold the resurrection, judgment and parousia, that unless these things are fulfilled, the entirety of the OT, including the animal sacrifices, remains valid. Engelsma seemed confused by the argument, and tried to counter that all Jesus said was that the types and shadows of the cultic system had to be fulfilled in order for the entirety of the Old Law to pass. When I pressed the point, he then ignored my argument entirely. The debate is archived at: www.thevoiceofreasonlive.com.

**122.** Stafford North, *Armageddon When?,* (Oklahoma University of Science and Arts, (Oklahoma City, 1982)48.

123. Wayne Jackson, article "The Menace of Radical Preterism." The entire article is found on his website <www.christiancourier.com> or his article and my response to it, can be found at <www.preteristarchive.com>.

124. Analytical Greek Lexicon, p.262.

125. Arndt and Gingrich, 500.

126. Kenneth Gentry, *Before Jerusalem Fell, Dating the Book of Revelation,* (Institute for Christian Economics, Tyler, Tx. 1989)142. It should be noted that Gentry has since modified his view of *mello*. In the smaller work on Revelation, revised and republished in 2002, Gentry refers to what he calls the "fluid nature of this term," that in his mind now, "makes it difficult to discern whether it signifies temporal proximity or simple futurity." He cites three lexicons that give up to four definitions of *mello*, and concludes that these various definitions have "led me to drop this evidentiary datum as inconclusive." *The Beast of Revelation,* (American Vision, Atlanta, Ga, 2002)33, n. 5. Interestingly, these lexicons said the same thing when he did accept the evidentiary nature of *mello* as indicative of imminence. Perhaps a key to why Gentry has abandoned *mello* as indicative of imminence is, **1.)** *Mello* is used in contexts predictive of the resurrection and judgment (Acts 17:30-31, 24:14-15), and, **2.)** Gentry is acutely aware of the rapid growth of the preterist movement, and the preterist movement is acutely aware of the meaning of *mello*. On page 34 of *Beast*, Gentry condemns Covenant Eschatology as heretical. So, the *possibility* exists that Gentry has changed his mind about *mello* due to *theology,* not because of a lack of "evidentiary datum." In spite of the fact that Gentry has been invited by me, and by several others, to meet me in formal debate to defend his charge of heresy, he has steadfastly maintained *total silence*. He has not even extended to me the courtesy of a response to my emails.

127. F. Blass and A. Debrunner, *A Greek Grammar of the New Testament,* (Chicago, University of Chicago Press, 1961)181.

128. Kenneth Wuest, Litt.D, "The Rapture–Precisely When?," Midnight Call Magazine, October, 2005, p. 3. The article can be found at: http://www.midnightcall.com/pdf/em0510.pdf .

129. Albert Pigeon, "Statistical Analysis of "Mello" in Various Translations," Unpublished MSS, (1227 Oakwood Ave. Norristown, PA. 19401.

**130.** I list these as *possible* exceptions to the rule of imminence. I am *not convinced* however, that they are exceptions. A closer look will reveal that Galatians 3, Hebrews 10:1, 11:8 can assuredly be understood to express imminence.

**131.** *Kittel's Theological Dictionary of the New Testament*, Vol. VI, (Grand Rapids, Eerdmans,1968)725+.

**132.** See John Bray's *The Man of Sin of 2 Thessalonians 2* for an excellent discussion of the first century appearance of the Man of Sin. The book is available from us.

**133.** See my book *Who Is This Babylon?* for a full discussion of the identity of Babylon as first century, Old Covenant Jerusalem. The book is available from our website, www.eschatology.org

**134.** It is lamentable that the millennialists insist that Peter was wrong to assert that the events of Pentecost were the beginning of the fulfillment of Joel. After a radio debate with Thomas Ice, in which I cited Peter and Acts 2, Mr. Ice sent me a three page letter by Arnold Fruchtenbaum, in which the author claims: "virtually nothing that happened on Pentecost was predicted in Joel 2." It surely is a wonder that Peter would say, "This is that which was spoken by the prophet Joel," when in fact, what he actually *meant* was, "virtually nothing that is happening here today was foretold by Joel!"

**135.** Burton Coffman, *Commentary on Luke*, (Firm Foundation, Austin, Tx. 1976)418.

**136.** G. K. Beale, *The Temple and the Church's Mission*, (Downer's Grove, Ill., InterVarsity Press, 2004)213, n. 29. I have had the highest regard for Beale, and yet, like so many others, he has been less than forthright in his dealings with preterism. On two different occasions, that *I* know of, he has publically called preterists *heretics*. I have challenged him, to his face on one occasion, to meet me in formal debate to defend that serious charge. Then, even after sending *repeated* emails to him reiterating my invitation to discuss these serious charges, he has not so much as had the courtesy to respond to my emails. It is surely less than honorable to charge believers with heresy, and then refuse to allow them to defend their beliefs, and refute the charge. Yet, Beale is not alone in this dishonorable action. Wayne Jackson, Larry Spargimino, Hal Lindsay, John MacArthur, Jack Van Impe, John Ankerberg and others have been challenged/invited to debate me, and have not, in the majority of the cases, extended the courtesy of a response.

137. In a radio debate with noted author F. LaGard Smith, I appealed to the imminence of the parousia, judgment and "end of all things" in 1 Peter. Smith rejoined that Peter did posit an imminent eschatology, but that the near things were mere types of the ultimate end. He suggested that I was "wooden" in my approach. My response was to ask, what *salvation of the soul* was Peter speaking of, foretold by the O.T. prophets, that was a mere type of the "real thing?" I asked what kind of *resurrection, i.e.* judgment of the living and the dead did occur imminently, but was a mere type of the real judgment of the living and the dead? The question clearly stunned him, and I received no response to my question, and he dropped that argument.

138. Jesus' words about the significance of the fall of Jerusalem betrays how far the modern church has strayed from Biblical truth. Most modern preachers deny that the fall of Jerusalem was linked with soteriology, ecclesiology, pnuematology, or eschatology. To many preachers, the fall of Jerusalem was nothing more than the final fall of the capital of Judaism. See Wayne Jackson's comments in this work, and read my dialogue with Dr. Russ Jurek on my website: www.eschatology.org under the heading "Responding to the Critics."

139. Edward Gibbon, *Rise and Fall of Roman Empire*, Vol. I, (New York, Random House)774f.

140. *Hays, (Conversion, p. 11)*. Commenting on 1 Corinthians 10:6, 11: "The events narrated in Scripture 'happened as *tupoi emon*' (10:6). The phrase does not mean–despite many translations–'warnings for us.' It means 'types of us,' prefigurations of the ekklesia. For Paul Scripture, rightly read, prefigures the formation of the eschatological community of the church."

141. John Owens, *Works*, 16 Vols, Banner of Truth Trust, Vol. 9, p. 134. Quoted in David Chilton's *Days of Vengeance*, (Ft. Wort, Dominion Press, 1987)543.

142. In his discussion of the new creation of Isaiah 65, Prof. David Engelsma begins at v. 17, ignoring the preceding verses that show that the new creation would come at the time of the judgment of Old Covenant Israel (v. 11-15). Engelsma believes that the new heavens comes at the end of time. But, this means that Israel is destroyed at the end of time in order to bring in the

new creation, and Engelsma has no place for such an event in his amillennialism. You can find Engelsma's comments at: http://www.prca.org/articles/amillennialism.html#No9

143. In my estimation, postmillennialists come closer to the proper grasp of Isaiah than the amillennialists and dispensationalists. Many postmillennialists, e.g. Gentry, properly note that Isaiah cannot be speaking of an "end of time" scenario. However they then divorce the prophecy from the N. T. eschatology, insisting that while Isaiah is the source for 2 Peter 3, that Peter "expands" on Isaiah to speak of something that Isaiah did not predict.

144. Richard Trench, *Synonyms of the New Testament*, (Grand Rapids, Eerdmans, 1975)220.

145. Several quotes from Owen, on 2 Peter 3, can be found at: http://www.preteristarchive.com/StudyArchive/o/owen-john_p uritan.html the website is www.PreteristArchive, run by Todd Dennis. The Archive is one of, if not *the* finest source, for research into the preterist perspective to be found anywhere. Todd Dennis has done a magnificent job in finding, documenting, and sharing a wealth of information.

146. Roderick Campbell, *Israel and the New Covenant*, (Tyler, Tx, Geneva Divinity School Press, [1954], [1981]. Listed by Gentry in *Dominion*, 301, n. 104.

147. It is always a frightening thought to claim "originality" for thought and research. There have been giants of intellect and thought that have gone before. I am sure that *someone*, somewhere, has presented the argument I am making here, but, even with the help of inter-library loan and the Internet, I have not been able to find it in any of the literature. If anyone who reads this can document anyone who has made the argument I am presenting, I would be indebted to know of it. I am a firm believer in the axiom: "give honor to whom honor is due."

148. It is significant that in *When Shall These Things Be?* three authors cite 2 Peter 3 no less than 24 times. Yet, unless I missed it, not one of them even stopped to ask of the significance of the relationship between 2 Peter 3 and Isaiah 64-66. How can it seriously be claimed that a person is properly interpreting 2 Peter 3 when the source of the prophecy is totally ignored?

149. In the O. T. there were times when God promised to a

"strange work," a "marvelous work and wonder" etc. And, anytime Jehovah did one of those strange works, a work so strange that when a person heard of its approach it "made his ears tingle," it was a time of judgment on Israel (1 Samuel 3:11; 2 Kings 21:12; Isaiah 28:21; 29:14; Jeremiah 19: 3).

150. This vital fact is lost on those who appeal to Romans 11:26: "all Israel shall be saved." Invariably, in the predictions of God's last days parousia to bring salvation to Israel, it is the righteous remnant that is saved, while *the wicked majority are destroyed*. This is true in the pivotal source prophecy for Romans 11:26, i.e. Isaiah 59. Salvation for Israel was promised to be sure. That is not debatable. The point is that salvation was promised to the righteous, "to those who turn from transgression" (v. 20), while the Lord would give "fury to His adversaries, recompense to His enemies" (Isaiah 59:18).

151. We cannot expand on it here, but Hebrews 1 directly cites Psalms 102, and many mistakenly take it as a prediction of the end of human history as we know it. However, if Psalms and Hebrews are predicting the passing of the material creation, one has the right to ask, *what people will perish, and what new people will be created, at the time of the destruction of physical creation?* Will the church cease to exist so that God can create a new people? Daniel 2:44 and other passages affirm that the church can never pass away. The only "people" that were ever predicted to cease as foretold by Psalms and Isaiah, was the Old Covenant nation of Israel. She was a type of the coming new creation people of the Messiah.

152. The promise of a new name in conjunction with the conversion/blessings on "eunuchs" in Isaiah 56 should be correlated with Acts 8. Under the Old Covenant eunuchs were "unclean" because they were "dry-wells" unable to contribute to the "marrying and giving in marriage" so critical to the well-being and sustaining of that Covenant World. However, under the New Covenant, "marrying and giving in marriage" is not necessary to sustain the kingdom, or to bring in the promised seed. Children of God are produced by faith in Christ, and are able now to help produce sons of God by bringing other sons to glory through the knowledge of Christ. I develop this concept in a tape series on "Acts and the Restoration of Israel." Series is available from me: www.eschatology.org.

153. In public debates with millennialists, I have had them

appeal to Isaiah's prediction of the wolf and lamb lying down together, with the appeal, "I have never seen anything like this, have you?" This *ad hominem* argument proves nothing. In Romans 15 Paul, who preached nothing but the hope of Israel, quotes verbatim from Isaiah's prophecy that "in that day" the day when the wolf and lamb would dwell in peace, the Lord would raise an ensign for the Gentiles. Paul affirms that it was his ministry to call the Gentiles! Therefore, "the day," foretold by Isaiah had arrived. Paul's inspired testimony about Isaiah is devastating against the dispensational view.

154. The prophecy of Isaiah 63-66 actually goes back further than chapter 63. It includes the prophecy of Isaiah 62 and the promise that in the last days Jehovah would once again marry Israel, and this would be in the Day of His coming for salvation (62:4f). This prophecy serves as the source for Jesus' prediction of his parousia in Matthew 16:27, and of course, he said that would occur in his generation (Matthew 16:28).

155. Tim LaHaye and Thomas Ice, *Charting the End Times*, (Harvest House, Eugene, Ore, 2001)75.

156. Many postmillennialists, as Gentry has noted, believe that Isaiah 65 was fulfilled with the destruction of Israel in A.D. 70. See Gentry, *Dominion*, 361f. Gentry clearly has not thought through the implications of positing Isaiah at A.D. 70, however.

157. In public debates with amillennialists, I have asked the following question: "At what point of time, and with what event, were all of God's OT promises made to Israel fulfilled, and His Covenant relationship with her terminated?" The answer has invariably been that no promises of God to Israel extended beyond A.D. 70. If Isaiah 65 is the promise of the destruction of the earth, and the creation of the new world, that Peter is referring to (2 Peter 3:1-2, 13), then patently, at least one OT promise to Israel remains valid. Of course, if any of the OT remains valid, and unfulfilled today, then Israel remains God's chosen, Covenant people, and the entirety of the OT remains valid as well (Matthew 5:17f). The public debates (Lockwood/Preston; Thrasher/Preston; Preston and Stevens-V-George and Hartley) are available from our website: www.eschatology.org.

158. Greg Bahnsen and Kenneth Gentry, *House Divided The Break Up of Dispensational Theology*, (Tyler, Tx. Institute for

Christian Economics, 1989)75, n. 30.

159. Gary DeMar, "A Response to Ed Hindson" (http://planetpreterist.com/news-2461.html)

160. Kenneth Gentry, *The Beast of Revelation*, revised, (Powder Springs, Ga., American Vision, 2002)27.

161. Kenneth Gentry, *Before Jerusalem Fell*, (Tyler, Tx.., Institute for Christian Economics, 1989)133.

162. Keith Mathison, *Dispensationalism Rightly Dividing the People of God?* (New Jersey, Philippsburg, P & R, 1995)130

163. The term "pantelist" seems to be a term coined by Seriah, to describe full preterists who take the Bible seriously that Jesus kept his word to come in the first century.

164. C. Jonathan Seriah, *The End of All Things*, (Moscow, Idaho, Canon Press, 1999) 64, note 9.

165. For a powerful, yet easy to understand presentation of the transitional period see Bill Fangio, *Time of Transition*, (Carlsbad, N. M., Biblical Publishing Corporation, 2002). The book can be ordered from me.

166. Jay Adams, *The Time is At Hand*, (A Press, Greenville, SC, 1987)14-15.

167. Dub McClish, Fourth Annual Houston College of the Bible Lectureship, (1996), David Brown, editor, (Isaiah Vol. II, Chapters 40-66)343. See also Ron Cosby, ibid, p. 315, who holds to the same distinctions between Isaiah and Revelation.

168. James D. Bales, *New Testament Interpretation of Old Testament Prophecies of the Kingdom*, (Searcy, Ark., Harding College Press, 1950)47.

169. Wayne Jackson, *Isaiah: Prophet of Doom and Deliverance*, (Abilene, Tx., Quality Publications, 1991). Jackson draws the same false distinctions between Isaiah, Peter and Revelation as McClish.

170. The word "remembered" as used in Jeremiah does not mean simple mental recall. It refers to a covenantal remembrance. In other words, traveling to Jerusalem and honoring the Ark of the Covenant would lose all theological and covenantal significance in the kingdom. This is naturally important in light of the modern emphasis and excitement over

the imagined imminent rebuilding of the Temple and discovery of the Ark. One "discoverer" Vendyl Jones, claimed that he knew just where the lost Ark was, and that with Rabbinic approval, he would announce that he had retrieved the Ark, on June 7, 2005. http://arutzsheva.com/news.php3?id=82226. Of course, nothing happened, and in a later release, Jones claimed that he was "misunderstood."

**171.** *Bauer's Arndt and Gingrich, A Greek-English Lexicon,* (Chicago, University of Chicago Press, 1979, second edition)92.

**172.** *Thayer's Greek English Lexicon,* (Grand Rapids, Zondervan, 1973)63.

**173.** I have prepared a 52 lesson MP3 study of Acts under the heading of "Acts and the Restoration of Israel."

**174.** J. W. McGarvey, *Commentary on Acts,* (Nashville, Gospel Advocate, seventh edition)59.

**175.** Lorraine Boettner, *Four Views of the Millennium,* (Downers Grove, InterVarsity,1977)102.

**176.** See my book *From Torah To Telos, The Passing of the Law of Moses. From Creation to Consummation,* available from my websites, Amazon and other retailers.

**177.** Peter is not alone in declaring that his eschatological hope was what Moses and all the prophets predicted. Paul affirmed the identical truth (Acts 24:14f; 26:6f).

**178.** Balz and Schneider, *Exegetical Dictionary of the New Testament,* (Grand Rapids, Eerdmans, 1990, Vol. 1)129.

**179.** Thayer's, p. 152; see also See *Kittel's Theological Dictionary of NT,* (Vol. V)449 under "orthos, diorthos."

**180.** Paul Ellingworth, *New International Greek Testament Commentary on Hebrews,* (Grand Rapids, Paternoster, 1993) 444.

**181.** Once again we must honor his chronological perspective. The verbs in the text are in the present tense. See the American Standard, New American Standard, Revised and New Revised Standard, New English Version, etc. .

**182.** The writer's point is not so much the continuance of the Temple edifice as it is the *continuing validity* of the Old Covenant world. See William Lane, *Word Biblical Commentary,*

*Hebrews 9-13*, (Waco, Word Publishing, Vol. 47b, 1991)223.

183. Ice's contention that the term "heaven and earth" is not used metaphorically falls to the ground in Matthew 5.17f. Jesus said "until heaven and earth pass away, not one jot or one tittle shall pass from the Law, until it is all fulfilled." The topic here is the Mosaic Covenant. Jesus said "heaven and earth" would not pass until the entirety of that Mosaic Torah was fulfilled. Thomas Ice believes that the Mosaic Torah has indeed passed away (*Prophecy Watch*, 258). If therefore, the Mosaic Law has passed away, then the "heaven and earth" of Matthew 5 has passed away. The dilemma here is acute for Dr. Ice. If he admits that the "heaven and earth" term is used metaphorically here, then his contention that the term is never so used falls to the ground. On the other hand, if he maintains his denial that the term is used metaphorically, then that means that until literal "heaven and earth" passes away, then the Mosaic Torah remains valid. This would demand that the Mosaic Law remains valid today. Ice cannot have it both ways.

184. Interestingly, in the article cited here, Ice insists that there is no lexical support for the metaphoric use of "heaven and earth." This is a strange argument indeed, coming from someone who has invented, out of thin air, a new definition for "imminent." Ice and other millennialists claim that "imminent" means, "the next thing on the prophetic calendar." They insist that if any other prophetic event has to be fulfilled, prior to an "imminent" event, that the "imminent event" is not truly imminent. Ice cannot find his "imminent, but not soon" definition in any dictionary or lexicon. All dictionaries agree that "imminent" means "near, soon, etc.". See my in-depth analysis of Ice's inventive definitions in my *Who Is This Babylon?*

185. Randolph O. Yeager, *The Renaissance New Testament*, 18 vols. (Bowling Green, KY: Renaissance Press, 1978), vol. 3. p. 322.

186. Thomas Ice, An Interpretation of Matthew 24-25 (part 32), http://www.pre-trib.org/article-view.php?id=233.

187. Arnold Fruchtenbaum, Israelology, CTS Journal, vol. 5, #4, (1999)6.

188. Crispin H. T. Fletcher-Louis, "The Destruction of the Temple and the Relativization of the Old Covenant," *Eschatology in the Bible and Theology, Evangelical Essays at*

*the Dawn of a New Millennium*, (Downer's Grove, Ill., InterVarsity, 1997)157.

189. Contrary to popular opinion, the Old Law did not pass away at the cross. The passages normally used to sustain such a view actually say that *the believer died to the Law* by entering Christ (Romans 7:4f; Ephesians 2;12f; Colossians 2 etc.) The objective reality, the body of the Law, did not pass until it was all fulfilled. And Jesus said that would be in the fall of Jerusalem (Luke 21:22). See my *Have Heaven and Earth Passed Away?* for a fuller discussion. In addition, In 2011 I had a formal written debate with Kurt Simmons on the passing of Torah. That book is available from my websites, from Amazon, and other retailers. See also my upcoming book: *From Torah To Telos, From Creation to Consummation.*

190. William Lane, *Word Biblical Commentary*, vol. 47b, Hebrews, (Dallas, Word Publishers, 1991)480.

191. Tom Holland, *Contours of Pauline Theology*, (Christian Focus Publications, Geanies House, Fearn, Ross-Shire IV20 1TW, Scotland, UK, 2004) 252. www.christianfocus.com or, www.tomholland.instant.org.uk.

192. Marvin R. Wilson, *Our Father Abraham. Jewish Roots of the Christian Faith*, (Dayton, Ohio, Center for Judaic-Christian Studies, 1989).

193. Jim McGuiggan, *The Book of Isaiah*, (Lubbock, Montex, 1985)260.

194. Marius Reiser, *Jesus and Judgment*, (Minneapolis, Fortress, 1997)146+. "Early Jewish expectation was thus directed 'entirely to the renewal of the concrete historical world, in the midst of which is a particular land, a particular city, and a particular people with an irreplaceable and unending history. But as the world that, in God's coming will be changed and renewed from its roots upward, it does not cease to be the same concrete, historical world. *Mutata eaeem resugit*; it remains also the new world, in different circumstances, but identical with itself."

195. Albert Barnes, *Commentary on Matthew*, (Grand Rapids, Baker, 1976)132.

196. Robertson Nicoll, *Expositors Greek Testament*, Vol. 1, (Grand Rapids, Eerdmans, 1970)188.

197. Emile Schurer, *The History of the Jewish People in the Age of Jesus Christ*, Vol. II, (Edinburgh, T and T Clark, 1979)537f.

198. Burton Coffman, *Commentary on Matthew*, (Austin, Firm Foundation, 1977)175.

199. Adam Clarke, *Clarke's Commentary*, Vol. V. (Nashville, Abingdon)138f.

200. *McGuiggan-King Debate*, (Letter Shop Inc., 387 Chestnut, N. E. Warren, Ohio, 44483, 1975)81.

201. Jim McGuiggan, *The Reign of God*, (Lubbock, Montex, 1979)61.

202. Please note that Jesus responds to the question of the resurrection by affirming the Father's words, "I am the God of Abraham, Isaac and Jacob, I am not the God of the dead, but of the living" (Matthew 22:32). In Matthew 8:11f, Jesus affirmed that, "Many shall come from the east and the west and sit down with Abraham, Isaac and Jacob, But the sons of the kingdom will be cast out into outer darkness." Now since the time of Abraham sitting in the banquet in the kingdom, must, by definition, be the time of the resurrection, and since Jesus posited the time of Abraham sitting down to the banquet as the time when "the sons of the kingdom will be cast out," it therefore follows that the time of the resurrection–and thus the age to come of Matthew 22:23f–would be *when the sons of the kingdom were cast out,* and that was unequivocally in AD 70. See my book *Seventy Weeks Are Determined... For the Resurrection*, for a discussion of the resurrection. The book is available from my websites, Amazon and other retailers.

203. In several public debates, my opponents have attempted to use that argument, at least initially. However, they soon abandoned that argument in light of the evidence from the text. Jesus' "this age" was patently the Mosaic age in which the Levirate marriage was being practiced. Jesus was anticipating the "age to come" in which that practice was no longer valid, and that most assuredly is true of the age of Christ and the New Covenant.

204. N. T. Wright, *Jesus and the Victory of God*, (Minneapolis, Fortress, 1996)402, n. 109.

205. F. F. Bruce, *Epistle to the Ephesians*, (Revell, 1970)42.

206. Edward Fudge, *Our Man in Heaven*, (Athens, Alabama, C.E.I. Publishing, 1973)28f.

207. F. F. Bruce, *New International Commentary on the New Testament, Hebrews*, Grand Rapids, Eerdmans, 1978)32f.

208. C. Marvin Pate, *Communities of the Last Days*, (Fortress, IVP, Downer's Grove, Ill. 2000)204.

209. John Calvin, *Calvin's Commentaries*, (Grand Rapids, AP and A, vol. 7)462.

210. There is a four-fold eschatological pattern in the NT. It is *preaching, persecution, power, parousia*. Jesus told his disciples to go *preach* the gospel. They would be *persecuted* as they did so. However, they would receive the Spirit (*power*) to guide them and confound their adversaries, and Jesus would come (*parousia*) in vindication of their suffering, in that generation. I develop this pattern extensively in my *book Into All the World, Then Comes the End*, available at, www.eschatology.org.

211. Here is another example of exegetes failing to honor the importance of God's promises to Israel. Paul said the charismata would end when "that which is perfect" arrived. That is, when the "face to face" reality arrived. But, the "face to face" reality was the time of Israel's salvation, i.e. the establishment of the kingdom. (See Isaiah 52:8-13). Thus, when Israel reached her destiny, the gifts that signaled that end (Joel 2:28f/ 1 Corinthians 14:20f), would end. Some preterists who affirm the parousia in A.D. 70, and the consummation of God's dealings with Israel, nonetheless seek to hold onto the charismata. But the charismata and the last days of Israel go inseparably hand in hand.

212. Lile's excellent article on the anaphoric article in 1 Peter 4:17 can be found on our website at: http://www.eschatology.org/articles/resurrection/1peter417.htm (7-11-05)

213. Kenneth Gentry, *The Beast of Revelation*, (Atlanta, Ga., American Vision, 2002)26.

214. See Daniel 12:4, 8-9, where Daniel foresaw the last days events, the events Peter said were near, and Daniel said he saw "but did not understand" (Daniel 12:8), and, he was told to seal his vision because it would not be fulfilled in his lifetime. We must take this temporal contrast seriously, and acknowledge the objective nearness therefore, of the parousia in Peter's day.

293

215. Wendell Winkler, "Premillennialism, True or False," First Annual Ft. Worth Lectures, (Ft. Worth, Tx., Winkler Publications, 1978)28.

216. *Vines Theological Dictionary,* (Revell, 1966, Foreword. (22).

217. See Max's series of articles on Hebrews 5-6 in "The Living Presence," Warren, Ohio, Vol. 6, no. 1, August, 1995. "The Living Presence" Journal is no longer active.

218. The word used in Hebrews for leaving behind the first principles is strong. It is far more than "grow up." So the idea is not that they should simply mature, but that the first principles of Christ in view should be removed from their lives as the power in their lives. This patently cannot refer to the gospel.

219. Milton S. Terry, *Biblical Hermeneutics*, (Grand Rapids, Zondervan, 1974)596, n.1.

220. John Lightfoot, *Commentary on NT from Talmud and Hebraica,* Vol. 3, (Peabody, Mass, Hendrickson, 1989 reprint)451.

221. Steven Kraftchick, *Jude and 2 Peter*, (Nashville, Abingdon, 2002)166.

222. Douglas Moo, *The NIV Application Commentary, 2 Peter and Jude*, (Grand Rapids, Zondervan, 1996)196.

223. Moo is an advocate of the inspiration of the scripture and says so in his commentary on 2 Peter 3.

224. Wayne Jackson, *Isaiah: God's Prophet of Doom and Deliverance*, (Quality Publications, P. O. Box 1060, Abilene, Tx. 79604-1060, 199)131.

225. Marvin R. Wilson, *Our Father Abraham*, (Grand Rapids, Eerdmans, 1989)167.

226. David Divin and Roy B. Blizzard, in *Understanding the Difficult Words of Jesus*, (Austin, Tx. Center for Judaic-Christian Studies, 1984) 22. Cited in *Our Father Abraham*, Marvin Wilson, (Grand Rapids, Eerdmans, 1989)30.

227. We are not talking about an "allegorical" approach to scripture here, in the mode of Origen. Allegory finds (invents!), a hint of a shadow, of a type, of a symbol, under every rock and in every word it the text. What we are suggesting however, is that

the N. T. writers tell us by inspiration, and the Hebraic source of their prophecies guides us to understand that the prophetic language was not woodenly literalistic. See 1 Corinthians 2:6f where Paul said that the scriptures were to be interpreted by "comparing spiritual things with spiritual things."

228. Graydon Snyder, "The Literalization of the Apocalyptic Form in the New Testament Church," Chicago Society of Biblical Research, Vol. 15, (1969)5-18.

229. Josephus, Ant. Bk. 1, chapter 7, 7 (p. 180-181). The Temple and even the garments of the priest represented land, sea and heaven. See also Ant. Bk. 3, chapter 6, 4 (p. 123) The Temple was "an imitation of the systems of the world. The rest was sea and land."

230. Gregory Stevenson, *Power and Place: Temple and Identity in the Book of Revelation*, (New York, Walter de Gruyter, 2001)156.

231. Dale Allison Jr., *The End of the Ages Has Come*, (Philadelphia, Fortress, 1985)35.

232. See my *Seventy Weeks Are Determined...For the Resurrection*, for a full discussion of Daniel's prediction and how the N. T. writers believed they were living in the days of its fulfillment. Paul's anticipating of the coming righteousness is nothing less than the consummation of the seventy week prophecy, and means that Daniel had not been postponed. This is extremely important.

233. See my *Seal Up Vision and Prophecy*, for a full demonstration that Daniel's prophecy was fulfilled in the fall of Jerusalem in AD 70. Available on my website: www.eschatology.org.

234. If Peter was anticipating the fulfillment of the 70th Week of Daniel 9, this presents huge problems for the millennial view. Most millennialists place 2 Peter 3 at the end of the millennium. Well, if 2 Peter 3 is Daniel 9, and if 2 Peter 3 is fulfilled at the end of the millennium, then the 70th Week of Daniel 9 will not be fulfilled until the end of the millennium! It is therefore, necessary for the millennialists to posit the coming of two totally different "worlds of righteousness" foretold by the prophets. Daniel was predicting one, and Isaiah must have been predicting another one. See my *Seventy Weeks Are Determined...For the*

*Resurrection* for a full discussion of the relationship of Daniel to 2 Peter 3.

**235.** See my *Seal Up Vision and Prophecy*, for a total refutation of the millennial gap theory, and demonstration that the 70th Week was fulfilled in A.D. 70.

**236.** If Daniel 9 is not fulfilled until the end of time, then that means that the 70th Week of Daniel does not begin with the rapture and signing of the peace treaty between Israel and the man of sin. If 2 Peter 3 anticipated the fulfillment of Daniel 9, this means that the entire millennial scheme of things is falsified.

**237.** The same is true of Paul's statement in Galatians 5:5, a passage alluded to earlier. He said they were eagerly expecting "the hope of righteousness." Paul's eschatological hope was "the hope of Israel." Thus, since Daniel foretold the arrival of the world of righteousness, and Paul said they were then *eagerly expecting* that hope of righteousness, this is powerful proof that Paul was anticipating the consummation of Daniel 9.

**238.** We are told that at his parousia, death is destroyed, and yet, here in Revelation 14, we have death existing after the parousia! Very clearly, *physical death is not the focus of "destruction"* at the Lord's coming.

**239.** As an example of the desperation of the millennial camp to avoid the unequivocal statement of Daniel 12:7, some millennialists now argue that the "power" of the holy people, i.e. Israel, was not the Temple, the altar, the priesthood, the Covenant, etc., but rather, *their stubborn will.* Ice affirms this in *Prophecy Watch*, p. 159. This is false. The word translated "power" is Strong's #3027. It is used literally hundreds of times in the O. T. and *not once* does it refer to Israel's stubborn will.

**240.** Worse than this charge, in my mind, is the view taken by some preterists, that since Christ has accomplished his work of salvation, that there is no such thing as sin, of evil, and that literally, no matter what a person might do, they are the recipient of God's salvation, i.e. universalism. I have in my files an email post from a person affirming that since the fulfillment of A.D. 70, that homosexuality, adultery, fornication, *or anything else* is any longer sinful! Now, unless *God's fundamental, intrinsic holy nature has changed*, then the things that from the beginning and onward, were *always contrary to His very nature*, and considered an abomination to Him, *are still an abomination to Him.*

Furthermore, to affirm that there is no such thing as sin since A.D. 70 means that Paul's statement of Romans 6 and Peter's affirmations in 2 Peter 2, are no longer applicable. After all, the antinomian claim was that God's grace covers anything, so there is no need for holy living. Paul emphatically condemned this view. However, the modern universalism being taught by some parties in the preterist movement would reject Paul's condemnation of sin, for there is now no sin to condemn, and the antinomians were/are right after all!

241. Thomas Ice in "Midnight Call," October 2002, (p. 3), under Prophetic Issues, and the article, "The Age to Come."

242. Believe it or not, Ice believes that the Second Coming of Christ was *supposed* to be in the first century *but was postponed!* (Midnight Call, 3). Ice is the first dispensationalist I have ever read to openly admit to this belief. The implications of this are incredible.

243. Thomas Ice and Timothy Demy, *Prophecy Watch*, (Eugene, Or., 1998)246+.

244. See for instance Kenneth Gentry in his response to Wayne Gruden, *The Charismatic Gift of Prophecy*, (Memphis, Tn., Footstool, Publications, 1989)53f.

245. Gary Workman, Denton Lectureship Book, *"Studies in 1 and 2 Thessalonians and Philemon,"* (Denton, Tx., Valid Publications, Dub McClish editor, 1988)165.

246. I have produced an 11 part tape series on John the Immerser, demonstrating how his message permeates the New Testament. His message of impending judgment is far too often divorced from the epistles, as if the message had become irrelevant by the time the epistles were written. This is unfortunate, since just the opposite is true. The message had become even more urgent.

247. Joseph Canfield, "Kingdom Counsel," Ed Stevens, editor, 122 Seaward Avenue, Bradford, Pa. 16701, Nov., 1989, p. 7f.

248. See my *We Shall Meet Him In the Air, the Wedding of the King of kings*. In that work, I bring forth many additional direct parallels between the Olivet Discourse and Thessalonians. It is undeniable that Paul is drawing his eschatology from the Discourse. This means that Paul was not predicting an end of time event, but the end of the age judgment on Israel. That book

is available from my websites, Amazon and other retailers.

249. Several attempts have been made by various individuals to get Gentry to meet me in formal public debate. I have personally issued that invitation myself, via email, and Mr. Gentry has not even extended the courtesy of a response to me, or to others. It is strange indeed that the leading apologist for postmillennial eschatology, an experienced debater, continues to refuse the opportunity to openly refute what he repeatedly calls heresy. If Gentry can refute preterism, and stop the digression, why will he not do it? He writes articles condemning preterists as heretics, but will not publicly defend his charges. This is less than honorable.

250. R. C. Sproul, *The Last Days According to Jesus*, (Grand Rapids, Baker, 1998)26.

251. See John Bray's *The Man of Sin* book for an excellent presentation on the Man of Sin. Bray does a fine job presenting a very plausible, and likely, scenario for the identification of that enigmatic personage. His book is available from us.

252. Keith Mathison, *Premillennialism, Rightly Dividing the People of God?*, (New Jersey, P and R Publishing,1995)49.

253. Wayne Jackson, *A Review of the A.D. 70 Theory*, (Stockton, Ca. Courier Publications1990)67.

254. David Engelsma, "A Defense of (Reformed) Amillennialism," a series of articles on the Internet. Found at www.prca.org.

255. Keith Mathison, *Postmillennialism An Eschatology of Hope*, (Phillipsburg, NJ, P and R Publishing, 1999)239.

256. Sam Frost, *Misplaced Hope*, (Colorado Springs, Co, BiMillennal Press, 2002)45. I highly recommend Frost's book as a refutation of the inordinate appeal to the creeds. Frost has a "creedal" background, and yet rightly sees the fallacy of trusting in them for doctrine and faith. Frost's position is that history is to be honored and respected, but should never be made the litmus test of orthodoxy.

257. The Jehovah's Witnesses leaders have consistently claimed to have divine insight, prophetic understanding *directly from God*. That is the highest kind of authority, right? Yet, the drafters of the historical creeds made no such claims. So, Mathison

rejects the Witnesses' claims to having "inspired" understanding, all the while claiming that uninspired creeds determine orthodoxy. This is the height of inconsistency. And how would Mathison condemn the Witnesses? Why, we assume from the *Bible, or yes, from those uninspired creeds*!

**258.** Cited in *Beyond Creation Science*, (Timothy Martin, Whitehall, Montana. www.truthinliving.org.

**259.** Merle D'Aubigne, D. D., *History of the Reformation of the Sixteenth Century*, Vol. II, Book VII, chapter 8, (American Tract Society, New York, 1848)247.

**260.** A relatively new book from the world of academia notes the current revival of interest and discussion of universalism. See *Universal Salvation? The Current Debate*, Editors Robin Parry and Christopher Partridge, (Grand Rapids, Eerdmans, 2003).

**261.** One has to prove that the implications that one thinks that they see in a doctrine, are indeed valid. I have had any number of opponents of Covenant Eschatology claim that it implies this or that, and therefore it is wrong, when in fact, what they *claimed* was an implication was just an over active imagination, based on faulty assumptions on their part.

**262.** The antinomian situation is far different from that of Hymenaeus and Philetus who said that the resurrection was past (2 Timothy 2:18f). The issue with Hymenaeus was that his doctrine demanded that New Covenant saints be identified by observance of Torah, and this is in no way related to the antinomian issue. See my audio book *The Hymenaean Heresy: Reverse the Charges!*. Available from my website: www.eschatology.org

**263.** Part of the issue here is the reality of objective right and wrong. Some might object by saying that adultery, homosexuality, thievery, murder are still "wrong" because they harm people, not because they are still considered dangerous sins in God's eyes. This is semantic sophistry. David realized that his adulterous sin was a sin against God, not just against Bathsheeba and her family (Psalms 51), "Against you and you only have I sinned." You cannot relegate "sin" to a simple matter of offending fellow humans. The atheist will argue that these things are wrong because they harm people, but that there is no objective standard of right or wrong, for which man must answer. So, will PU adopt the humanistic relativist mentality, wrapping it up in theological robes? The end result is the same, a rejection of the righteousness of God.

264. There is a "tension" in the NT in regard to Christians and sin. On the one hand the authors affirm the security of the believer, "There is therefore no condemnation to those who are in Christ." On the other hand they warn that those who walk "according to the flesh" shall not inherit the kingdom. Part of the solution is that when the authors affirm the security of the believer, they have in mind the "walking after the Spirit" i.e. walking by faith (1 John 1:7). When they warn against the danger of walking after the flesh, that they are speaking of being guilty of "the sin" of open rebellion, i.e. the sin of Adam. Paul did not expect Christ to remove his human desires when he became a Christian. But Christ delivered, and delivers, from the guilt of "sin," i.e the *weakness* of humanity, while still condemning "the sin" in the mode of Adam. God's *grace* covers weakness and humanity. God's *justice* rejects the sin of Adam.

265. In other words, Paul was not warning that simple "weakness of the flesh" would result in loss of kingdom blessings. He was addressing the danger of committing "the sin" i.e. the sin of Adam, by open rebellion against God. In Paul's writings, there is a difference between "the sin" and "sin." For Paul, "sin" is the human in weakness, struggling with his desire to serve the Lord. "The sin" is man in open rebellion. He is not struggling. He wants to be his own god, ruler of his own destiny. It is the later Paul has in mind in 1 Corinthians 6, Galatians, Hebrews 6, 10. etc.

266. In the discussion of universalism, *it does not matter who Paul is addressing*. His statements that those who give themselves to rebellion against God's moral law *excludes someone* from enjoying the kingdom blessings, *after the time of the end*.

267. Only God can *provide* salvation. So, in that sense, salvation is a Fiat act of God. However, that is not John's point, nor mine. My point is that John affirms that a person must be *actively involved* in *accepting Christ* in order to receive the blessings that the Father has offered. If there is no active acceptance of Christ, there are no blessings from the Father.

268. A. T. Robertson, *Word Pictures of the N. T.* Vol. V., (Nashville, Broadman, 1932)414.

**269.** Very clearly, the author does not have any kind of temporal chastisement in mind, because any kind of temporal "chastening of His children," could never be worse than the physical death of the text's comparison. This threat is exponentially worse than any temporal chastisement, and that can only be spiritual death.

**270.** It is my personal conviction that too much emphasis is being placed on a supposed distinction between the atonement of Christ, reconciliation, redemption and salvation. In the mind of a Jewish reader, the completion of the work of Christ, in the antitypical fulfillment of the High Priestly function, would bring about reconciliation. That reconciliation would be accomplished through forgiveness, because sin is what alienated. However, the forgiveness of sin is the climax of the atonement, and the climax of the atonement was in fact *salvation*. For Paul, redemption is inalienably linked with forgiveness (Ephesians 1:7). So, while there may be, and are, nuances in the different words with variation of emphasis, nonetheless, *substantively* one would be hard pressed to draw sharp distinction between these terms.